TOM ST … K 6



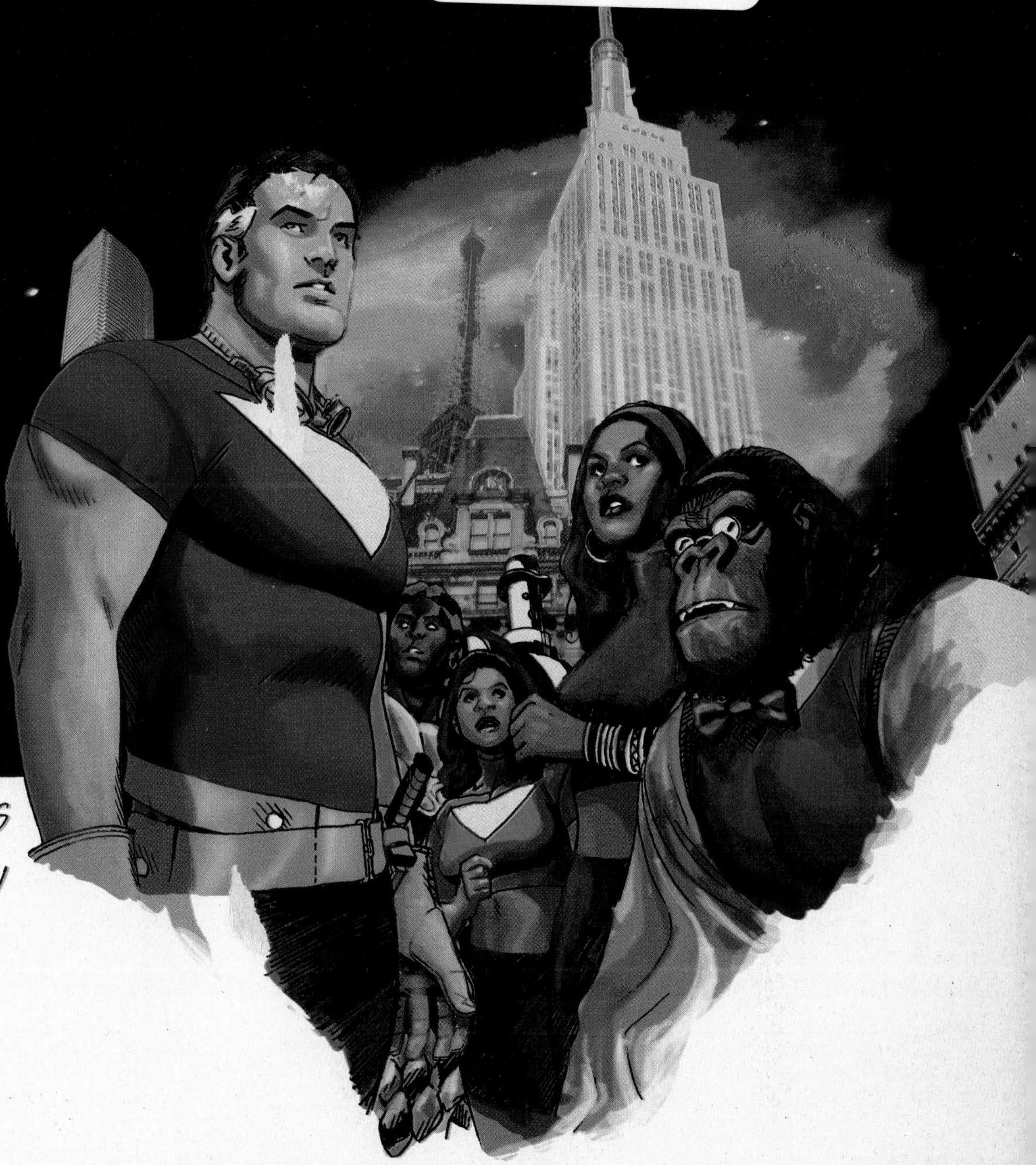

CHRIS SPROUSE
JOSE VILLARRUBIA

**JIM LEE**
Editorial Director

**JOHN NEE**
VP – Business Development

**SCOTT DUNBIER**
Executive Editor

**KRISTY QUINN**
Assistant Editor

TOM STRONG BOOK SIX. Published by America's Best Comics, LLC. Editorial offices: 888 Prospect St, Suite 240, La Jolla, CA 92037. Compilation, cover and sketches © 2006 America's Best Comics, LLC. TOM STRONG and all related characters and elements are trademarks of America's Best Comics. All Rights Reserved. SIR SEATON BEGG and CAPTAIN ZODIAC are © and TM Michael Moorcock, used with permission. Originally published in single magazine form as TOM STRONG #31-36 © 2005, 2006 America's Best Comics.  Any similarities to persons living or dead are purely coincidental. America's Best Comics does not read or accept unsolicited submissions of ideas, stories, or artwork. PRINTED IN CANADA. FIRST PRINTING.

Hardcover ISBN 1-4012-1108-9          Softcover ISBN 1-4012-1109-7
Hardcover ISBN-13: 978-1-4012-1108-0          Softcover ISBN-13: 978-1-4012-1109-7

# TOM STRONG

## COLLECTED EDITION
### BOOK 6

ALAN MOORE

MICHAEL MOORCOCK

JOE CASEY

STEVE MOORE

PETER HOGAN

writers

CHRIS SPROUSE

JERRY ORDWAY

BEN OLIVER

PAUL GULACY

JIMMY PALMIOTTI

KARL STORY

artists

MICHELLE MADSEN
JD METTLER
WILDSTORM FX
JOSE VILLARRUBIA
coloring

TODD KLEIN
lettering,
logos and
design

**TOM STRONG** created by
Alan Moore & Chris Sprouse

AMERICA'S
BEST COMICS

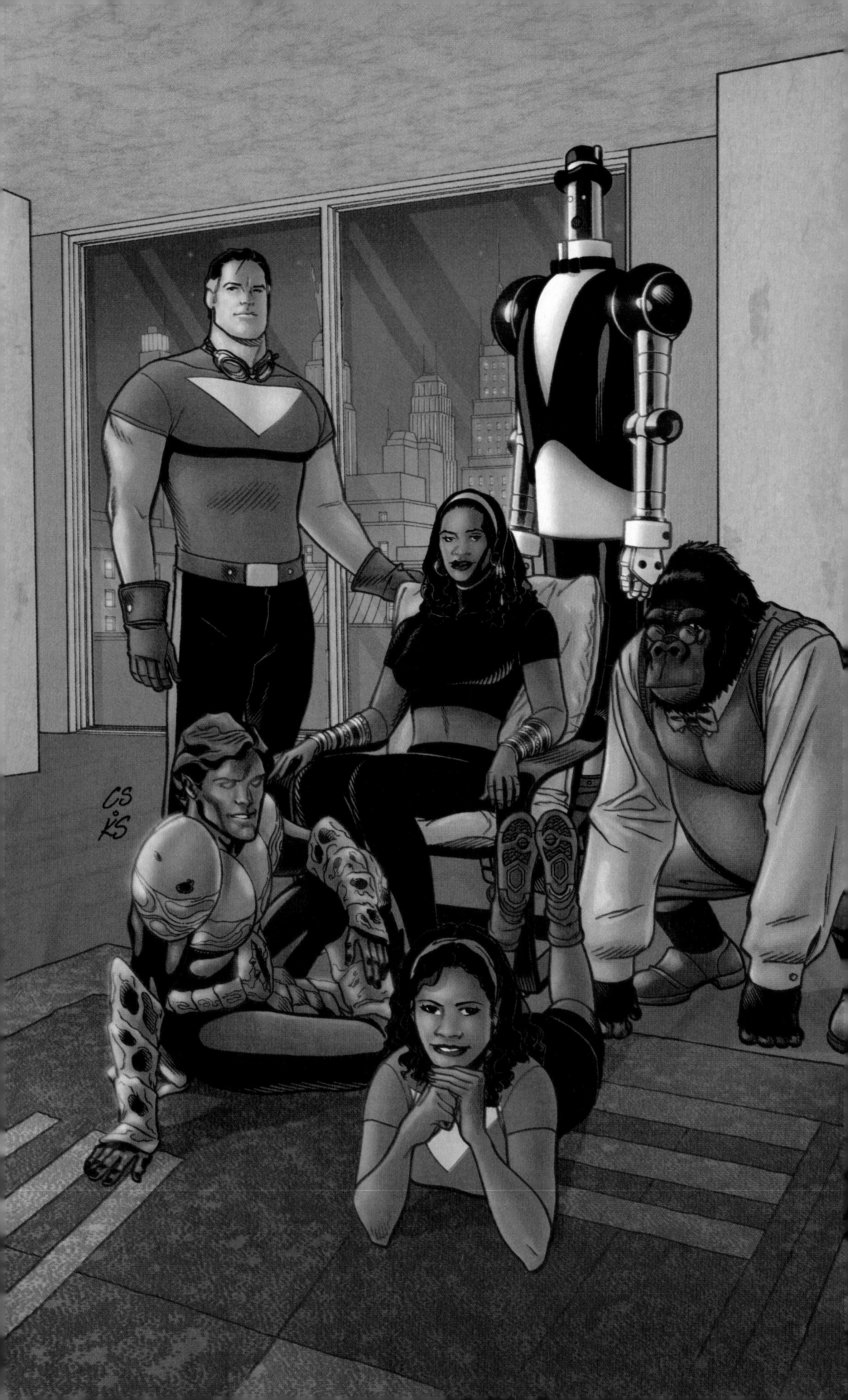
CS
KS

# CHAPTER ONE

In which Tom returns to a piratical past,
King Solomon mans the rigging,
and Pneuman takes the helm.

Cover art:
Jerry Ordway
Cover colors:
Carrie Strachan

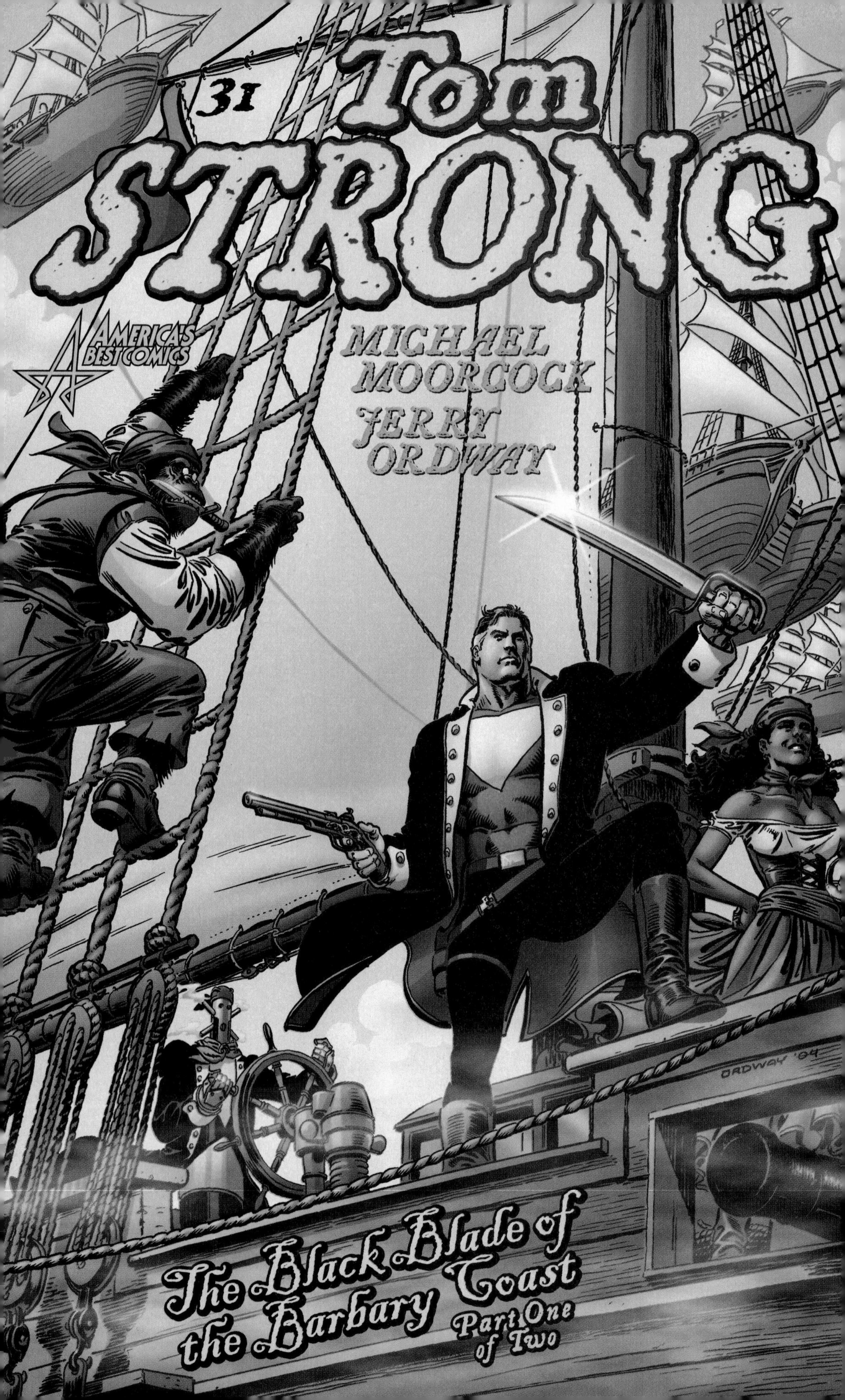
31
Tom STRONG
AMERICA'S BEST COMICS
MICHAEL MOORCOCK
JERRY ORDWAY
ORDWAY '04
The Black Blade of the Barbary Coast
Part One of Two

America's Best Comics Presents:

# Tom STRONG and The Black Blade of the Barbary Coast

Created by Alan Moore & Chris Sprouse


Michael Moorcock writer

Jerry Ordway artist

Michelle Madsen: colors
Todd Klein: letters
Kristy Quinn: asst. ed
Scott Dunbier: editor


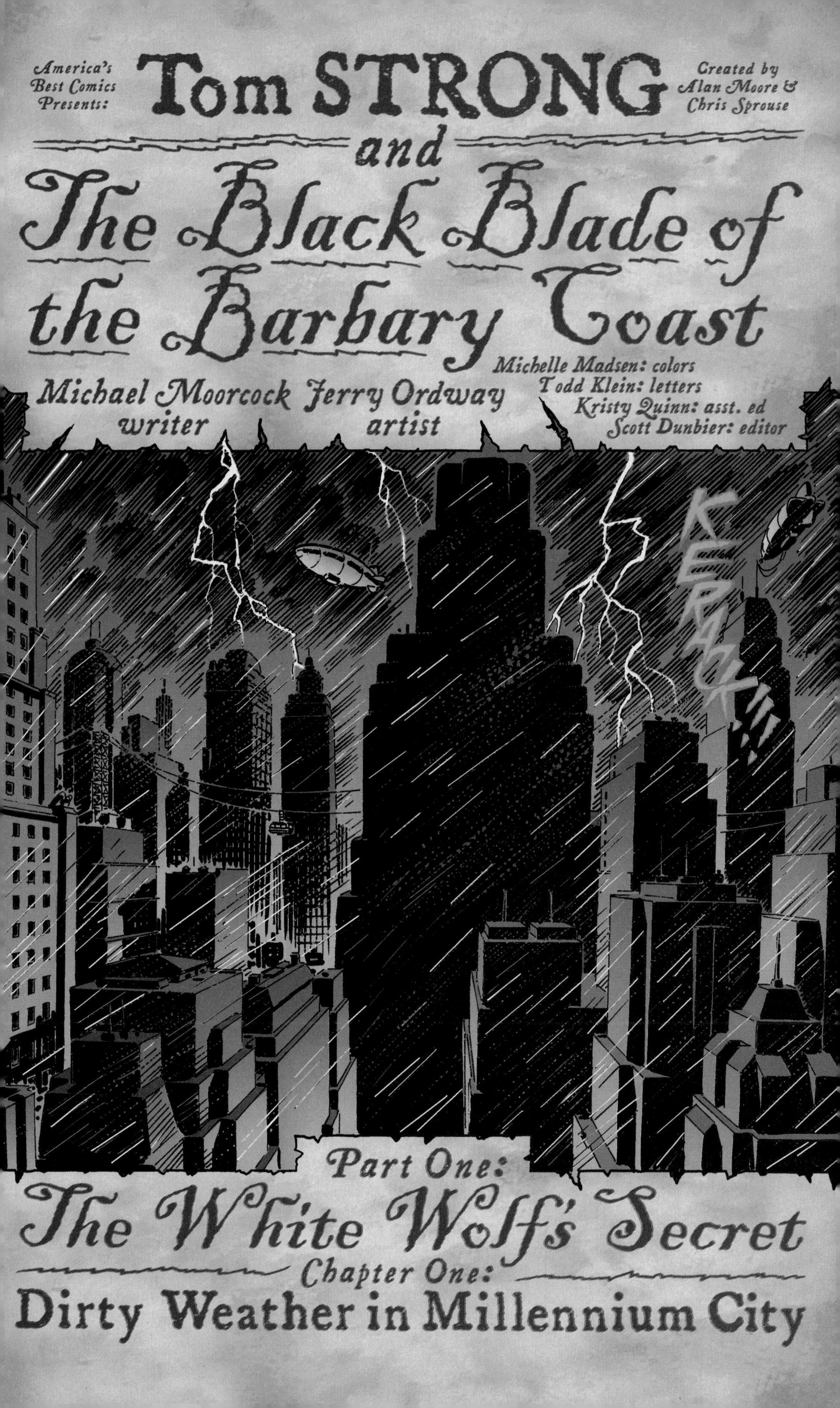
KERACK!!!

## Part One: The White Wolf's Secret

### Chapter One: Dirty Weather in Millennium City

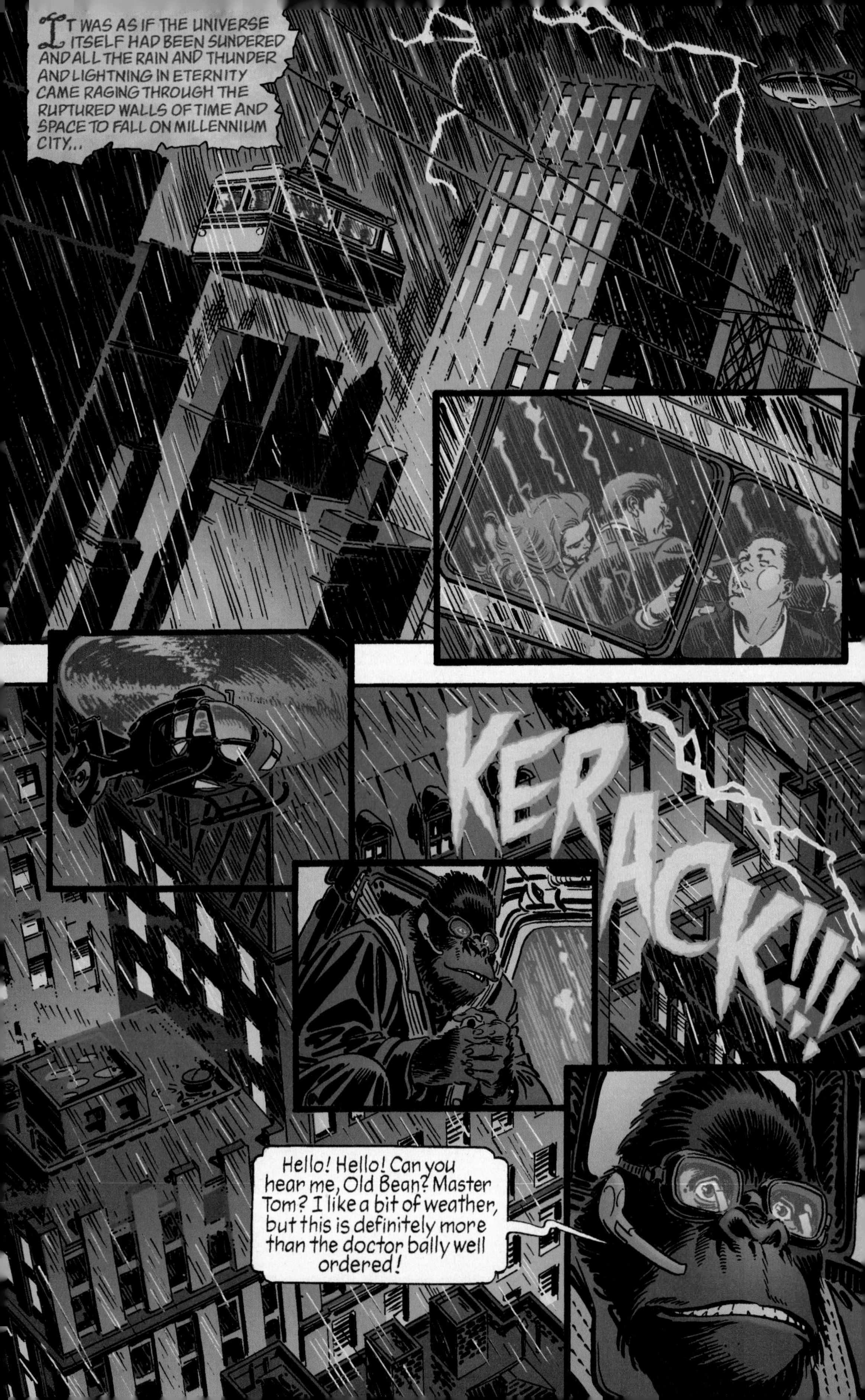
IT WAS AS IF THE UNIVERSE ITSELF HAD BEEN SUNDERED AND ALL THE RAIN AND THUNDER AND LIGHTNING IN ETERNITY CAME RAGING THROUGH THE RUPTURED WALLS OF TIME AND SPACE TO FALL ON MILLENNIUM CITY...
KERACK!!!
Hello! Hello! Can you hear me, Old Bean? Master Tom? I like a bit of weather, but this is definitely more than the doctor bally well ordered!

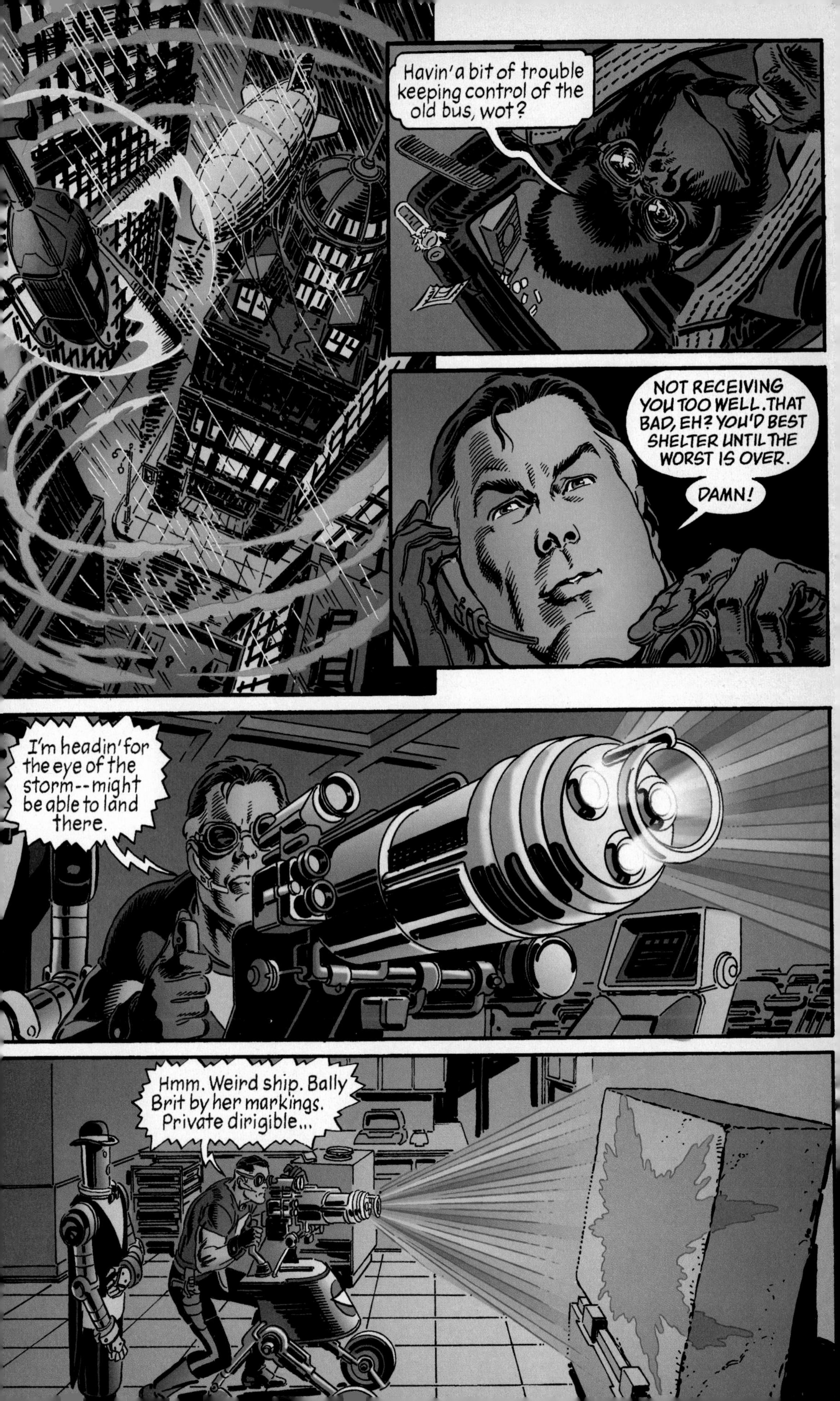
Havin' a bit of trouble keeping control of the old bus, wot?
NOT RECEIVING YOU TOO WELL. THAT BAD, EH? YOU'D BEST SHELTER UNTIL THE WORST IS OVER.
DAMN!
I'm headin' for the eye of the storm--might be able to land there.
Hmm. Weird ship. Bally Brit by her markings. Private dirigible...

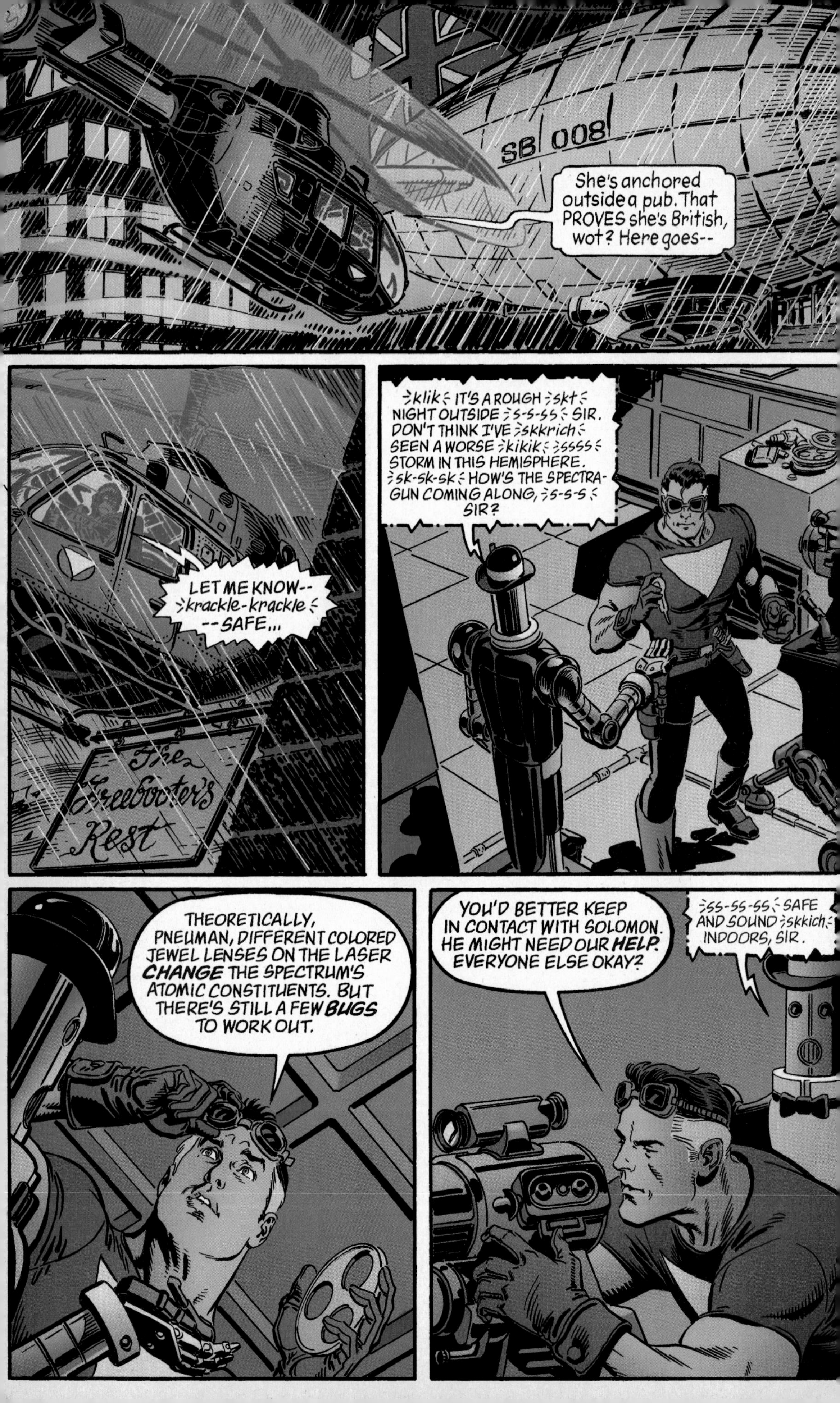
SB 008
She's anchored outside a pub. That PROVES she's British, wot? Here goes--
LET ME KNOW-- ⋚krackle-krackle⋚ --SAFE...
The Freebooter's Rest
⋚klik⋚ IT'S A ROUGH ⋚skt⋚ NIGHT OUTSIDE ⋚s-s-ss⋚ SIR. DON'T THINK I'VE ⋚skkrich⋚ SEEN A WORSE ⋚kikik⋚ ⋚ssss⋚ STORM IN THIS HEMISPHERE. ⋚sk-sk-sk⋚ HOW'S THE SPECTRA-GUN COMING ALONG, ⋚s-s-s⋚ SIR?
THEORETICALLY, PNEUMAN, DIFFERENT COLORED JEWEL LENSES ON THE LASER **CHANGE** THE SPECTRUM'S ATOMIC CONSTITUENTS. BUT THERE'S STILL A FEW **BUGS** TO WORK OUT.
YOU'D BETTER KEEP IN CONTACT WITH SOLOMON. HE MIGHT NEED OUR **HELP**. EVERYONE ELSE OKAY?
⋚ss-ss-ss⋚ SAFE AND SOUND ⋚skkich⋚ INDOORS, SIR.

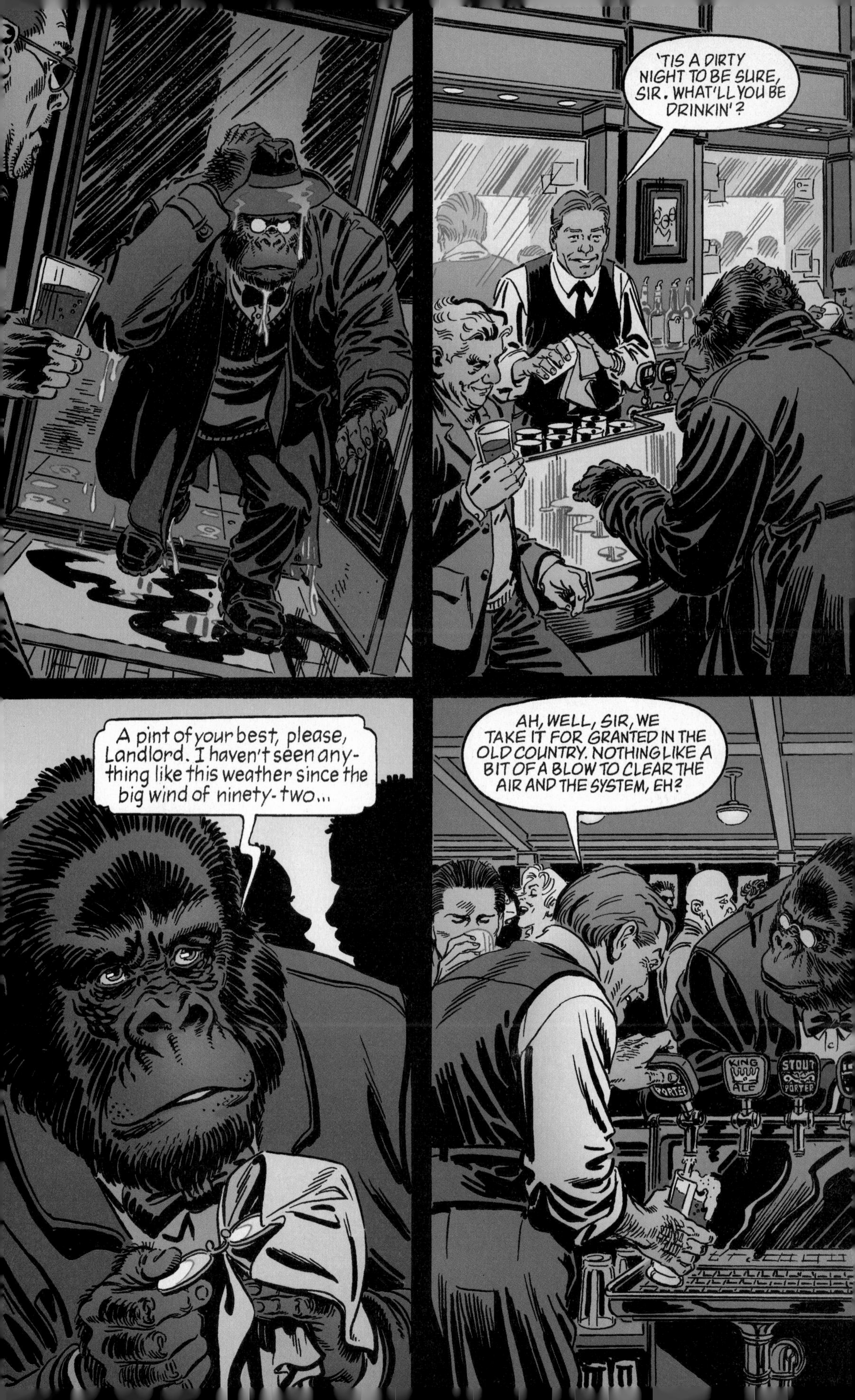

'TIS A DIRTY NIGHT TO BE SURE, SIR. WHAT'LL YOU BE DRINKIN'?
A pint of your best, please, Landlord. I haven't seen anything like this weather since the big wind of ninety-two...
AH, WELL, SIR, WE TAKE IT FOR GRANTED IN THE OLD COUNTRY. NOTHING LIKE A BIT OF A BLOW TO CLEAR THE AIR AND THE SYSTEM, EH?
KING ALE
STOUT PORTER
PORTER

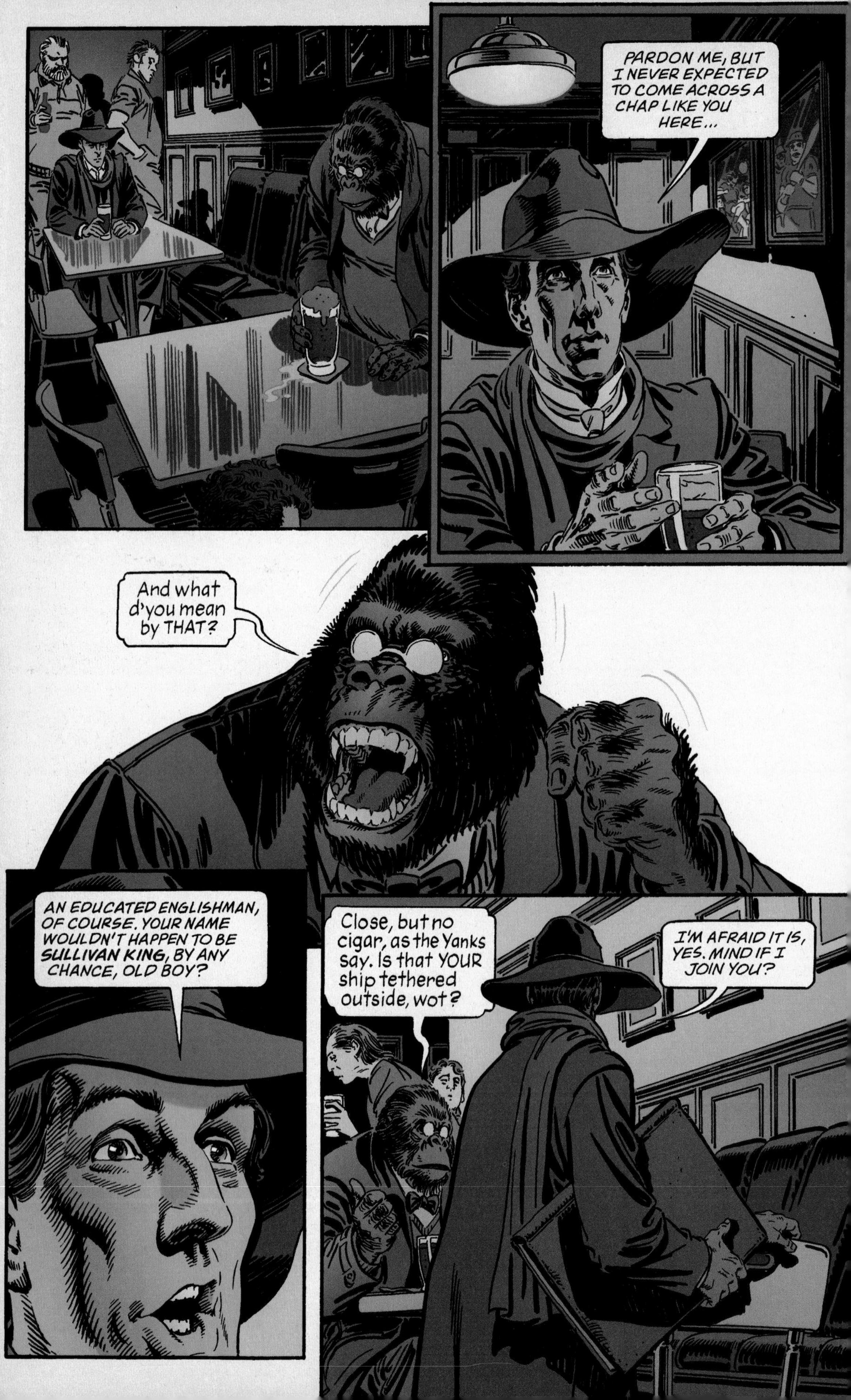
PARDON ME, BUT I NEVER EXPECTED TO COME ACROSS A CHAP LIKE YOU HERE...
And what d'you mean by THAT?
AN EDUCATED ENGLISHMAN, OF COURSE. YOUR NAME WOULDN'T HAPPEN TO BE SULLIVAN KING, BY ANY CHANCE, OLD BOY?
Close, but no cigar, as the Yanks say. Is that YOUR ship tethered outside, wot?
I'M AFRAID IT IS, YES. MIND IF I JOIN YOU?

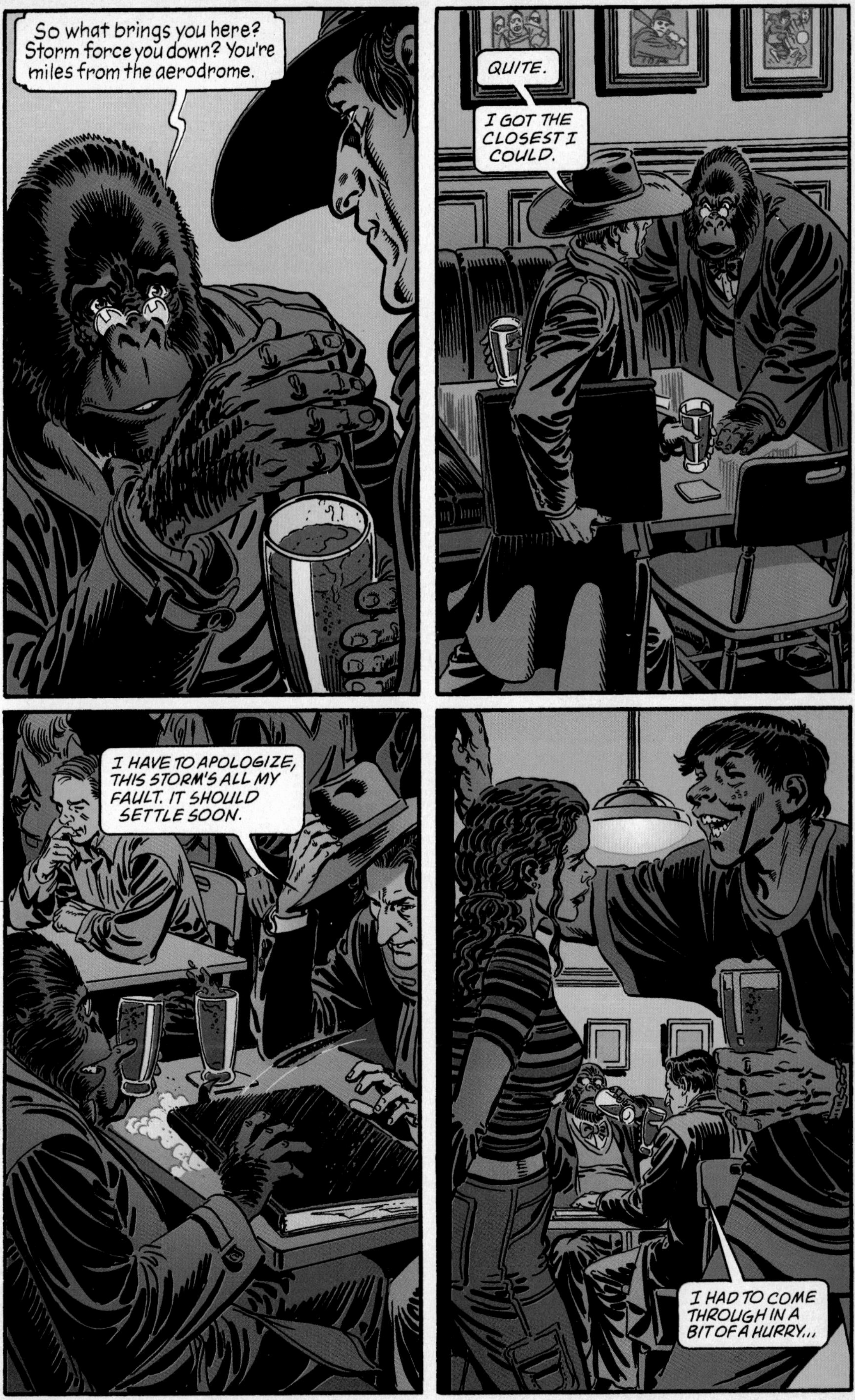
So what brings you here? Storm force you down? You're miles from the aerodrome.
QUITE.
I GOT THE CLOSEST I COULD.
I HAVE TO APOLOGIZE, THIS STORM'S ALL MY FAULT. IT SHOULD SETTLE SOON.
I HAD TO COME THROUGH IN A BIT OF A HURRY...

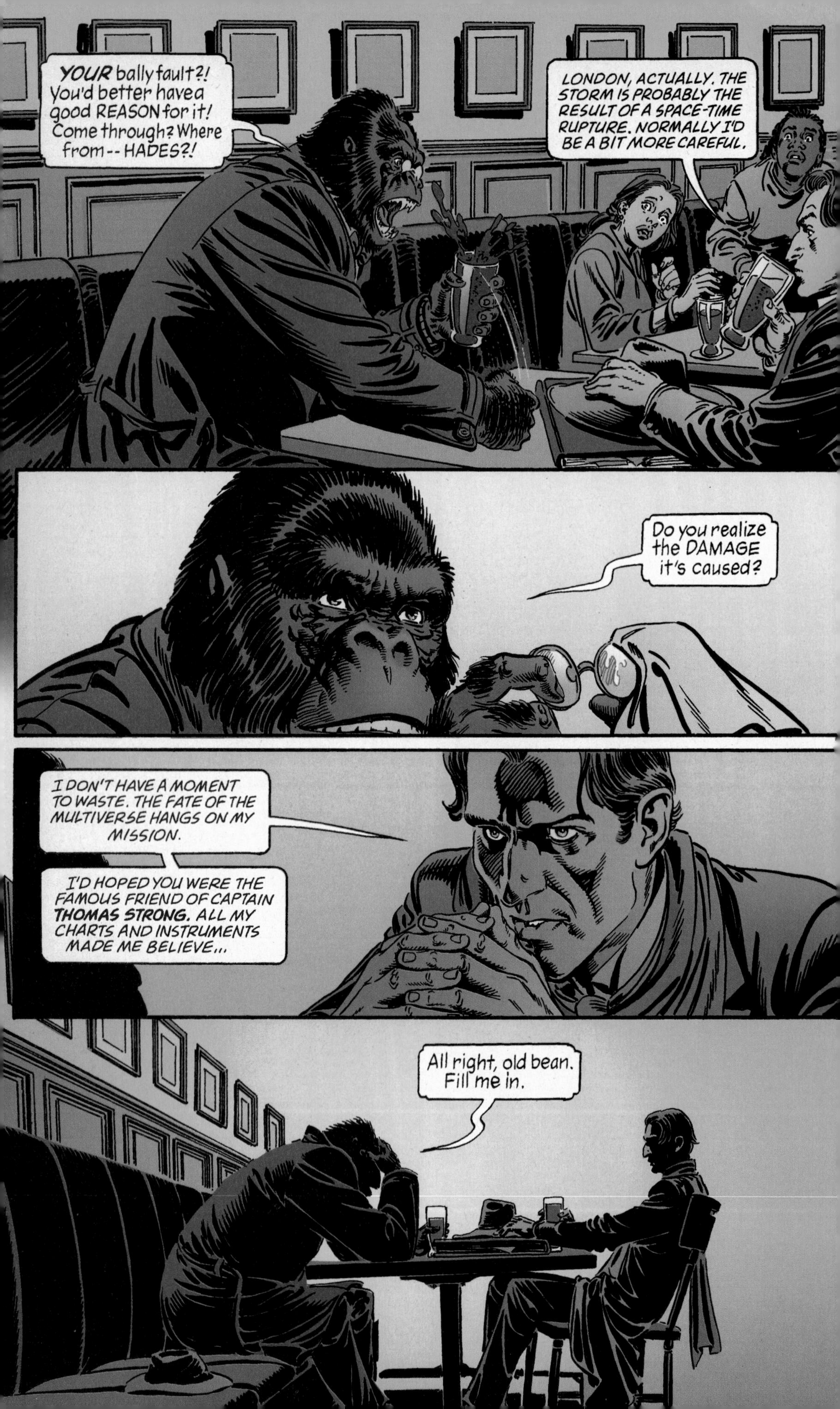
YOUR bally fault?! You'd better have a good REASON for it! Come through? Where from -- HADES?!
LONDON, ACTUALLY. THE STORM IS PROBABLY THE RESULT OF A SPACE-TIME RUPTURE. NORMALLY I'D BE A BIT MORE CAREFUL.
Do you realize the DAMAGE it's caused?
I DON'T HAVE A MOMENT TO WASTE. THE FATE OF THE MULTIVERSE HANGS ON MY MISSION.
I'D HOPED YOU WERE THE FAMOUS FRIEND OF CAPTAIN THOMAS STRONG. ALL MY CHARTS AND INSTRUMENTS MADE ME BELIEVE...
All right, old bean. Fill me in.

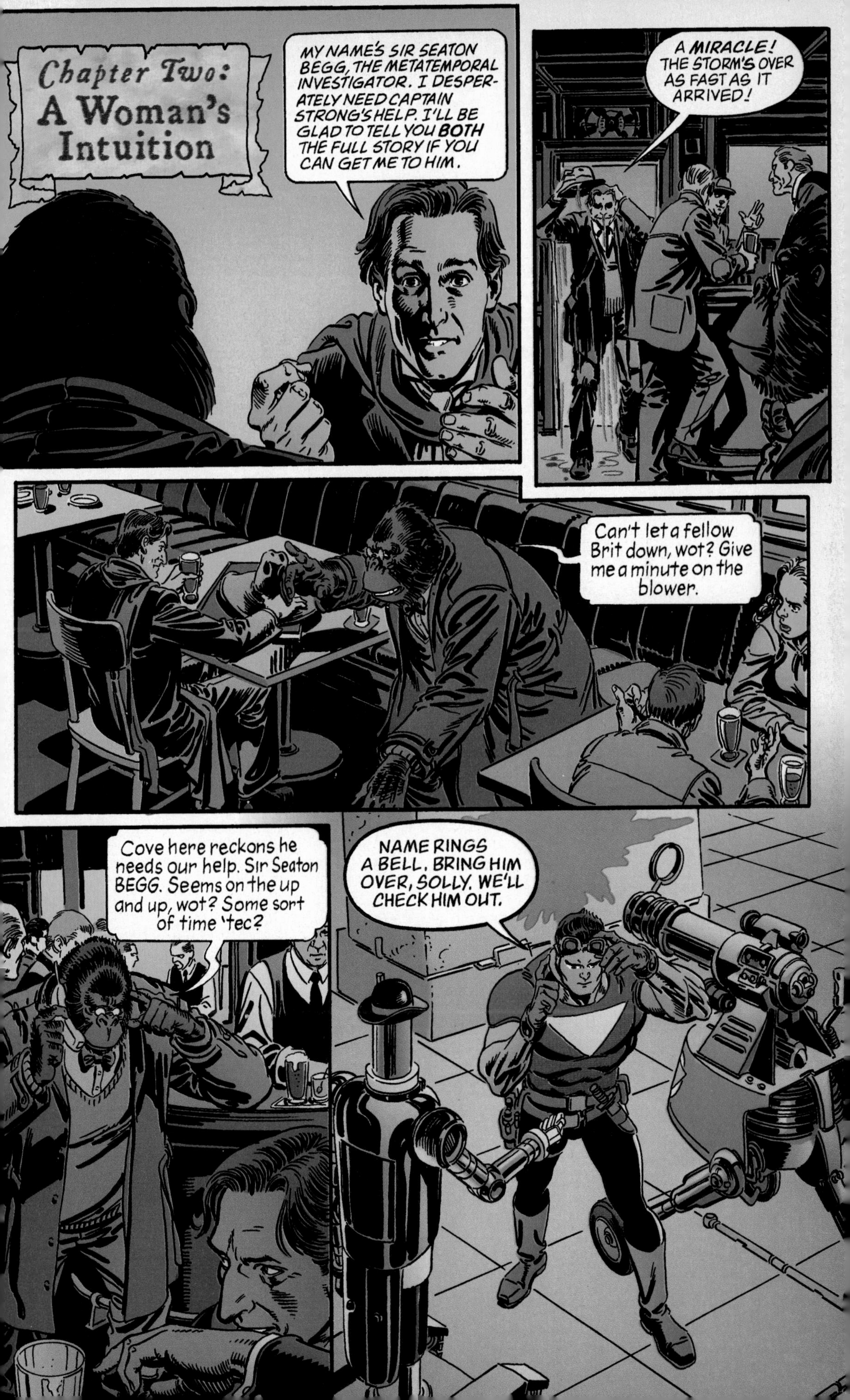
Chapter Two:
A Woman's Intuition
MY NAME'S SIR SEATON BEGG, THE METATEMPORAL INVESTIGATOR. I DESPERATELY NEED CAPTAIN STRONG'S HELP. I'LL BE GLAD TO TELL YOU BOTH THE FULL STORY IF YOU CAN GET ME TO HIM.
A MIRACLE! THE STORM'S OVER AS FAST AS IT ARRIVED!
Can't let a fellow Brit down, wot? Give me a minute on the blower.
Cove here reckons he needs our help. Sir Seaton BEGG. Seems on the up and up, wot? Some sort of time 'tec?
NAME RINGS A BELL. BRING HIM OVER, SOLLY. WE'LL CHECK HIM OUT.

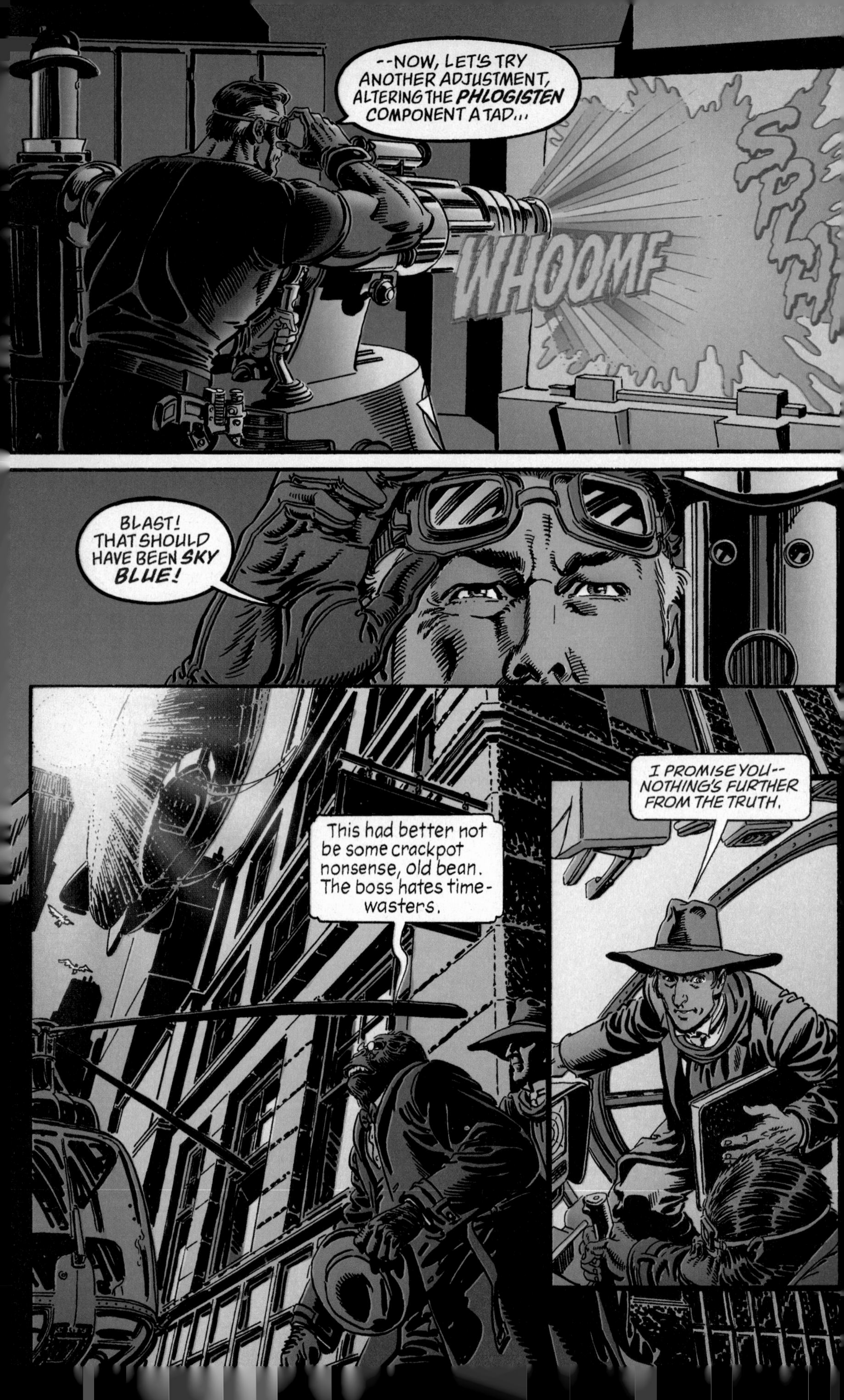
--NOW, LET'S TRY ANOTHER ADJUSTMENT, ALTERING THE **PHLOGISTEN** COMPONENT A TAD...
WHOOMF
BLAST! THAT SHOULD HAVE BEEN **SKY BLUE!**
This had better not be some crackpot nonsense, old bean. The boss hates time-wasters.
I PROMISE YOU-- NOTHING'S FURTHER FROM THE TRUTH.

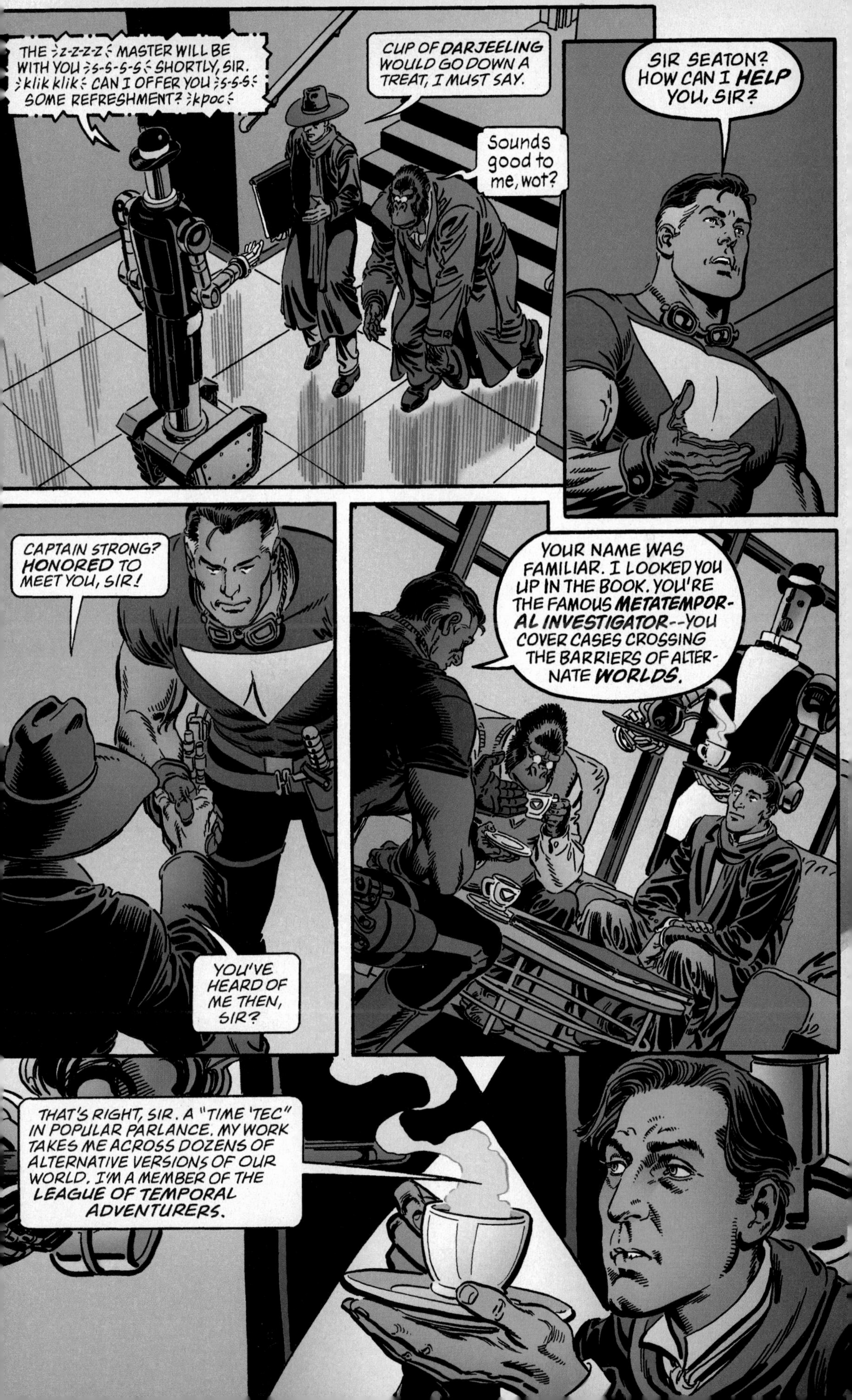
THE ≷z-z-z-z≶ MASTER WILL BE WITH YOU ≷s-s-s-s≶ SHORTLY, SIR. ≷klik klik≶ CAN I OFFER YOU ≷s-s-s≶ SOME REFRESHMENT? ≷kpoc≶
CUP OF DARJEELING WOULD GO DOWN A TREAT, I MUST SAY.
Sounds good to me, wot?
SIR SEATON? HOW CAN I HELP YOU, SIR?
CAPTAIN STRONG? HONORED TO MEET YOU, SIR!
YOU'VE HEARD OF ME THEN, SIR?
YOUR NAME WAS FAMILIAR. I LOOKED YOU UP IN THE BOOK. YOU'RE THE FAMOUS METATEMPORAL INVESTIGATOR--YOU COVER CASES CROSSING THE BARRIERS OF ALTERNATE WORLDS.
THAT'S RIGHT, SIR. A "TIME 'TEC" IN POPULAR PARLANCE. MY WORK TAKES ME ACROSS DOZENS OF ALTERNATIVE VERSIONS OF OUR WORLD. I'M A MEMBER OF THE LEAGUE OF TEMPORAL ADVENTURERS.

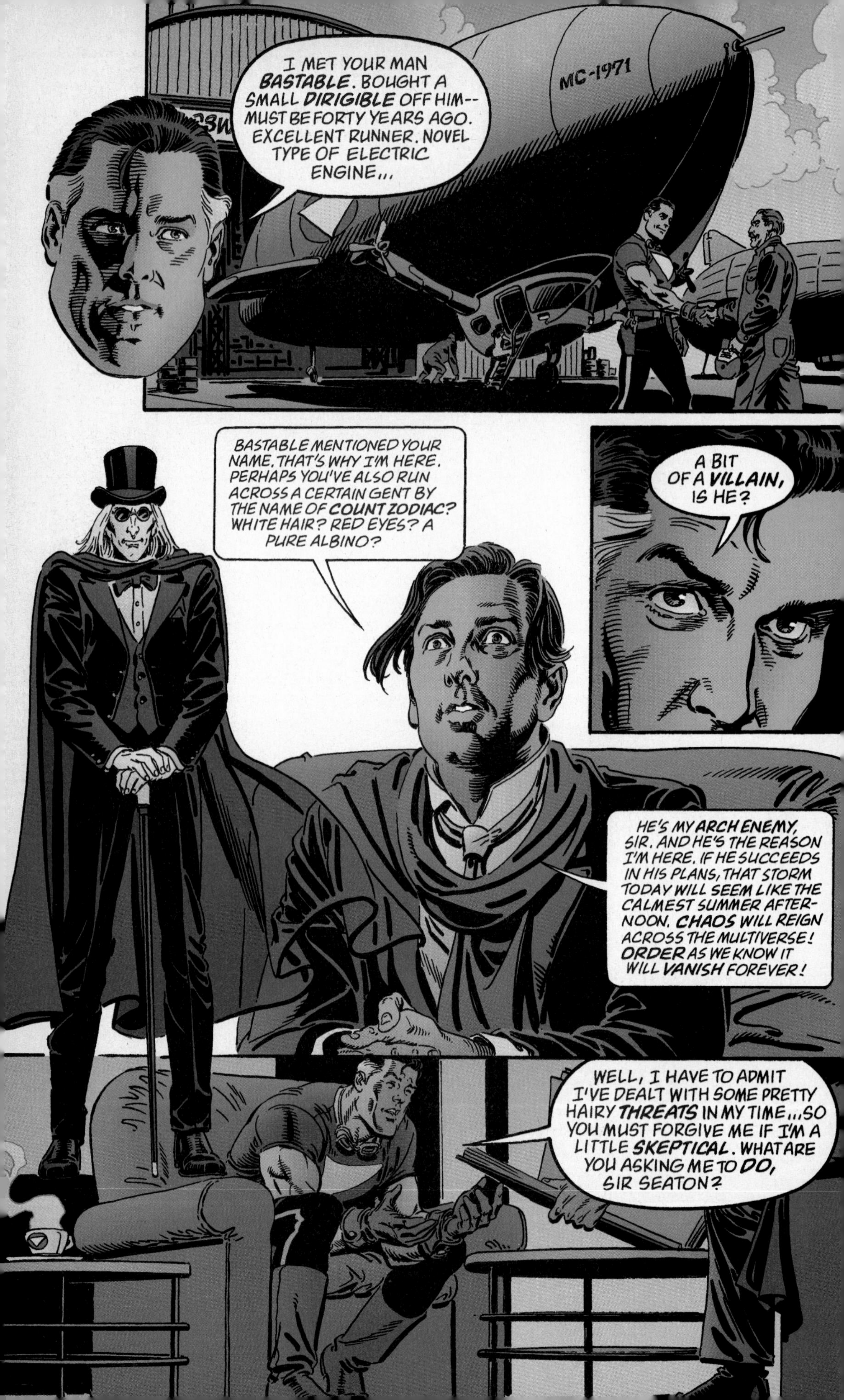
MC-1971
I MET YOUR MAN BASTABLE. BOUGHT A SMALL DIRIGIBLE OFF HIM-- MUST BE FORTY YEARS AGO. EXCELLENT RUNNER. NOVEL TYPE OF ELECTRIC ENGINE...
BASTABLE MENTIONED YOUR NAME. THAT'S WHY I'M HERE. PERHAPS YOU'VE ALSO RUN ACROSS A CERTAIN GENT BY THE NAME OF COUNT ZODIAC? WHITE HAIR? RED EYES? A PURE ALBINO?
A BIT OF A VILLAIN, IS HE?
HE'S MY ARCH ENEMY, SIR. AND HE'S THE REASON I'M HERE. IF HE SUCCEEDS IN HIS PLANS, THAT STORM TODAY WILL SEEM LIKE THE CALMEST SUMMER AFTERNOON. CHAOS WILL REIGN ACROSS THE MULTIVERSE! ORDER AS WE KNOW IT WILL VANISH FOREVER!
WELL, I HAVE TO ADMIT I'VE DEALT WITH SOME PRETTY HAIRY THREATS IN MY TIME...SO YOU MUST FORGIVE ME IF I'M A LITTLE SKEPTICAL. WHAT ARE YOU ASKING ME TO DO, SIR SEATON?

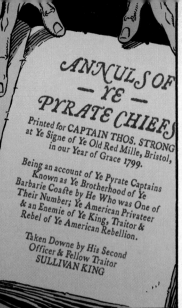

ANNULS OF
-- YE --
PYRATE CHIEFS

Printed for CAPTAIN THOS. STRONG
at Ye Signe of Ye Old Red Mille, Bristol,
in our Year of Grace 1799.

Being an account of Ye Pyrate Captains
Known as Ye Brotherhood of Ye
Barbarie Coaste by He Who was One of
Their Number; Ye American Privateer
& an Enemie of Ye King, Traitor &
Rebel of Ye American Rebellion.

Taken Downe by His Second
Officer & Fellow Traitor
SULLIVAN KING

Traitor! I say, that's a bit steep. I might have my bally faults, wot? But--

SO YOU **ARE** MR. SULLIVAN?

You can call me that, if you're callin' me a traitor, too...

THIS ISN'T **YOU**, SIR, BUT A CHAP WHO INHABITED THE ALTERNATE EARTH TO MY OWN ABOUT TWO CENTURIES BEFORE MY TIME --

--YESTERDAY'S TRAITORS ARE TODAY'S HEROES, ESPECIALLY WHERE OUR TWO GREAT NATIONS ARE CONCERNED! WE'VE ALWAYS BEEN A TRIFLE CONFUSED ON THAT SCORE, EH?

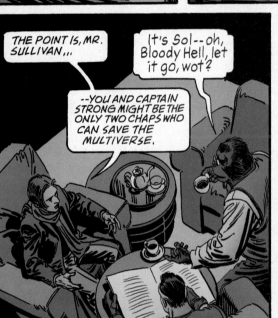

THE POINT IS, MR. SULLIVAN,...

It's Sol--oh, Bloody Hell, let it go, wot?

--YOU AND CAPTAIN STRONG MIGHT BE THE ONLY TWO CHAPS WHO CAN SAVE THE MULTIVERSE.

I'D BETTER MAKE IT **CLEAR**, SIR SEATON. I DON'T USE A MILITARY OR NAVAL TITLE.

QUITE SO, SIR. I APOLOGIZE, BUT IF YOU ARE TO HELP ME, IT MIGHT BE GOOD TO GET **USED** TO IT.

I HAVEN'T SAID I'D HELP...

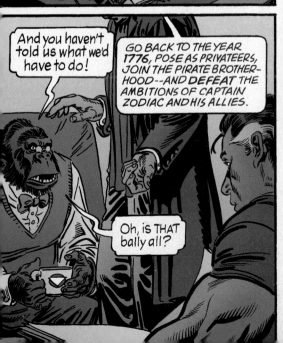

And you haven't told us what we'd have to do!

GO BACK TO THE YEAR 1776, POSE AS PRIVATEERS, JOIN THE PIRATE BROTHERHOOD--AND **DEFEAT** THE AMBITIONS OF CAPTAIN ZODIAC AND HIS ALLIES.

Oh, is THAT bally all?

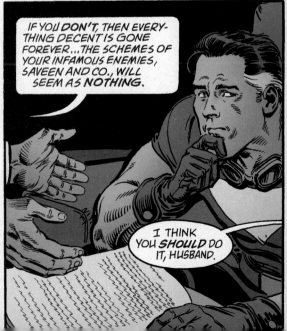

IF YOU **DON'T**, THEN EVERYTHING DECENT IS GONE FOREVER...THE SCHEMES OF YOUR INFAMOUS ENEMIES, SAVEEN AND CO., WILL SEEM AS **NOTHING**.

I THINK YOU **SHOULD** DO IT, HUSBAND.

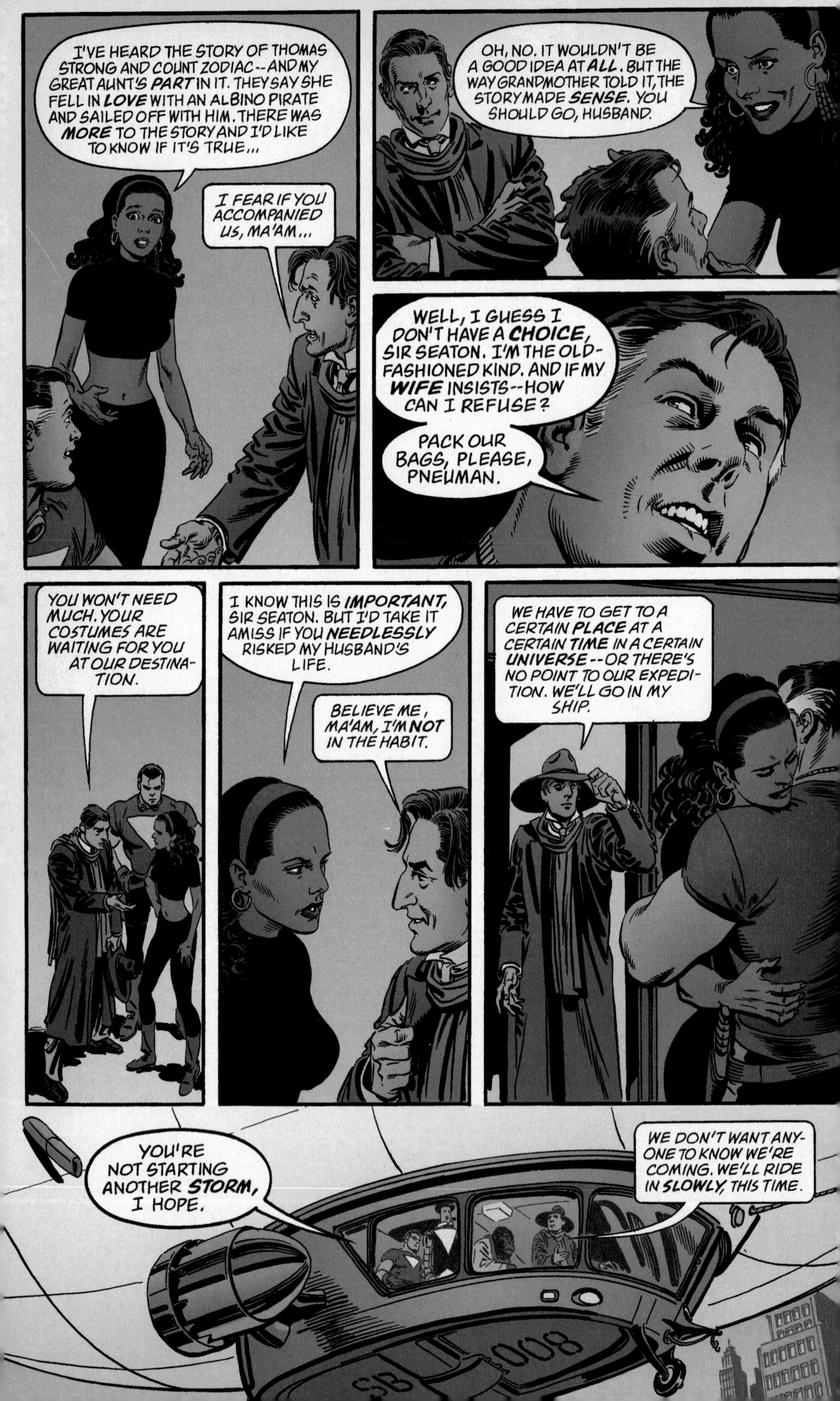
I'VE HEARD THE STORY OF THOMAS STRONG AND COUNT ZODIAC--AND MY GREAT AUNT'S PART IN IT. THEY SAY SHE FELL IN LOVE WITH AN ALBINO PIRATE AND SAILED OFF WITH HIM. THERE WAS MORE TO THE STORY AND I'D LIKE TO KNOW IF IT'S TRUE...
I FEAR IF YOU ACCOMPANIED US, MA'AM...
OH, NO. IT WOULDN'T BE A GOOD IDEA AT ALL. BUT THE WAY GRANDMOTHER TOLD IT, THE STORY MADE SENSE. YOU SHOULD GO, HUSBAND.
WELL, I GUESS I DON'T HAVE A CHOICE, SIR SEATON. I'M THE OLD-FASHIONED KIND. AND IF MY WIFE INSISTS--HOW CAN I REFUSE?
PACK OUR BAGS, PLEASE, PNEUMAN.
YOU WON'T NEED MUCH. YOUR COSTUMES ARE WAITING FOR YOU AT OUR DESTINATION.
I KNOW THIS IS IMPORTANT, SIR SEATON. BUT I'D TAKE IT AMISS IF YOU NEEDLESSLY RISKED MY HUSBAND'S LIFE.
BELIEVE ME, MA'AM, I'M NOT IN THE HABIT.
WE HAVE TO GET TO A CERTAIN PLACE AT A CERTAIN TIME IN A CERTAIN UNIVERSE--OR THERE'S NO POINT TO OUR EXPEDITION. WE'LL GO IN MY SHIP.
YOU'RE NOT STARTING ANOTHER STORM, I HOPE.
WE DON'T WANT ANYONE TO KNOW WE'RE COMING. WE'LL RIDE IN SLOWLY, THIS TIME.
SB 008

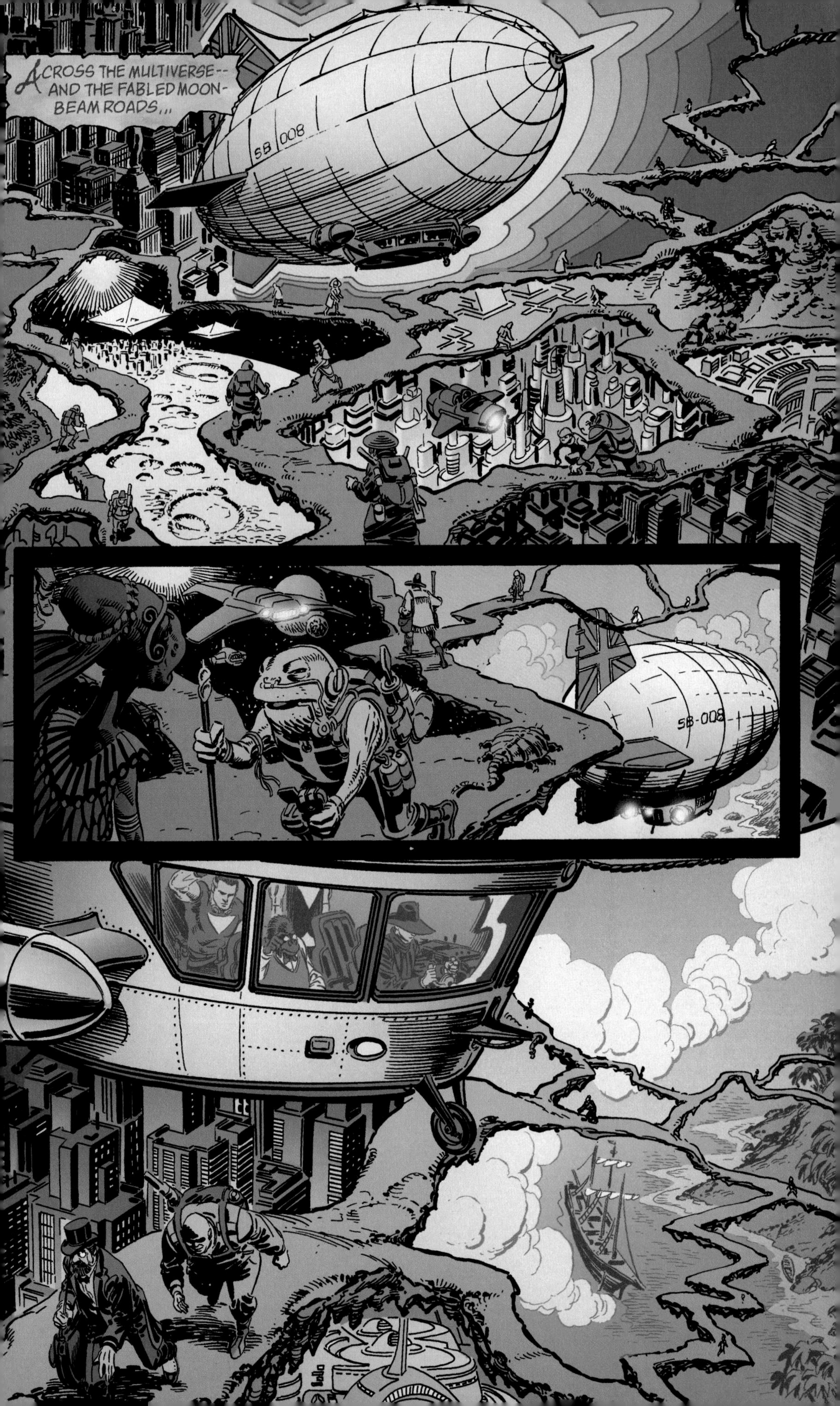
ACROSS THE MULTIVERSE-- AND THE FABLED MOON-BEAM ROADS,,,
SB 008
SB-008

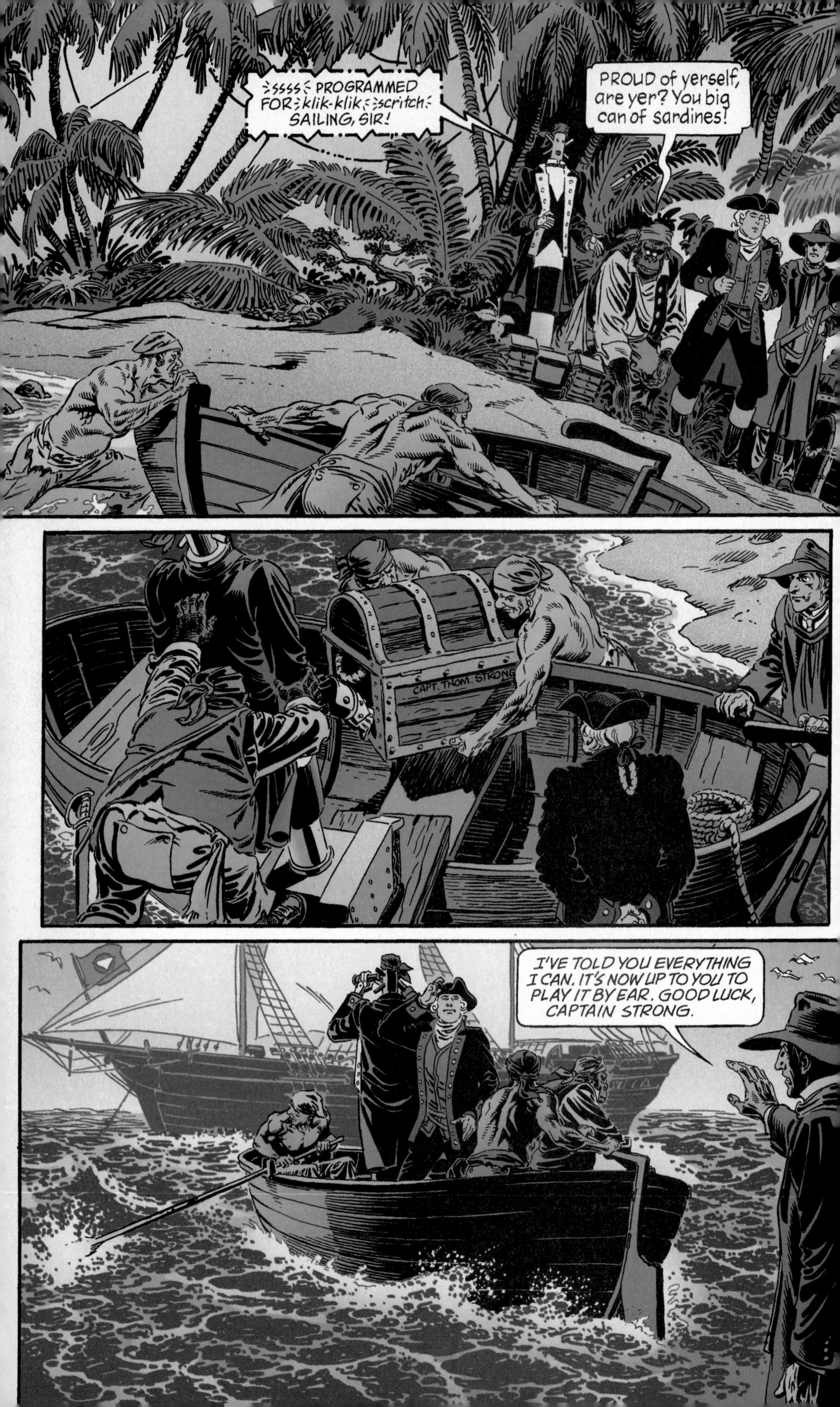

ssss PROGRAMMED FOR klik-klik scritch SAILING, SIR!
PROUD of yerself, are yer? You big can of sardines!
CAPT. THOM. STRONG
I'VE TOLD YOU EVERYTHING I CAN. IT'S NOW UP TO YOU TO PLAY IT BY EAR. GOOD LUCK, CAPTAIN STRONG.

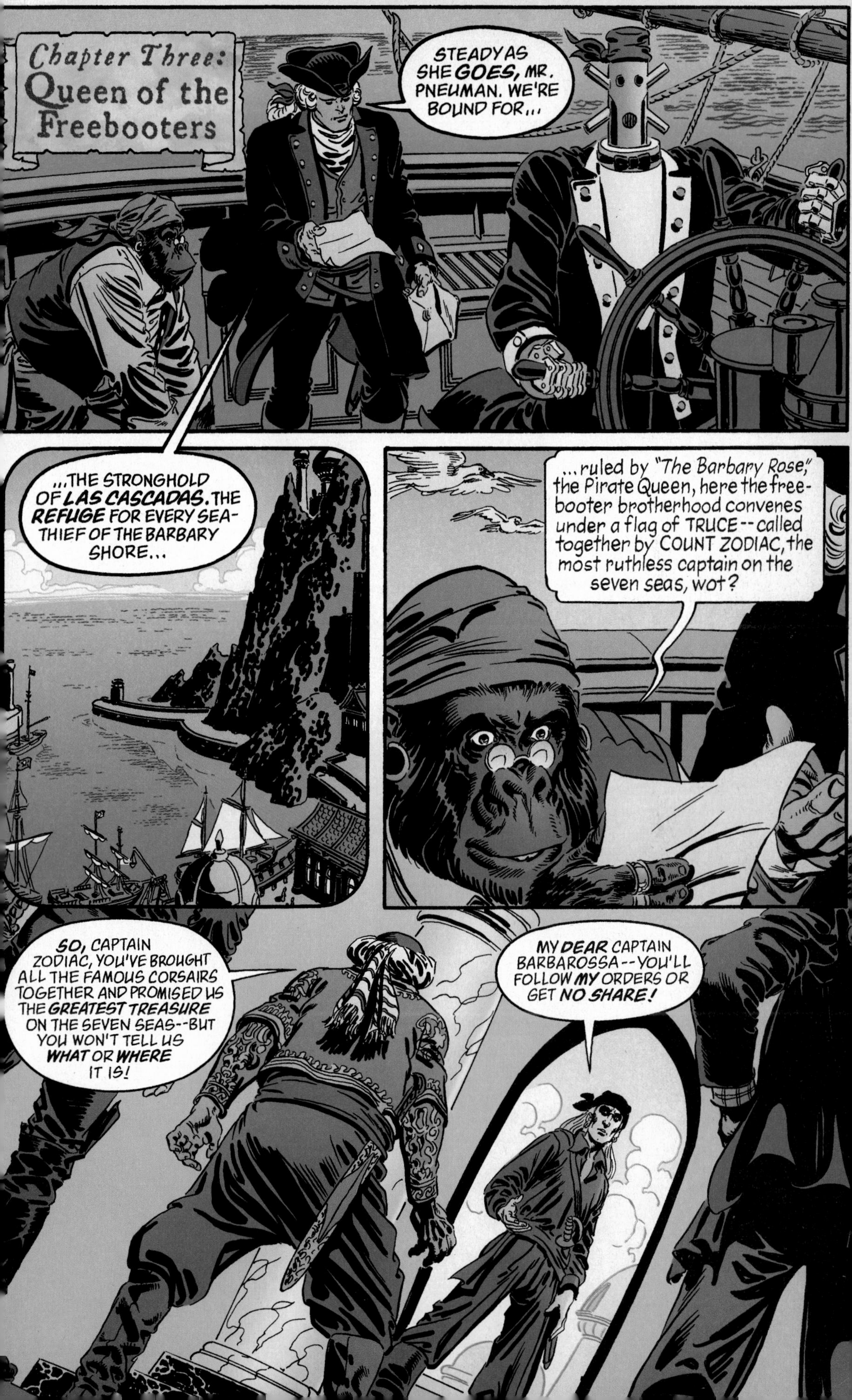
Chapter Three:
Queen of the Freebooters
STEADY AS SHE GOES, MR. PNEUMAN. WE'RE BOUND FOR...
...THE STRONGHOLD OF LAS CASCADAS. THE REFUGE FOR EVERY SEA-THIEF OF THE BARBARY SHORE...
...ruled by "The Barbary Rose," the Pirate Queen, here the free-booter brotherhood convenes under a flag of TRUCE--called together by COUNT ZODIAC, the most ruthless captain on the seven seas, wot?
SO, CAPTAIN ZODIAC, YOU'VE BROUGHT ALL THE FAMOUS CORSAIRS TOGETHER AND PROMISED US THE GREATEST TREASURE ON THE SEVEN SEAS--BUT YOU WON'T TELL US WHAT OR WHERE IT IS!
MY DEAR CAPTAIN BARBAROSSA--YOU'LL FOLLOW MY ORDERS OR GET NO SHARE!

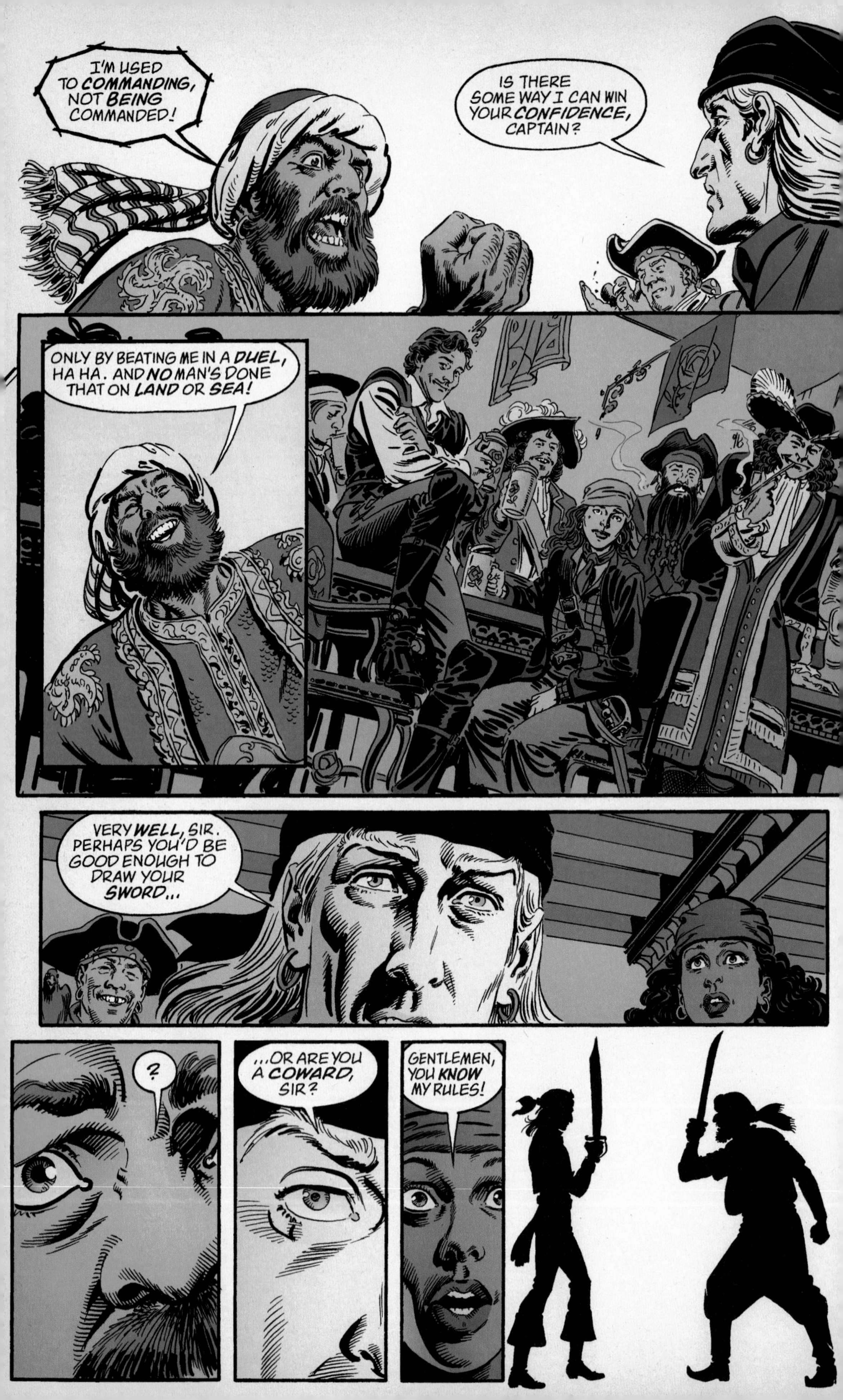

I'M USED TO COMMANDING, NOT BEING COMMANDED!
IS THERE SOME WAY I CAN WIN YOUR CONFIDENCE, CAPTAIN?
ONLY BY BEATING ME IN A DUEL, HA HA. AND NO MAN'S DONE THAT ON LAND OR SEA!
VERY WELL, SIR. PERHAPS YOU'D BE GOOD ENOUGH TO DRAW YOUR SWORD...
?
...OR ARE YOU A COWARD, SIR?
GENTLEMEN, YOU KNOW MY RULES!

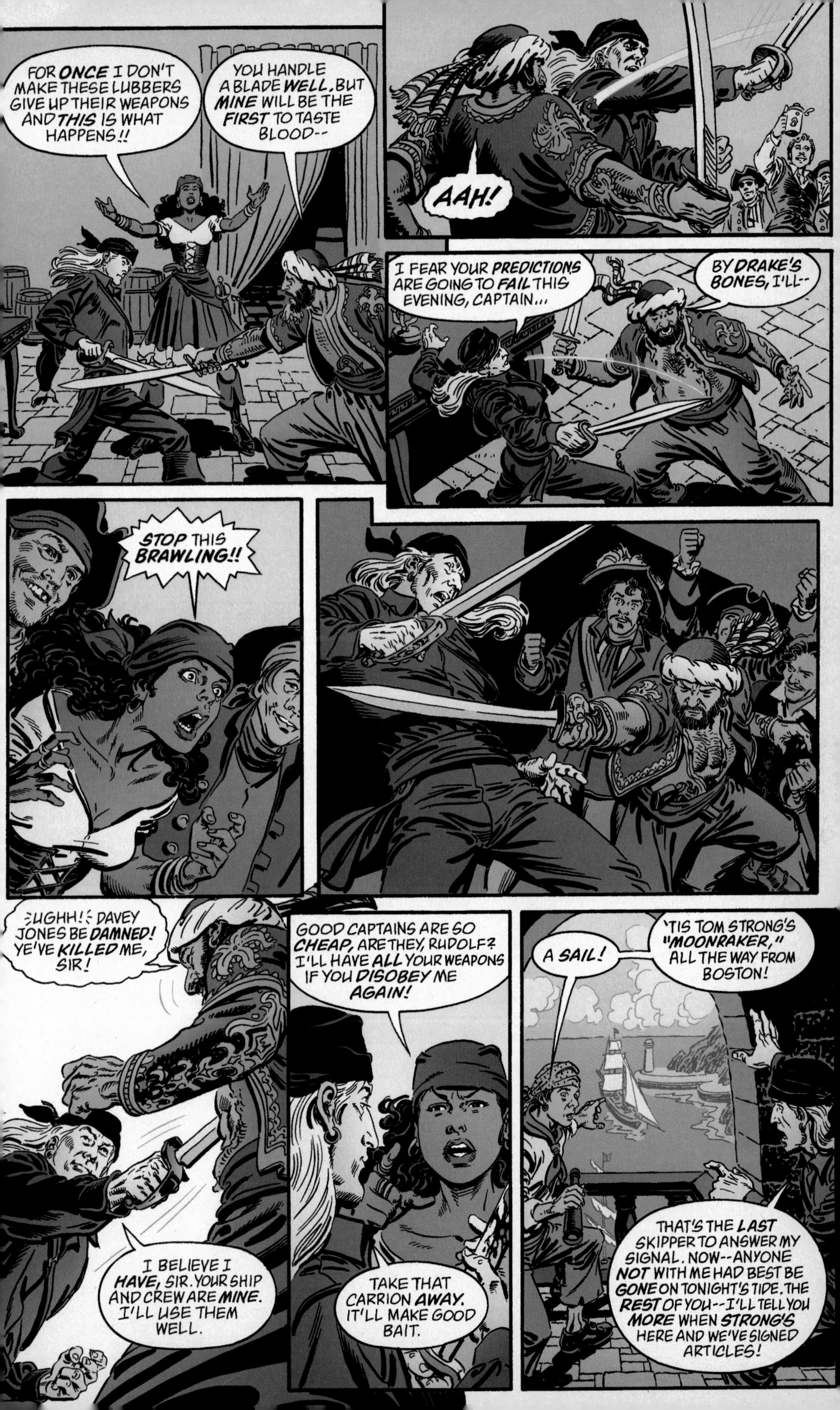
FOR ONCE I DON'T MAKE THESE LUBBERS GIVE UP THEIR WEAPONS AND THIS IS WHAT HAPPENS!!
YOU HANDLE A BLADE WELL. BUT MINE WILL BE THE FIRST TO TASTE BLOOD--
AAH!
I FEAR YOUR PREDICTIONS ARE GOING TO FAIL THIS EVENING, CAPTAIN...
BY DRAKE'S BONES, I'LL--
STOP THIS BRAWLING!!
UGHH! DAVEY JONES BE DAMNED! YE'VE KILLED ME, SIR!
I BELIEVE I HAVE, SIR. YOUR SHIP AND CREW ARE MINE. I'LL USE THEM WELL.
GOOD CAPTAINS ARE SO CHEAP, ARE THEY, RUDOLF? I'LL HAVE ALL YOUR WEAPONS IF YOU DISOBEY ME AGAIN!
TAKE THAT CARRION AWAY. IT'LL MAKE GOOD BAIT.
A SAIL!
'TIS TOM STRONG'S "MOONRAKER," ALL THE WAY FROM BOSTON!
THAT'S THE LAST SKIPPER TO ANSWER MY SIGNAL. NOW--ANYONE NOT WITH ME HAD BEST BE GONE ON TONIGHT'S TIDE. THE REST OF YOU--I'LL TELL YOU MORE WHEN STRONG'S HERE AND WE'VE SIGNED ARTICLES!

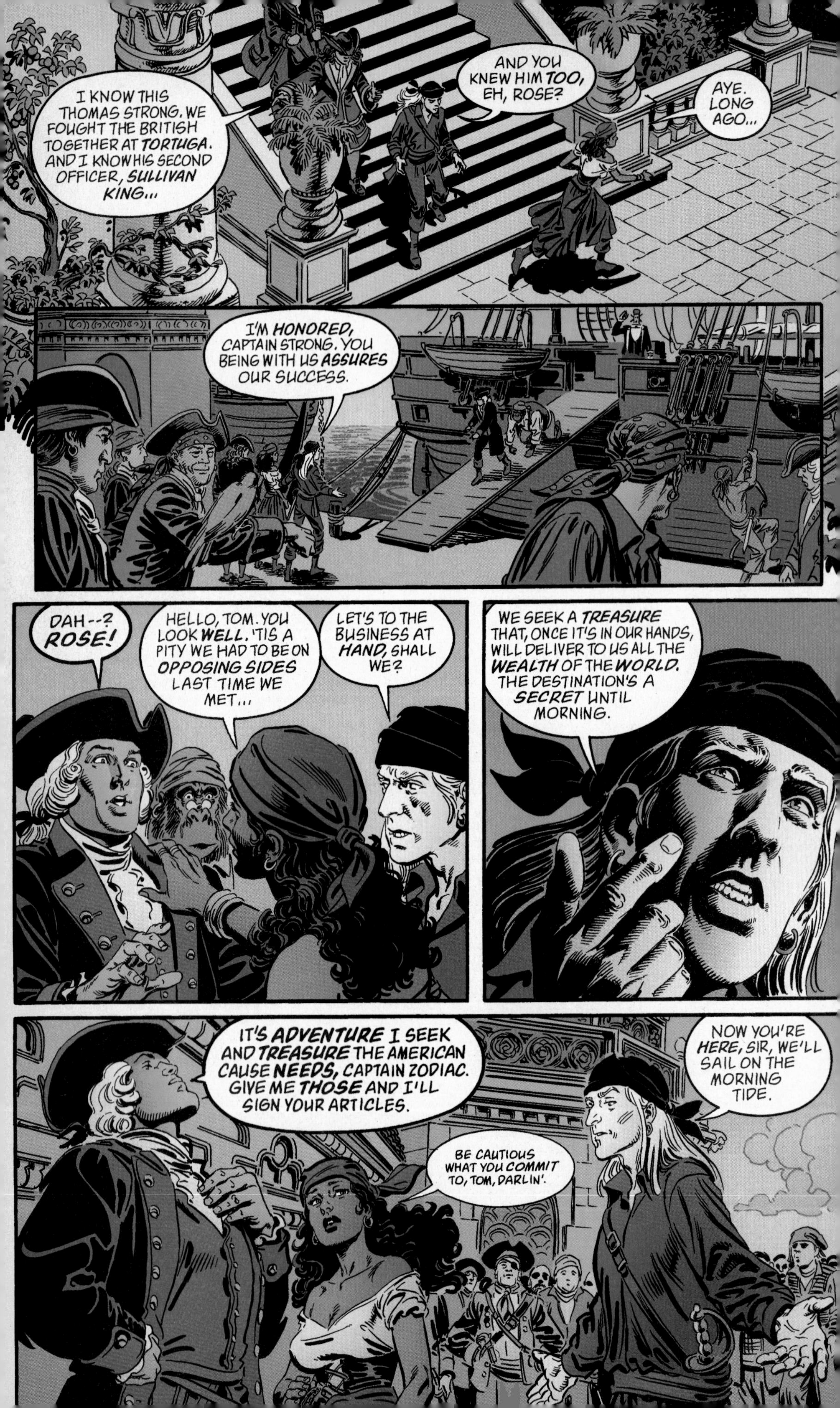
I KNOW THIS THOMAS STRONG. WE FOUGHT THE BRITISH TOGETHER AT TORTUGA. AND I KNOW HIS SECOND OFFICER, SULLIVAN KING...
AND YOU KNEW HIM TOO, EH, ROSE?
AYE. LONG AGO...
I'M HONORED, CAPTAIN STRONG. YOU BEING WITH US ASSURES OUR SUCCESS.
DAH--? ROSE!
HELLO, TOM. YOU LOOK WELL. 'TIS A PITY WE HAD TO BE ON OPPOSING SIDES LAST TIME WE MET...
LET'S TO THE BUSINESS AT HAND, SHALL WE?
WE SEEK A TREASURE THAT, ONCE IT'S IN OUR HANDS, WILL DELIVER TO US ALL THE WEALTH OF THE WORLD. THE DESTINATION'S A SECRET UNTIL MORNING.
IT'S ADVENTURE I SEEK AND TREASURE THE AMERICAN CAUSE NEEDS, CAPTAIN ZODIAC. GIVE ME THOSE AND I'LL SIGN YOUR ARTICLES.
BE CAUTIOUS WHAT YOU COMMIT TO, TOM, DARLIN'.
NOW YOU'RE HERE, SIR, WE'LL SAIL ON THE MORNING TIDE.

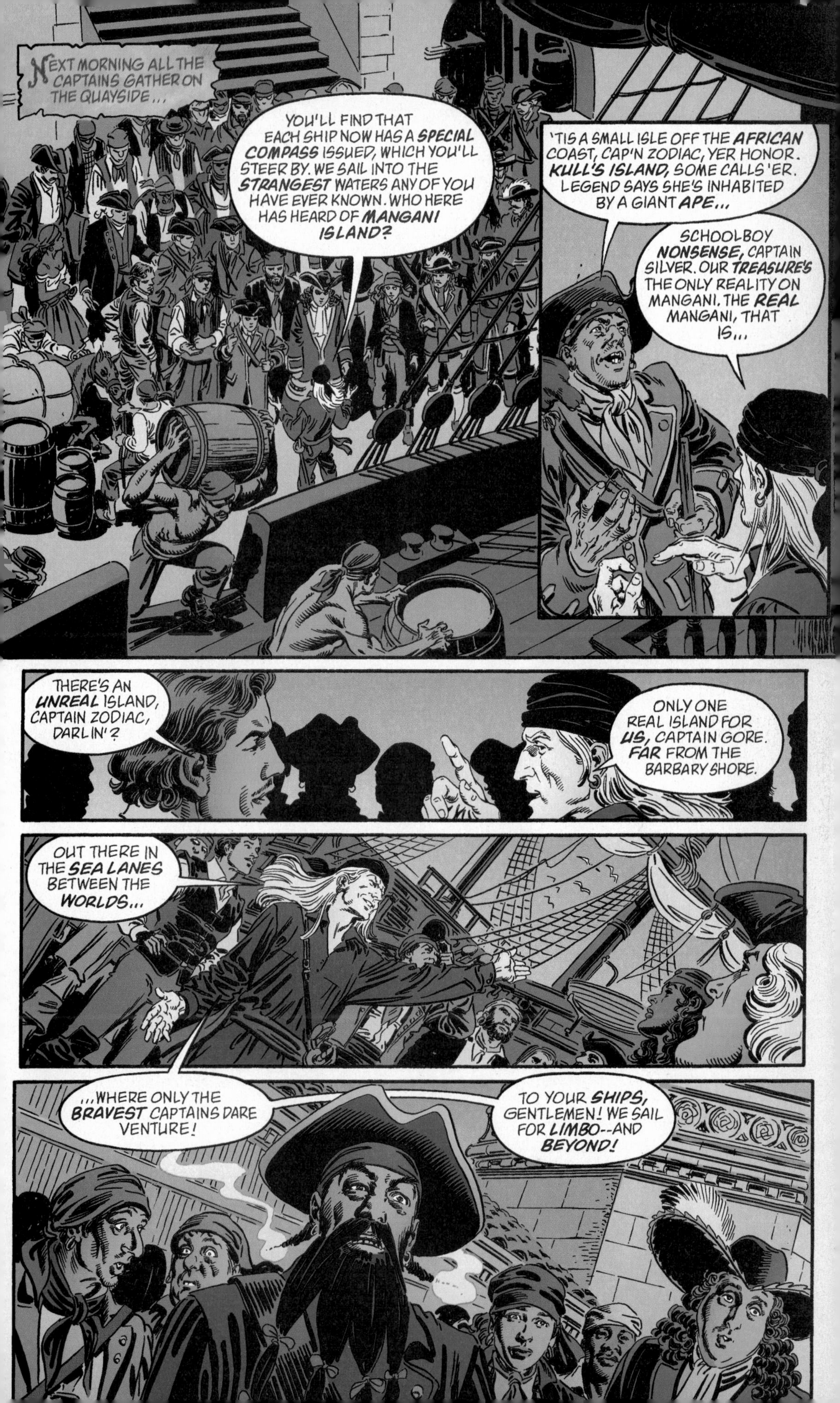
NEXT MORNING ALL THE CAPTAINS GATHER ON THE QUAYSIDE...
YOU'LL FIND THAT EACH SHIP NOW HAS A SPECIAL COMPASS ISSUED, WHICH YOU'LL STEER BY. WE SAIL INTO THE STRANGEST WATERS ANY OF YOU HAVE EVER KNOWN. WHO HERE HAS HEARD OF MANGANI ISLAND?
'TIS A SMALL ISLE OFF THE AFRICAN COAST, CAP'N ZODIAC, YER HONOR. KULL'S ISLAND, SOME CALLS 'ER. LEGEND SAYS SHE'S INHABITED BY A GIANT APE...
SCHOOLBOY NONSENSE, CAPTAIN SILVER. OUR TREASURE'S THE ONLY REALITY ON MANGANI. THE REAL MANGANI, THAT IS...
THERE'S AN UNREAL ISLAND, CAPTAIN ZODIAC, DARLIN'?
ONLY ONE REAL ISLAND FOR US, CAPTAIN GORE. FAR FROM THE BARBARY SHORE.
OUT THERE IN THE SEA LANES BETWEEN THE WORLDS...
...WHERE ONLY THE BRAVEST CAPTAINS DARE VENTURE!
TO YOUR SHIPS, GENTLEMEN! WE SAIL FOR LIMBO--AND BEYOND!

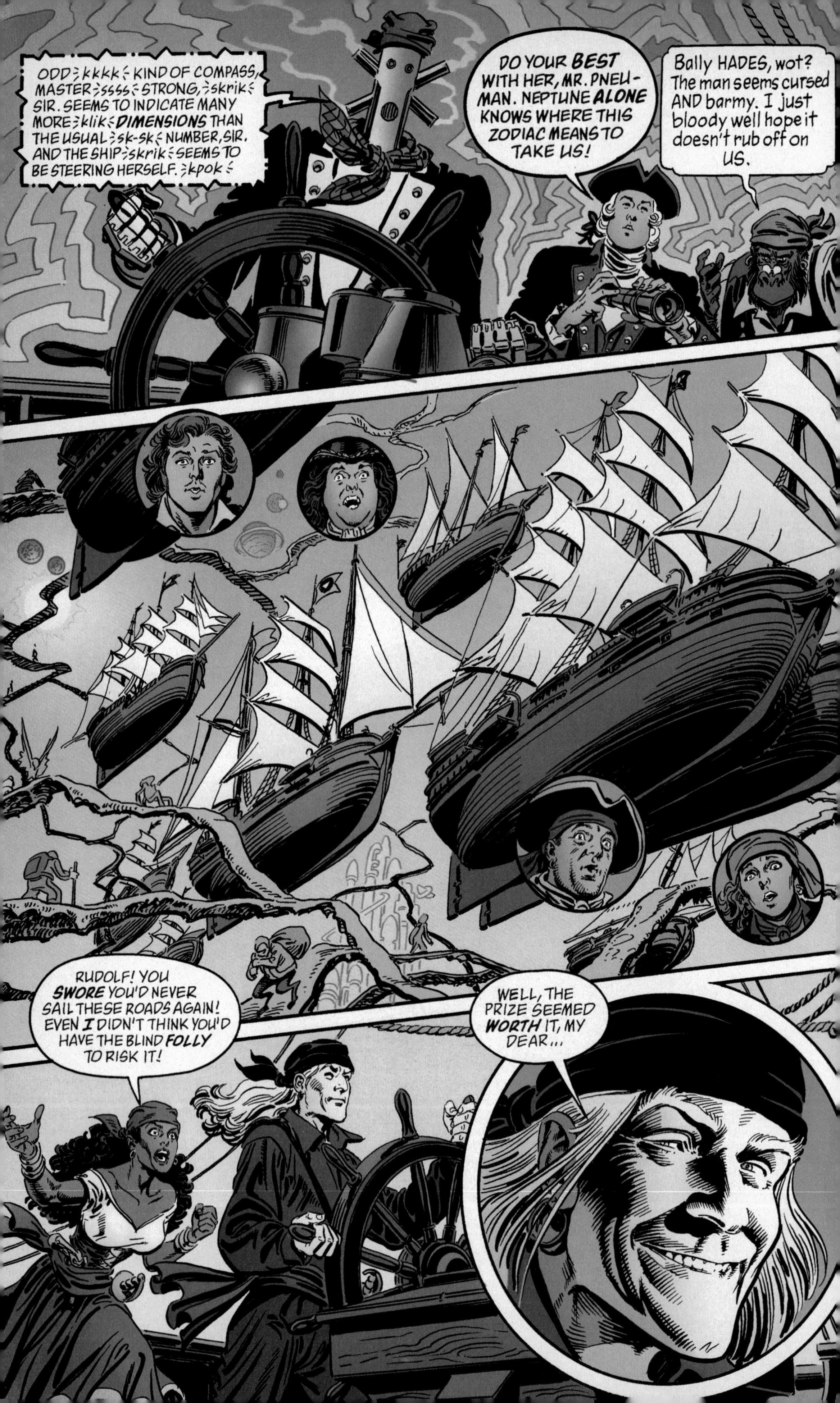

ODD ≷kkkk≶ KIND OF COMPASS, MASTER ≷ssss≶ STRONG, ≷skrik≶ SIR. SEEMS TO INDICATE MANY MORE ≷klik≶ **DIMENSIONS** THAN THE USUAL ≷sk-sk≶ NUMBER, SIR. AND THE SHIP ≷skrik≶ SEEMS TO BE STEERING HERSELF. ≷kpok≶
DO YOUR **BEST** WITH HER, MR. PNEUMAN. NEPTUNE **ALONE** KNOWS WHERE THIS ZODIAC MEANS TO TAKE US!
Bally HADES, wot? The man seems cursed AND barmy. I just bloody well hope it doesn't rub off on US.
RUDOLF! YOU **SWORE** YOU'D NEVER SAIL THESE ROADS AGAIN! EVEN **I** DIDN'T THINK YOU'D HAVE THE BLIND **FOLLY** TO RISK IT!
WELL, THE PRIZE SEEMED **WORTH** IT, MY DEAR...

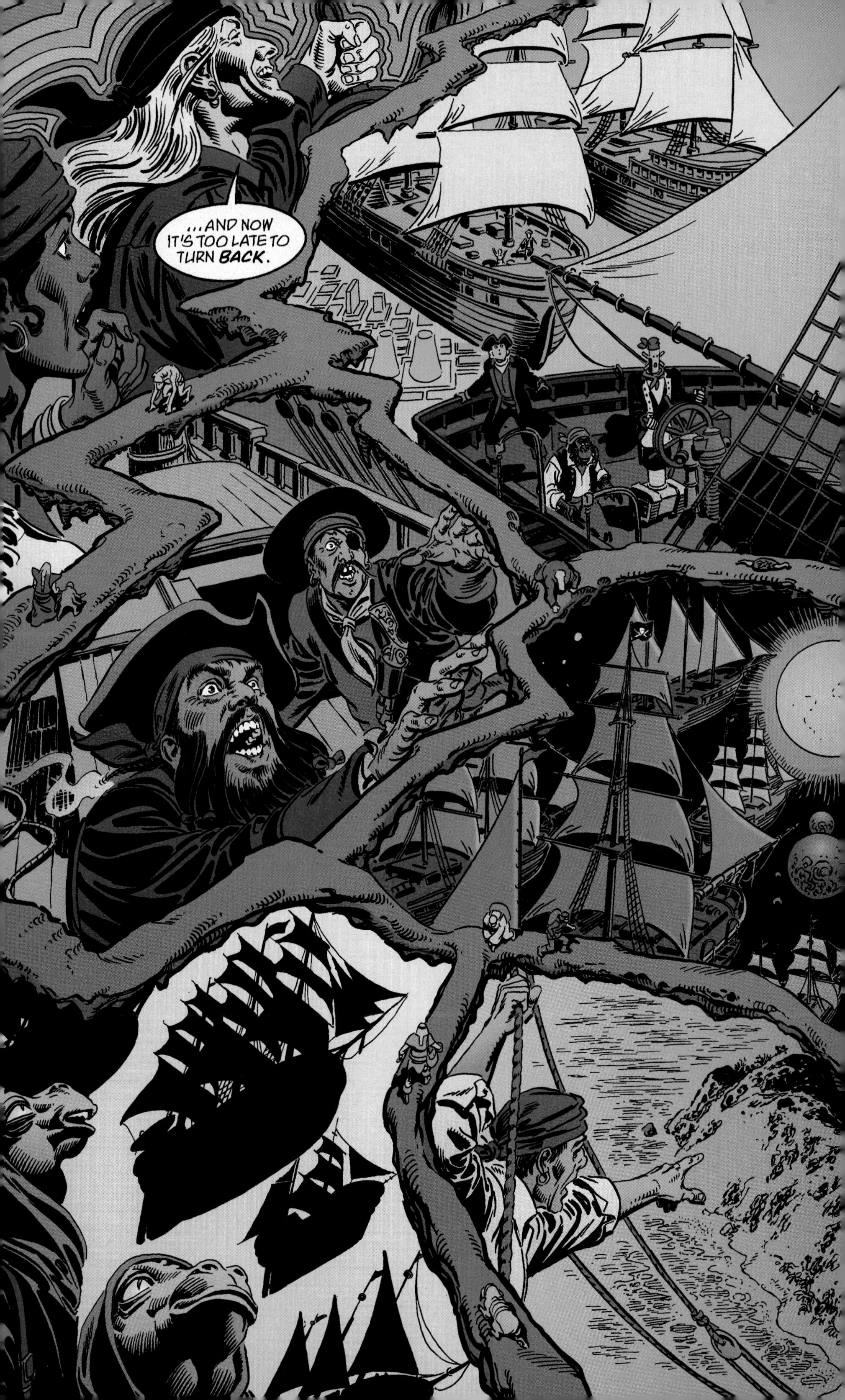
...AND NOW IT'S TOO LATE TO TURN BACK.

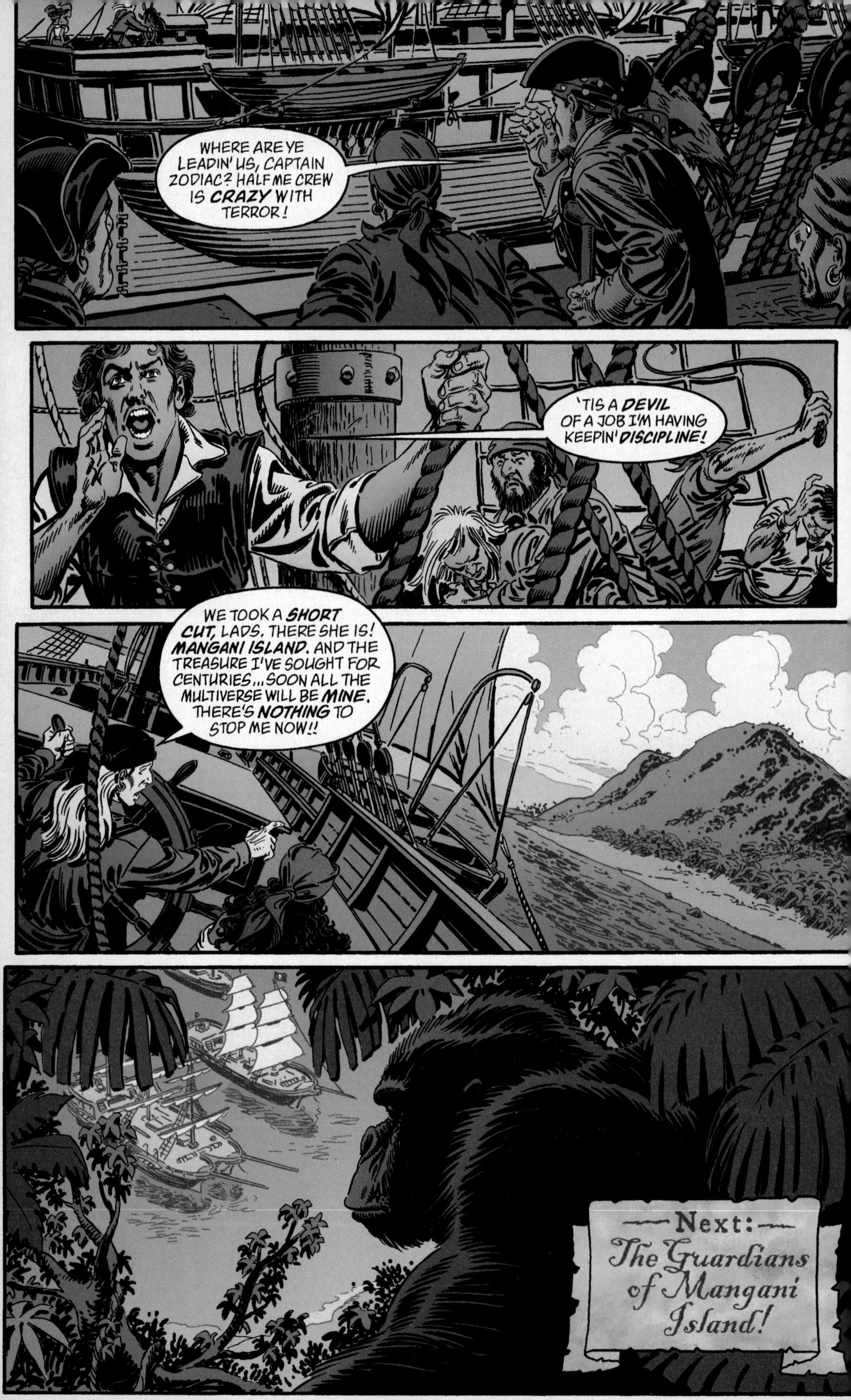
WHERE ARE YE LEADIN' US, CAPTAIN ZODIAC? HALF ME CREW IS CRAZY WITH TERROR!
'TIS A DEVIL OF A JOB I'M HAVING KEEPIN' DISCIPLINE!
WE TOOK A SHORT CUT, LADS. THERE SHE IS! MANGANI ISLAND. AND THE TREASURE I'VE SOUGHT FOR CENTURIES... SOON ALL THE MULTIVERSE WILL BE MINE. THERE'S NOTHING TO STOP ME NOW!!
Next:
The Guardians of Mangani Island!

# CHAPTER TWO

In which Tom and the pirates battle dinosaurs,
King Solomon parleys with distant relatives,
and a deadly cutlass is taken in hand.

Cover art:
Jerry Ordway
Cover colors:
Darlene Royer

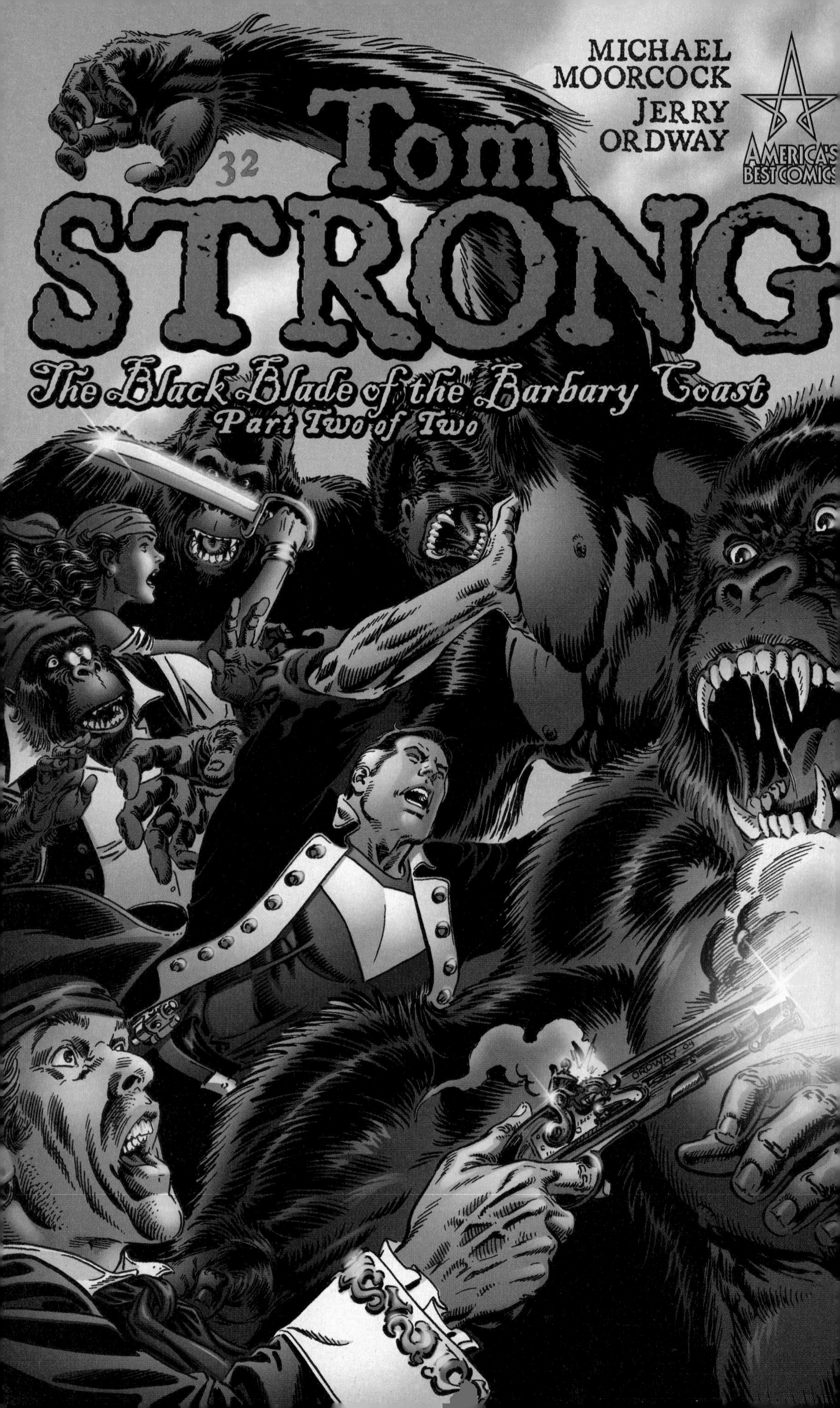

MICHAEL
MOORCOCK
JERRY
ORDWAY
AMERICA'S
BEST COMICS
32
Tom
STRONG
The Black Blade of the Barbary Coast
Part Two of Two
ORDWAY 04

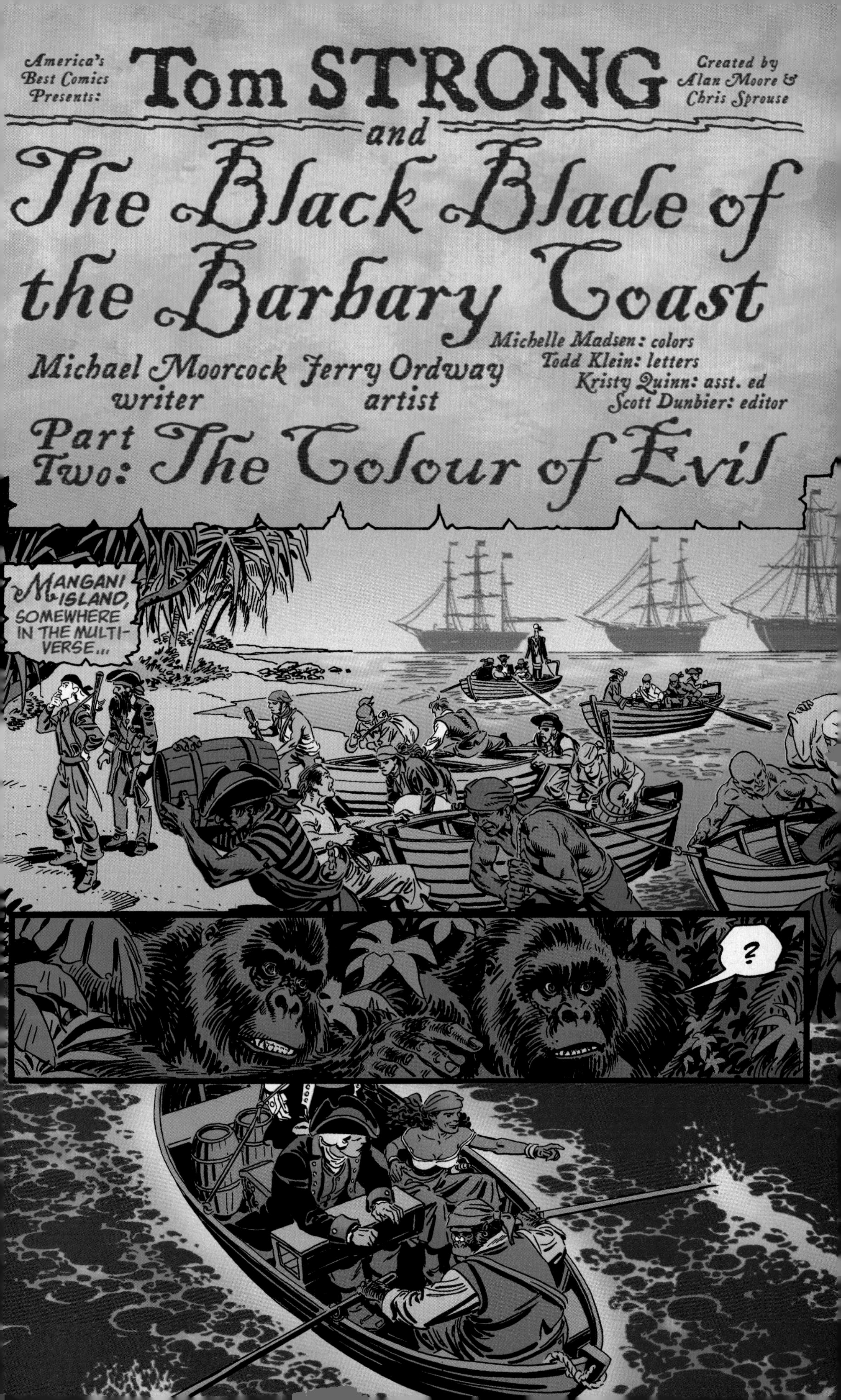
America's Best Comics Presents:
Tom STRONG
Created by Alan Moore & Chris Sprouse
and
The Black Blade of the Barbary Coast
Michelle Madsen: colors
Todd Klein: letters
Kristy Quinn: asst. ed
Scott Dunbier: editor
Michael Moorcock writer
Jerry Ordway artist
Part Two: The Colour of Evil
MANGANI ISLAND, SOMEWHERE IN THE MULTI-VERSE...
?

THIS HAD BETTER BE WORTH IT, CAP'N ZODIAC!

WORTH MORE THAN YOU CAN *IMAGINE*, CAPTAIN GORE...

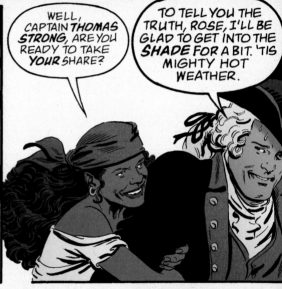

WELL, CAPTAIN *THOMAS STRONG*, ARE YOU READY TO TAKE *YOUR* SHARE?

TO TELL YOU THE TRUTH, ROSE, I'LL BE GLAD TO GET INTO THE *SHADE* FOR A BIT. 'TIS MIGHTY HOT WEATHER.

TOO bloody hot for a decent English gent, wot?

BEGGIN YER PARDON, CAP'N, BUT I THINK 'TIS BEST IF OLD *SILVER* STAYS YERE ON THE BEACH TER LOOK AFTER OUR *BOATS*...AYE...

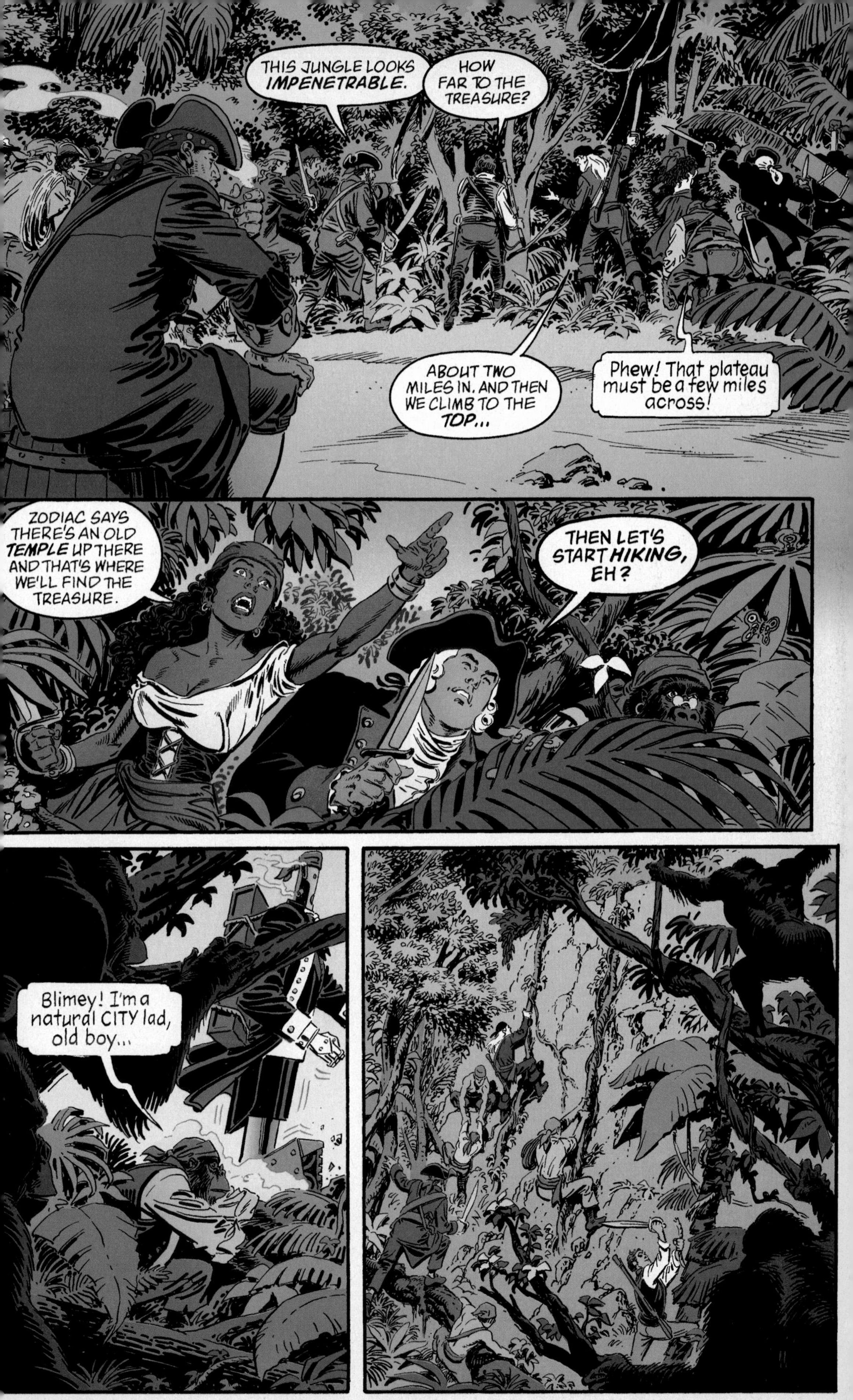

THIS JUNGLE LOOKS IMPENETRABLE.
HOW FAR TO THE TREASURE?
ABOUT TWO MILES IN. AND THEN WE CLIMB TO THE TOP...
Phew! That plateau must be a few miles across!
ZODIAC SAYS THERE'S AN OLD TEMPLE UP THERE AND THAT'S WHERE WE'LL FIND THE TREASURE.
THEN LET'S START HIKING, EH?
Blimey! I'm a natural CITY lad, old boy...

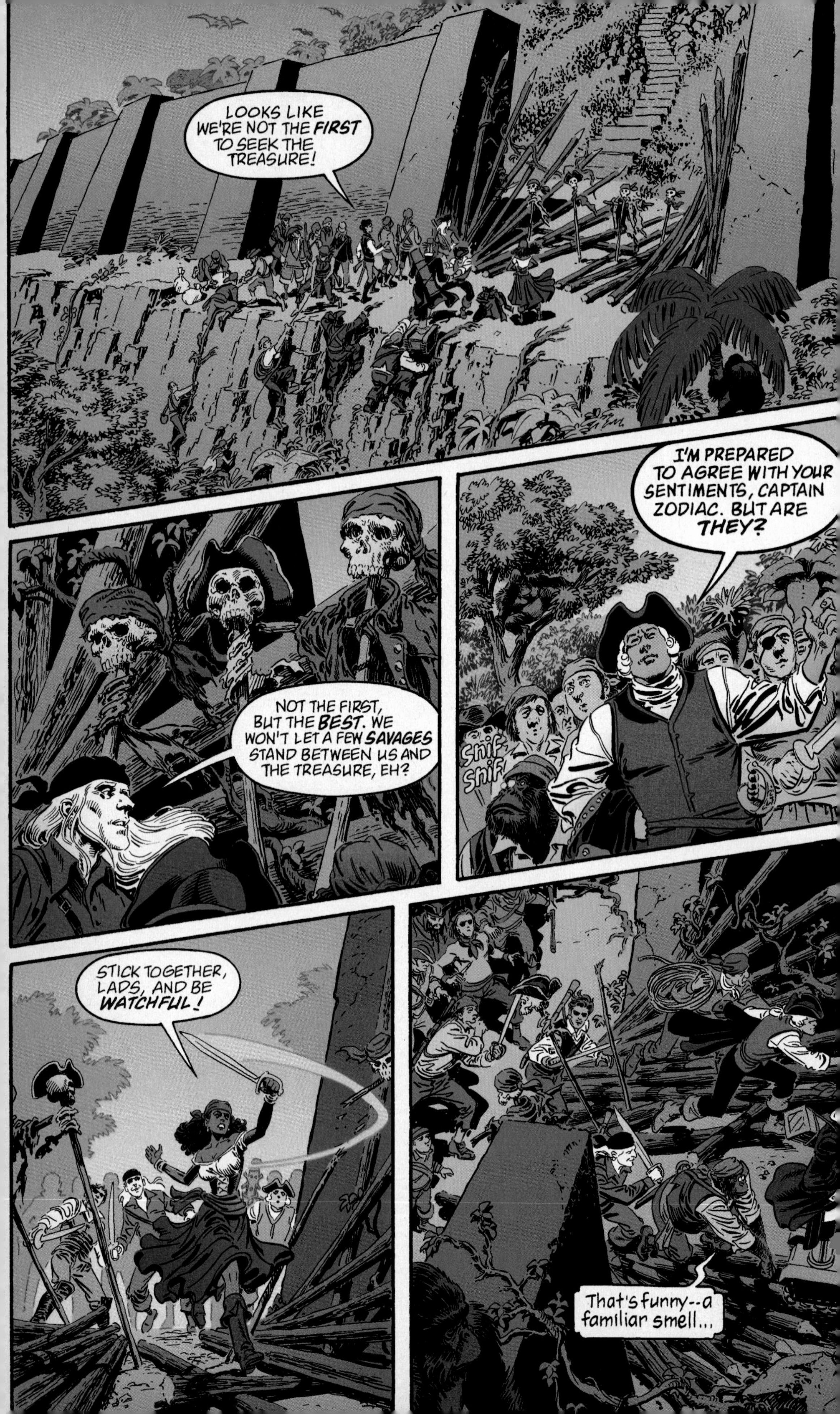
LOOKS LIKE WE'RE NOT THE FIRST TO SEEK THE TREASURE!
NOT THE FIRST, BUT THE BEST. WE WON'T LET A FEW SAVAGES STAND BETWEEN US AND THE TREASURE, EH?
I'M PREPARED TO AGREE WITH YOUR SENTIMENTS, CAPTAIN ZODIAC. BUT ARE THEY?
Snif Snif
STICK TOGETHER, LADS, AND BE WATCHFUL!
That's funny--a familiar smell...

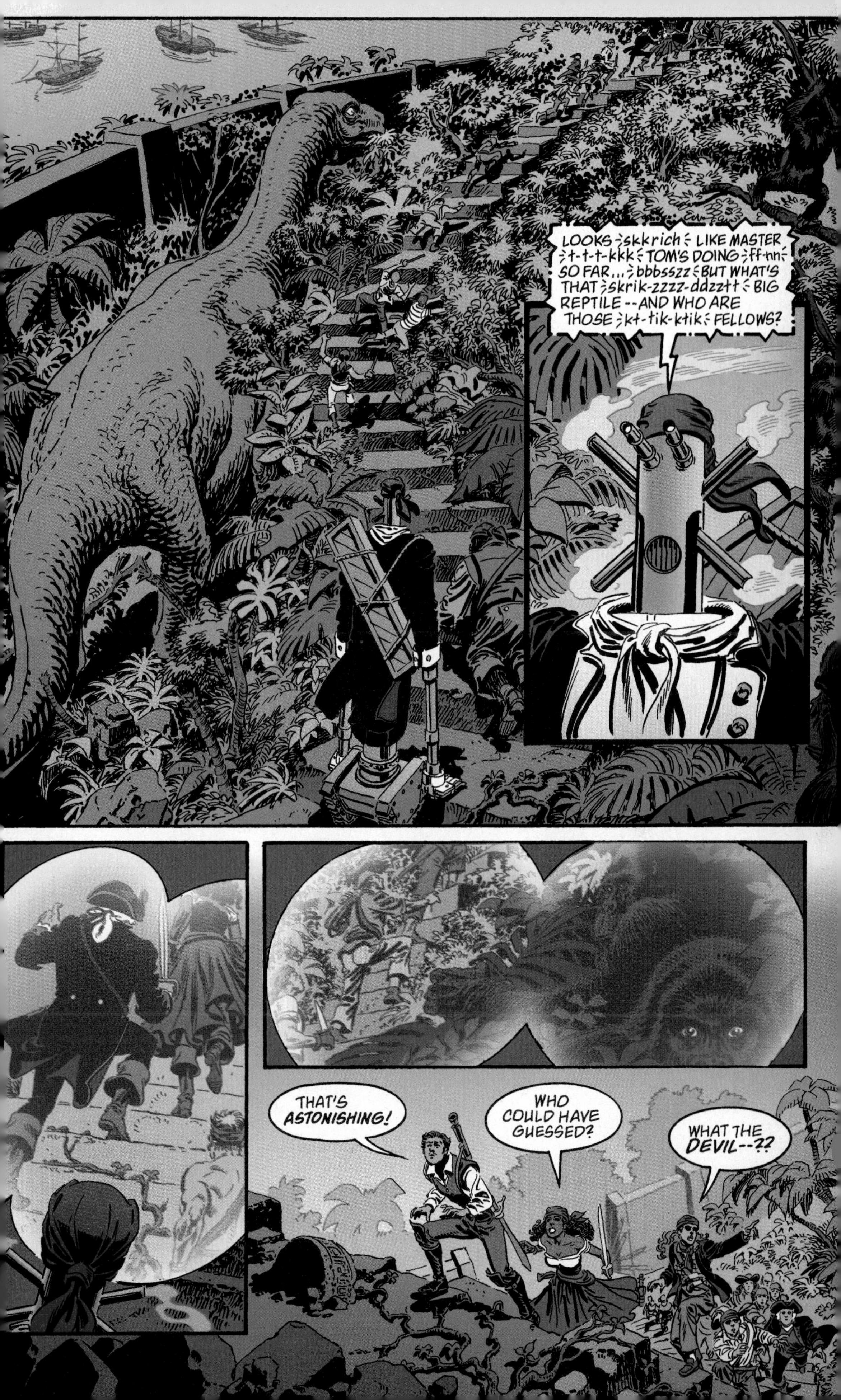

LOOKS skkrich LIKE MASTER t-t-t-kkk TOM'S DOING ff-nn SO FAR... bbbsszz BUT WHAT'S THAT skrik-zzzz-ddzztt BIG REPTILE --AND WHO ARE THOSE kt-tik-ktik FELLOWS?
THAT'S ASTONISHING!
WHO COULD HAVE GUESSED?
WHAT THE DEVIL--??

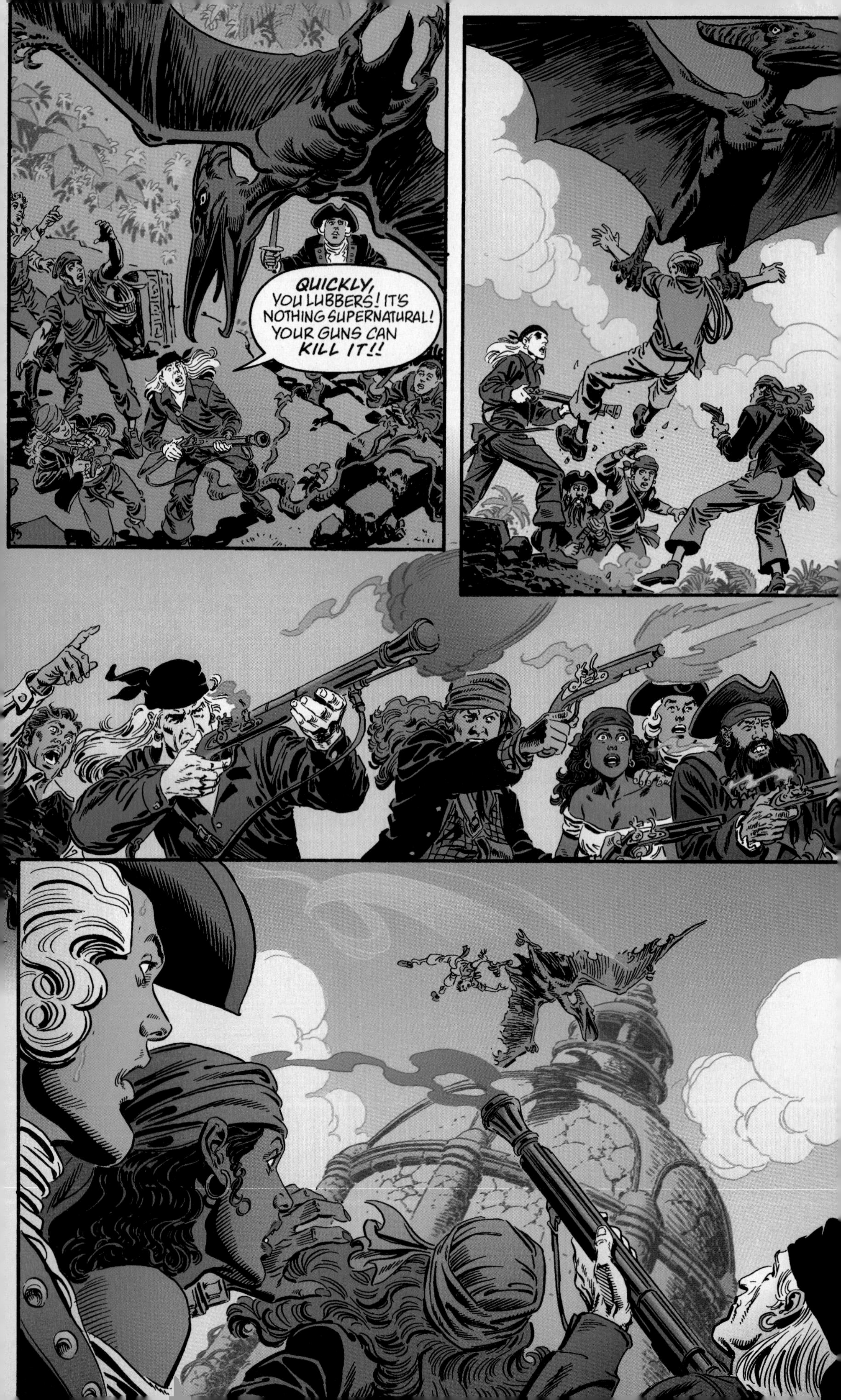
QUICKLY, YOU LUBBERS! IT'S NOTHING SUPERNATURAL! YOUR GUNS CAN KILL IT!!

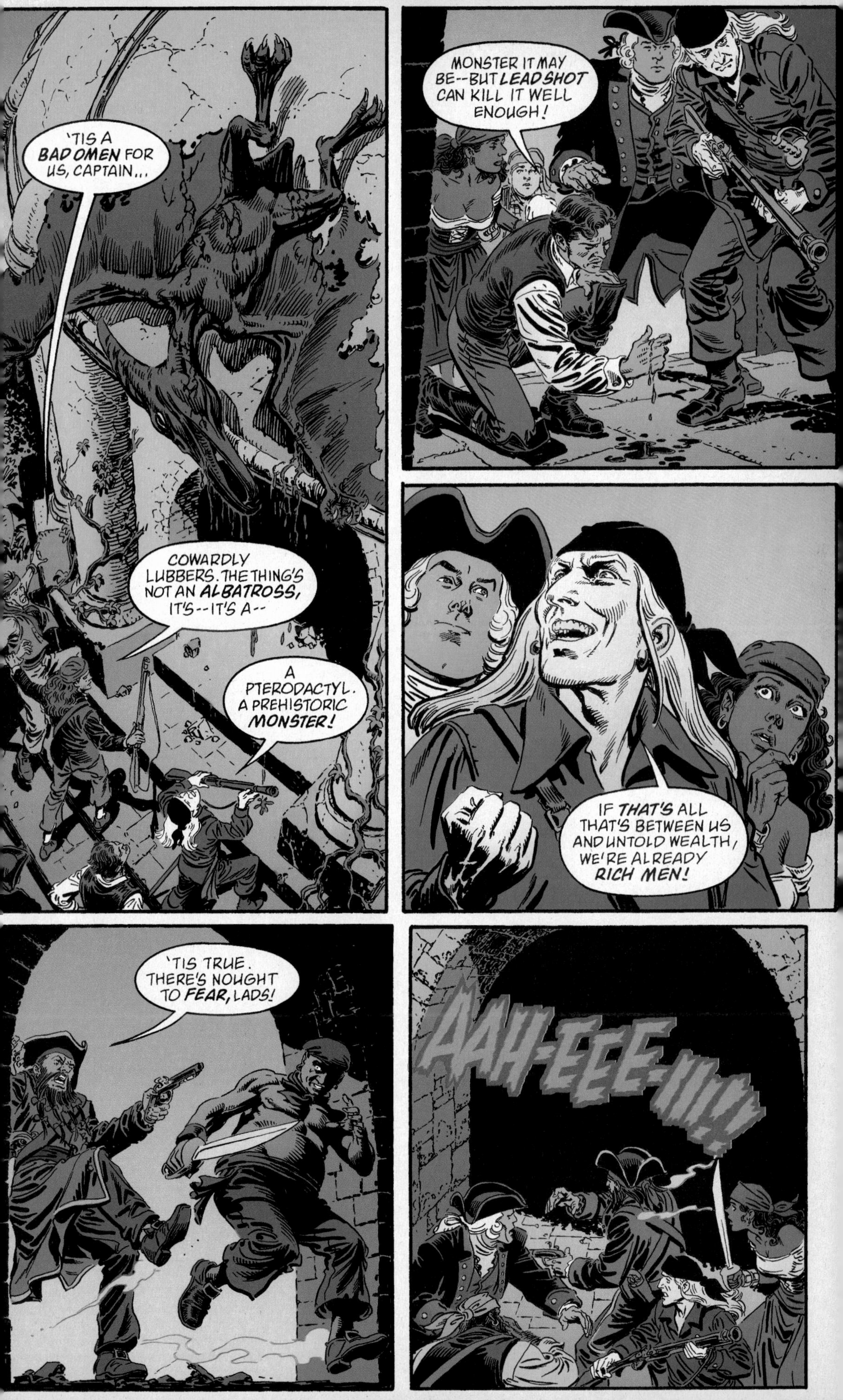
'TIS A BAD OMEN FOR US, CAPTAIN...
COWARDLY LUBBERS. THE THING'S NOT AN ALBATROSS, IT'S--IT'S A--
A PTERODACTYL. A PREHISTORIC MONSTER!
MONSTER IT MAY BE--BUT LEAD SHOT CAN KILL IT WELL ENOUGH!
IF THAT'S ALL THAT'S BETWEEN US AND UNTOLD WEALTH, WE'RE ALREADY RICH MEN!
'TIS TRUE. THERE'S NOUGHT TO FEAR, LADS!
AAH-EEE-IIII!

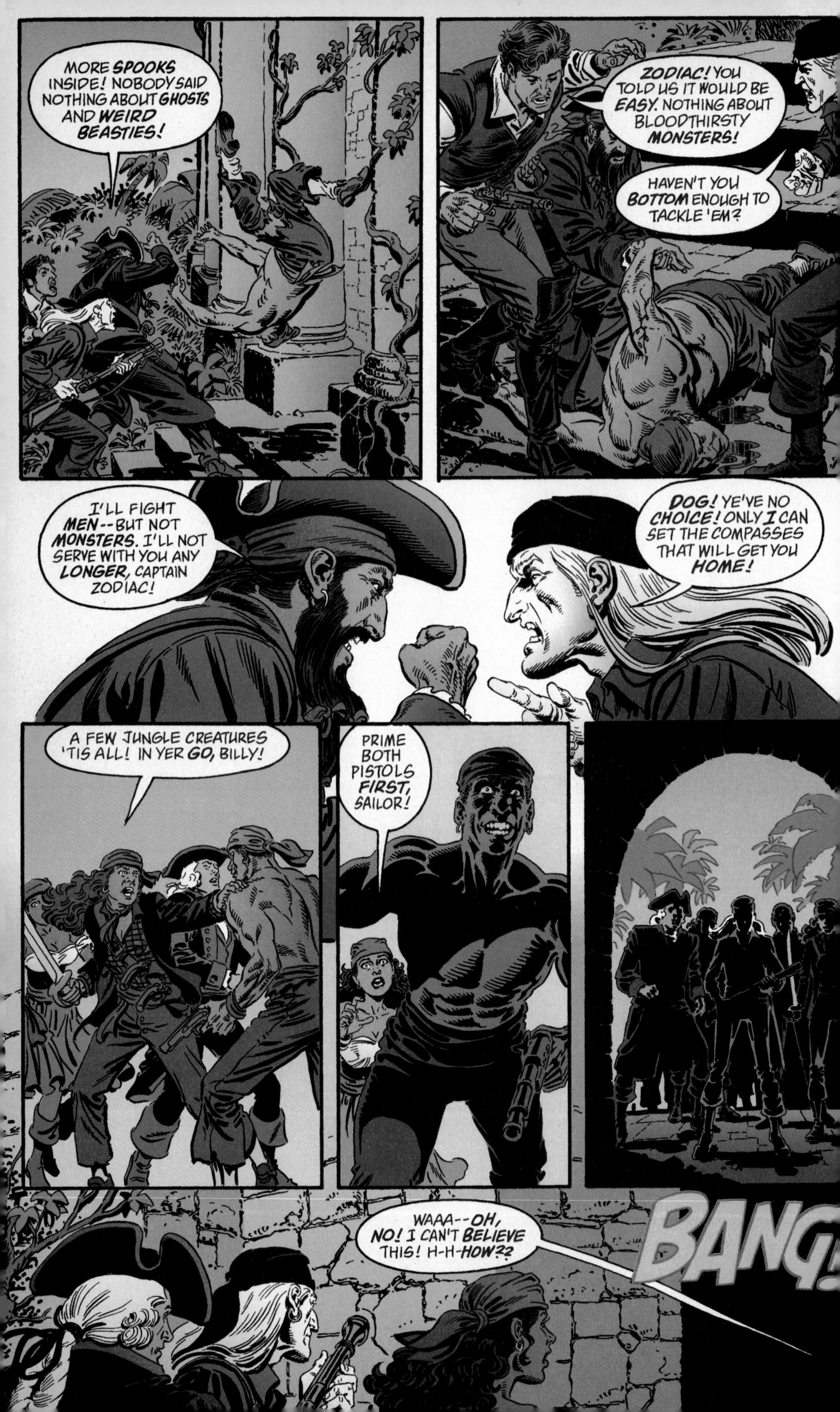
MORE SPOOKS INSIDE! NOBODY SAID NOTHING ABOUT GHOSTS AND WEIRD BEASTIES!
ZODIAC! YOU TOLD US IT WOULD BE EASY. NOTHING ABOUT BLOODTHIRSTY MONSTERS!
HAVEN'T YOU BOTTOM ENOUGH TO TACKLE 'EM?
I'LL FIGHT MEN--BUT NOT MONSTERS. I'LL NOT SERVE WITH YOU ANY LONGER, CAPTAIN ZODIAC!
DOG! YE'VE NO CHOICE! ONLY I CAN SET THE COMPASSES THAT WILL GET YOU HOME!
A FEW JUNGLE CREATURES 'TIS ALL! IN YER GO, BILLY!
PRIME BOTH PISTOLS FIRST, SAILOR!
WAAA--OH, NO! I CAN'T BELIEVE THIS! H-H-HOW??
BANG!

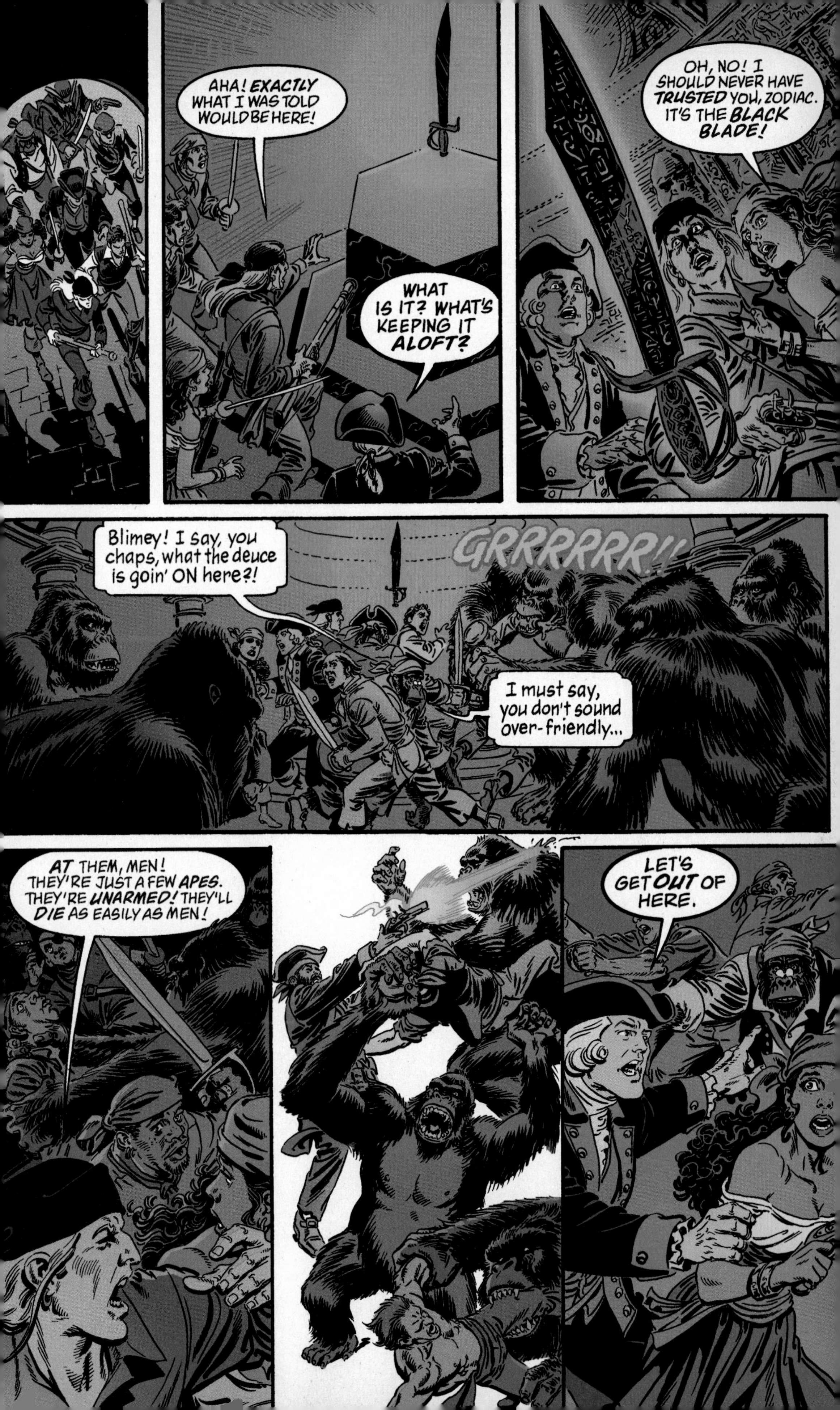
AHA! EXACTLY WHAT I WAS TOLD WOULD BE HERE!
WHAT IS IT? WHAT'S KEEPING IT ALOFT?
OH, NO! I SHOULD NEVER HAVE TRUSTED YOU, ZODIAC. IT'S THE BLACK BLADE!
Blimey! I say, you chaps, what the deuce is goin' ON here?!
GRRRRRR!!
I must say, you don't sound over-friendly...
AT THEM, MEN! THEY'RE JUST A FEW APES. THEY'RE UNARMED! THEY'LL DIE AS EASILY AS MEN!
LET'S GET OUT OF HERE.

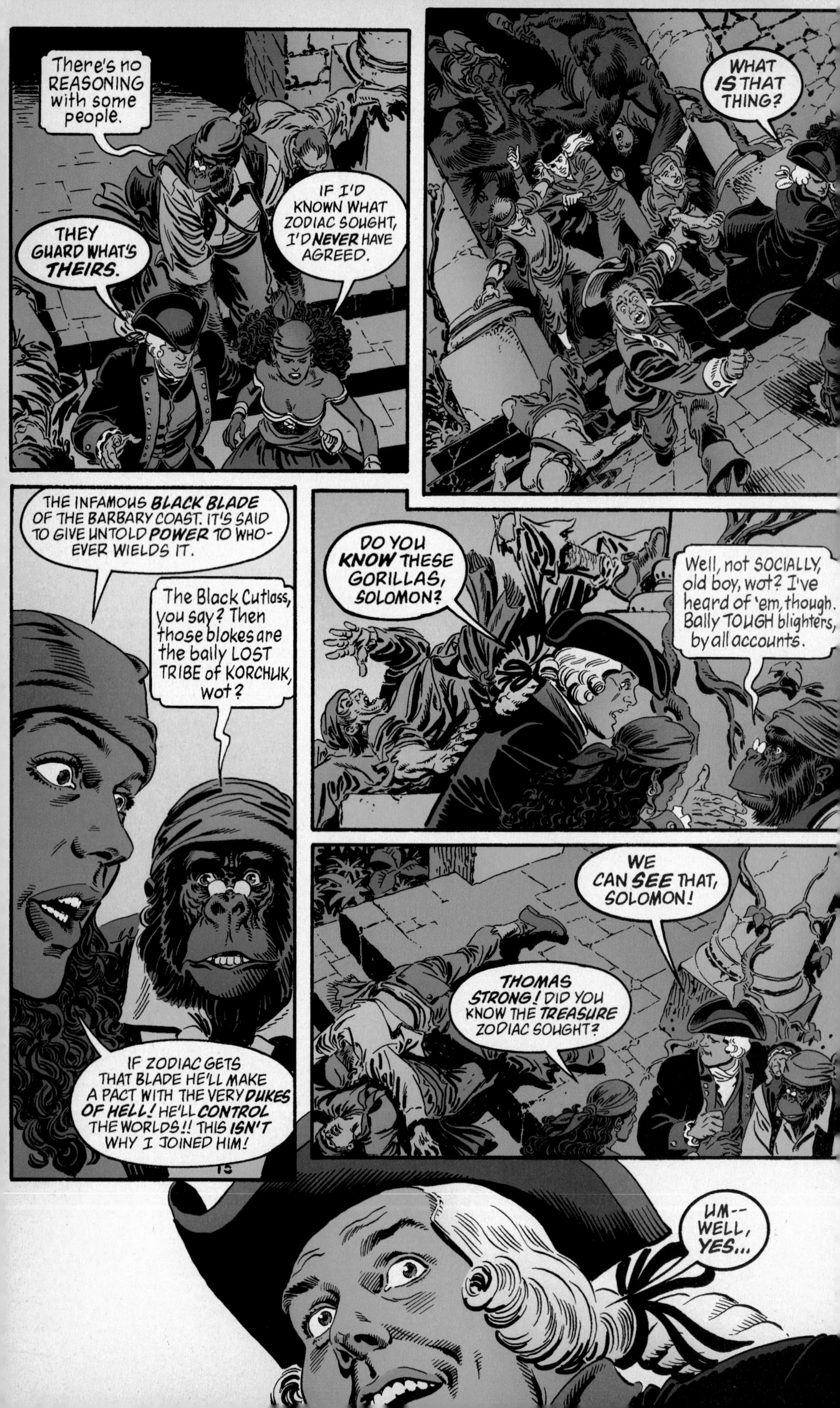
There's no REASONING with some people.
THEY GUARD WHAT'S THEIRS.
IF I'D KNOWN WHAT ZODIAC SOUGHT, I'D NEVER HAVE AGREED.
WHAT IS THAT THING?
THE INFAMOUS BLACK BLADE OF THE BARBARY COAST. IT'S SAID TO GIVE UNTOLD POWER TO WHO-EVER WIELDS IT.
The Black Cutlass, you say? Then those blokes are the bally LOST TRIBE of KORCHUK, wot?
IF ZODIAC GETS THAT BLADE HE'LL MAKE A PACT WITH THE VERY DUKES OF HELL! HE'LL CONTROL THE WORLDS!! THIS ISN'T WHY I JOINED HIM!
DO YOU KNOW THESE GORILLAS, SOLOMON?
Well, not SOCIALLY, old boy, wot? I've heard of 'em, though. Bally TOUGH blighters, by all accounts.
WE CAN SEE THAT, SOLOMON!
THOMAS STRONG! DID YOU KNOW THE TREASURE ZODIAC SOUGHT?
UM-- WELL, YES...

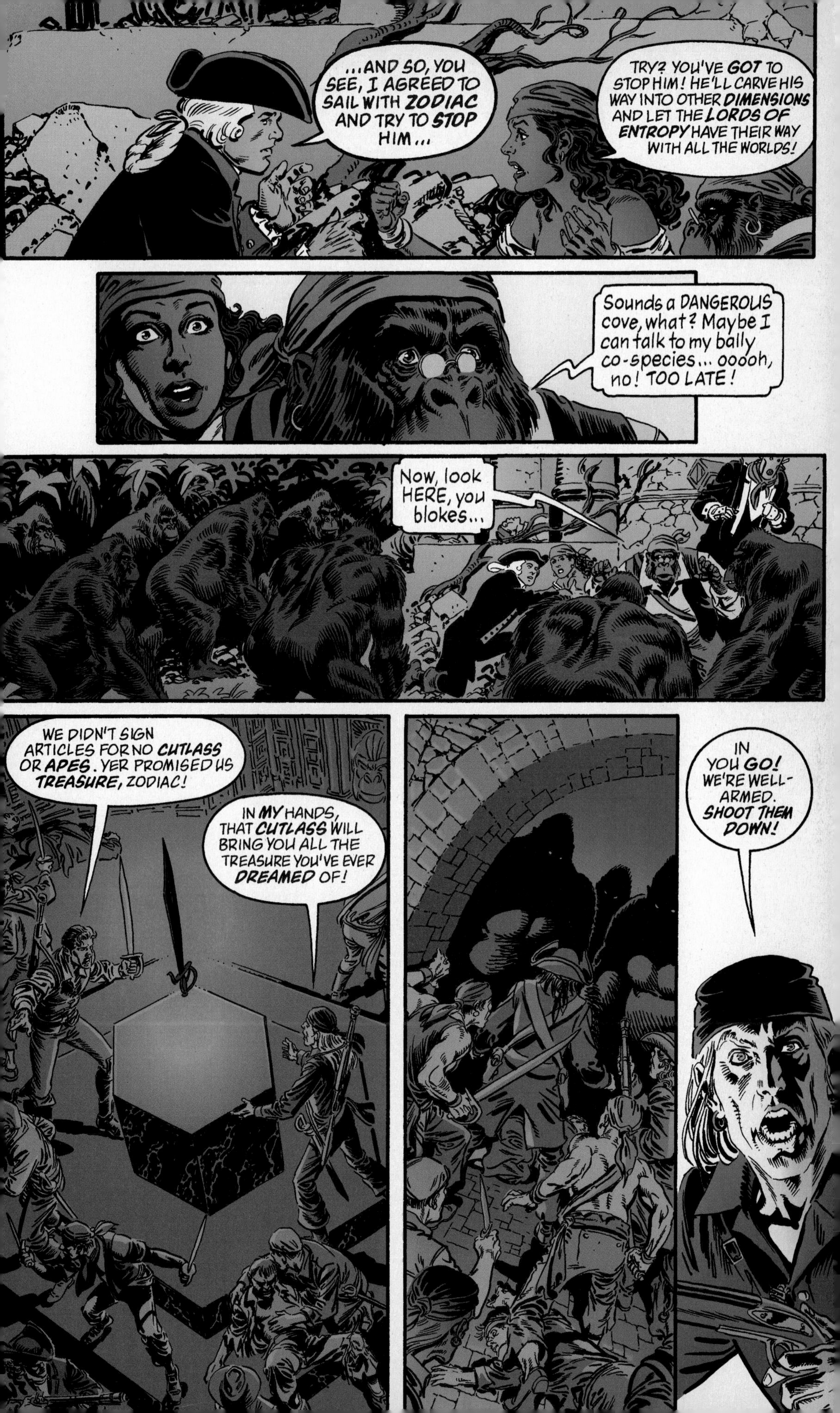
...AND SO, YOU SEE, I AGREED TO SAIL WITH ZODIAC AND TRY TO STOP HIM...
TRY? YOU'VE GOT TO STOP HIM! HE'LL CARVE HIS WAY INTO OTHER DIMENSIONS AND LET THE LORDS OF ENTROPY HAVE THEIR WAY WITH ALL THE WORLDS!
Sounds a DANGEROUS cove, what? Maybe I can talk to my bally co-species... ooooh, no! TOO LATE!
Now, look HERE, you blokes...
WE DIDN'T SIGN ARTICLES FOR NO CUTLASS OR APES. YER PROMISED US TREASURE, ZODIAC!
IN MY HANDS, THAT CUTLASS WILL BRING YOU ALL THE TREASURE YOU'VE EVER DREAMED OF!
IN YOU GO! WE'RE WELL-ARMED. SHOOT THEM DOWN!

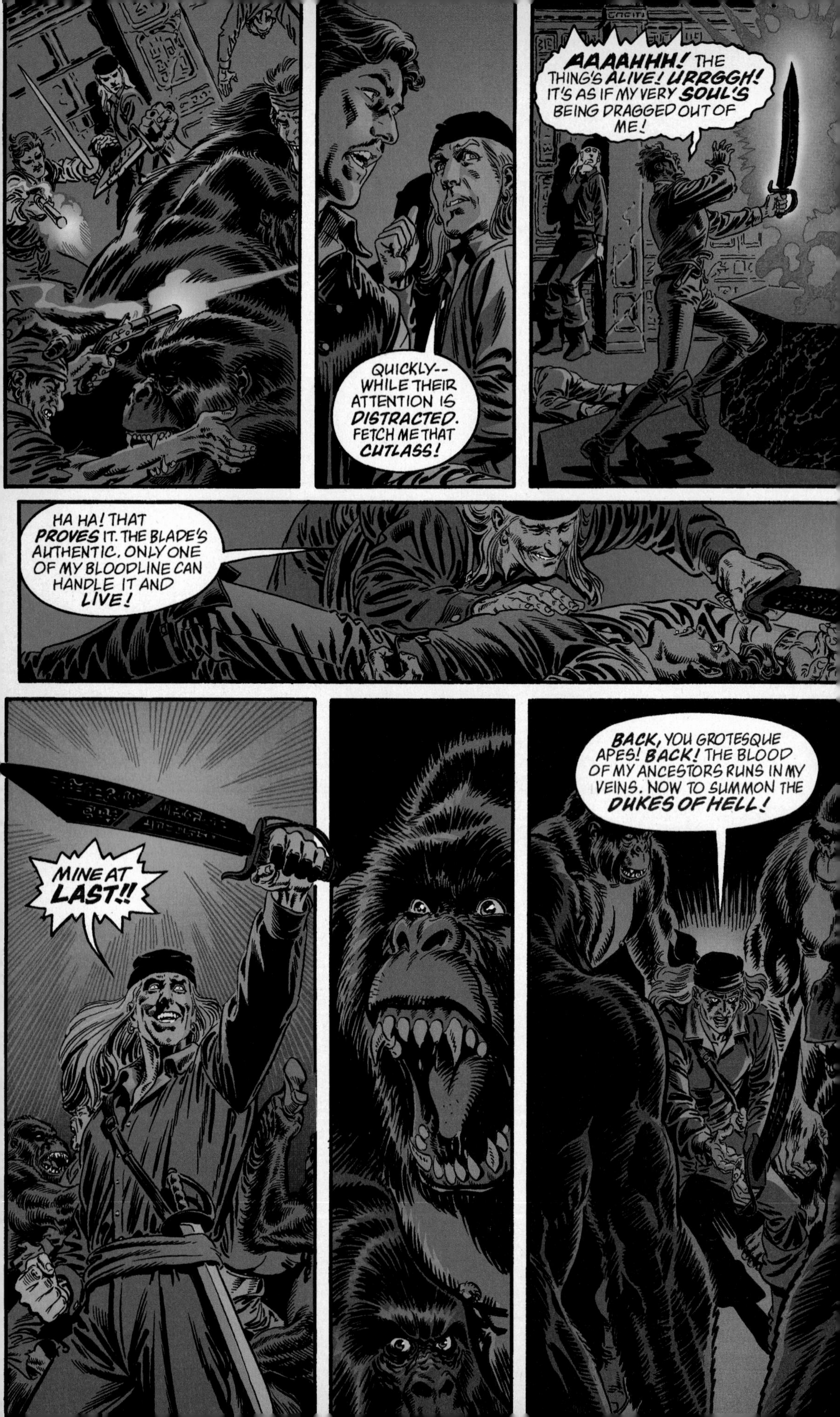
QUICKLY-- WHILE THEIR ATTENTION IS DISTRACTED. FETCH ME THAT CUTLASS!
AAAAHHH! THE THING'S ALIVE! URRGGH! IT'S AS IF MY VERY SOUL'S BEING DRAGGED OUT OF ME!
HA HA! THAT PROVES IT. THE BLADE'S AUTHENTIC. ONLY ONE OF MY BLOODLINE CAN HANDLE IT AND LIVE!
MINE AT LAST!!
BACK, YOU GROTESQUE APES! BACK! THE BLOOD OF MY ANCESTORS RUNS IN MY VEINS. NOW TO SUMMON THE DUKES OF HELL!

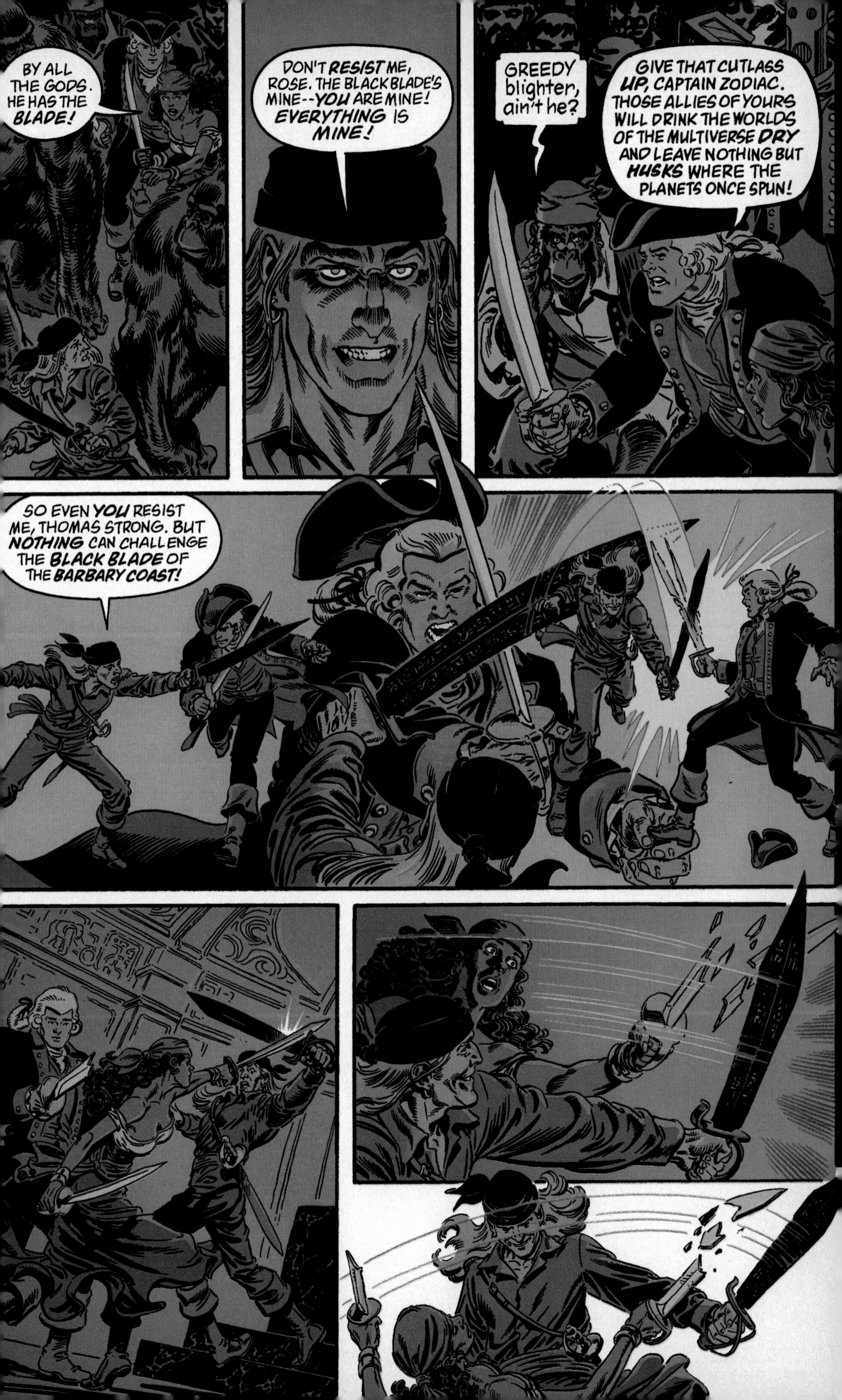
BY ALL THE GODS. HE HAS THE BLADE!
DON'T RESIST ME, ROSE. THE BLACK BLADE'S MINE--YOU ARE MINE! EVERYTHING IS MINE!
GREEDY blighter, ain't he?
GIVE THAT CUTLASS UP, CAPTAIN ZODIAC. THOSE ALLIES OF YOURS WILL DRINK THE WORLDS OF THE MULTIVERSE DRY AND LEAVE NOTHING BUT HUSKS WHERE THE PLANETS ONCE SPUN!
SO EVEN YOU RESIST ME, THOMAS STRONG. BUT NOTHING CAN CHALLENGE THE BLACK BLADE OF THE BARBARY COAST!

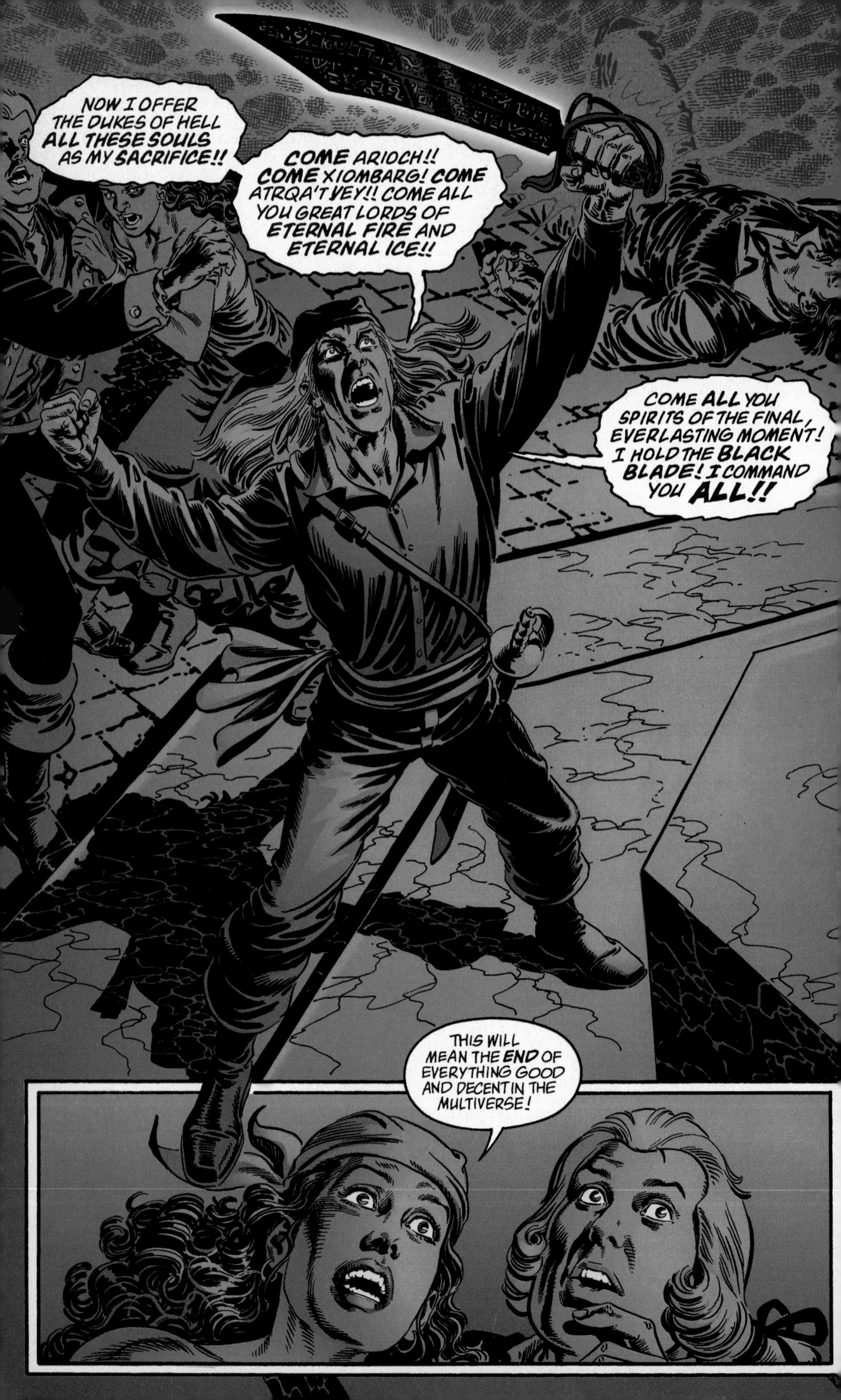
NOW I OFFER THE DUKES OF HELL ALL THESE SOULS AS MY SACRIFICE!!
COME ARIOCH!! COME XIOMBARG! COME ATRQA'T VEY!! COME ALL YOU GREAT LORDS OF ETERNAL FIRE AND ETERNAL ICE!!
COME ALL YOU SPIRITS OF THE FINAL, EVERLASTING MOMENT! I HOLD THE BLACK BLADE! I COMMAND YOU ALL!!
THIS WILL MEAN THE END OF EVERYTHING GOOD AND DECENT IN THE MULTIVERSE!

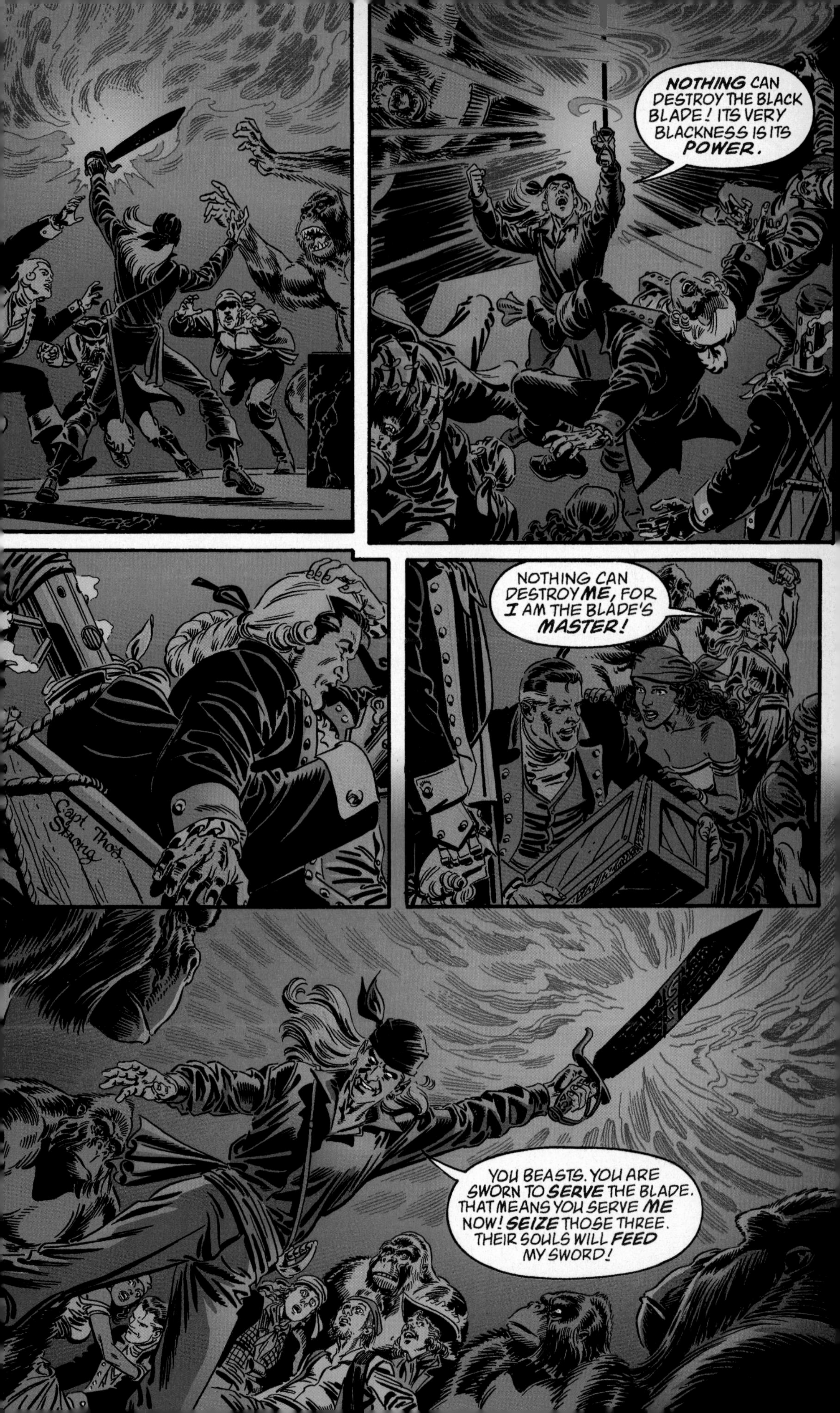
NOTHING CAN DESTROY THE BLACK BLADE! ITS VERY BLACKNESS IS ITS POWER.
Capt. Thos. Strong
NOTHING CAN DESTROY ME, FOR I AM THE BLADE'S MASTER!
YOU BEASTS. YOU ARE SWORN TO SERVE THE BLADE. THAT MEANS YOU SERVE ME NOW! SEIZE THOSE THREE. THEIR SOULS WILL FEED MY SWORD!

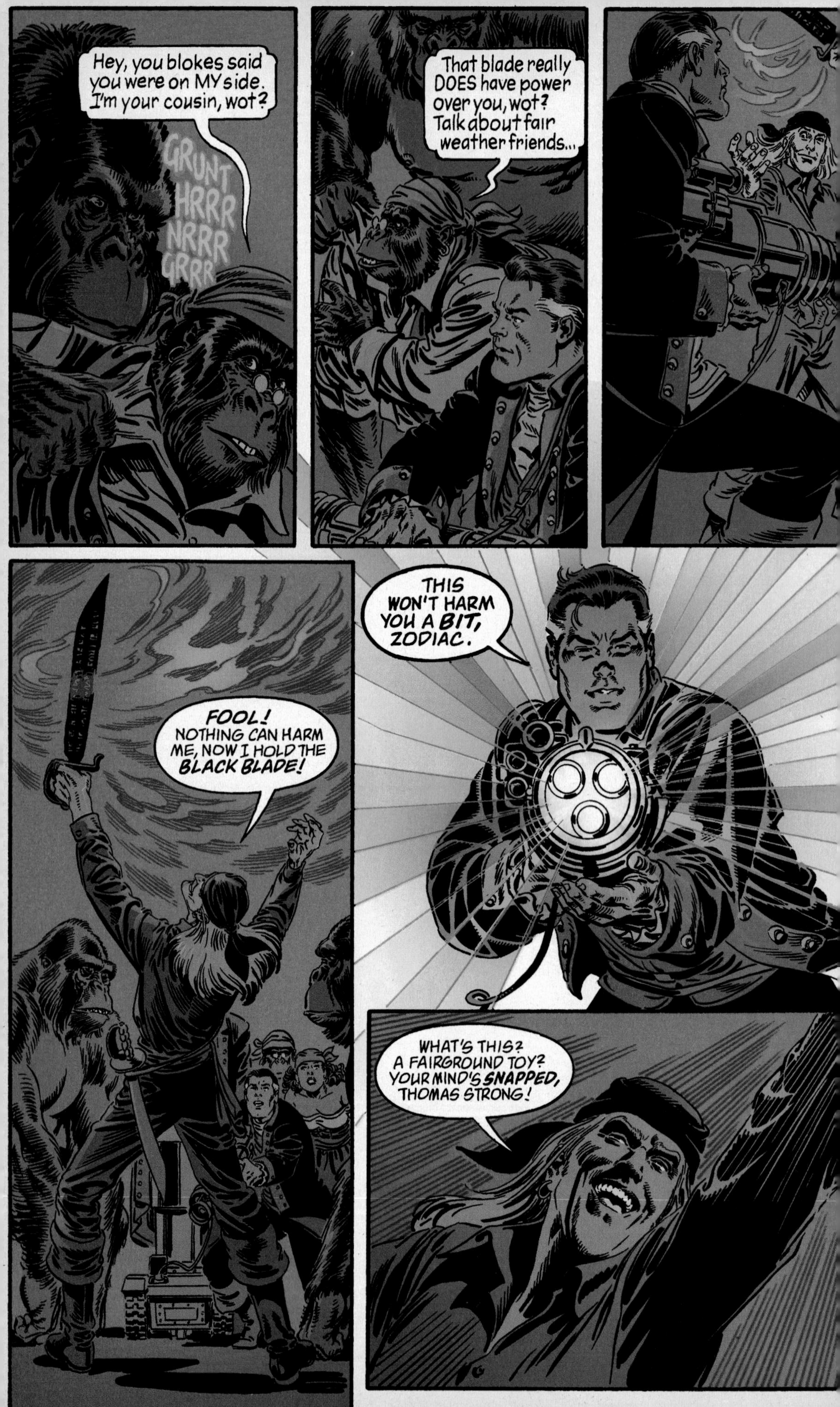
Hey, you blokes said you were on MY side. I'm your cousin, wot?
GRUNT HRRR NRRR GRRR
That blade really DOES have power over you, wot? Talk about fair weather friends...
FOOL! NOTHING CAN HARM ME, NOW I HOLD THE BLACK BLADE!
THIS WON'T HARM YOU A BIT, ZODIAC.
WHAT'S THIS? A FAIRGROUND TOY? YOUR MIND'S SNAPPED, THOMAS STRONG!

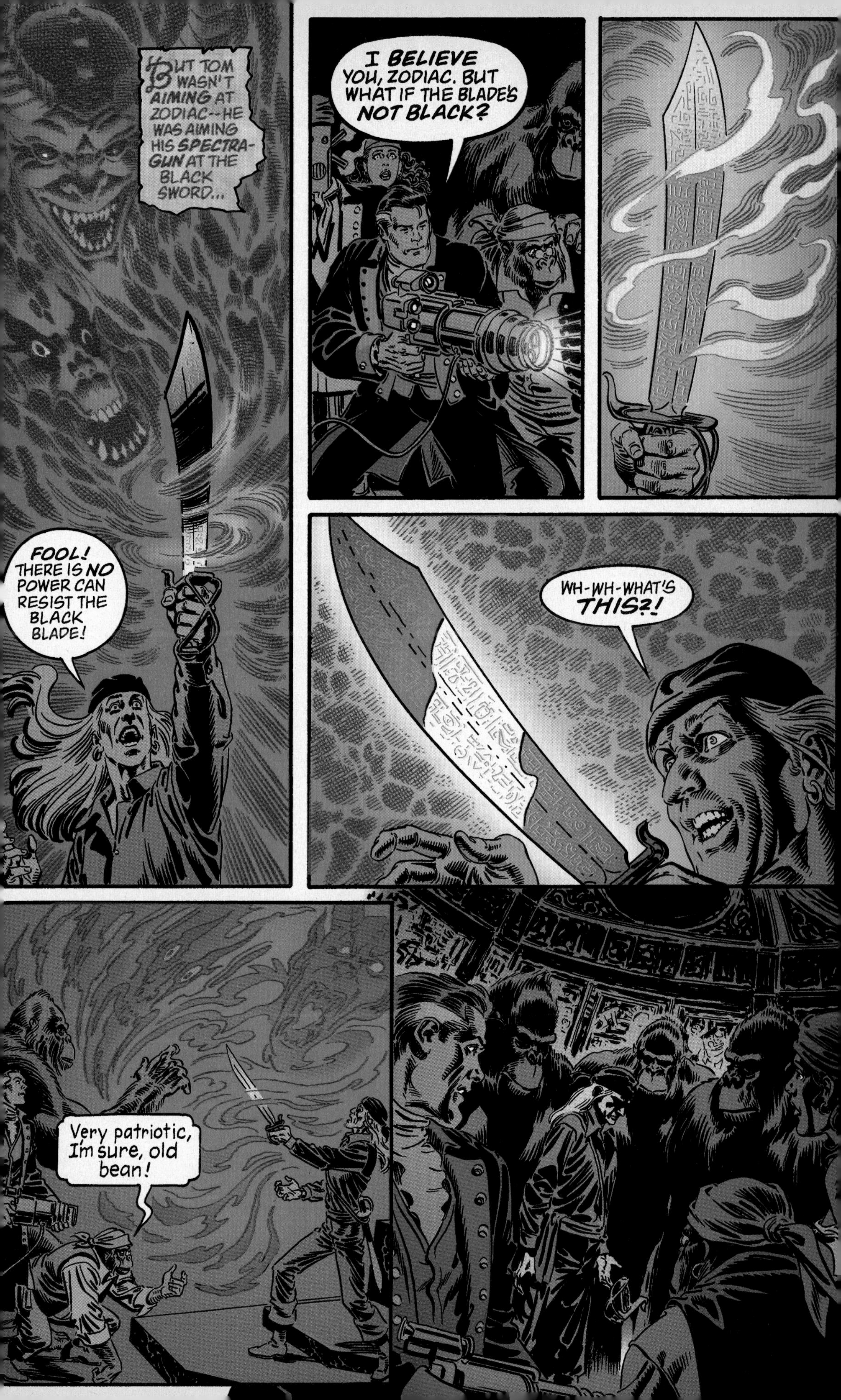
BUT TOM WASN'T AIMING AT ZODIAC--HE WAS AIMING HIS SPECTRA-GUN AT THE BLACK SWORD...
I BELIEVE YOU, ZODIAC. BUT WHAT IF THE BLADE'S NOT BLACK?
FOOL! THERE IS NO POWER CAN RESIST THE BLACK BLADE!
WH-WH-WHAT'S THIS?!
Very patriotic, I'm sure, old bean!

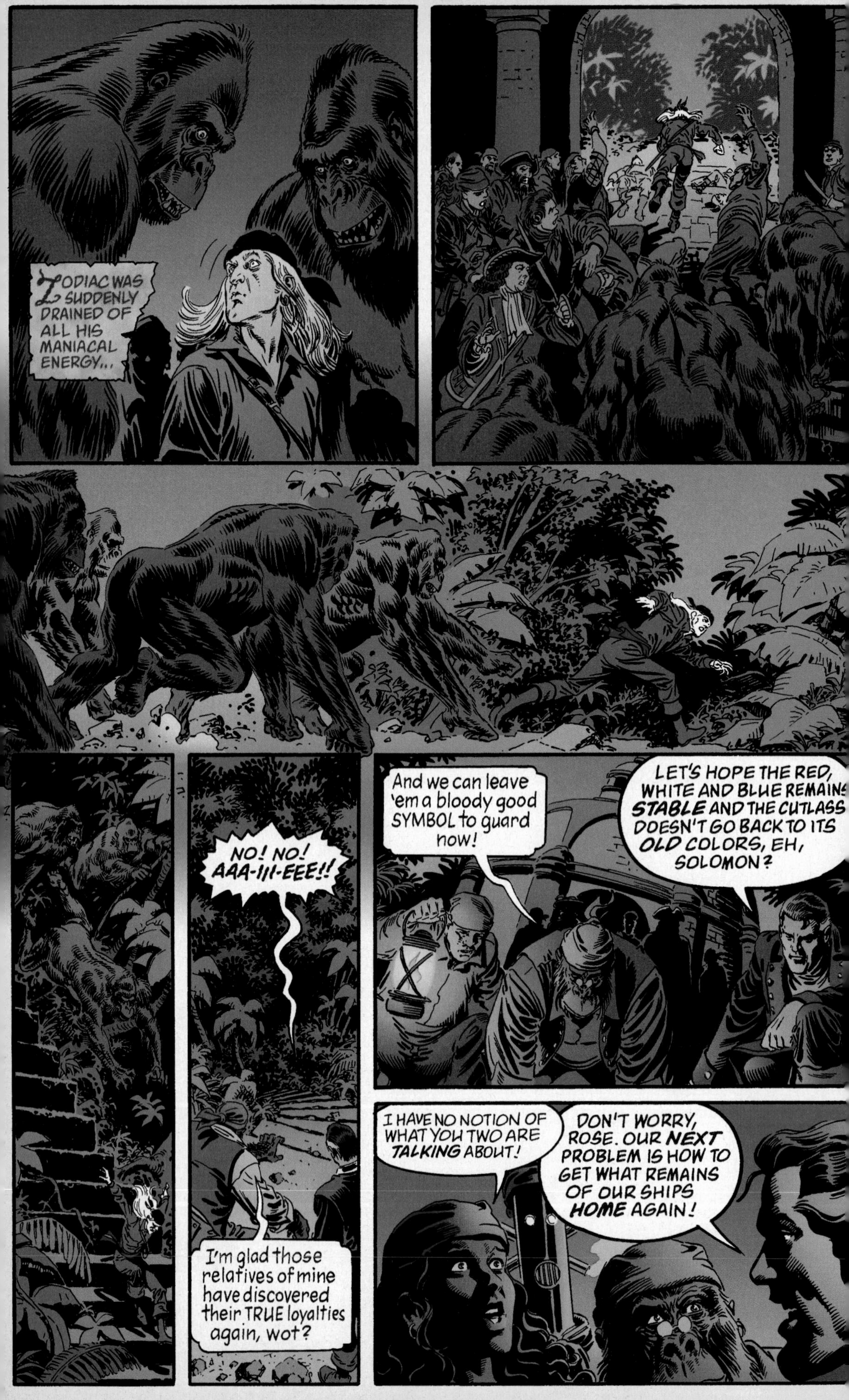
ZODIAC WAS SUDDENLY DRAINED OF ALL HIS MANIACAL ENERGY...
NO! NO! AAA-III-EEE!!
I'm glad those relatives of mine have discovered their TRUE loyalties again, wot?
And we can leave 'em a bloody good SYMBOL to guard now!
LET'S HOPE THE RED, WHITE AND BLUE REMAINS STABLE AND THE CUTLASS DOESN'T GO BACK TO ITS OLD COLORS, EH, SOLOMON?
I HAVE NO NOTION OF WHAT YOU TWO ARE TALKING ABOUT!
DON'T WORRY, ROSE. OUR NEXT PROBLEM IS HOW TO GET WHAT REMAINS OF OUR SHIPS HOME AGAIN!

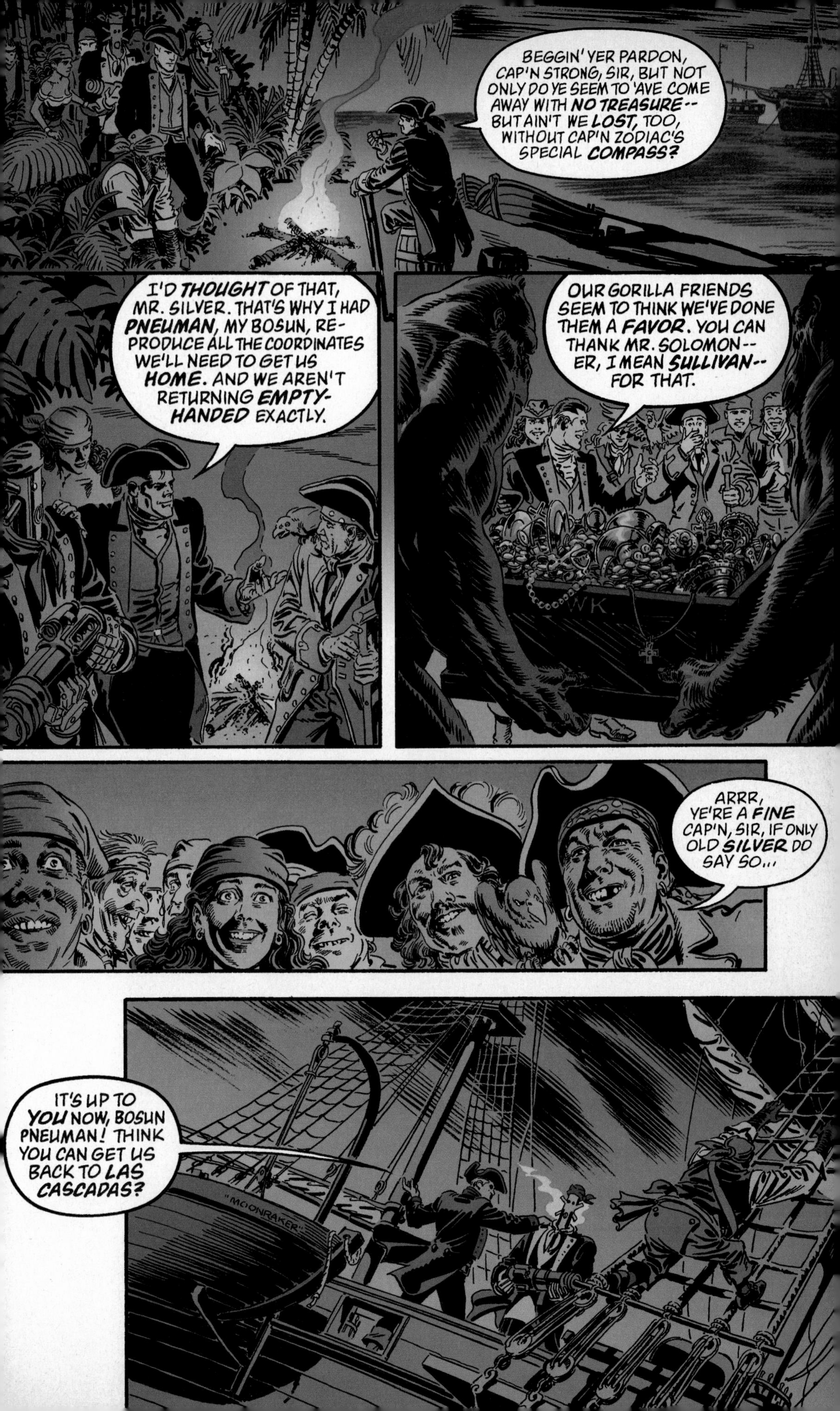
BEGGIN' YER PARDON, CAP'N STRONG, SIR, BUT NOT ONLY DO YE SEEM TO 'AVE COME AWAY WITH NO TREASURE-- BUT AIN'T WE LOST, TOO, WITHOUT CAP'N ZODIAC'S SPECIAL COMPASS?
I'D THOUGHT OF THAT, MR. SILVER. THAT'S WHY I HAD PNEUMAN, MY BOSUN, REPRODUCE ALL THE COORDINATES WE'LL NEED TO GET US HOME. AND WE AREN'T RETURNING EMPTY-HANDED EXACTLY.
OUR GORILLA FRIENDS SEEM TO THINK WE'VE DONE THEM A FAVOR. YOU CAN THANK MR. SOLOMON-- ER, I MEAN SULLIVAN-- FOR THAT.
ARRR, YE'RE A FINE CAP'N, SIR, IF ONLY OLD SILVER DO SAY SO...
IT'S UP TO YOU NOW, BOSUN PNEUMAN! THINK YOU CAN GET US BACK TO LAS CASCADAS?
"MOONRAKER"

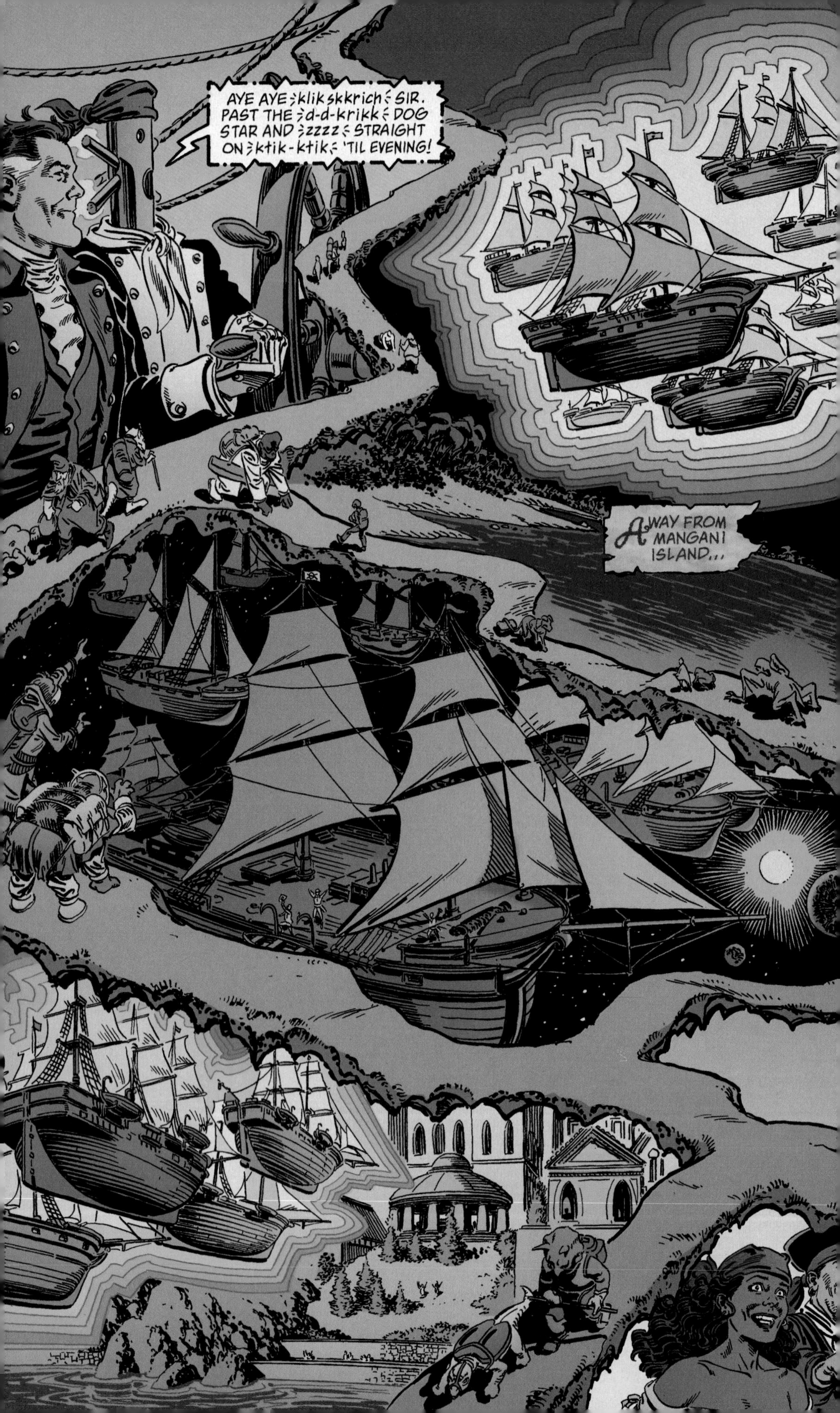
AYE AYE klikskkrich SIR. PAST THE d-d-krikk DOG STAR AND zzzz STRAIGHT ON ktik-ktik 'TIL EVENING!
AWAY FROM MANGANI ISLAND...

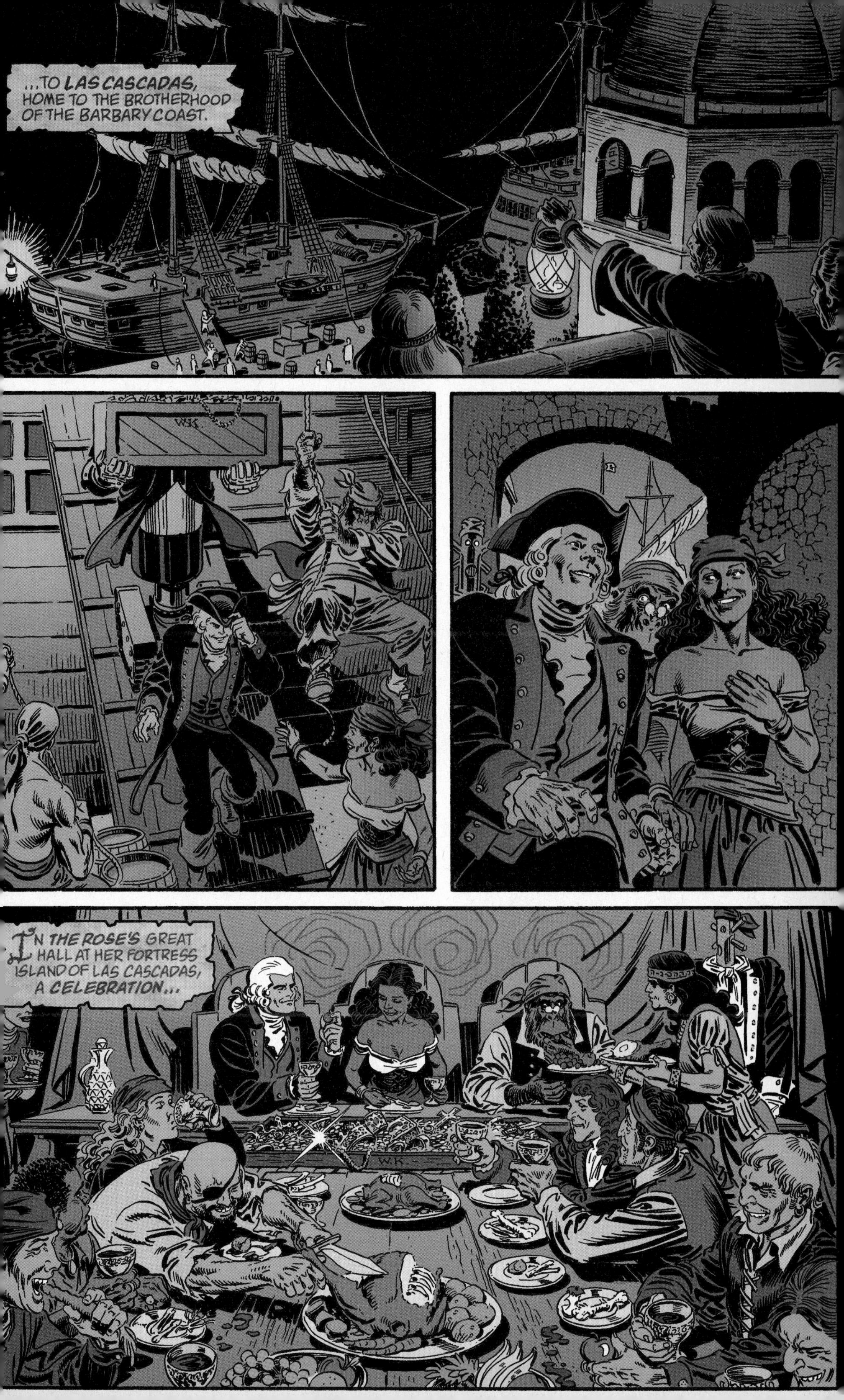
...TO LAS CASCADAS, HOME TO THE BROTHERHOOD OF THE BARBARY COAST.
W.K.
IN THE ROSE'S GREAT HALL AT HER FORTRESS ISLAND OF LAS CASCADAS, A CELEBRATION...
W.K.

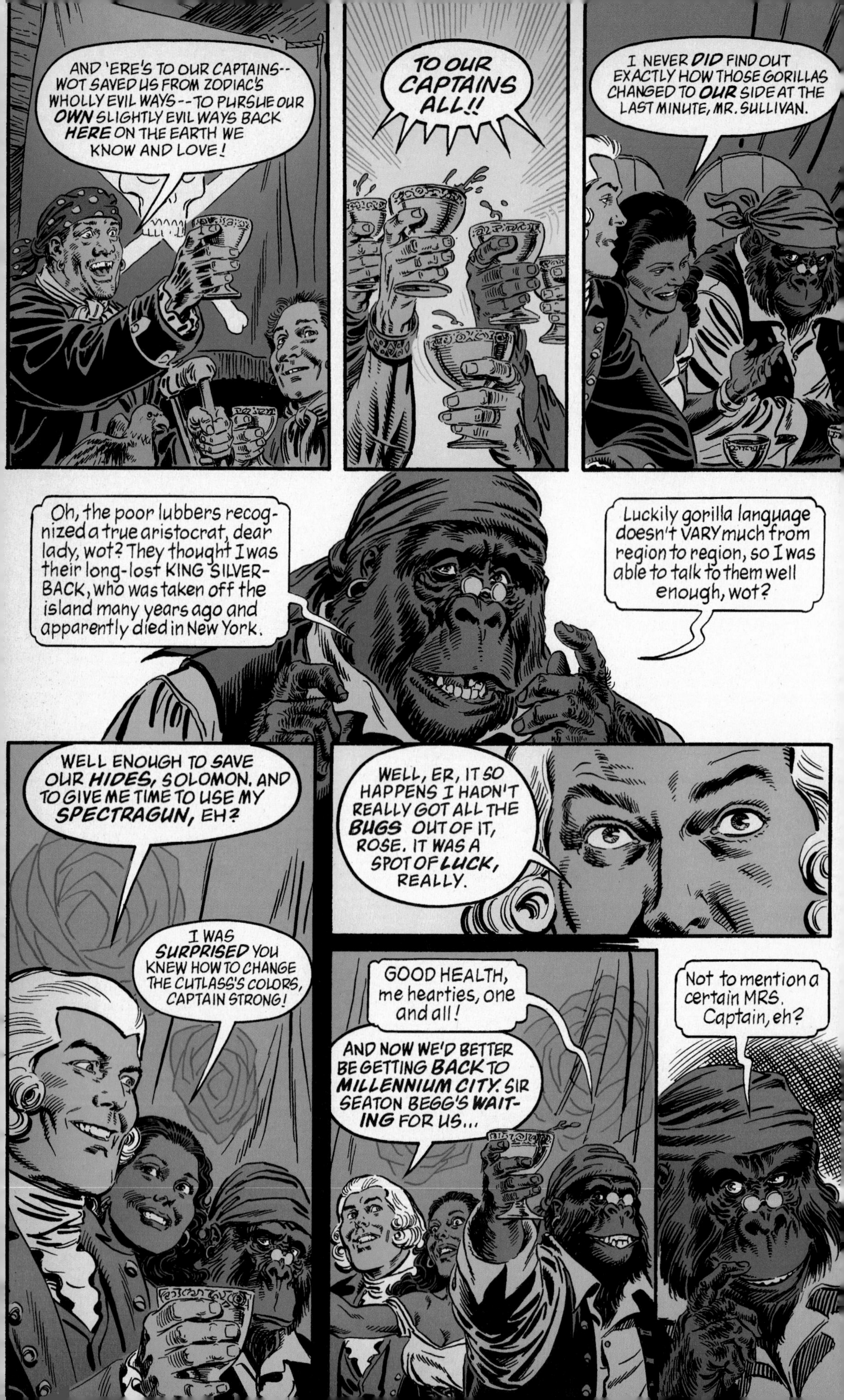
AND 'ERE'S TO OUR CAPTAINS-- WOT SAVED US FROM ZODIAC'S WHOLLY EVIL WAYS--TO PURSUE OUR OWN SLIGHTLY EVIL WAYS BACK HERE ON THE EARTH WE KNOW AND LOVE!
TO OUR CAPTAINS ALL!!
I NEVER DID FIND OUT EXACTLY HOW THOSE GORILLAS CHANGED TO OUR SIDE AT THE LAST MINUTE, MR. SULLIVAN.
Oh, the poor lubbers recognized a true aristocrat, dear lady, wot? They thought I was their long-lost KING SILVER-BACK, who was taken off the island many years ago and apparently died in New York.
Luckily gorilla language doesn't VARY much from region to region, so I was able to talk to them well enough, wot?
WELL ENOUGH TO SAVE OUR HIDES, SOLOMON. AND TO GIVE ME TIME TO USE MY SPECTRAGUN, EH?
WELL, ER, IT SO HAPPENS I HADN'T REALLY GOT ALL THE BUGS OUT OF IT, ROSE. IT WAS A SPOT OF LUCK, REALLY.
I WAS SURPRISED YOU KNEW HOW TO CHANGE THE CUTLASS'S COLORS, CAPTAIN STRONG!
GOOD HEALTH, me hearties, one and all!
AND NOW WE'D BETTER BE GETTING BACK TO MILLENNIUM CITY. SIR SEATON BEGG'S WAITING FOR US...
Not to mention a certain MRS. Captain, eh?

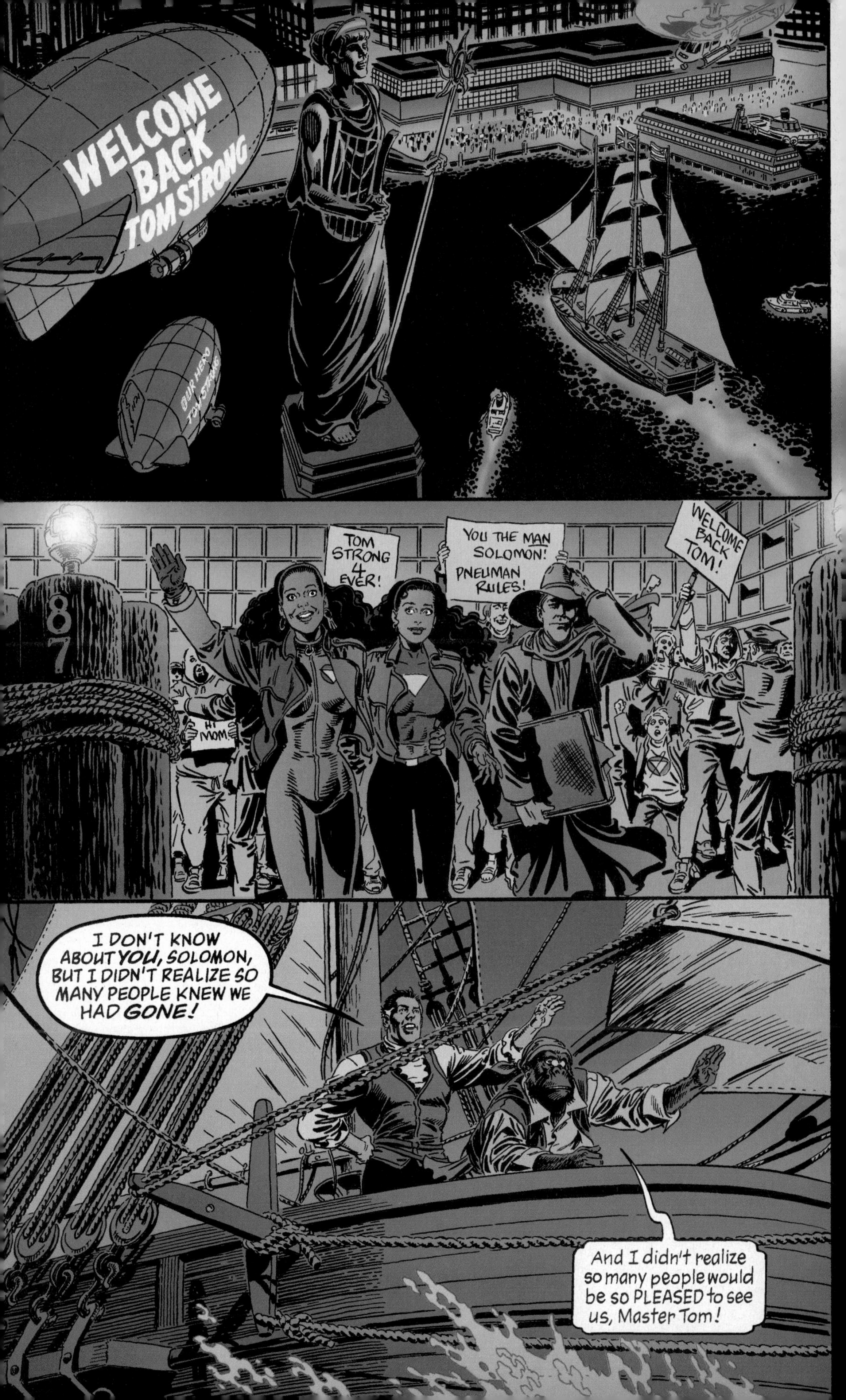
WELCOME BACK TOM STRONG
OUR HERO TOM STRONG
TOM STRONG 4 EVER!
YOU THE MAN SOLOMON!
PNEUMAN RULES!
WELCOME BACK TOM!
8 7
HI MOM
I DON'T KNOW ABOUT YOU, SOLOMON, BUT I DIDN'T REALIZE SO MANY PEOPLE KNEW WE HAD GONE!
And I didn't realize so many people would be so PLEASED to see us, Master Tom!

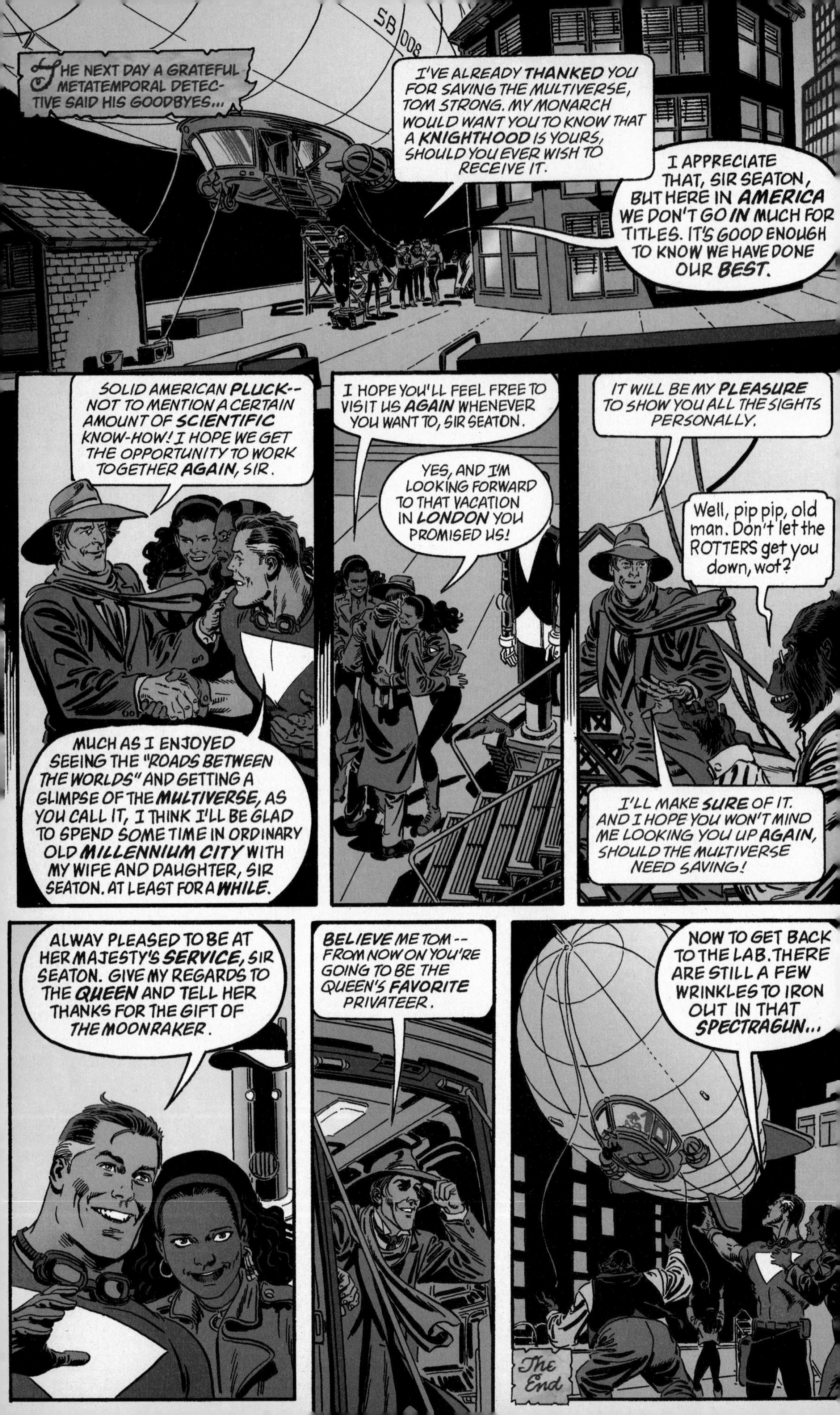
SB 008
THE NEXT DAY A GRATEFUL METATEMPORAL DETECTIVE SAID HIS GOODBYES...
I'VE ALREADY THANKED YOU FOR SAVING THE MULTIVERSE, TOM STRONG. MY MONARCH WOULD WANT YOU TO KNOW THAT A KNIGHTHOOD IS YOURS, SHOULD YOU EVER WISH TO RECEIVE IT.
I APPRECIATE THAT, SIR SEATON, BUT HERE IN AMERICA WE DON'T GO IN MUCH FOR TITLES. IT'S GOOD ENOUGH TO KNOW WE HAVE DONE OUR BEST.
SOLID AMERICAN PLUCK-- NOT TO MENTION A CERTAIN AMOUNT OF SCIENTIFIC KNOW-HOW! I HOPE WE GET THE OPPORTUNITY TO WORK TOGETHER AGAIN, SIR.
MUCH AS I ENJOYED SEEING THE "ROADS BETWEEN THE WORLDS" AND GETTING A GLIMPSE OF THE MULTIVERSE, AS YOU CALL IT, I THINK I'LL BE GLAD TO SPEND SOME TIME IN ORDINARY OLD MILLENNIUM CITY WITH MY WIFE AND DAUGHTER, SIR SEATON. AT LEAST FOR A WHILE.
I HOPE YOU'LL FEEL FREE TO VISIT US AGAIN WHENEVER YOU WANT TO, SIR SEATON.
YES, AND I'M LOOKING FORWARD TO THAT VACATION IN LONDON YOU PROMISED US!
IT WILL BE MY PLEASURE TO SHOW YOU ALL THE SIGHTS PERSONALLY.
Well, pip pip, old man. Don't let the ROTTERS get you down, wot?
I'LL MAKE SURE OF IT. AND I HOPE YOU WON'T MIND ME LOOKING YOU UP AGAIN, SHOULD THE MULTIVERSE NEED SAVING!
ALWAY PLEASED TO BE AT HER MAJESTY'S SERVICE, SIR SEATON. GIVE MY REGARDS TO THE QUEEN AND TELL HER THANKS FOR THE GIFT OF THE MOONRAKER.
BELIEVE ME TOM -- FROM NOW ON YOU'RE GOING TO BE THE QUEEN'S FAVORITE PRIVATEER.
NOW TO GET BACK TO THE LAB. THERE ARE STILL A FEW WRINKLES TO IRON OUT IN THAT SPECTRAGUN...
The End

# CHAPTER THREE

In which Pneuman exhibits unusual behavior,
Tom and King Solomon go in to investigate,
and an incredible voyage opens new vistas.

Cover art:
Chris Sprouse & Karl Story
Cover colors:
Michelle Madsen

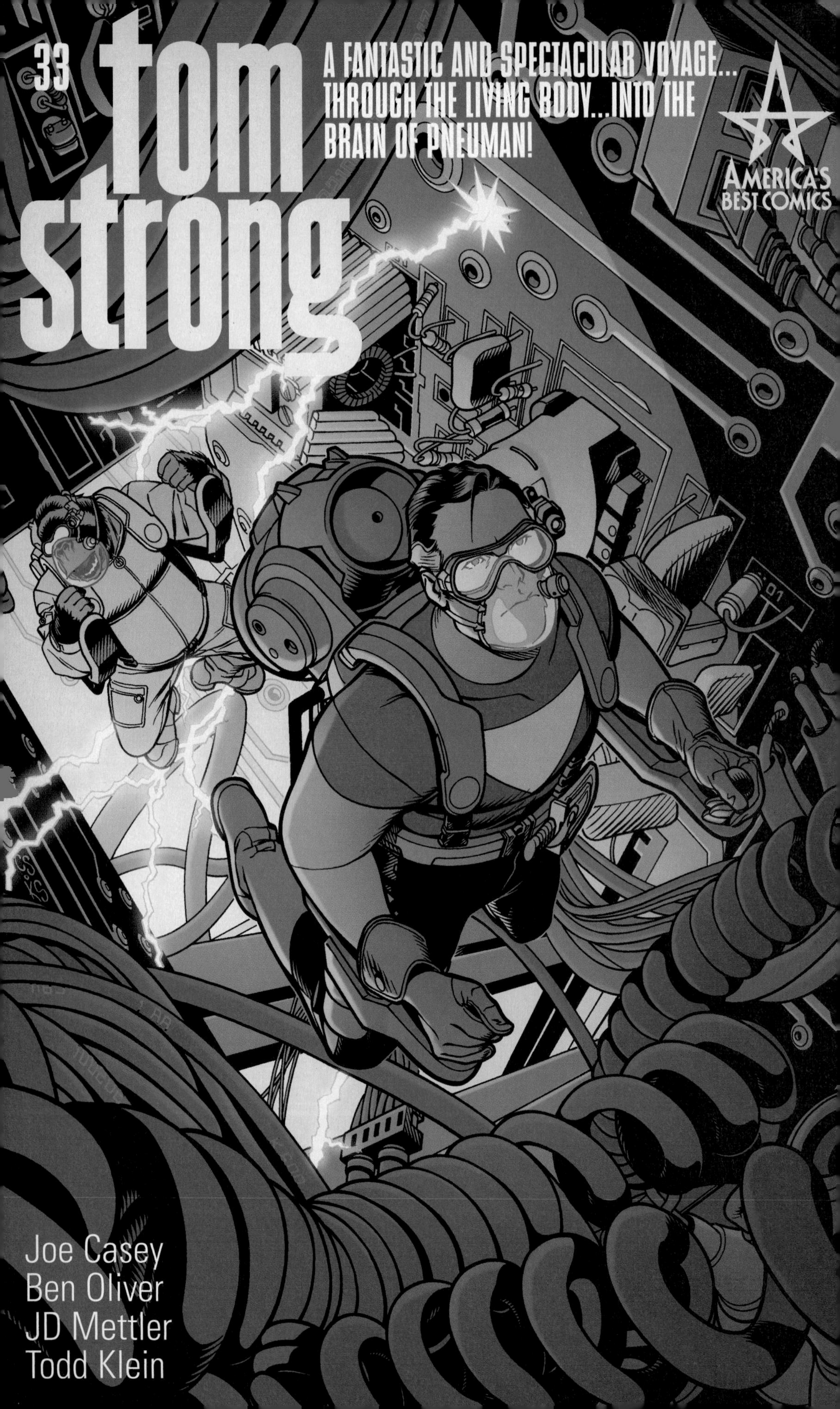
33
tom strong
A FANTASTIC AND SPECTACULAR VOYAGE... THROUGH THE LIVING BODY...INTO THE BRAIN OF PNEUMAN!
AMERICA'S BEST COMICS
Joe Casey
Ben Oliver
JD Mettler
Todd Klein

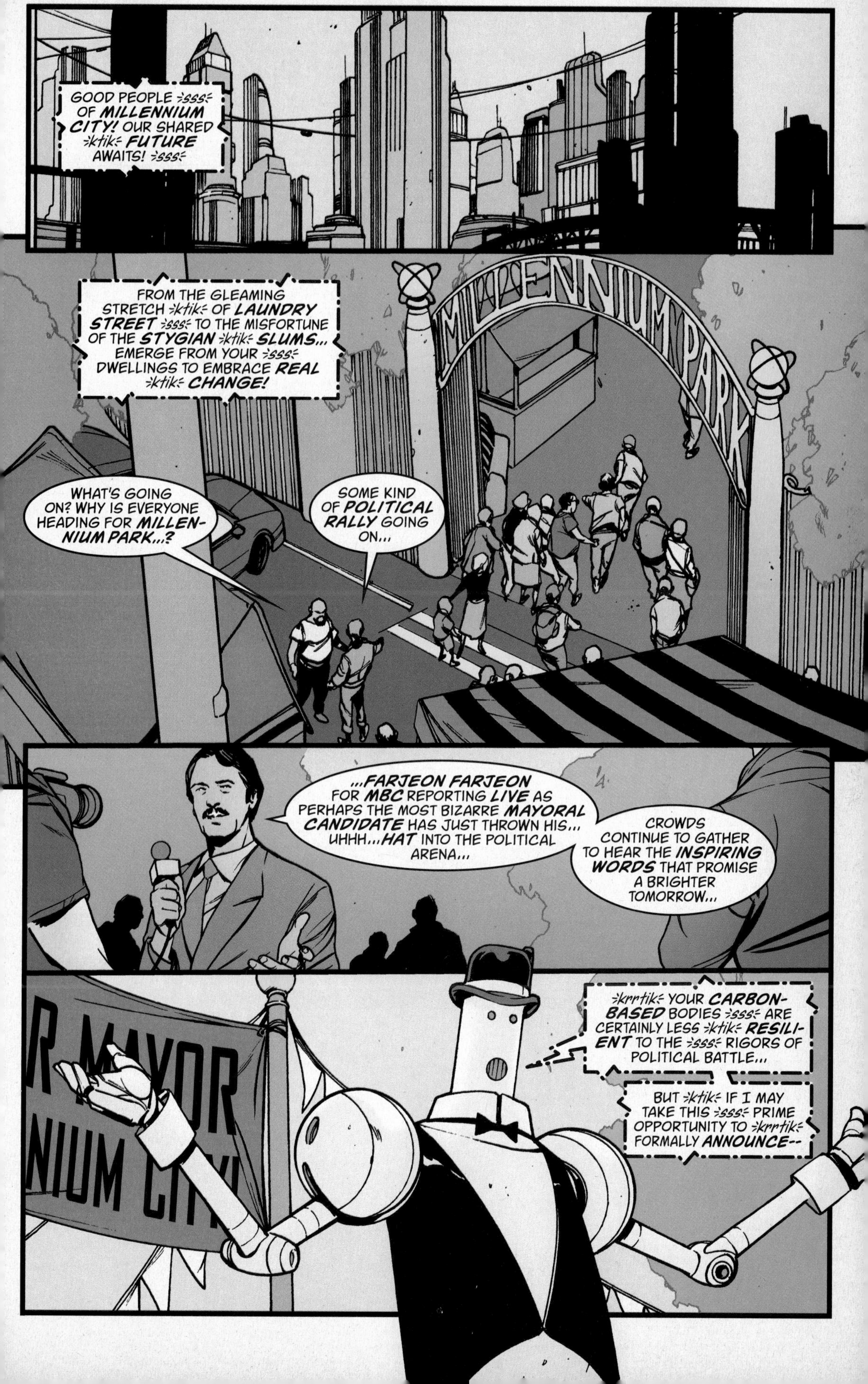
GOOD PEOPLE >sss< OF MILLENNIUM CITY! OUR SHARED >ktik< FUTURE AWAITS! >sss<
FROM THE GLEAMING STRETCH >ktik< OF LAUNDRY STREET >sss< TO THE MISFORTUNE OF THE STYGIAN >ktik< SLUMS... EMERGE FROM YOUR >sss< DWELLINGS TO EMBRACE REAL >ktik< CHANGE!
MILLENNIUM PARK
WHAT'S GOING ON? WHY IS EVERYONE HEADING FOR MILLENNIUM PARK...?
SOME KIND OF POLITICAL RALLY GOING ON...
...FARJEON FARJEON FOR MBC REPORTING LIVE AS PERHAPS THE MOST BIZARRE MAYORAL CANDIDATE HAS JUST THROWN HIS... UHHH...HAT INTO THE POLITICAL ARENA...
CROWDS CONTINUE TO GATHER TO HEAR THE INSPIRING WORDS THAT PROMISE A BRIGHTER TOMORROW...
R MAYOR
NIUM CIT
>krrtik< YOUR CARBON-BASED BODIES >sss< ARE CERTAINLY LESS >ktik< RESILIENT TO THE >sss< RIGORS OF POLITICAL BATTLE...
BUT >ktik< IF I MAY TAKE THIS >sss< PRIME OPPORTUNITY TO >krrtik< FORMALLY ANNOUNCE--

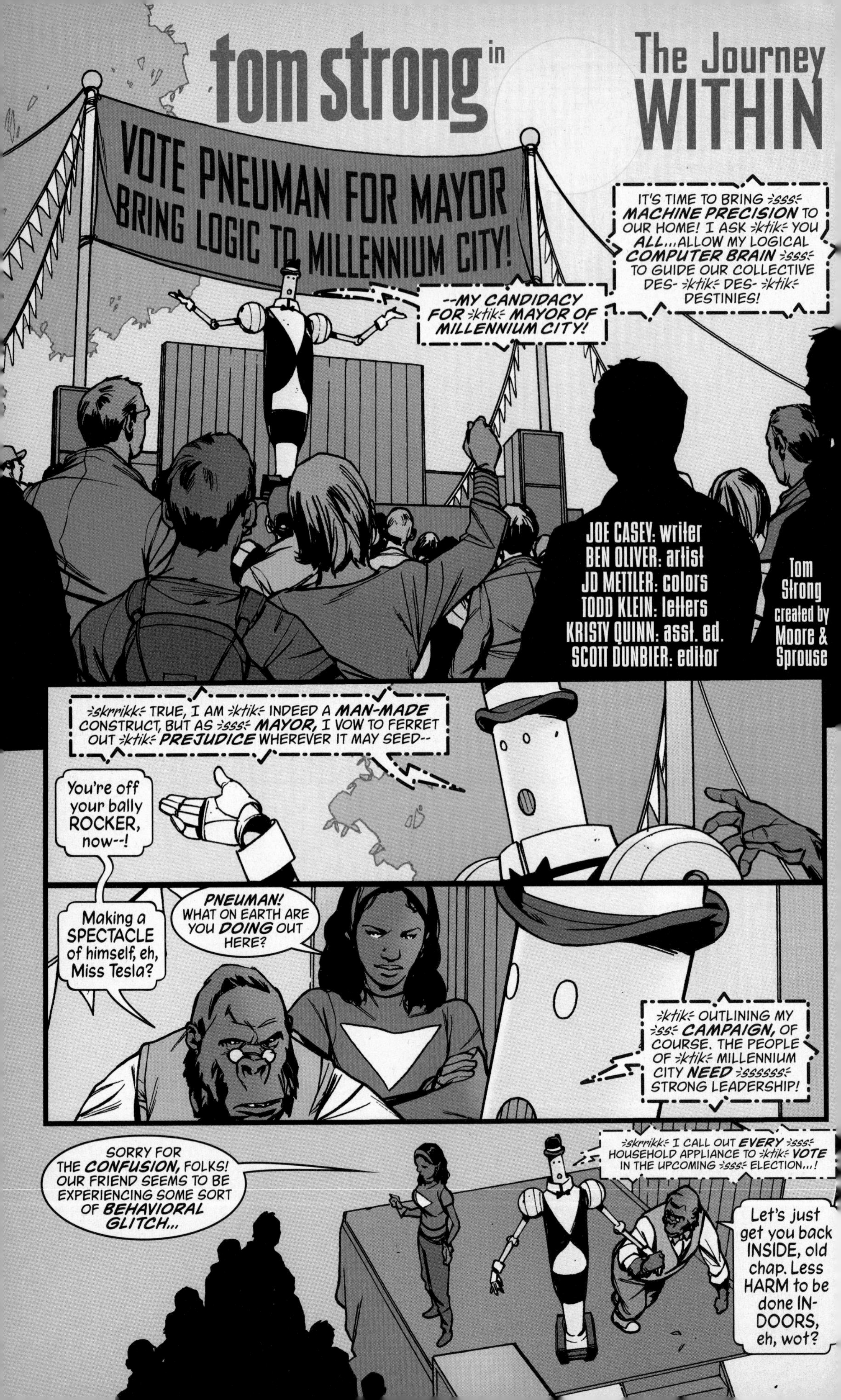
tom strong in
The Journey WITHIN
VOTE PNEUMAN FOR MAYOR
BRING LOGIC TO MILLENNIUM CITY!
--MY CANDIDACY FOR ≈ktik≈ MAYOR OF MILLENNIUM CITY!
IT'S TIME TO BRING ≈sss≈ MACHINE PRECISION TO OUR HOME! I ASK ≈ktik≈ YOU ALL...ALLOW MY LOGICAL COMPUTER BRAIN ≈sss≈ TO GUIDE OUR COLLECTIVE DES- ≈ktik≈ DES- ≈ktik≈ DESTINIES!
JOE CASEY: writer
BEN OLIVER: artist
JD METTLER: colors
TODD KLEIN: letters
KRISTY QUINN: asst. ed.
SCOTT DUNBIER: editor
Tom Strong created by Moore & Sprouse
≈skrrikk≈ TRUE, I AM ≈ktik≈ INDEED A MAN-MADE CONSTRUCT, BUT AS ≈sss≈ MAYOR, I VOW TO FERRET OUT ≈ktik≈ PREJUDICE WHEREVER IT MAY SEED--
You're off your bally ROCKER, now--!
Making a SPECTACLE of himself, eh, Miss Tesla?
PNEUMAN! WHAT ON EARTH ARE YOU DOING OUT HERE?
≈ktik≈ OUTLINING MY ≈sss≈ CAMPAIGN, OF COURSE. THE PEOPLE OF ≈ktik≈ MILLENNIUM CITY NEED ≈ssssss≈ STRONG LEADERSHIP!
SORRY FOR THE CONFUSION, FOLKS! OUR FRIEND SEEMS TO BE EXPERIENCING SOME SORT OF BEHAVIORAL GLITCH...
≈skrrikk≈ I CALL OUT EVERY ≈sss≈ HOUSEHOLD APPLIANCE TO ≈ktik≈ VOTE IN THE UPCOMING ≈sss≈ ELECTION...!
Let's just get you back INSIDE, old chap. Less HARM to be done IN-DOORS, eh, wot?

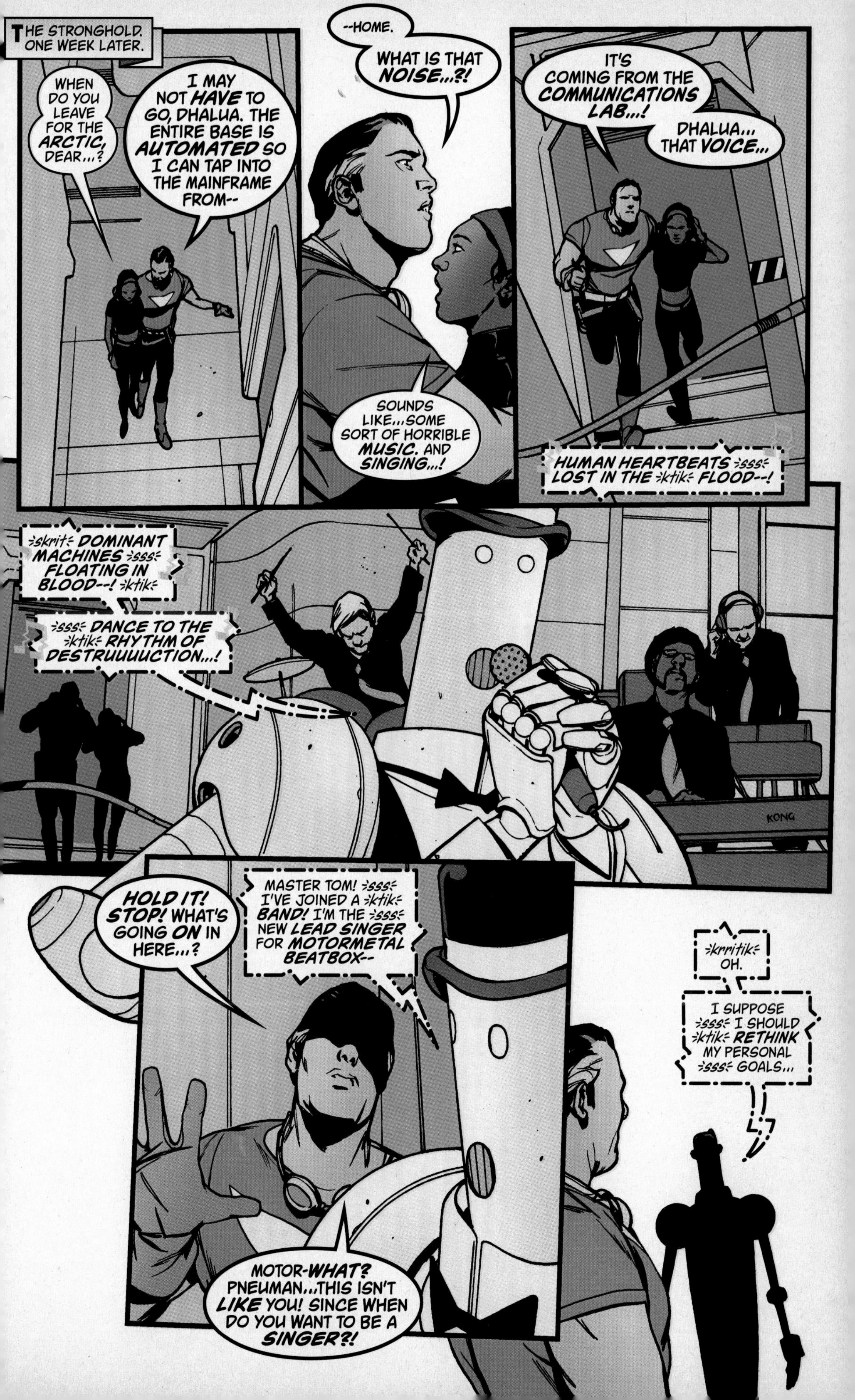
THE STRONGHOLD. ONE WEEK LATER.
WHEN DO YOU LEAVE FOR THE ARCTIC, DEAR...?
I MAY NOT HAVE TO GO, DHALUA. THE ENTIRE BASE IS AUTOMATED SO I CAN TAP INTO THE MAINFRAME FROM--
--HOME.
WHAT IS THAT NOISE...?!
SOUNDS LIKE...SOME SORT OF HORRIBLE MUSIC. AND SINGING...!
IT'S COMING FROM THE COMMUNICATIONS LAB...!
DHALUA... THAT VOICE...
HUMAN HEARTBEATS sss LOST IN THE ktik FLOOD--!
skrit DOMINANT MACHINES sss FLOATING IN BLOOD--! ktik
sss DANCE TO THE ktik RHYTHM OF DESTRUUUUCTION...!
KONG
HOLD IT! STOP! WHAT'S GOING ON IN HERE...?
MASTER TOM! sss I'VE JOINED A ktik BAND! I'M THE sss NEW LEAD SINGER FOR MOTORMETAL BEATBOX--
MOTOR-WHAT? PNEUMAN...THIS ISN'T LIKE YOU! SINCE WHEN DO YOU WANT TO BE A SINGER?!
krritik OH.
I SUPPOSE sss I SHOULD ktik RETHINK MY PERSONAL sss GOALS...

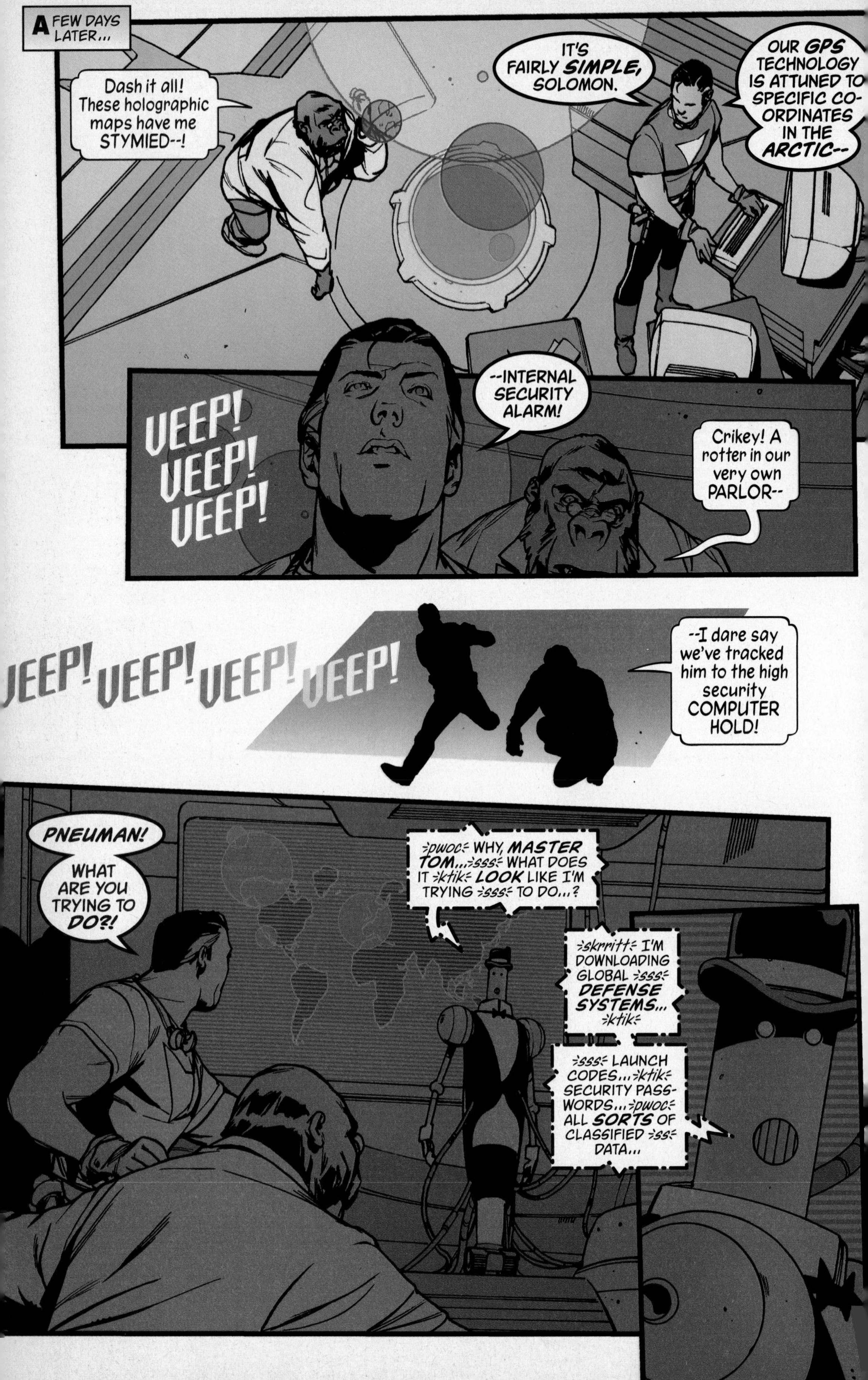
A FEW DAYS LATER...
Dash it all! These holographic maps have me STYMIED--!
IT'S FAIRLY SIMPLE, SOLOMON.
OUR GPS TECHNOLOGY IS ATTUNED TO SPECIFIC CO-ORDINATES IN THE ARCTIC--
VEEP! VEEP! VEEP!
--INTERNAL SECURITY ALARM!
Crikey! A rotter in our very own PARLOR--
VEEP! VEEP! VEEP! VEEP!
--I dare say we've tracked him to the high security COMPUTER HOLD!
PNEUMAN! WHAT ARE YOU TRYING TO DO?!
=pwoc= WHY, MASTER TOM... =sss= WHAT DOES IT =ktik= LOOK LIKE I'M TRYING =sss= TO DO...?
=skrritt= I'M DOWNLOADING GLOBAL =sss= DEFENSE SYSTEMS... =ktik=
=sss= LAUNCH CODES... =ktik= SECURITY PASS-WORDS... =pwoc= ALL SORTS OF CLASSIFIED =ss= DATA...

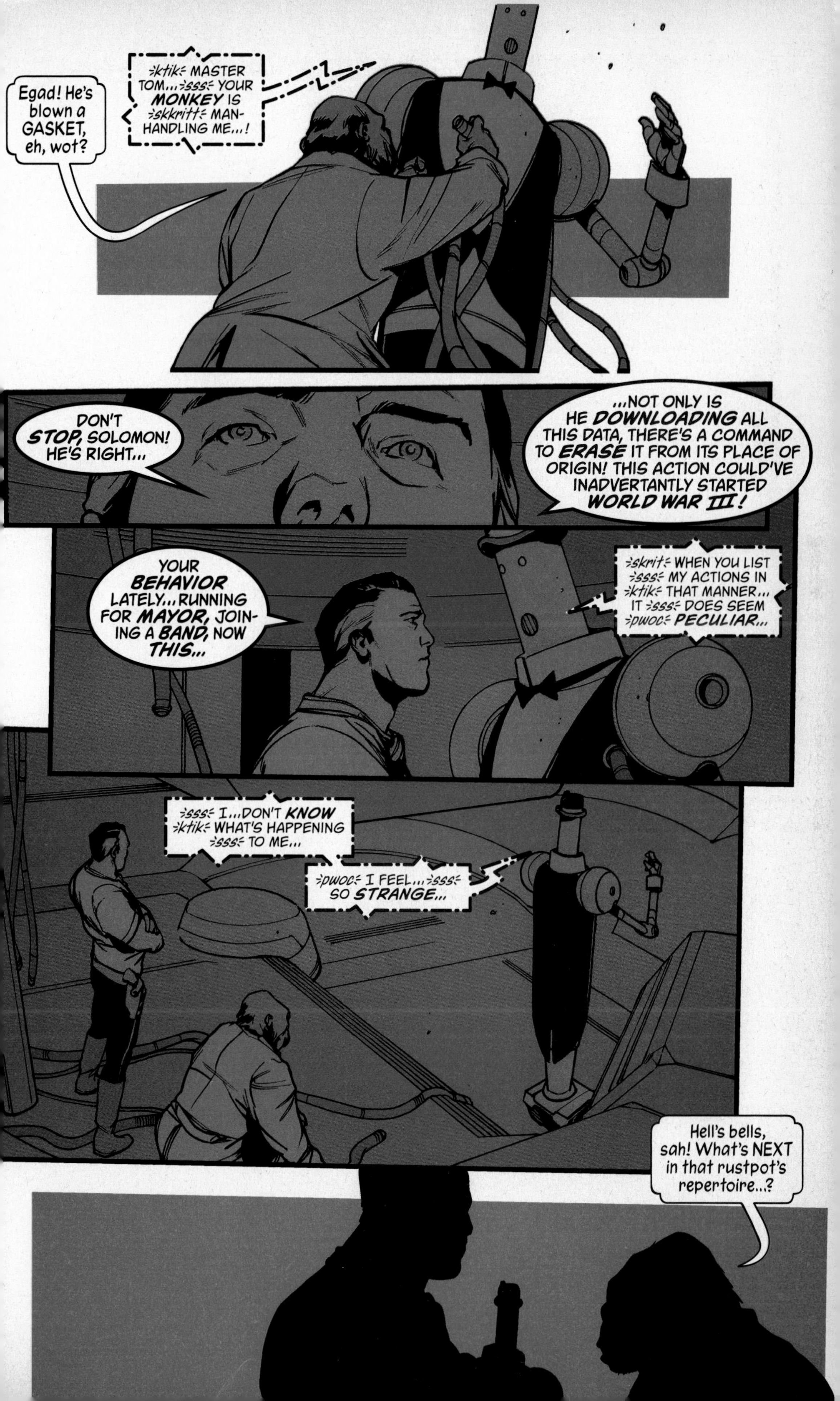

Egad! He's blown a GASKET, eh, wot?
ktik MASTER TOM... sss YOUR MONKEY IS skkritt MAN-HANDLING ME...!
DON'T STOP, SOLOMON! HE'S RIGHT...
...NOT ONLY IS HE DOWNLOADING ALL THIS DATA, THERE'S A COMMAND TO ERASE IT FROM ITS PLACE OF ORIGIN! THIS ACTION COULD'VE INADVERTANTLY STARTED WORLD WAR III!
YOUR BEHAVIOR LATELY...RUNNING FOR MAYOR, JOIN-ING A BAND, NOW THIS...
skrit WHEN YOU LIST sss MY ACTIONS IN ktik THAT MANNER... IT sss DOES SEEM pwoc PECULIAR...
sss I...DON'T KNOW ktik WHAT'S HAPPENING sss TO ME...
pwoc I FEEL... sss SO STRANGE...
Hell's bells, sah! What's NEXT in that rustpot's repertoire...?

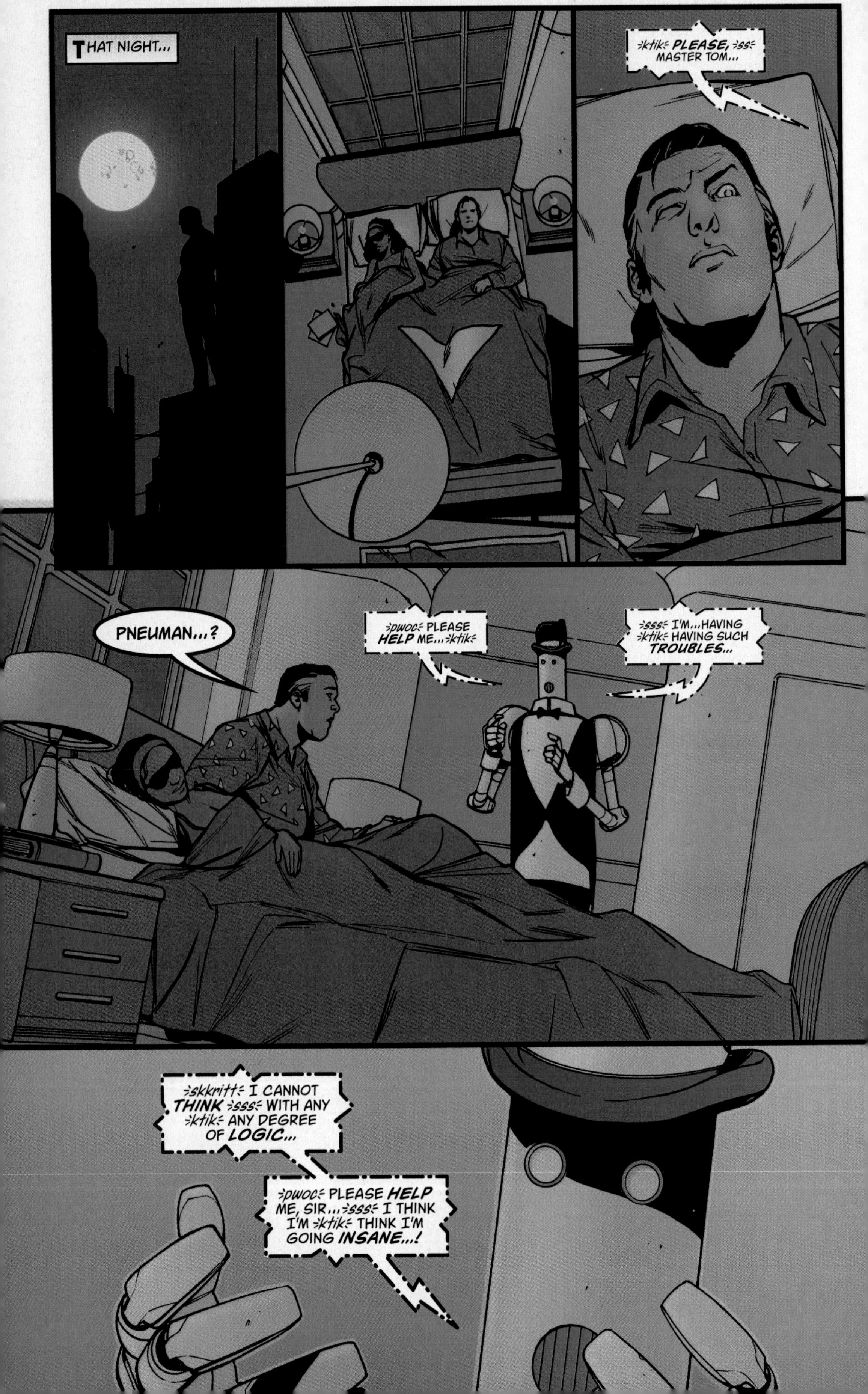
THAT NIGHT...
≈ktik≈ PLEASE, ≈ss≈ MASTER TOM...
PNEUMAN...?
≈pwoc≈ PLEASE HELP ME... ≈ktik≈
≈sss≈ I'M... HAVING ≈ktik≈ HAVING SUCH TROUBLES...
≈skkritt≈ I CANNOT THINK ≈sss≈ WITH ANY ≈ktik≈ ANY DEGREE OF LOGIC...
≈pwoc≈ PLEASE HELP ME, SIR... ≈sss≈ I THINK I'M ≈ktik≈ THINK I'M GOING INSANE...!

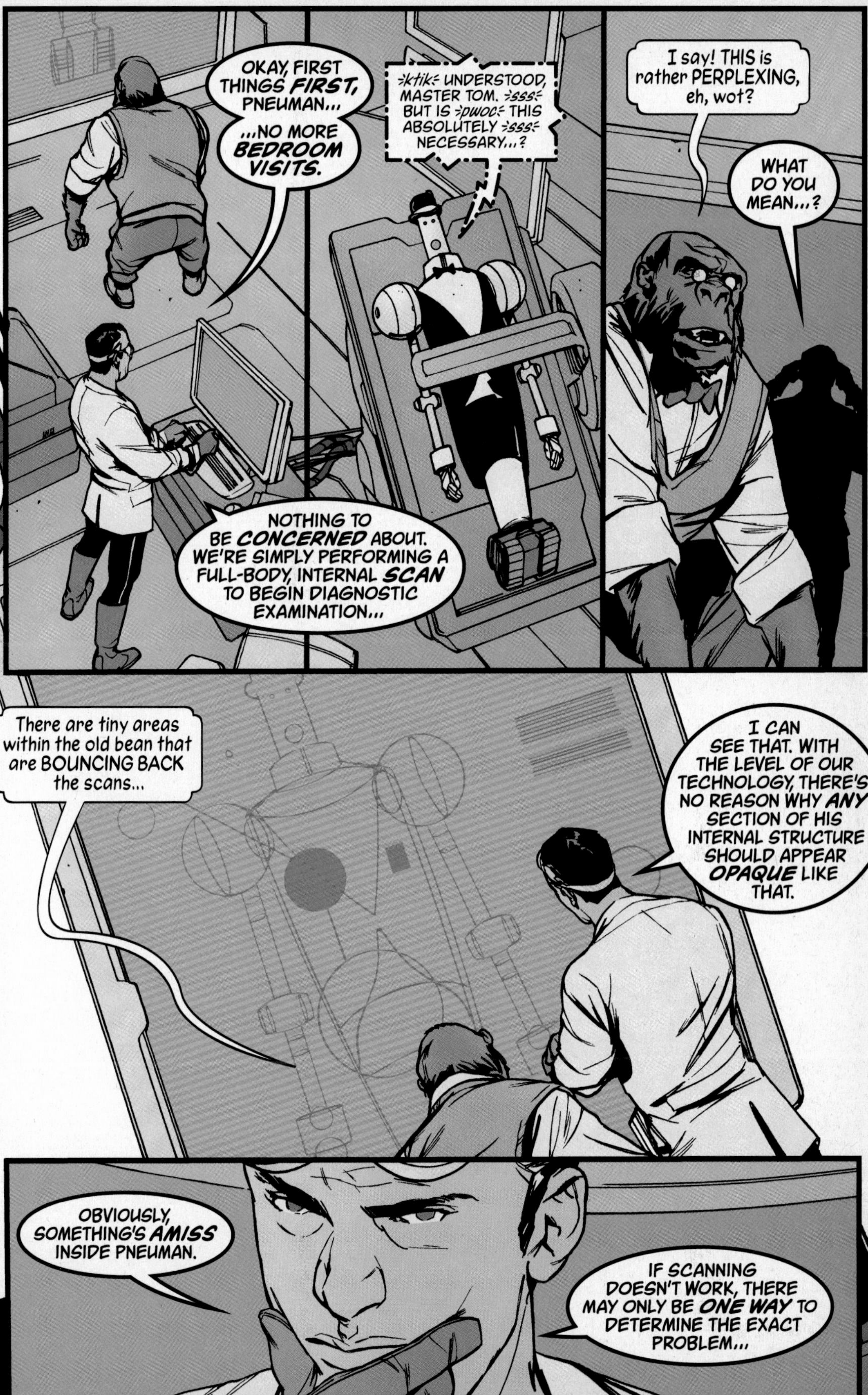
OKAY, FIRST THINGS FIRST, PNEUMAN...
...NO MORE BEDROOM VISITS.
≠ktik≠ UNDERSTOOD, MASTER TOM. ≠sss≠ BUT IS ≠pwoc≠ THIS ABSOLUTELY ≠sss≠ NECESSARY...?
NOTHING TO BE CONCERNED ABOUT. WE'RE SIMPLY PERFORMING A FULL-BODY, INTERNAL SCAN TO BEGIN DIAGNOSTIC EXAMINATION...
I say! THIS is rather PERPLEXING, eh, wot?
WHAT DO YOU MEAN...?
There are tiny areas within the old bean that are BOUNCING BACK the scans...
I CAN SEE THAT. WITH THE LEVEL OF OUR TECHNOLOGY, THERE'S NO REASON WHY ANY SECTION OF HIS INTERNAL STRUCTURE SHOULD APPEAR OPAQUE LIKE THAT.
OBVIOUSLY, SOMETHING'S AMISS INSIDE PNEUMAN.
IF SCANNING DOESN'T WORK, THERE MAY ONLY BE ONE WAY TO DETERMINE THE EXACT PROBLEM...

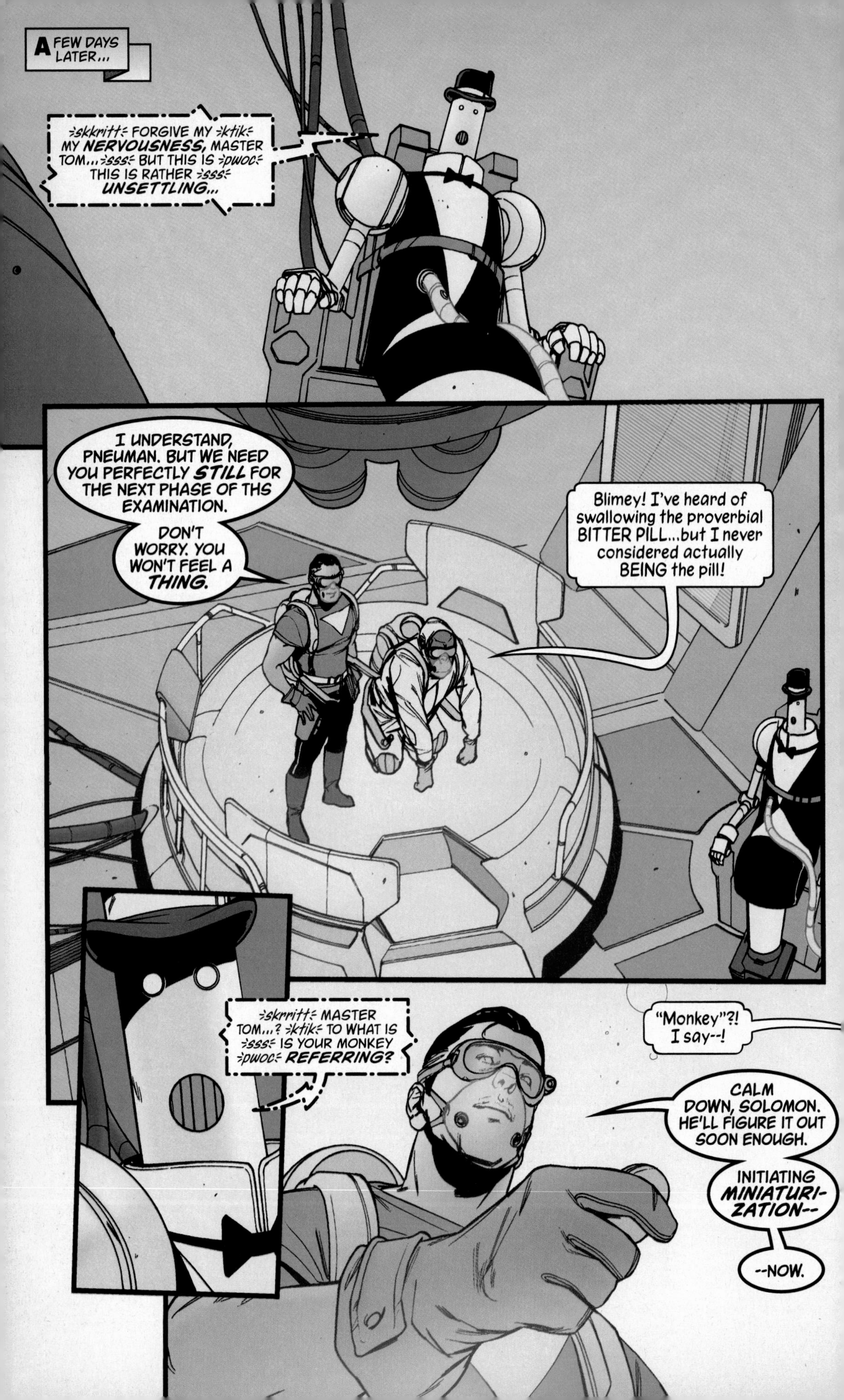

A FEW DAYS LATER...
⚡skkritt⚡ FORGIVE MY ⚡ktik⚡ MY NERVOUSNESS, MASTER TOM... ⚡sss⚡ BUT THIS IS ⚡pwoc⚡ THIS IS RATHER ⚡sss⚡ UNSETTLING...
I UNDERSTAND, PNEUMAN. BUT WE NEED YOU PERFECTLY STILL FOR THE NEXT PHASE OF THS EXAMINATION.
DON'T WORRY. YOU WON'T FEEL A THING.
Blimey! I've heard of swallowing the proverbial BITTER PILL...but I never considered actually BEING the pill!
⚡skritt⚡ MASTER TOM...? ⚡ktik⚡ TO WHAT IS ⚡sss⚡ IS YOUR MONKEY ⚡pwoc⚡ REFERRING?
"Monkey"?! I say--!
CALM DOWN, SOLOMON. HE'LL FIGURE IT OUT SOON ENOUGH.
INITIATING MINIATURIZATION--
--NOW.

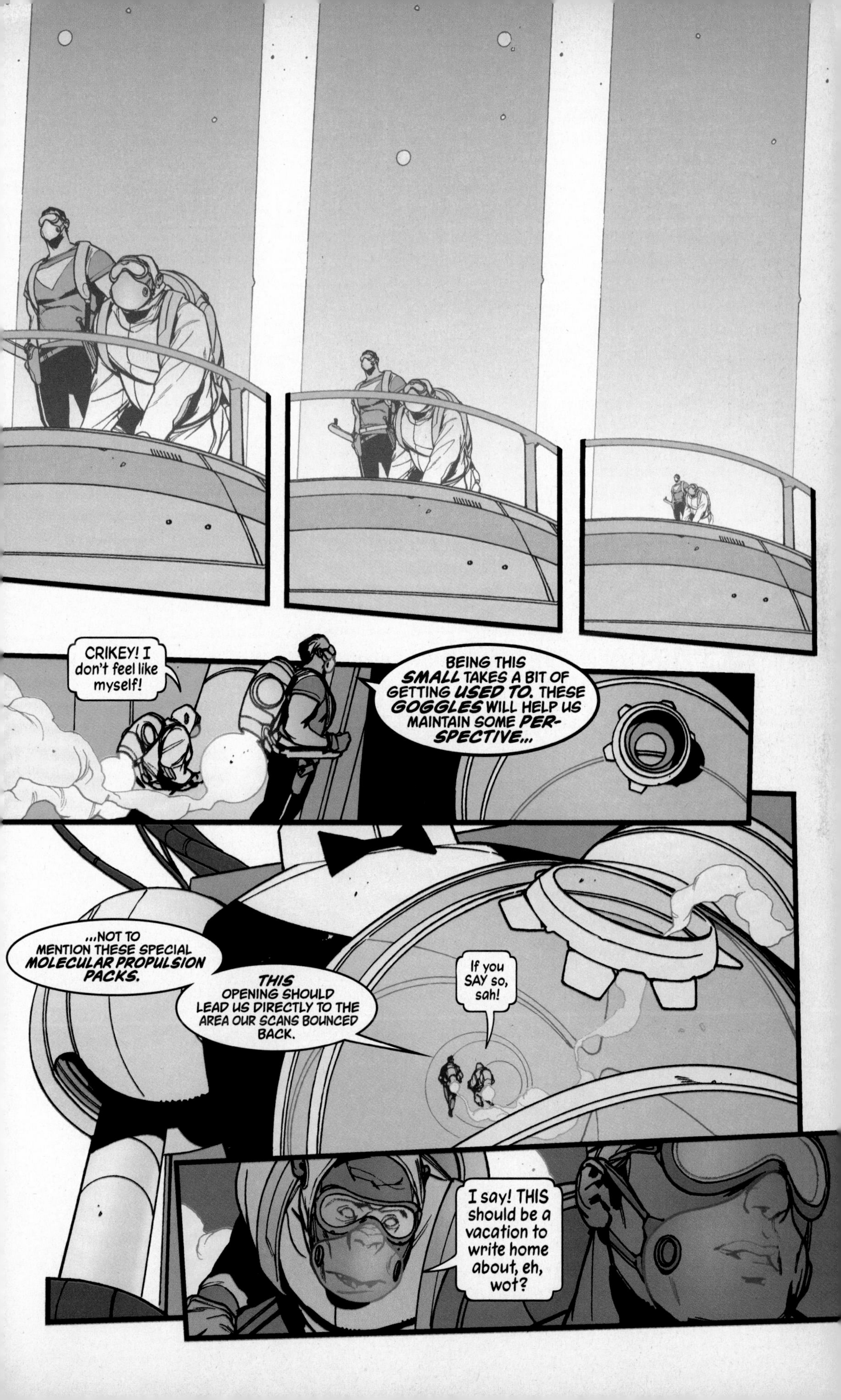
CRIKEY! I don't feel like myself!
BEING THIS SMALL TAKES A BIT OF GETTING USED TO. THESE GOGGLES WILL HELP US MAINTAIN SOME PER-SPECTIVE...
...NOT TO MENTION THESE SPECIAL MOLECULAR PROPULSION PACKS.
THIS OPENING SHOULD LEAD US DIRECTLY TO THE AREA OUR SCANS BOUNCED BACK.
If you SAY so, sah!
I say! THIS should be a vacation to write home about, eh, wot?

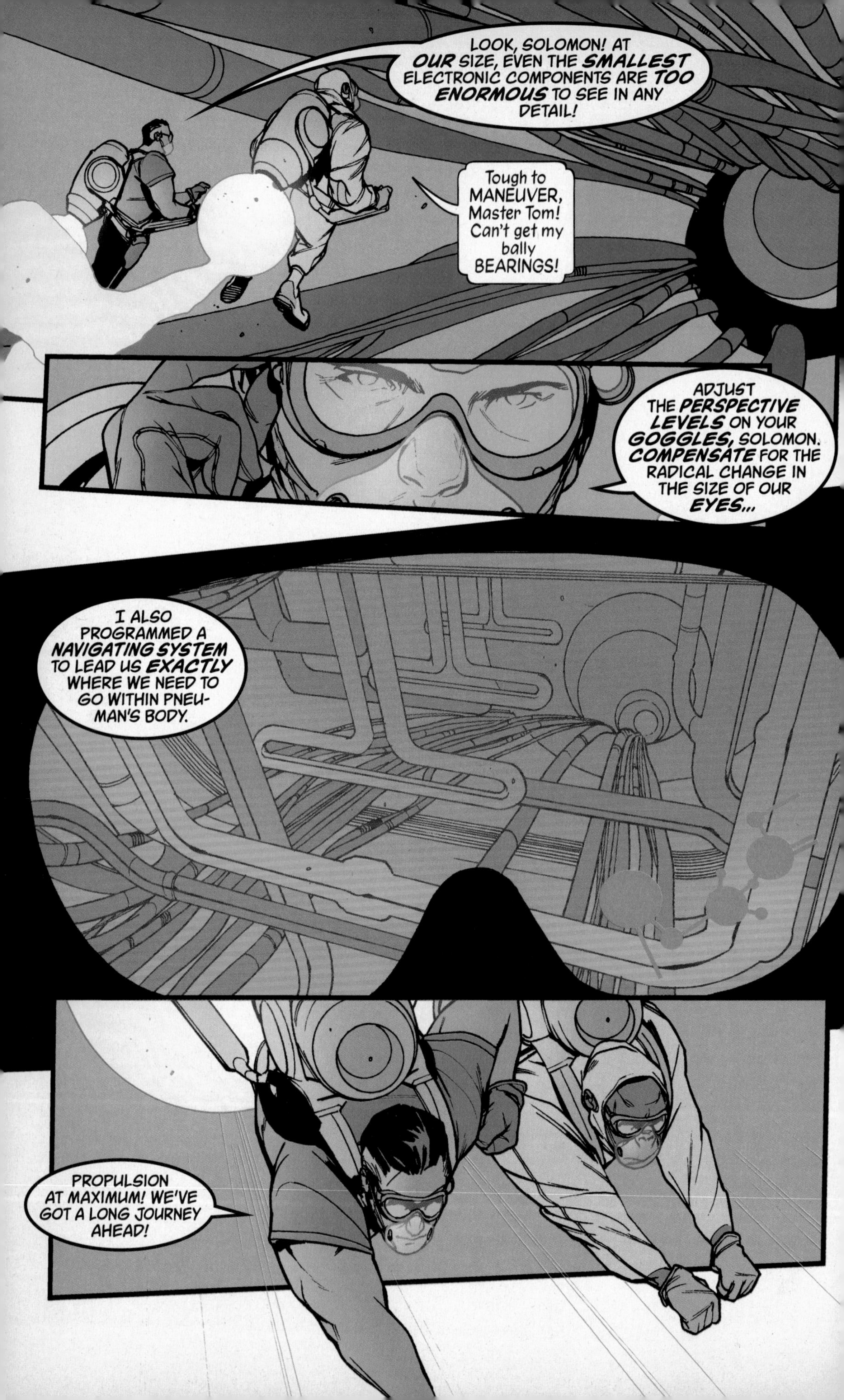
LOOK, SOLOMON! AT OUR SIZE, EVEN THE SMALLEST ELECTRONIC COMPONENTS ARE TOO ENORMOUS TO SEE IN ANY DETAIL!
Tough to MANEUVER, Master Tom! Can't get my bally BEARINGS!
ADJUST THE PERSPECTIVE LEVELS ON YOUR GOGGLES, SOLOMON. COMPENSATE FOR THE RADICAL CHANGE IN THE SIZE OF OUR EYES...
I ALSO PROGRAMMED A NAVIGATING SYSTEM TO LEAD US EXACTLY WHERE WE NEED TO GO WITHIN PNEU-MAN'S BODY.
PROPULSION AT MAXIMUM! WE'VE GOT A LONG JOURNEY AHEAD!

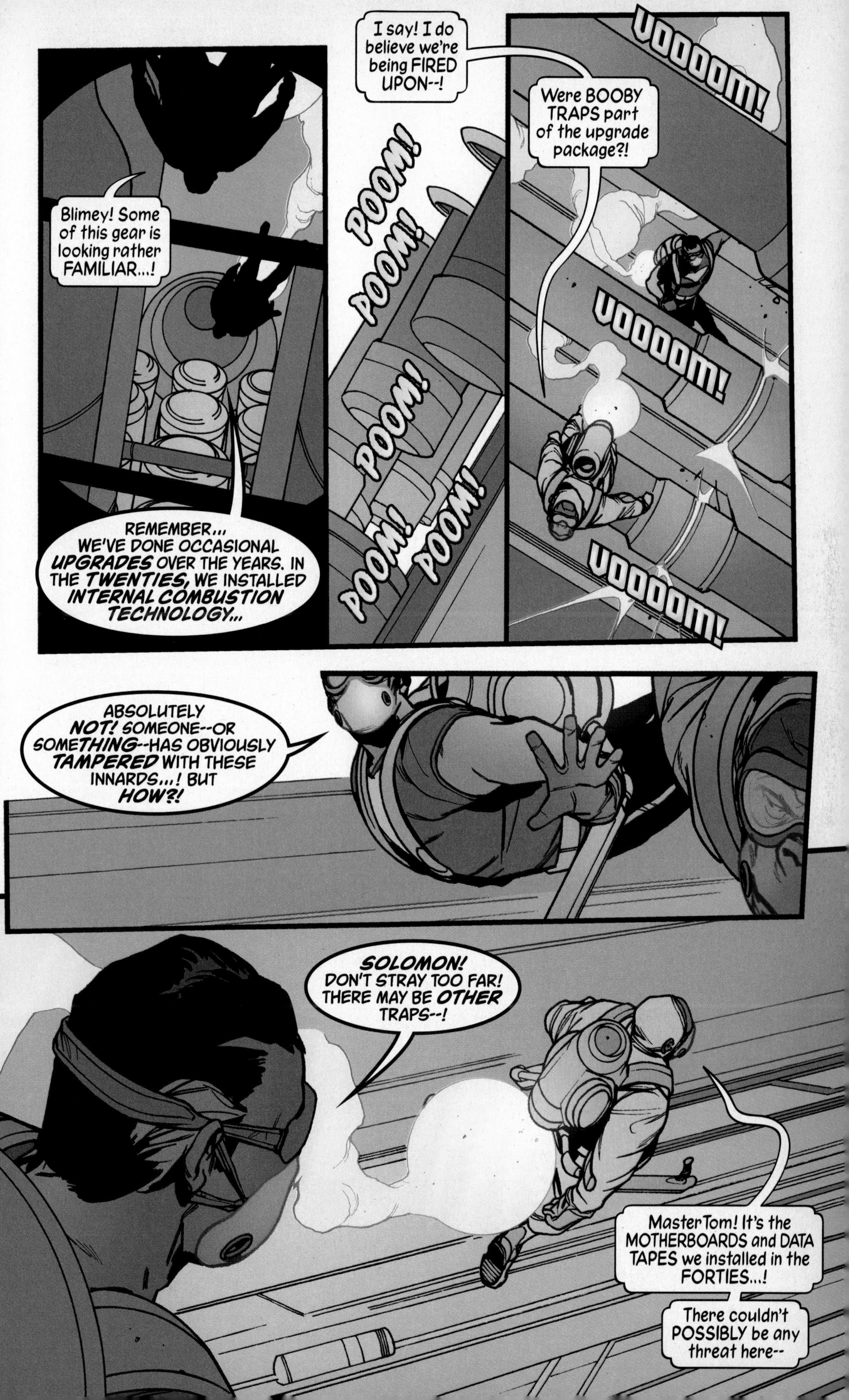

Blimey! Some of this gear is looking rather FAMILIAR...!
REMEMBER... WE'VE DONE OCCASIONAL UPGRADES OVER THE YEARS. IN THE TWENTIES, WE INSTALLED INTERNAL COMBUSTION TECHNOLOGY...
POOM! POOM! POOM! POOM! POOM! POOM!
I say! I do believe we're being FIRED UPON--!
VOOOOM!
Were BOOBY TRAPS part of the upgrade package?!
VOOOOM!
VOOOOM!
ABSOLUTELY NOT! SOMEONE--OR SOMETHING--HAS OBVIOUSLY TAMPERED WITH THESE INNARDS...! BUT HOW?!
SOLOMON! DON'T STRAY TOO FAR! THERE MAY BE OTHER TRAPS--!
MasterTom! It's the MOTHERBOARDS and DATA TAPES we installed in the FORTIES...!
There couldn't POSSIBLY be any threat here--

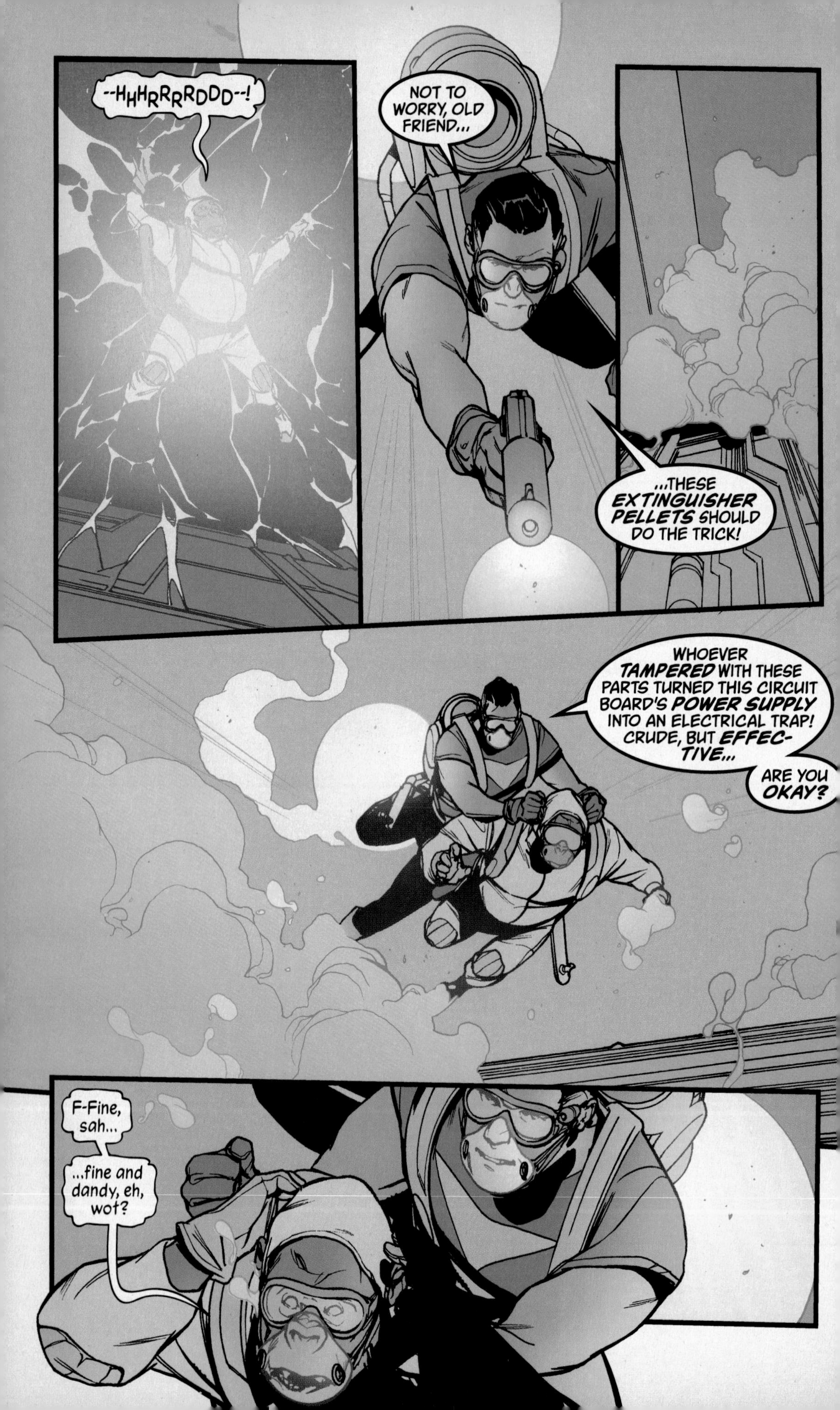

--HHHRRRRDDD--!
NOT TO WORRY, OLD FRIEND...
...THESE EXTINGUISHER PELLETS SHOULD DO THE TRICK!
WHOEVER TAMPERED WITH THESE PARTS TURNED THIS CIRCUIT BOARD'S POWER SUPPLY INTO AN ELECTRICAL TRAP! CRUDE, BUT EFFECTIVE...
ARE YOU OKAY?
F-Fine, sah...
...fine and dandy, eh, wot?

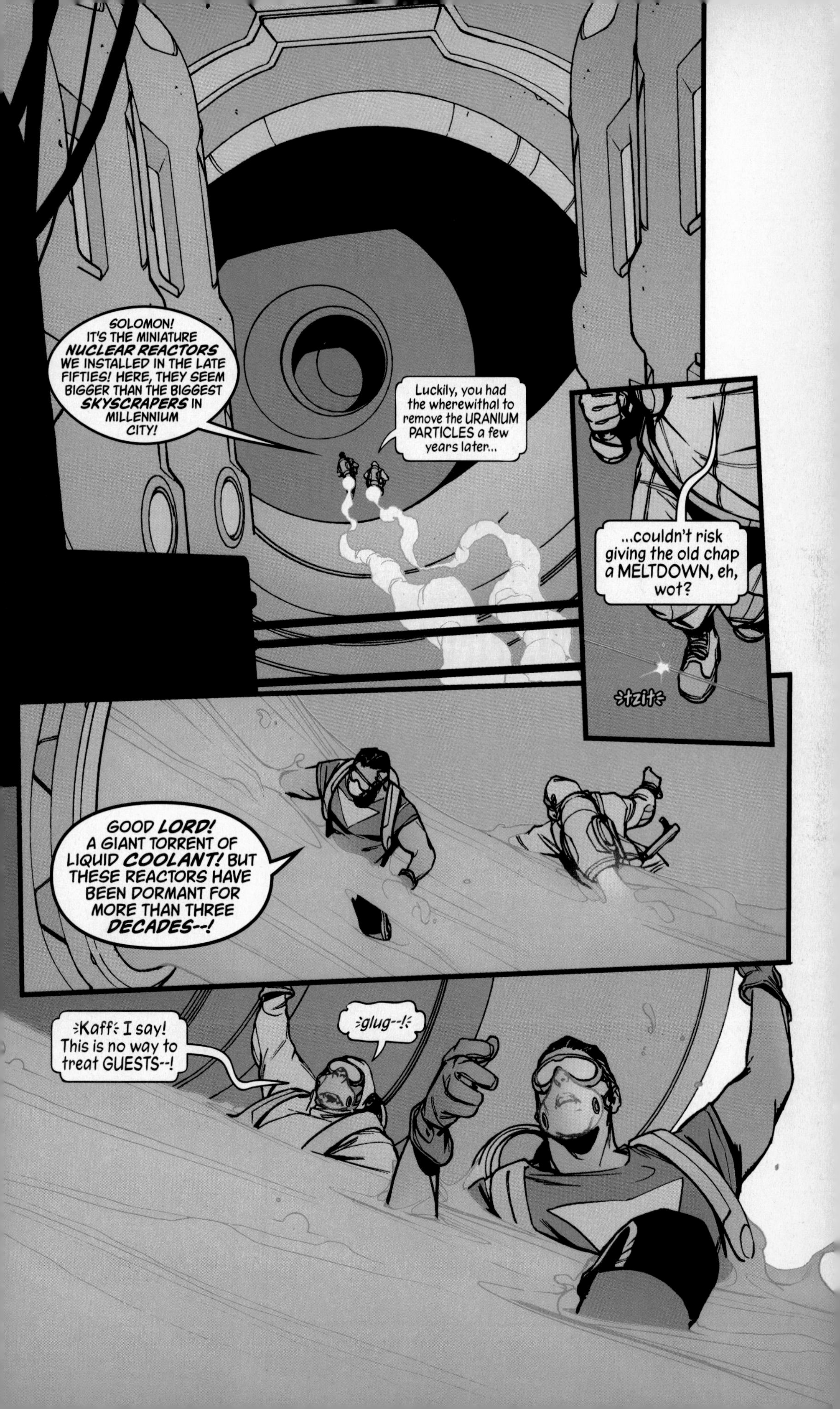
SOLOMON! IT'S THE MINIATURE NUCLEAR REACTORS WE INSTALLED IN THE LATE FIFTIES! HERE, THEY SEEM BIGGER THAN THE BIGGEST SKYSCRAPERS IN MILLENNIUM CITY!
Luckily, you had the wherewithal to remove the URANIUM PARTICLES a few years later...
...couldn't risk giving the old chap a MELTDOWN, eh, wot?
tzit
GOOD LORD! A GIANT TORRENT OF LIQUID COOLANT! BUT THESE REACTORS HAVE BEEN DORMANT FOR MORE THAN THREE DECADES--!
Kaff I say! This is no way to treat GUESTS--!
glug--!

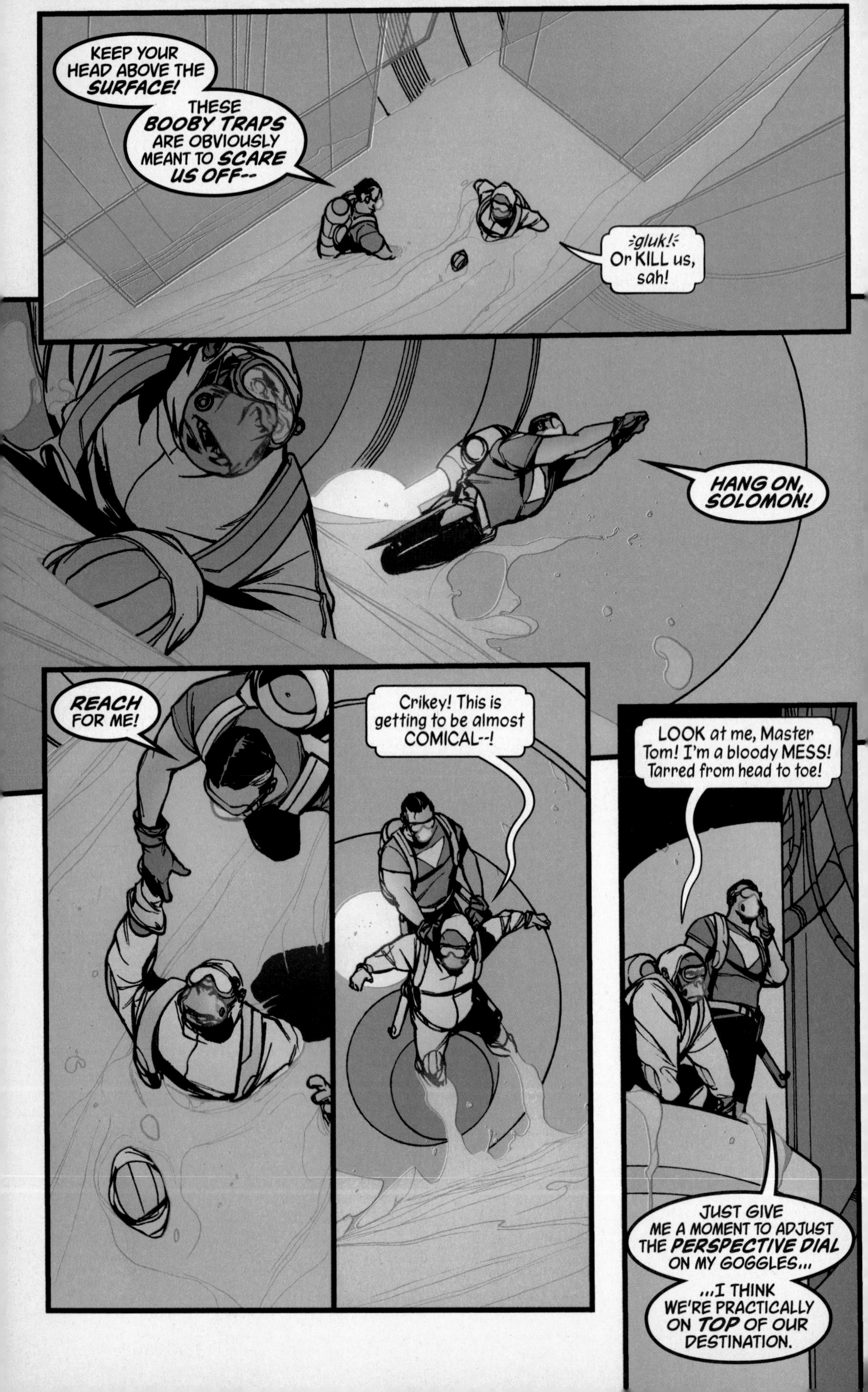
KEEP YOUR HEAD ABOVE THE SURFACE!
THESE BOOBY TRAPS ARE OBVIOUSLY MEANT TO SCARE US OFF--
gluk! Or KILL us, sah!
HANG ON, SOLOMON!
REACH FOR ME!
Crikey! This is getting to be almost COMICAL--!
LOOK at me, Master Tom! I'm a bloody MESS! Tarred from head to toe!
JUST GIVE ME A MOMENT TO ADJUST THE PERSPECTIVE DIAL ON MY GOGGLES...
...I THINK WE'RE PRACTICALLY ON TOP OF OUR DESTINATION.

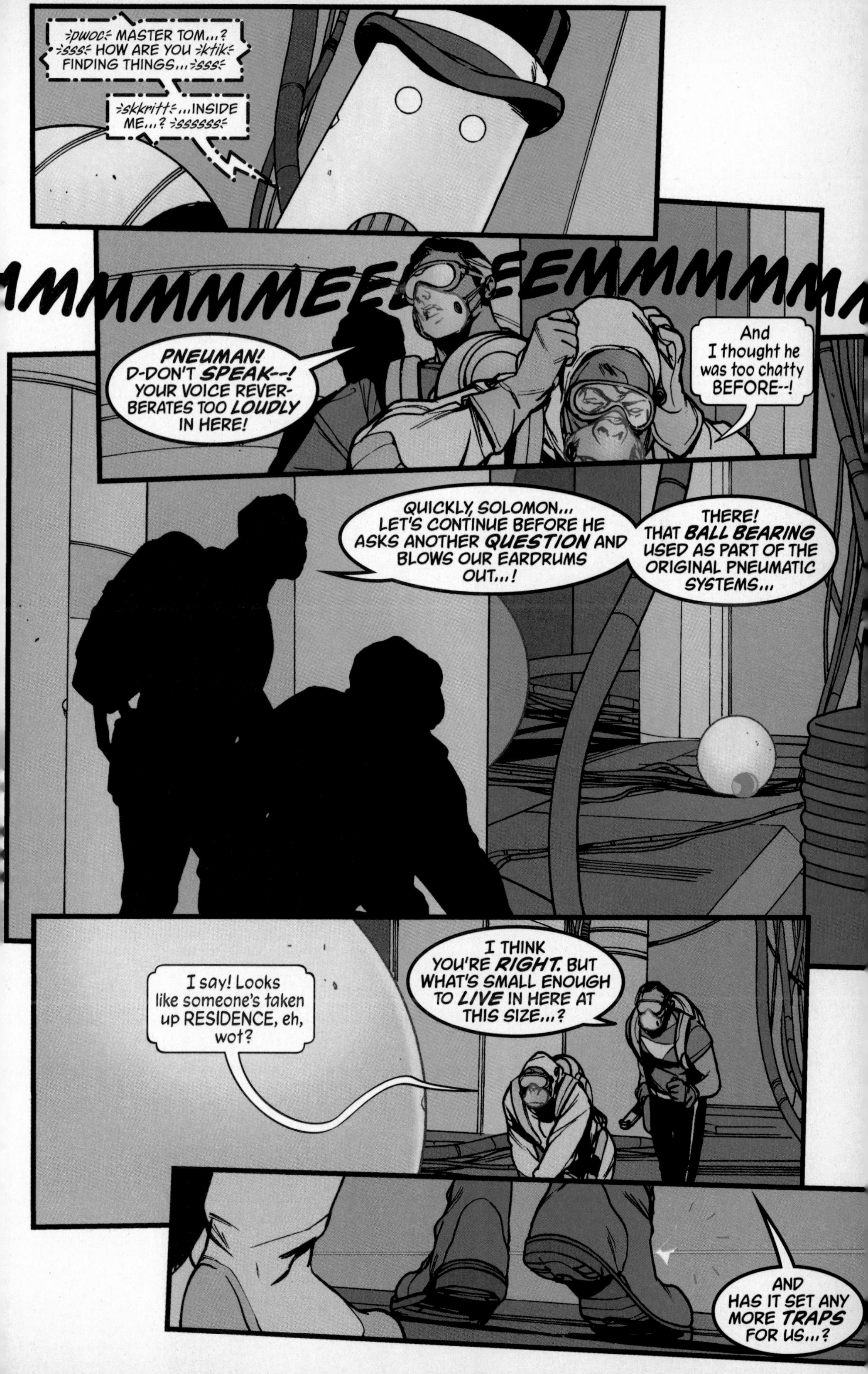

>pwoc< MASTER TOM...? >sss< HOW ARE YOU >ktik< FINDING THINGS... >sss<
>skkritt< ...INSIDE ME...? >ssssss<
MMMMMMEEEEEMMMMMM
PNEUMAN! D-DON'T SPEAK--! YOUR VOICE REVERBERATES TOO LOUDLY IN HERE!
And I thought he was too chatty BEFORE--!
QUICKLY, SOLOMON... LET'S CONTINUE BEFORE HE ASKS ANOTHER QUESTION AND BLOWS OUR EARDRUMS OUT...!
THERE! THAT BALL BEARING USED AS PART OF THE ORIGINAL PNEUMATIC SYSTEMS...
I say! Looks like someone's taken up RESIDENCE, eh, wot?
I THINK YOU'RE RIGHT. BUT WHAT'S SMALL ENOUGH TO LIVE IN HERE AT THIS SIZE...?
AND HAS IT SET ANY MORE TRAPS FOR US...?

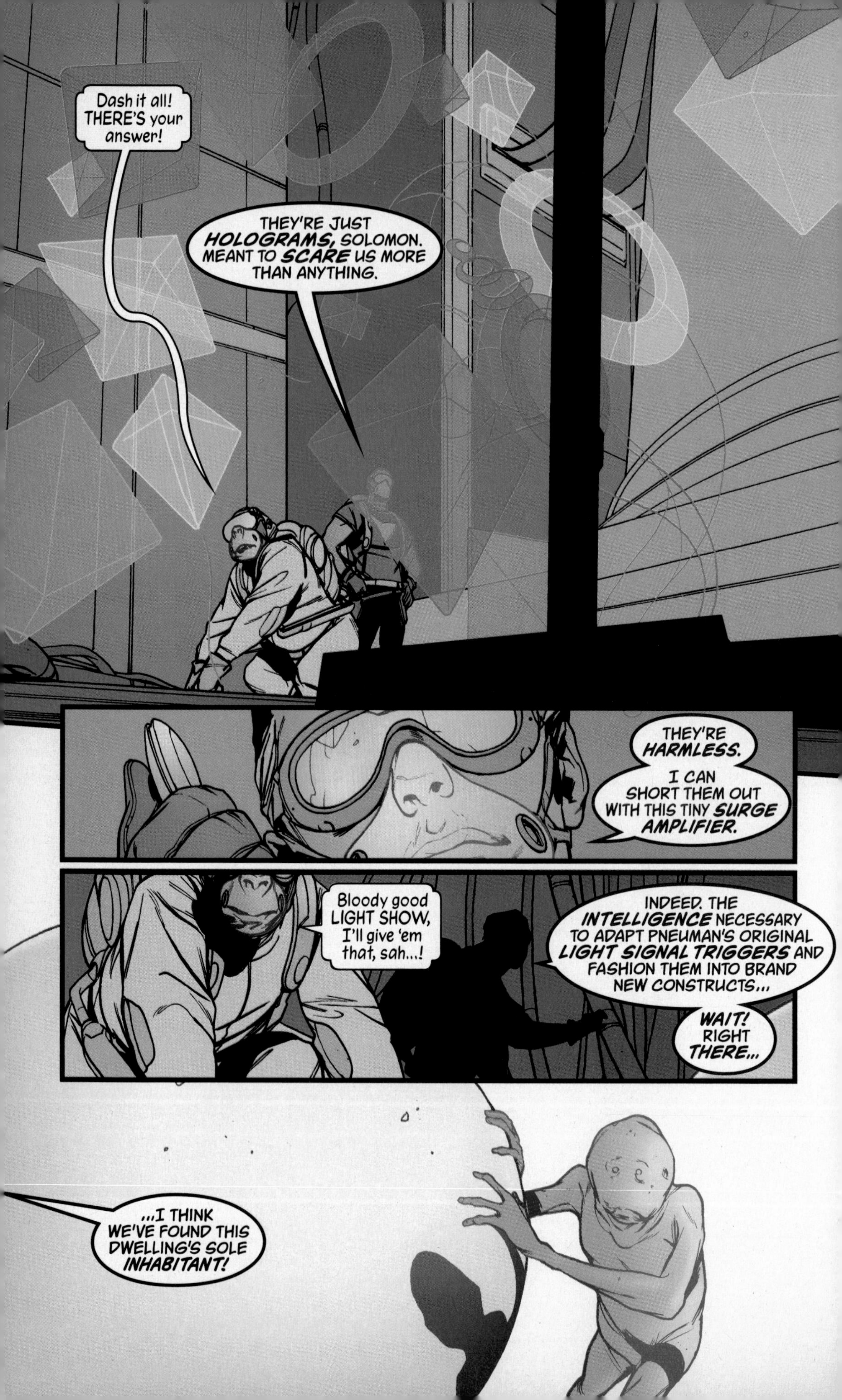
Dash it all! THERE'S your answer!
THEY'RE JUST HOLOGRAMS, SOLOMON. MEANT TO SCARE US MORE THAN ANYTHING.
THEY'RE HARMLESS.
I CAN SHORT THEM OUT WITH THIS TINY SURGE AMPLIFIER.
Bloody good LIGHT SHOW, I'll give 'em that, sah...!
INDEED. THE INTELLIGENCE NECESSARY TO ADAPT PNEUMAN'S ORIGINAL LIGHT SIGNAL TRIGGERS AND FASHION THEM INTO BRAND NEW CONSTRUCTS...
WAIT! RIGHT THERE...
...I THINK WE'VE FOUND THIS DWELLING'S SOLE INHABITANT!

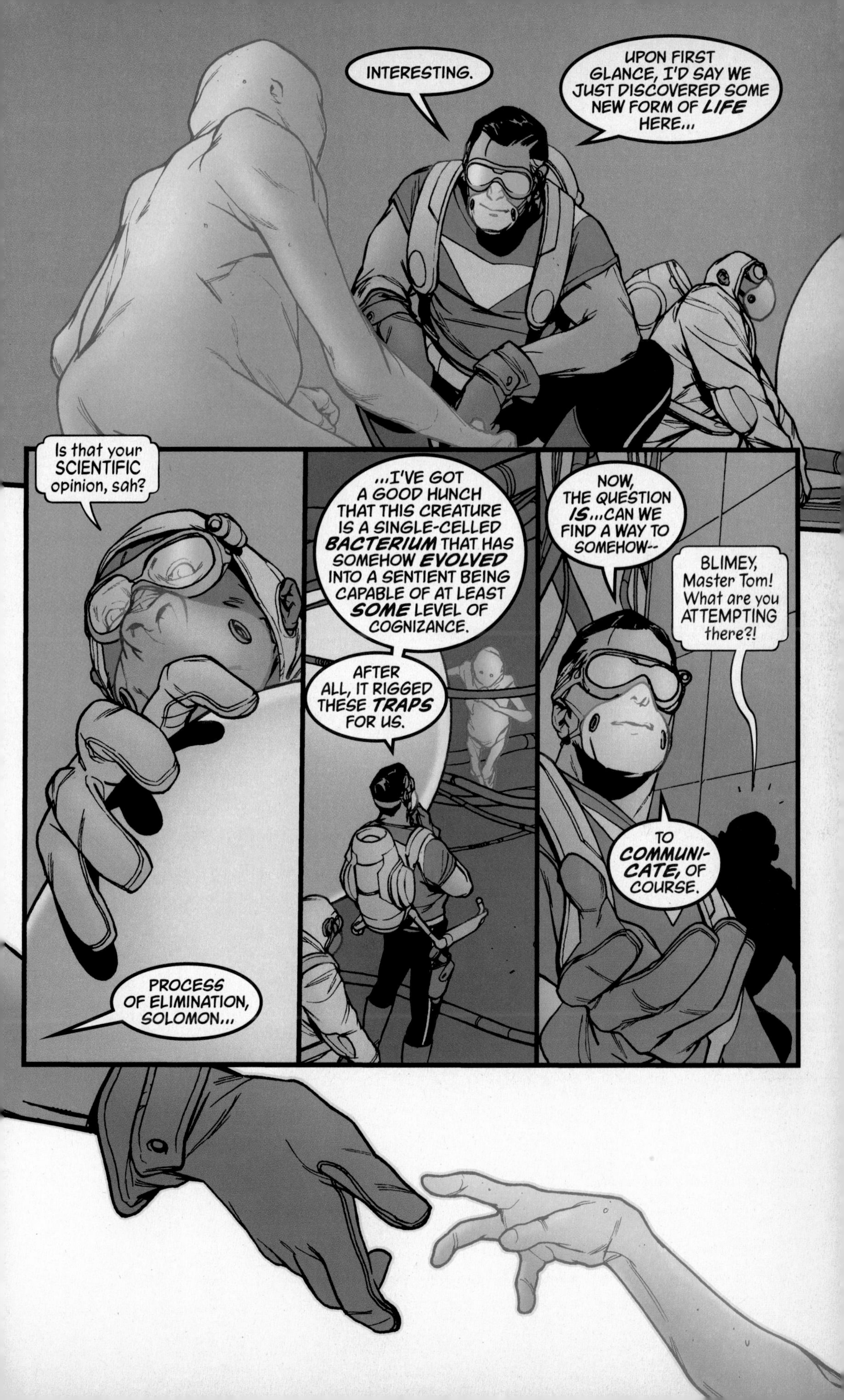
INTERESTING.
UPON FIRST GLANCE, I'D SAY WE JUST DISCOVERED SOME NEW FORM OF LIFE HERE...
Is that your SCIENTIFIC opinion, sah?
PROCESS OF ELIMINATION, SOLOMON...
...I'VE GOT A GOOD HUNCH THAT THIS CREATURE IS A SINGLE-CELLED BACTERIUM THAT HAS SOMEHOW EVOLVED INTO A SENTIENT BEING CAPABLE OF AT LEAST SOME LEVEL OF COGNIZANCE.
AFTER ALL, IT RIGGED THESE TRAPS FOR US.
NOW, THE QUESTION IS...CAN WE FIND A WAY TO SOMEHOW--
BLIMEY, Master Tom! What are you ATTEMPTING there?!
TO COMMUNI-CATE, OF COURSE.

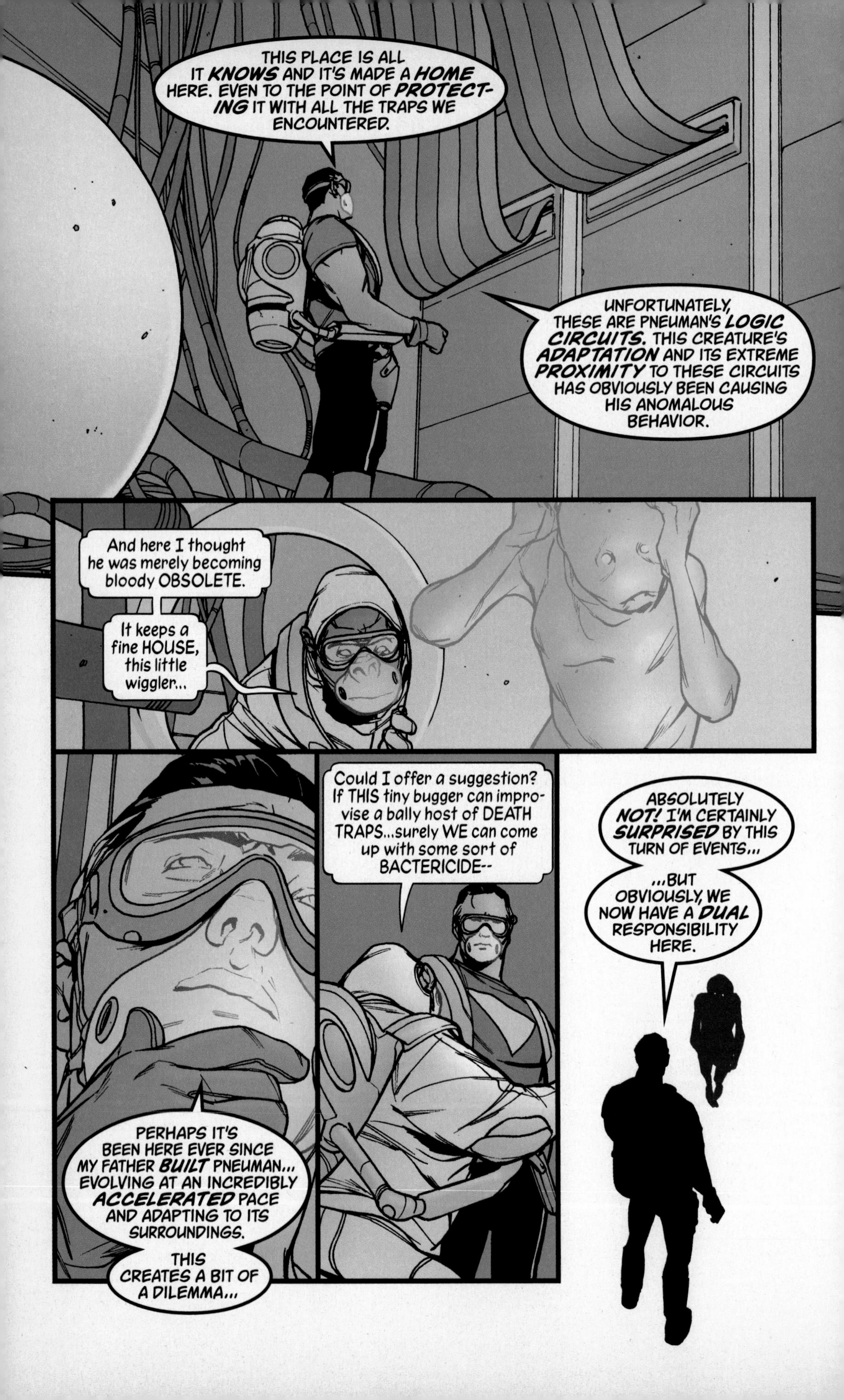
THIS PLACE IS ALL IT KNOWS AND IT'S MADE A HOME HERE. EVEN TO THE POINT OF PROTECTING IT WITH ALL THE TRAPS WE ENCOUNTERED.
UNFORTUNATELY, THESE ARE PNEUMAN'S LOGIC CIRCUITS. THIS CREATURE'S ADAPTATION AND ITS EXTREME PROXIMITY TO THESE CIRCUITS HAS OBVIOUSLY BEEN CAUSING HIS ANOMALOUS BEHAVIOR.
And here I thought he was merely becoming bloody OBSOLETE.
It keeps a fine HOUSE, this little wiggler...
PERHAPS IT'S BEEN HERE EVER SINCE MY FATHER BUILT PNEUMAN... EVOLVING AT AN INCREDIBLY ACCELERATED PACE AND ADAPTING TO ITS SURROUNDINGS.
THIS CREATES A BIT OF A DILEMMA...
Could I offer a suggestion? If THIS tiny bugger can improvise a bally host of DEATH TRAPS...surely WE can come up with some sort of BACTERICIDE--
ABSOLUTELY NOT! I'M CERTAINLY SURPRISED BY THIS TURN OF EVENTS...
...BUT OBVIOUSLY, WE NOW HAVE A DUAL RESPONSIBILITY HERE.

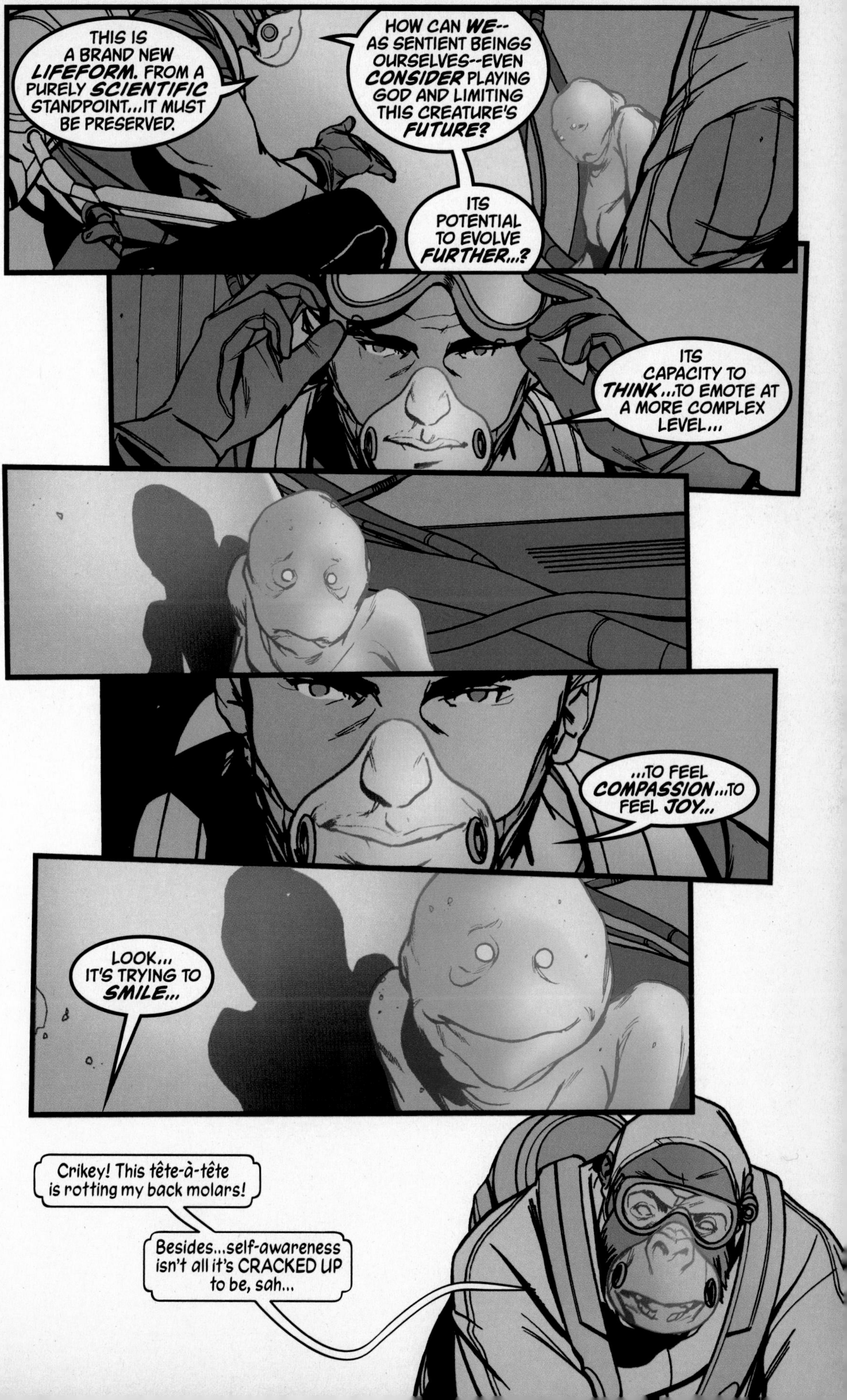
THIS IS A BRAND NEW LIFEFORM. FROM A PURELY SCIENTIFIC STANDPOINT...IT MUST BE PRESERVED.
HOW CAN WE--AS SENTIENT BEINGS OURSELVES--EVEN CONSIDER PLAYING GOD AND LIMITING THIS CREATURE'S FUTURE?
ITS POTENTIAL TO EVOLVE FURTHER...?
ITS CAPACITY TO THINK...TO EMOTE AT A MORE COMPLEX LEVEL...
...TO FEEL COMPASSION...TO FEEL JOY...
LOOK... IT'S TRYING TO SMILE...
Crikey! This tête-à-tête is rotting my back molars!
Besides...self-awareness isn't all it's CRACKED UP to be, sah...

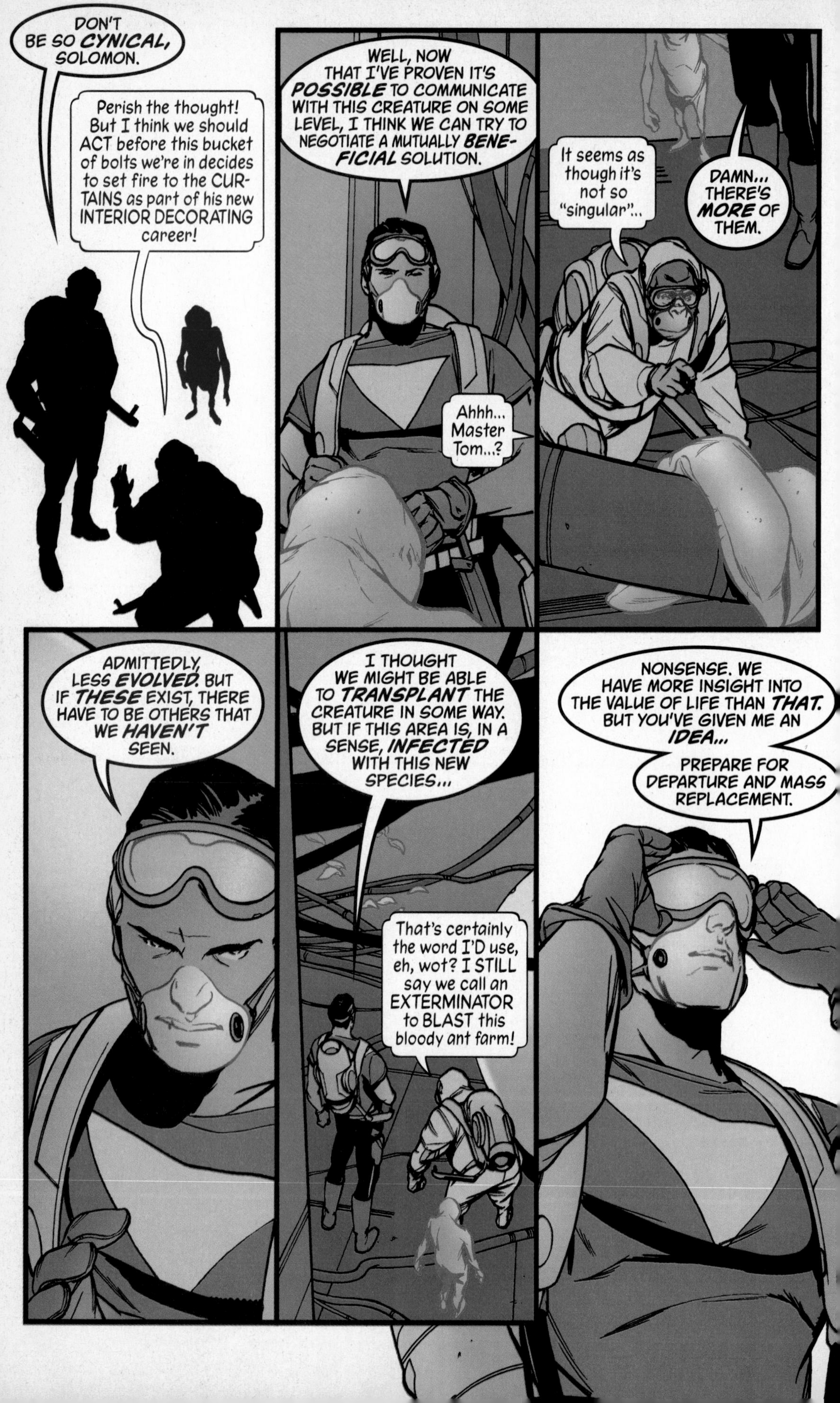
DON'T BE SO CYNICAL, SOLOMON.
Perish the thought! But I think we should ACT before this bucket of bolts we're in decides to set fire to the CURTAINS as part of his new INTERIOR DECORATING career!
WELL, NOW THAT I'VE PROVEN IT'S POSSIBLE TO COMMUNICATE WITH THIS CREATURE ON SOME LEVEL, I THINK WE CAN TRY TO NEGOTIATE A MUTUALLY BENEFICIAL SOLUTION.
Ahhh... Master Tom...?
It seems as though it's not so "singular"...
DAMN... THERE'S MORE OF THEM.
ADMITTEDLY, LESS EVOLVED. BUT IF THESE EXIST, THERE HAVE TO BE OTHERS THAT WE HAVEN'T SEEN.
I THOUGHT WE MIGHT BE ABLE TO TRANSPLANT THE CREATURE IN SOME WAY. BUT IF THIS AREA IS, IN A SENSE, INFECTED WITH THIS NEW SPECIES...
That's certainly the word I'D use, eh, wot? I STILL say we call an EXTERMINATOR to BLAST this bloody ant farm!
NONSENSE. WE HAVE MORE INSIGHT INTO THE VALUE OF LIFE THAN THAT. BUT YOU'VE GIVEN ME AN IDEA...
PREPARE FOR DEPARTURE AND MASS REPLACEMENT.

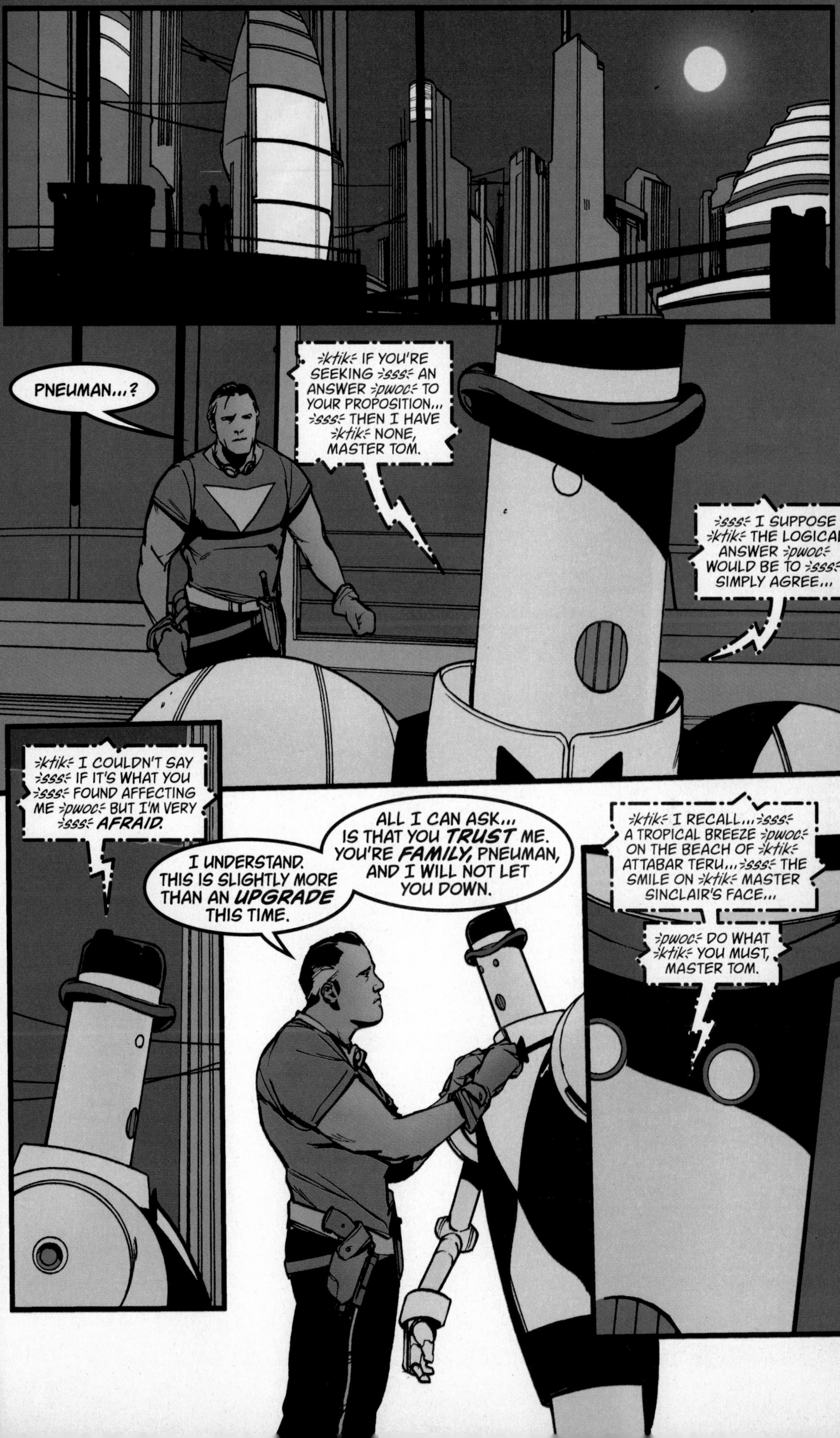
PNEUMAN...?
=ktik= IF YOU'RE SEEKING =sss= AN ANSWER =pwoc= TO YOUR PROPOSITION... =sss= THEN I HAVE =ktik= NONE, MASTER TOM.
=sss= I SUPPOSE =ktik= THE LOGICAL ANSWER =pwoc= WOULD BE TO =sss= SIMPLY AGREE...
=ktik= I COULDN'T SAY =sss= IF IT'S WHAT YOU =sss= FOUND AFFECTING ME =pwoc= BUT I'M VERY =sss= AFRAID.
I UNDERSTAND. THIS IS SLIGHTLY MORE THAN AN UPGRADE THIS TIME.
ALL I CAN ASK... IS THAT YOU TRUST ME. YOU'RE FAMILY, PNEUMAN, AND I WILL NOT LET YOU DOWN.
=ktik= I RECALL... =sss= A TROPICAL BREEZE =pwoc= ON THE BEACH OF =ktik= ATTABAR TERU... =sss= THE SMILE ON =ktik= MASTER SINCLAIR'S FACE...
=pwoc= DO WHAT =ktik= YOU MUST, MASTER TOM.

THE FOLLOWING DAY.

...A COMPLETE AND TOTAL *SUCCESS!*

÷ktik÷ I FEEL ÷sss÷ LIKE MY OLD SELF ÷pwoo÷ AGAIN!

Back to merely ANNOYING instead of DANGEROUS, old bean!

YOU LOOK AS GOOD AS *NEW*, PNEUMAN. I CAN'T EVEN TELL THE *DIFFERENCE.*

WELL, THAT MAKES SENSE.

I *REPLACED* PNEUMAN'S *MIDSECTION* WITH AN *EXACT REPLICA.* COMPLETELY *BACTERIA FREE*, OF COURSE.

AS FOR THE *ORIGINAL*, IT WILL REMAIN SAFE UNDER GLASS HERE IN THE LAB.

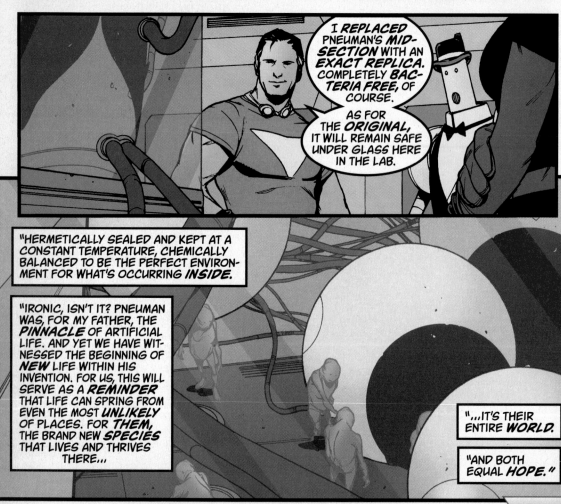

"HERMETICALLY SEALED AND KEPT AT A CONSTANT TEMPERATURE, CHEMICALLY BALANCED TO BE THE PERFECT ENVIRONMENT FOR WHAT'S OCCURRING *INSIDE.*

"IRONIC, ISN'T IT? PNEUMAN WAS, FOR MY FATHER, THE *PINNACLE* OF ARTIFICIAL LIFE. AND YET WE HAVE WITNESSED THE BEGINNING OF *NEW* LIFE WITHIN HIS INVENTION. FOR US, THIS WILL SERVE AS A *REMINDER* THAT LIFE CAN SPRING FROM EVEN THE MOST *UNLIKELY* OF PLACES. FOR *THEM*, THE BRAND NEW *SPECIES* THAT LIVES AND THRIVES THERE...

"...IT'S THEIR ENTIRE *WORLD.*

"AND BOTH EQUAL *HOPE.*"

**THE END**

# CHAPTER FOUR

In which Tom treks to a fabled lost desert city,
uncovers denizens both alien and familiar,
and faces destruction with a new ally.

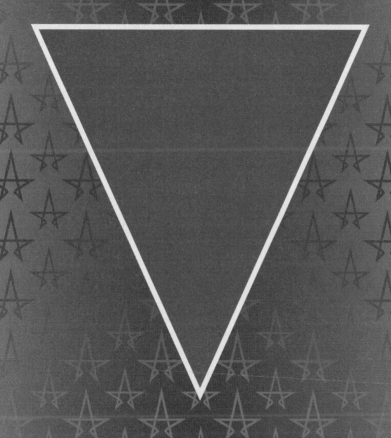

**Cover art:**
Chris Sprouse & Karl Story
**Cover colors:**
Darlene Royer

# TOM STRONG
## AND THE
## SPIRES OF SAMAKHARA

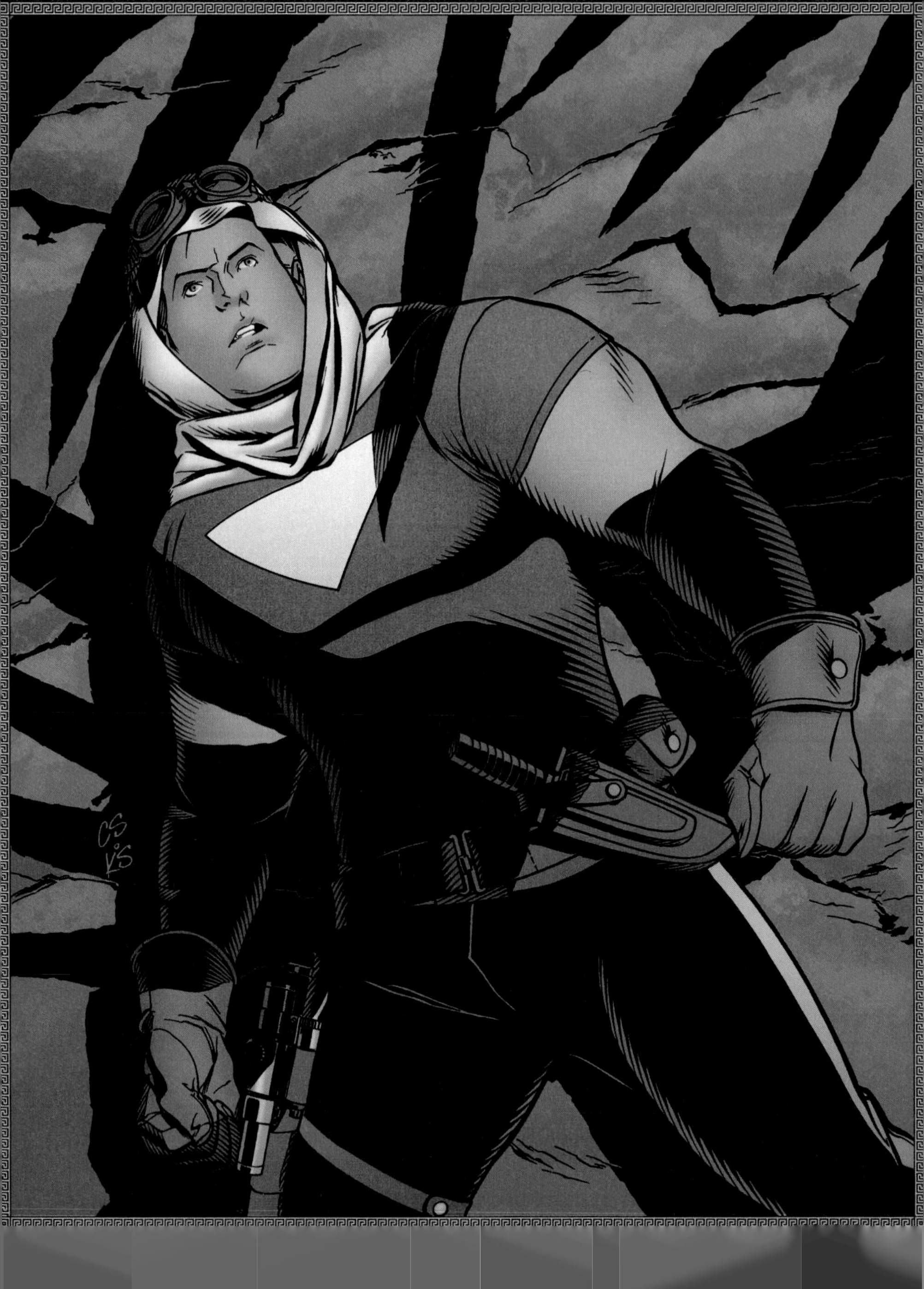

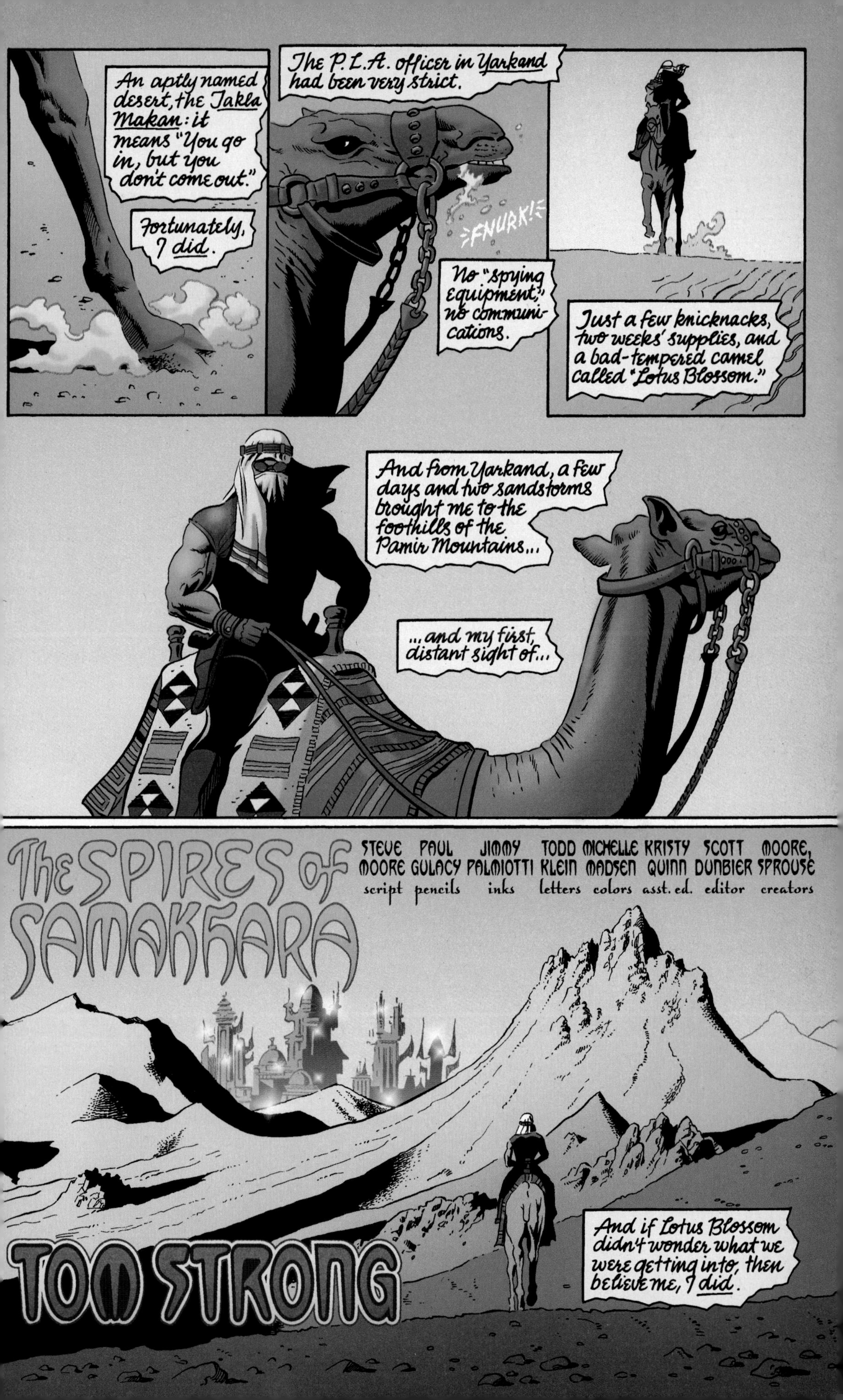
An aptly named desert, the Takla Makan: it means "You go in, but you don't come out."
Fortunately, I did.
The P.L.A. officer in Yarkand had been very strict.
FNURK!
No "spying equipment," no communications.
Just a few knicknacks, two weeks' supplies, and a bad-tempered camel called "Lotus Blossom."
And from Yarkand, a few days and two sandstorms brought me to the foothills of the Pamir Mountains...
...and my first, distant sight of...
The SPIRES of SAMAKHARA
STEVE MOORE script
PAUL GULACY pencils
JIMMY PALMIOTTI inks
TODD KLEIN letters
MICHELLE MADSEN colors
KRISTY QUINN asst. ed.
SCOTT DUNBIER editor
MOORE, SPROUSE creators
TOM STRONG
And if Lotus Blossom didn't wonder what we were getting into, then believe me, I did.

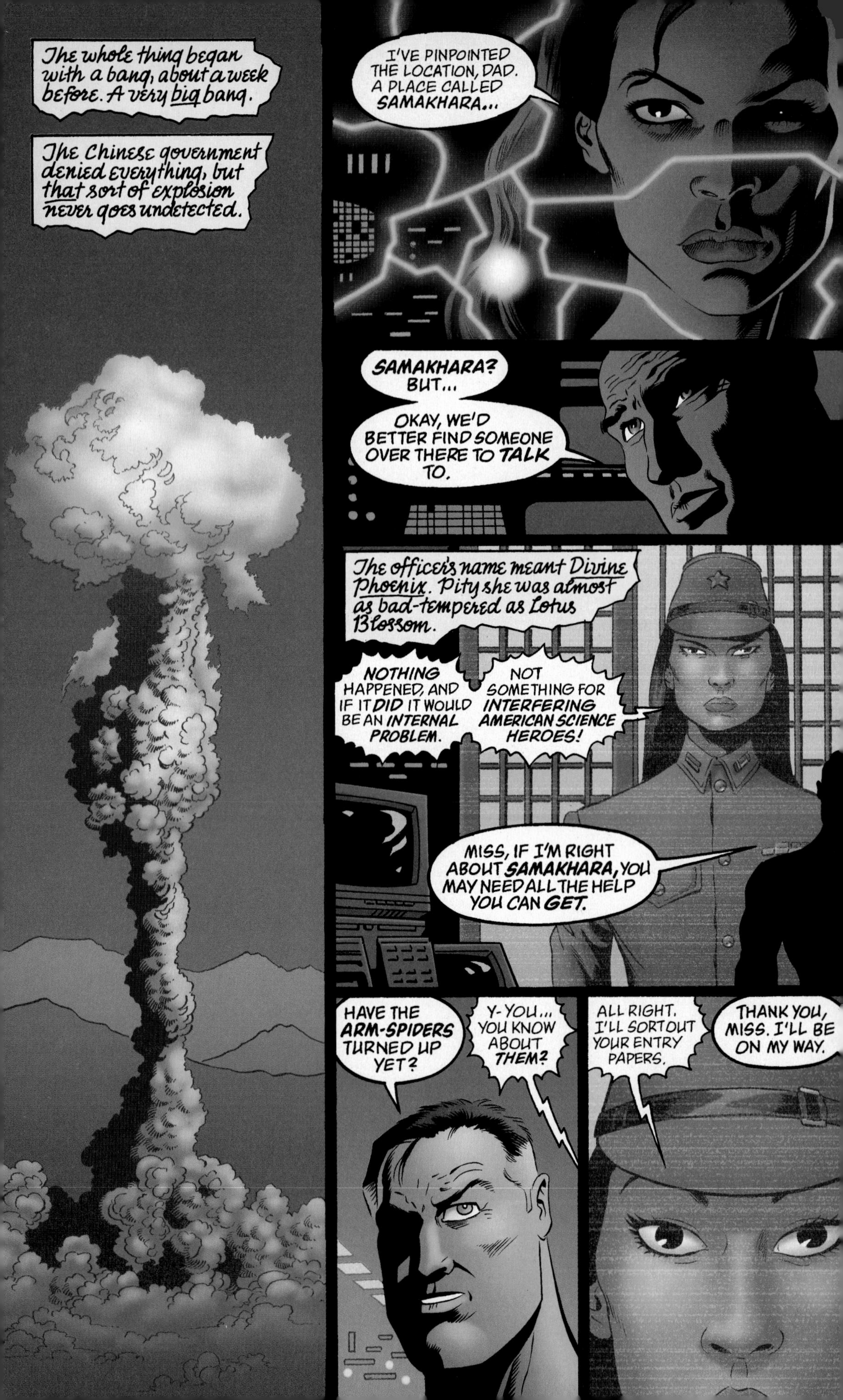

The whole thing began with a bang, about a week before. A very big bang.
The Chinese government denied everything, but that sort of explosion never goes undetected.
I'VE PINPOINTED THE LOCATION, DAD. A PLACE CALLED SAMAKHARA...
SAMAKHARA? BUT...
OKAY, WE'D BETTER FIND SOMEONE OVER THERE TO TALK TO.
The officer's name meant Divine Phoenix. Pity she was almost as bad-tempered as Lotus Blossom.
NOTHING HAPPENED, AND IF IT DID IT WOULD BE AN INTERNAL PROBLEM.
NOT SOMETHING FOR INTERFERING AMERICAN SCIENCE HEROES!
MISS, IF I'M RIGHT ABOUT SAMAKHARA, YOU MAY NEED ALL THE HELP YOU CAN GET.
HAVE THE ARM-SPIDERS TURNED UP YET?
Y-YOU... YOU KNOW ABOUT THEM?
ALL RIGHT. I'LL SORT OUT YOUR ENTRY PAPERS.
THANK YOU, MISS. I'LL BE ON MY WAY.

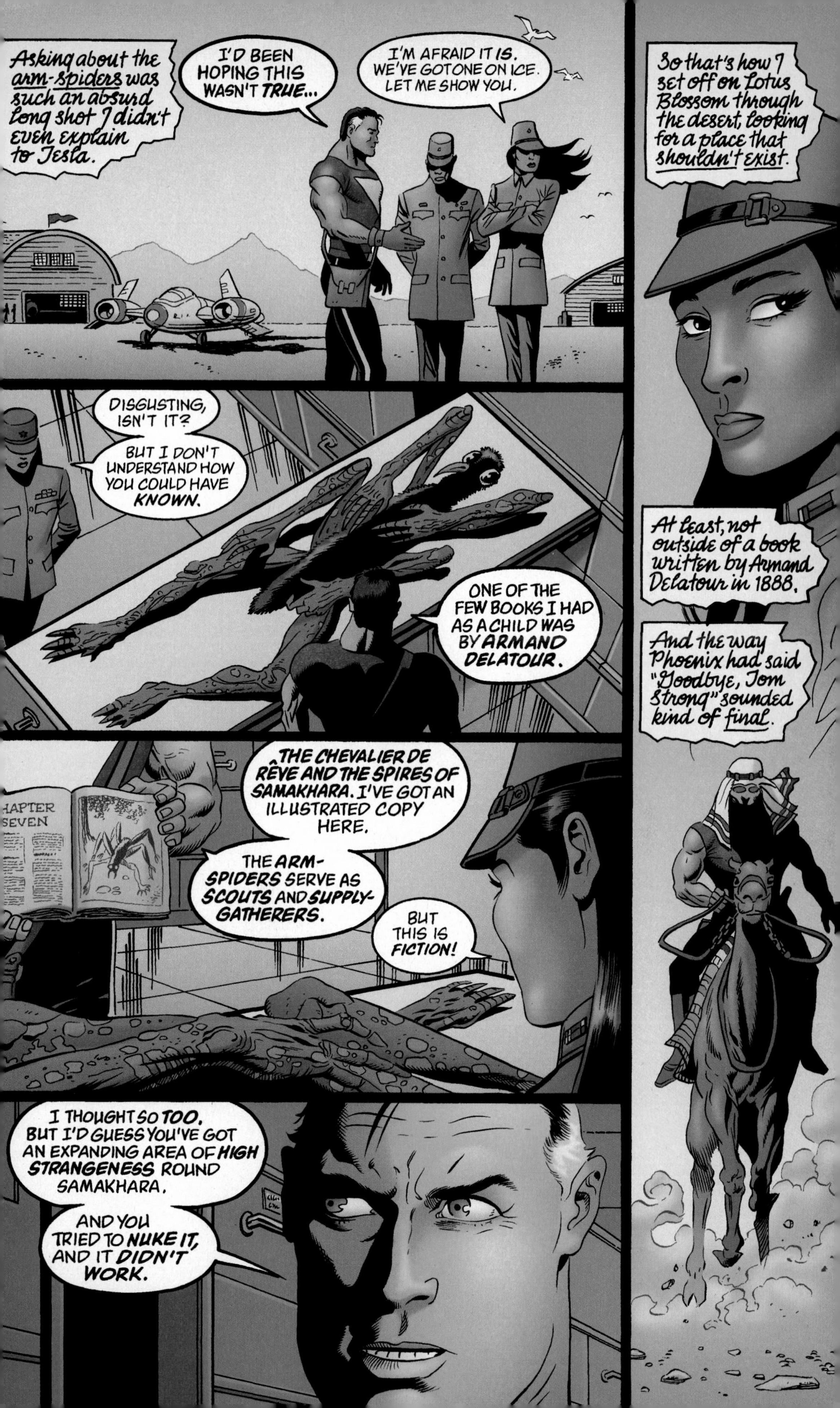
Asking about the arm-spiders was such an absurd long shot I didn't even explain to Tesla.
I'D BEEN HOPING THIS WASN'T TRUE...
I'M AFRAID IT IS. WE'VE GOT ONE ON ICE. LET ME SHOW YOU.
DISGUSTING, ISN'T IT?
BUT I DON'T UNDERSTAND HOW YOU COULD HAVE KNOWN.
ONE OF THE FEW BOOKS I HAD AS A CHILD WAS BY ARMAND DELATOUR.
THE CHEVALIER DE RÊVE AND THE SPIRES OF SAMAKHARA. I'VE GOT AN ILLUSTRATED COPY HERE.
HAPTER SEVEN
THE ARM-SPIDERS SERVE AS SCOUTS AND SUPPLY-GATHERERS.
BUT THIS IS FICTION!
I THOUGHT SO TOO. BUT I'D GUESS YOU'VE GOT AN EXPANDING AREA OF HIGH STRANGENESS ROUND SAMAKHARA.
AND YOU TRIED TO NUKE IT, AND IT DIDN'T WORK.
So that's how I set off on Lotus Blossom through the desert, looking for a place that shouldn't exist.
At least, not outside of a book written by Armand Delatour in 1888.
And the way Phoenix had said "Goodbye, Tom Strong" sounded kind of final.

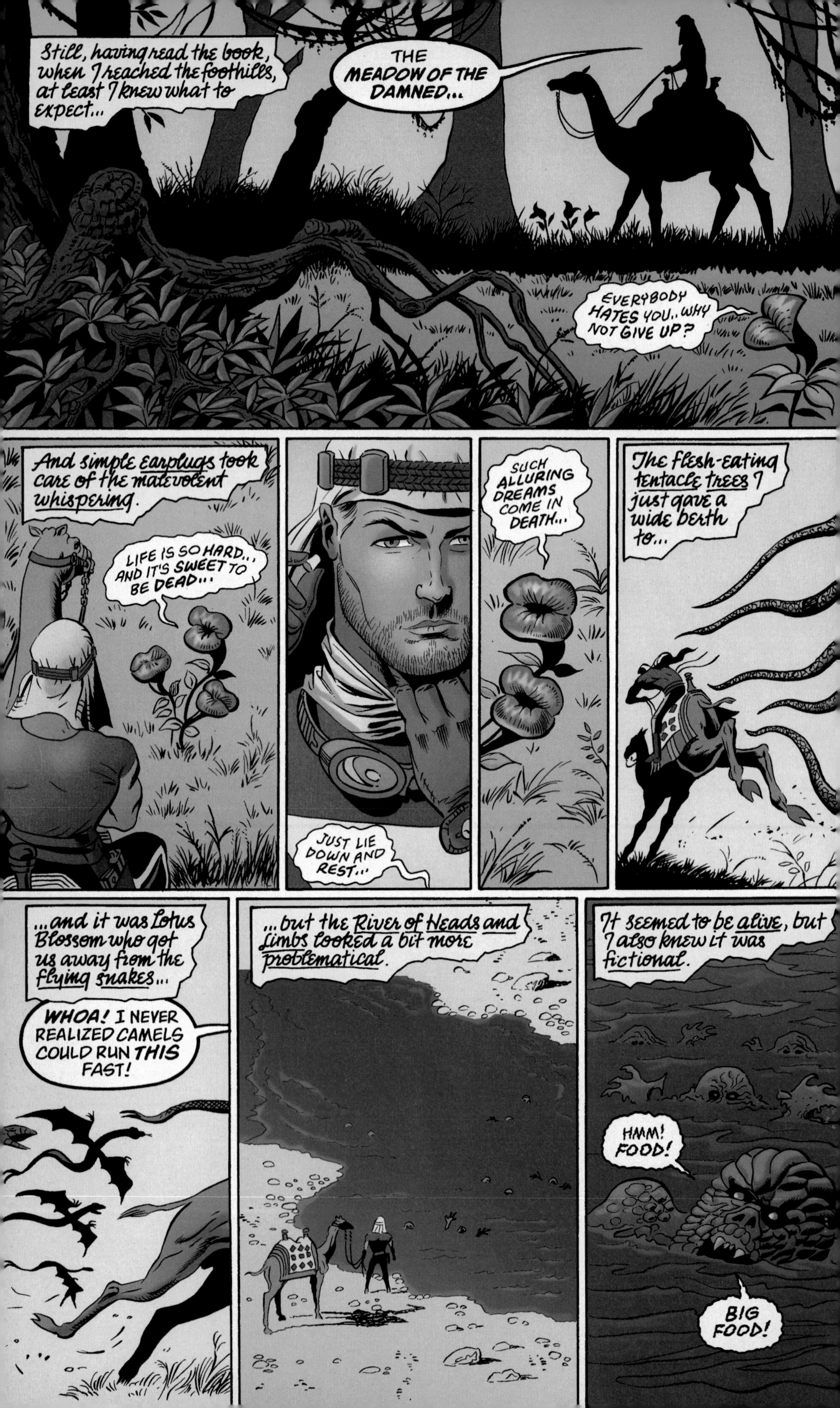
Still, having read the book, when I reached the foothills, at least I knew what to expect...
THE MEADOW OF THE DAMNED...
EVERYBODY HATES YOU.. WHY NOT GIVE UP?
And simple earplugs took care of the malevolent whispering.
LIFE IS SO HARD... AND IT'S SWEET TO BE DEAD...
JUST LIE DOWN AND REST...
SUCH ALLURING DREAMS COME IN DEATH...
The flesh-eating tentacle trees I just gave a wide berth to...
...and it was Lotus Blossom who got us away from the flying snakes...
WHOA! I NEVER REALIZED CAMELS COULD RUN THIS FAST!
...but the River of Heads and Limbs looked a bit more problematical.
It seemed to be alive, but I also knew it was fictional.
HMM! FOOD!
BIG FOOD!

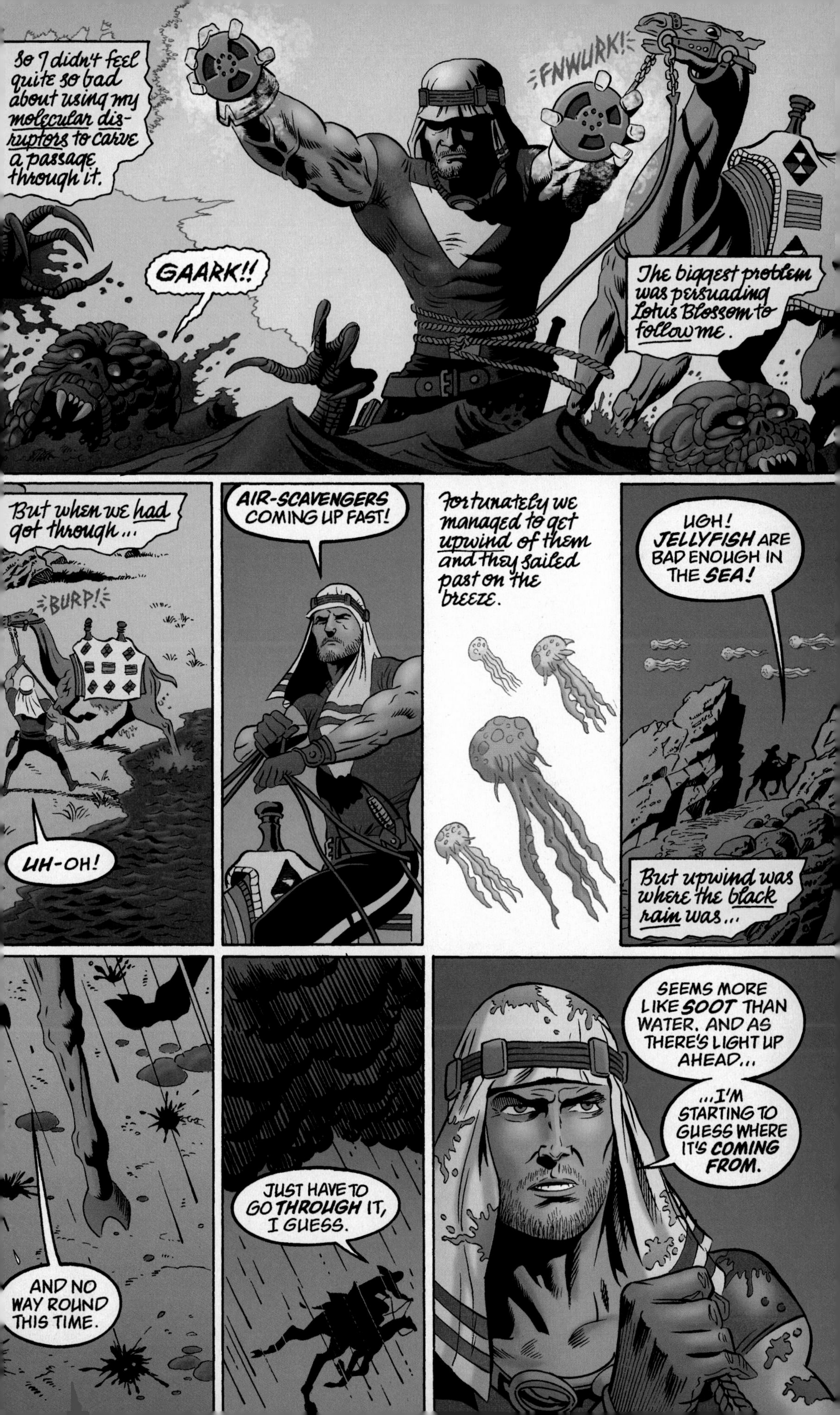
So I didn't feel quite so bad about using my molecular disruptors to carve a passage through it.
FNWURK!
GAARK!!
The biggest problem was persuading Lotus Blossom to follow me.
But when we had got through...
BURP!
UH-OH!
AIR-SCAVENGERS COMING UP FAST!
Fortunately we managed to get upwind of them and they sailed past on the breeze.
UGH! JELLYFISH ARE BAD ENOUGH IN THE SEA!
But upwind was where the black rain was...
AND NO WAY ROUND THIS TIME.
JUST HAVE TO GO THROUGH IT, I GUESS.
SEEMS MORE LIKE SOOT THAN WATER. AND AS THERE'S LIGHT UP AHEAD...
...I'M STARTING TO GUESS WHERE IT'S COMING FROM.

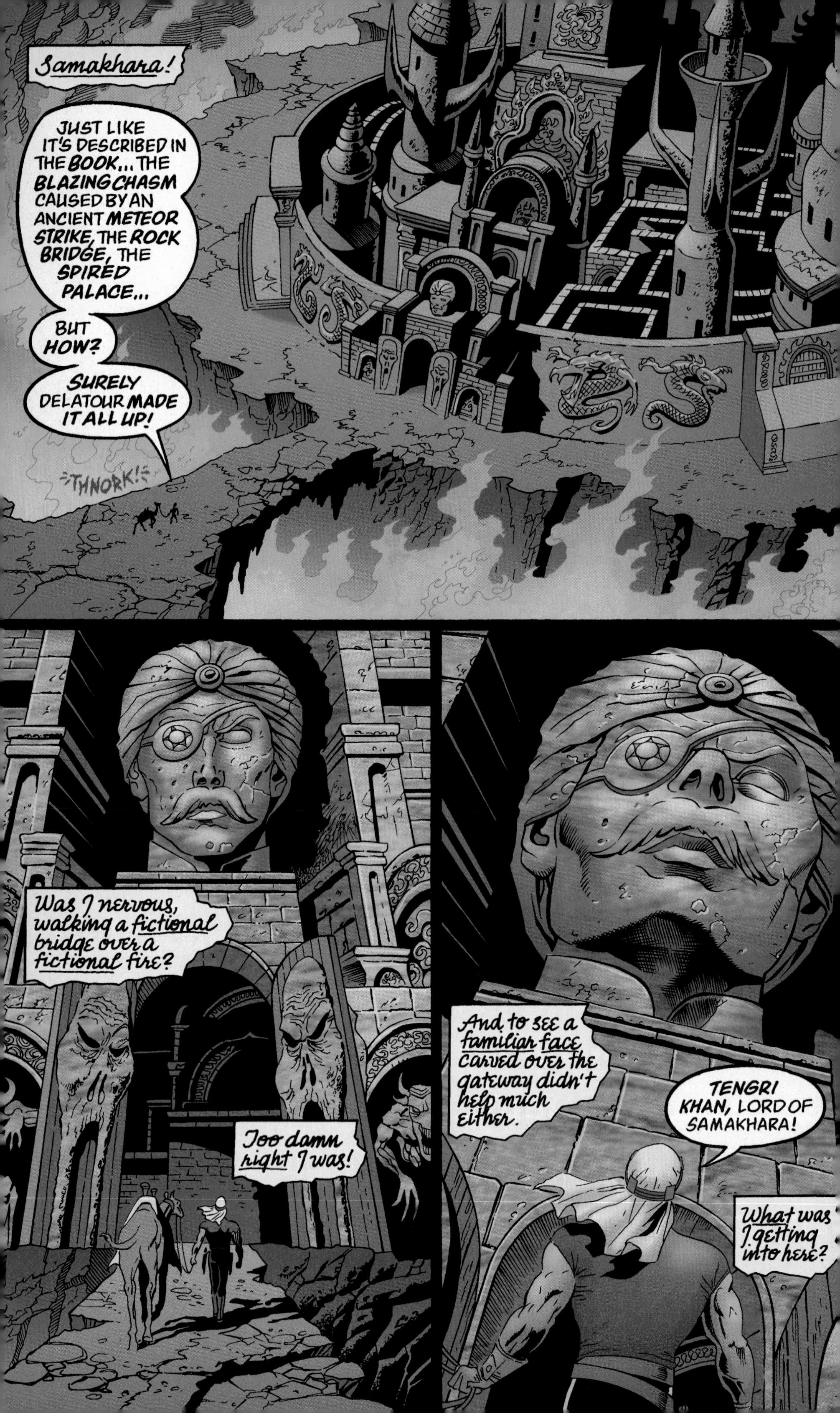

Samakhara!
JUST LIKE IT'S DESCRIBED IN THE BOOK... THE BLAZING CHASM CAUSED BY AN ANCIENT METEOR STRIKE, THE ROCK BRIDGE, THE SPIRED PALACE...
BUT HOW?
SURELY DELATOUR MADE IT ALL UP!
THNORK!
Was I nervous, walking a fictional bridge over a fictional fire?
Too damn right I was!
And to see a familiar face carved over the gateway didn't help much either.
TENGRI KHAN, LORD OF SAMAKHARA!
What was I getting into here?

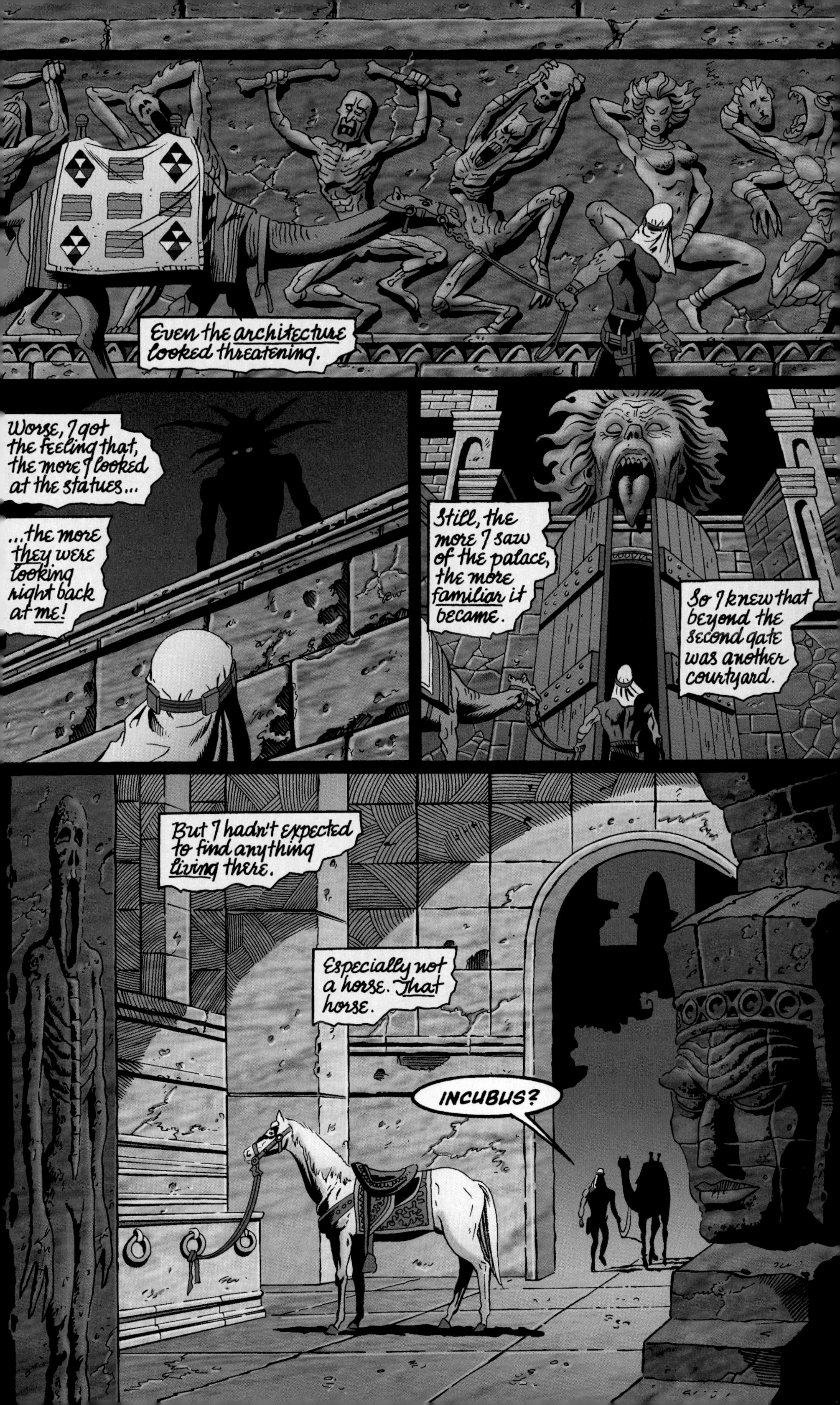
Even the architecture looked threatening.
Worse, I got the feeling that, the more I looked at the statues...
...the more they were looking right back at me!
Still, the more I saw of the palace, the more familiar it became.
So I knew that beyond the second gate was another courtyard.
But I hadn't expected to find anything living there.
Especially not a horse. That horse.
INCUBUS?

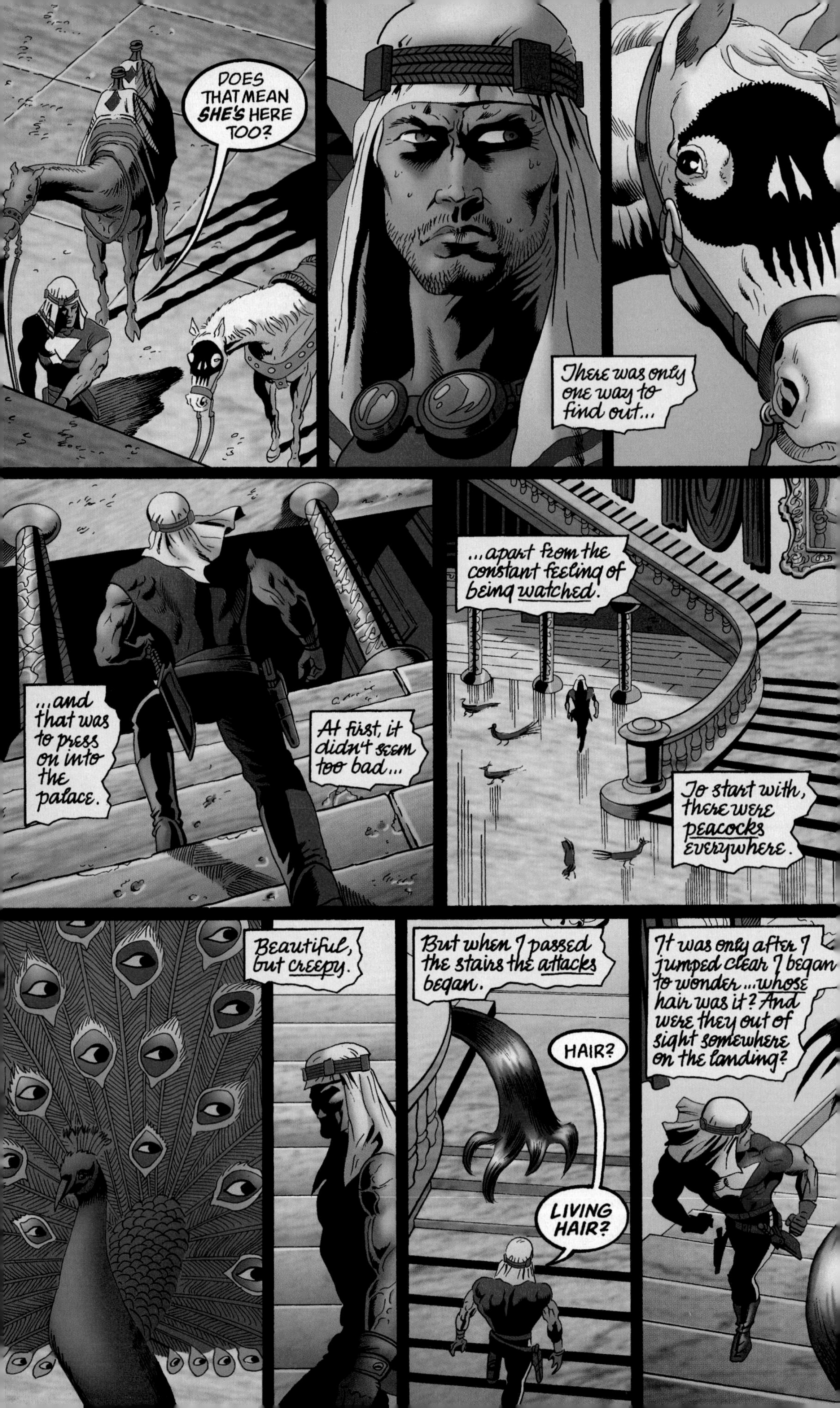
DOES THAT MEAN SHE'S HERE TOO?
There was only one way to find out...
...and that was to press on into the palace.
At first, it didn't seem too bad...
...apart from the constant feeling of being watched.
To start with, there were peacocks everywhere.
Beautiful, but creepy.
But when I passed the stairs the attacks began.
HAIR?
LIVING HAIR?
It was only after I jumped clear I began to wonder... whose hair was it? And were they out of sight somewhere on the landing?

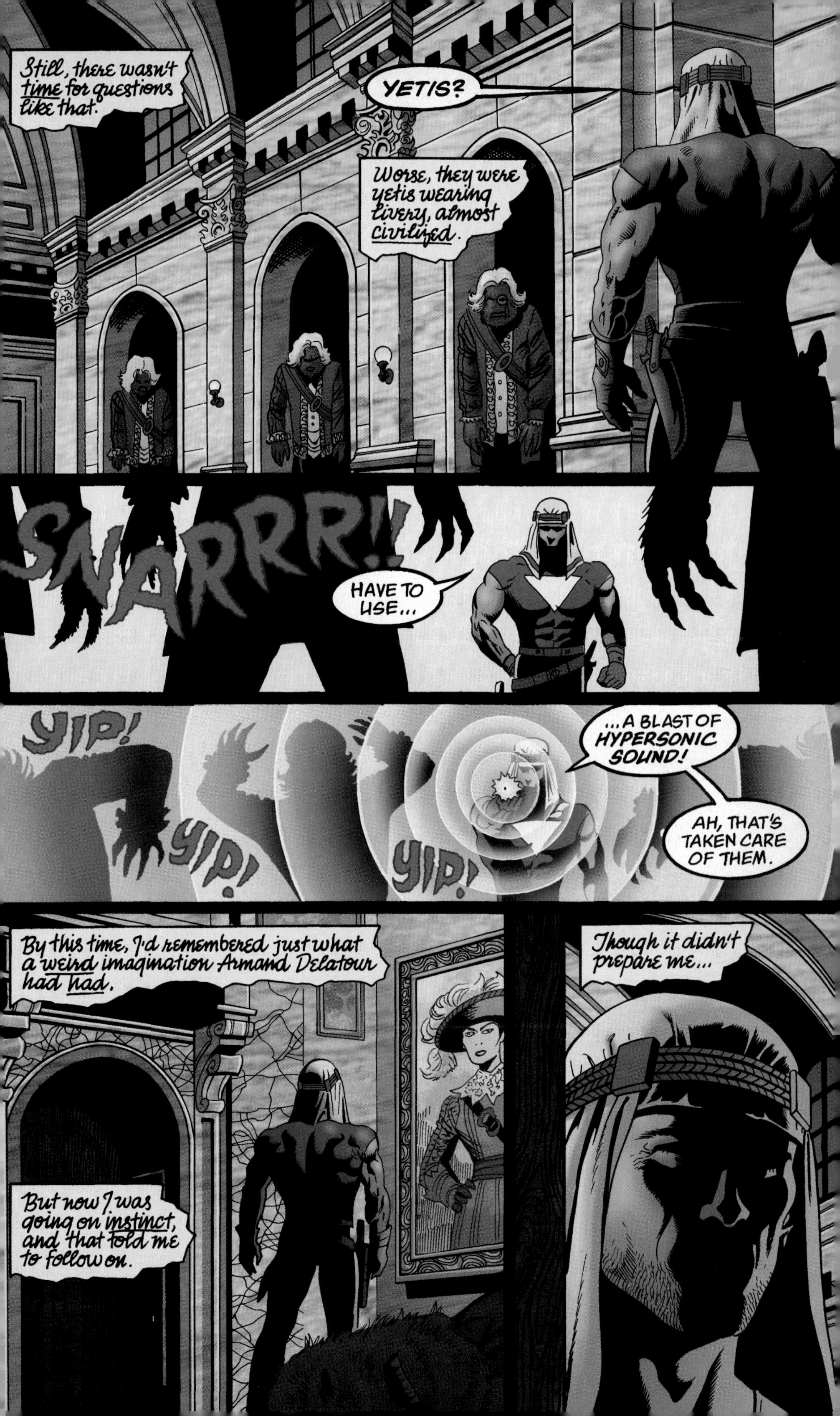
Still, there wasn't time for questions like that.
YETIS?
Worse, they were yetis wearing livery, almost civilized.
SNARRR!!
HAVE TO USE...
YIP!
YIP!
YIP!
...A BLAST OF HYPERSONIC SOUND!
AH, THAT'S TAKEN CARE OF THEM.
By this time, I'd remembered just what a weird imagination Armand Delatour had had.
But now I was going on instinct, and that told me to follow on.
Though it didn't prepare me...

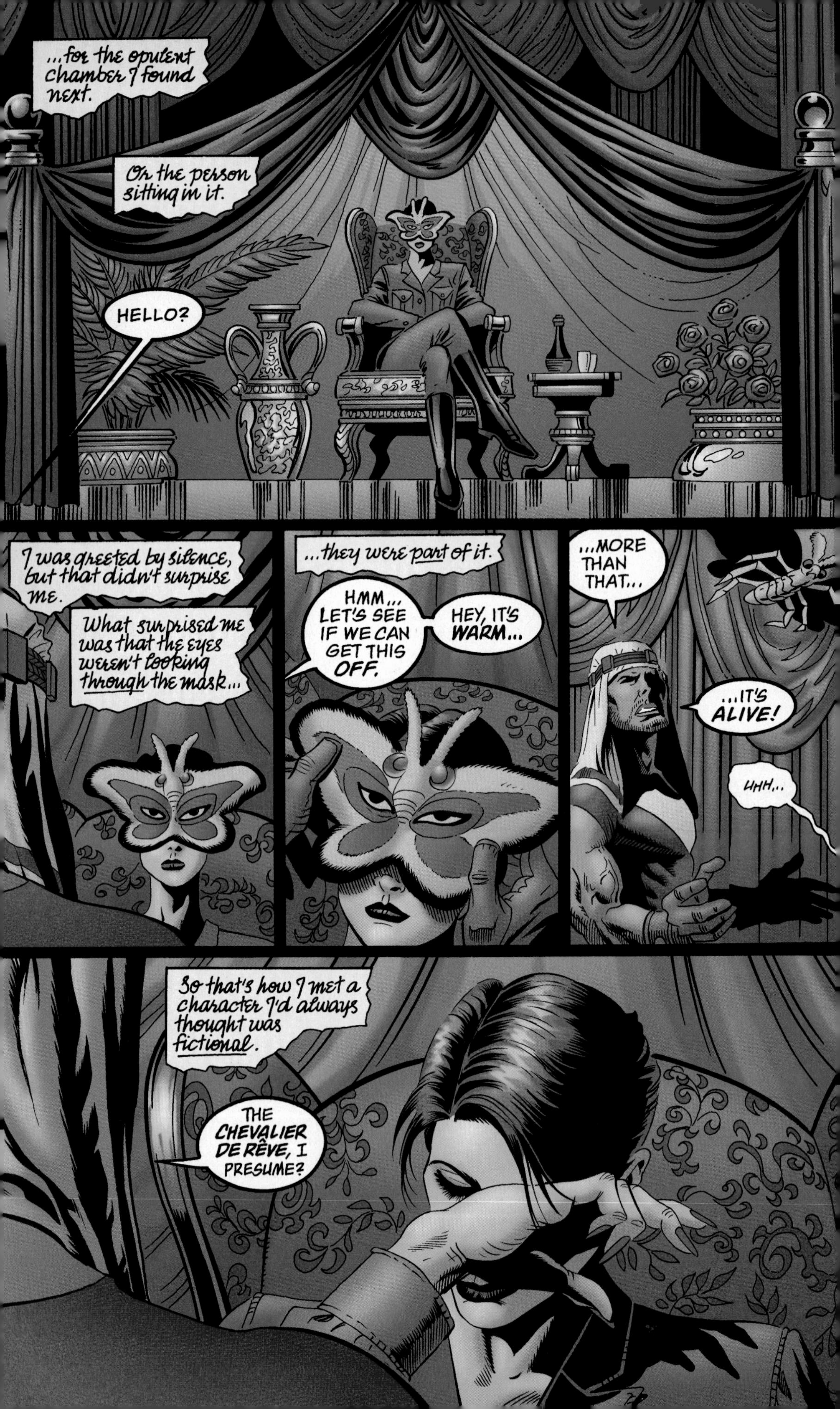
...for the opulent chamber I found next.
Or the person sitting in it.
HELLO?
I was greeted by silence, but that didn't surprise me.
What surprised me was that the eyes weren't looking through the mask...
...they were part of it.
HMM... LET'S SEE IF WE CAN GET THIS OFF.
HEY, IT'S WARM...
...MORE THAN THAT...
...IT'S ALIVE!
UHH...
So that's how I met a character I'd always thought was fictional.
THE CHEVALIER DE RÊVE, I PRESUME?

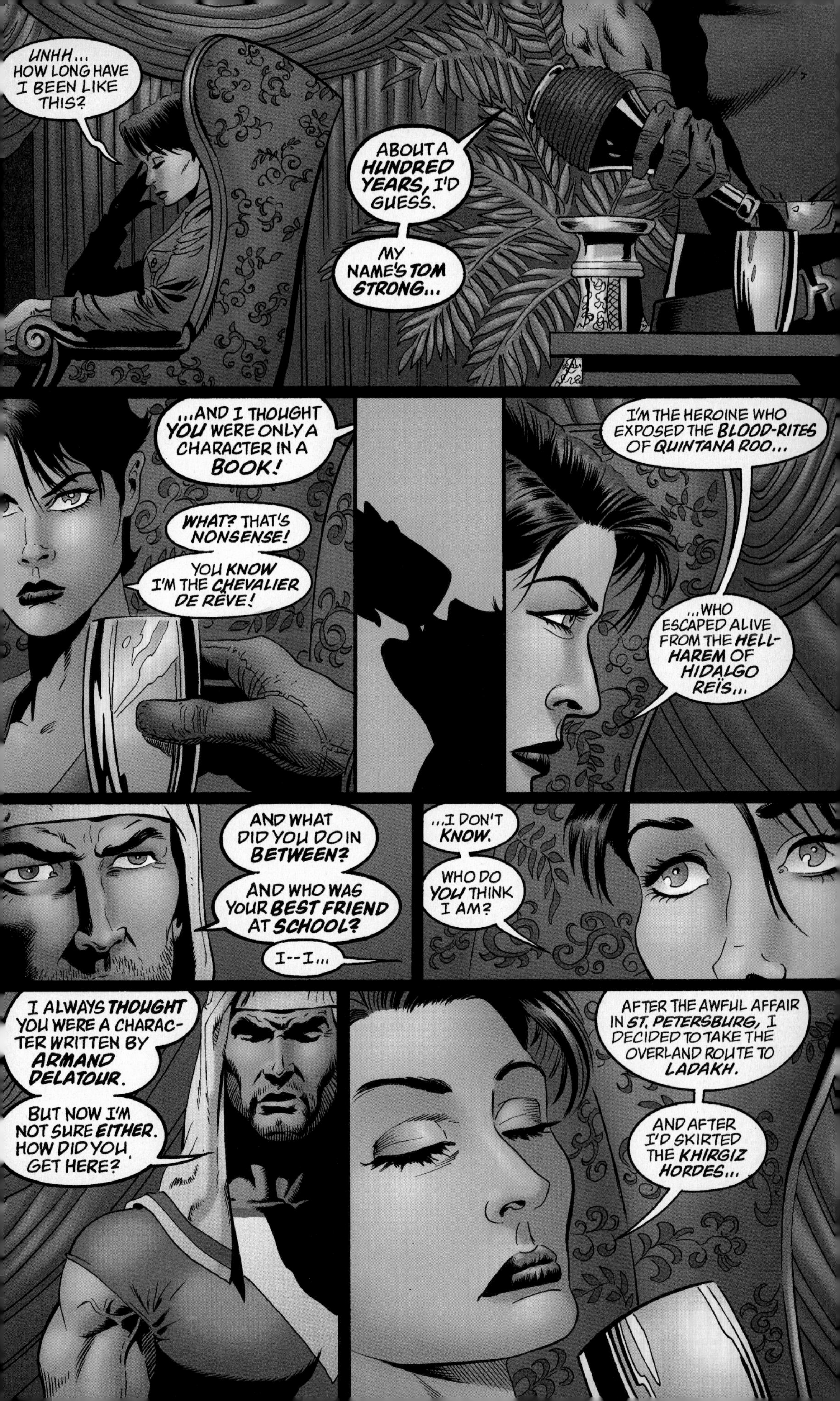
UNHH... HOW LONG HAVE I BEEN LIKE THIS?
ABOUT A HUNDRED YEARS, I'D GUESS.
MY NAME'S TOM STRONG...
...AND I THOUGHT YOU WERE ONLY A CHARACTER IN A BOOK!
WHAT? THAT'S NONSENSE!
YOU KNOW I'M THE CHEVALIER DE RÊVE!
I'M THE HEROINE WHO EXPOSED THE BLOOD-RITES OF QUINTANA ROO...
...WHO ESCAPED ALIVE FROM THE HELL-HAREM OF HIDALGO REÏS...
AND WHAT DID YOU DO IN BETWEEN?
AND WHO WAS YOUR BEST FRIEND AT SCHOOL?
I--I...
...I DON'T KNOW.
WHO DO YOU THINK I AM?
I ALWAYS THOUGHT YOU WERE A CHARACTER WRITTEN BY ARMAND DELATOUR.
BUT NOW I'M NOT SURE EITHER. HOW DID YOU GET HERE?
AFTER THE AWFUL AFFAIR IN ST. PETERSBURG, I DECIDED TO TAKE THE OVERLAND ROUTE TO LADAKH.
AND AFTER I'D SKIRTED THE KHIRGIZ HORDES...

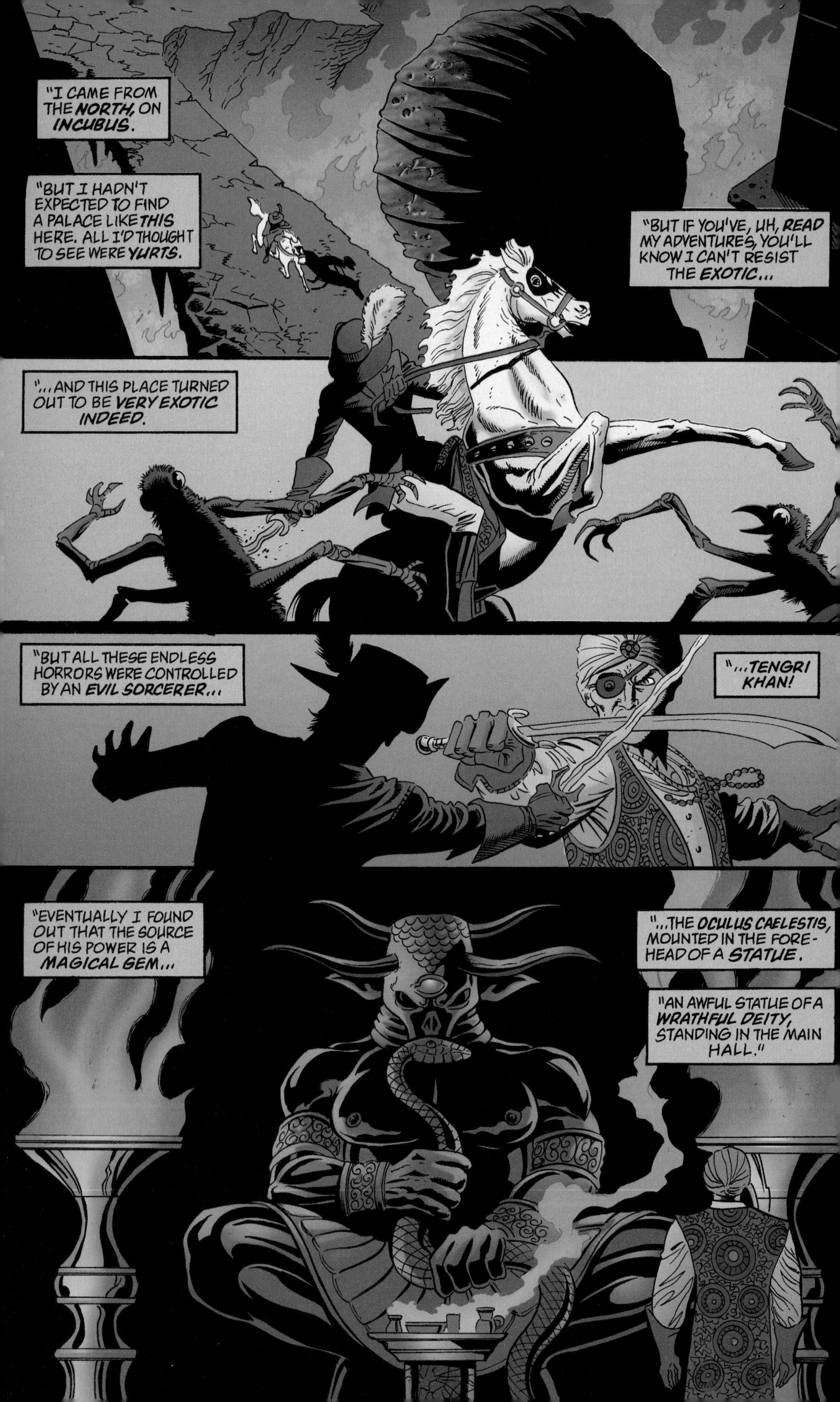
"I CAME FROM THE NORTH, ON INCUBUS.
"BUT I HADN'T EXPECTED TO FIND A PALACE LIKE THIS HERE. ALL I'D THOUGHT TO SEE WERE YURTS.
"BUT IF YOU'VE, UH, READ MY ADVENTURES, YOU'LL KNOW I CAN'T RESIST THE EXOTIC...
"...AND THIS PLACE TURNED OUT TO BE VERY EXOTIC INDEED.
"BUT ALL THESE ENDLESS HORRORS WERE CONTROLLED BY AN EVIL SORCERER...
"...TENGRI KHAN!
"EVENTUALLY I FOUND OUT THAT THE SOURCE OF HIS POWER IS A MAGICAL GEM...
"...THE OCULUS CAELESTIS, MOUNTED IN THE FORE-HEAD OF A STATUE.
"AN AWFUL STATUE OF A WRATHFUL DEITY, STANDING IN THE MAIN HALL."

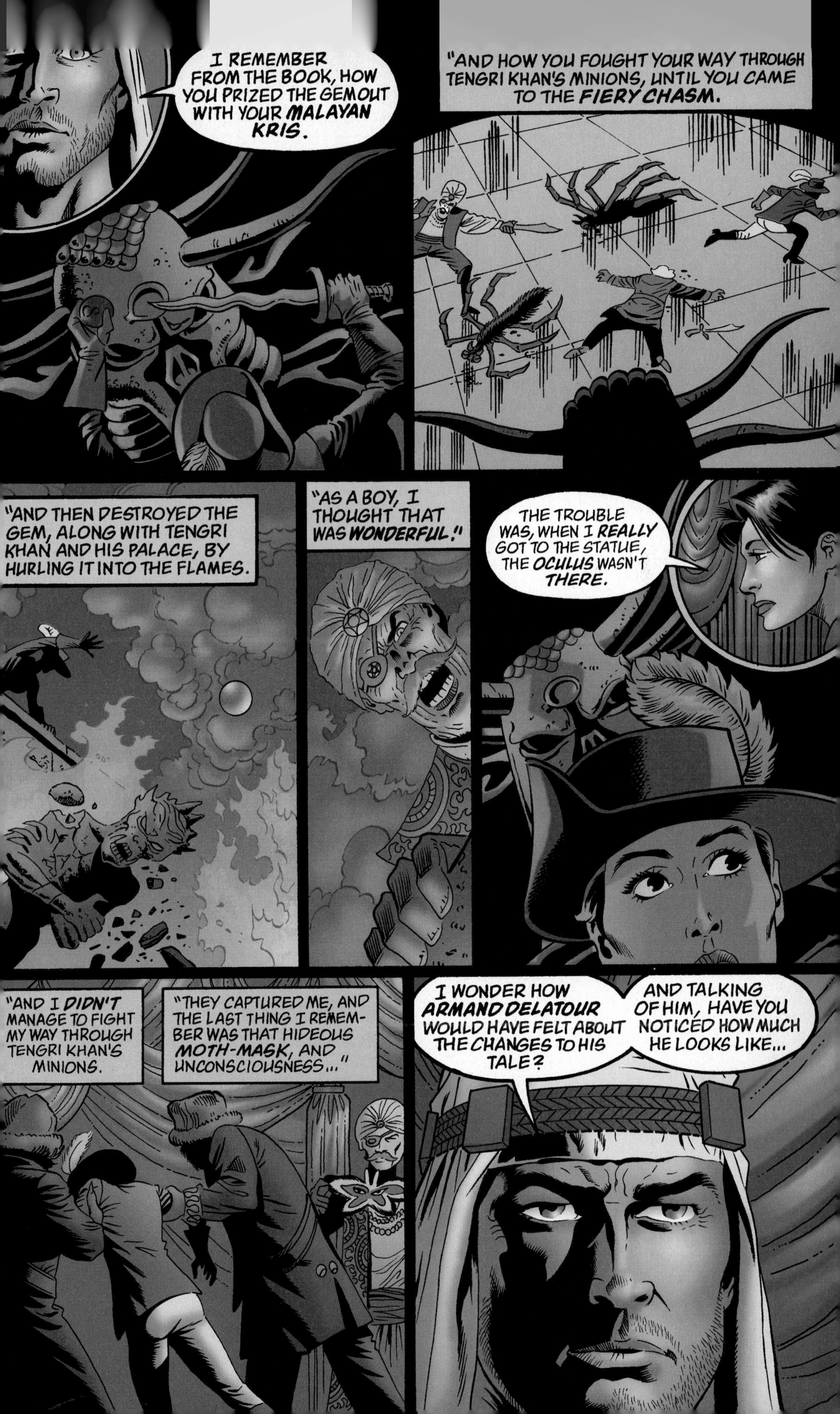
I REMEMBER FROM THE BOOK, HOW YOU PRIZED THE GEM OUT WITH YOUR MALAYAN KRIS.
"AND HOW YOU FOUGHT YOUR WAY THROUGH TENGRI KHAN'S MINIONS, UNTIL YOU CAME TO THE FIERY CHASM.
"AND THEN DESTROYED THE GEM, ALONG WITH TENGRI KHAN AND HIS PALACE, BY HURLING IT INTO THE FLAMES.
"AS A BOY, I THOUGHT THAT WAS WONDERFUL."
THE TROUBLE WAS, WHEN I REALLY GOT TO THE STATUE, THE OCULUS WASN'T THERE.
"AND I DIDN'T MANAGE TO FIGHT MY WAY THROUGH TENGRI KHAN'S MINIONS.
"THEY CAPTURED ME, AND THE LAST THING I REMEMBER WAS THAT HIDEOUS MOTH-MASK, AND UNCONSCIOUSNESS..."
I WONDER HOW ARMAND DELATOUR WOULD HAVE FELT ABOUT THE CHANGES TO HIS TALE?
AND TALKING OF HIM, HAVE YOU NOTICED HOW MUCH HE LOOKS LIKE...

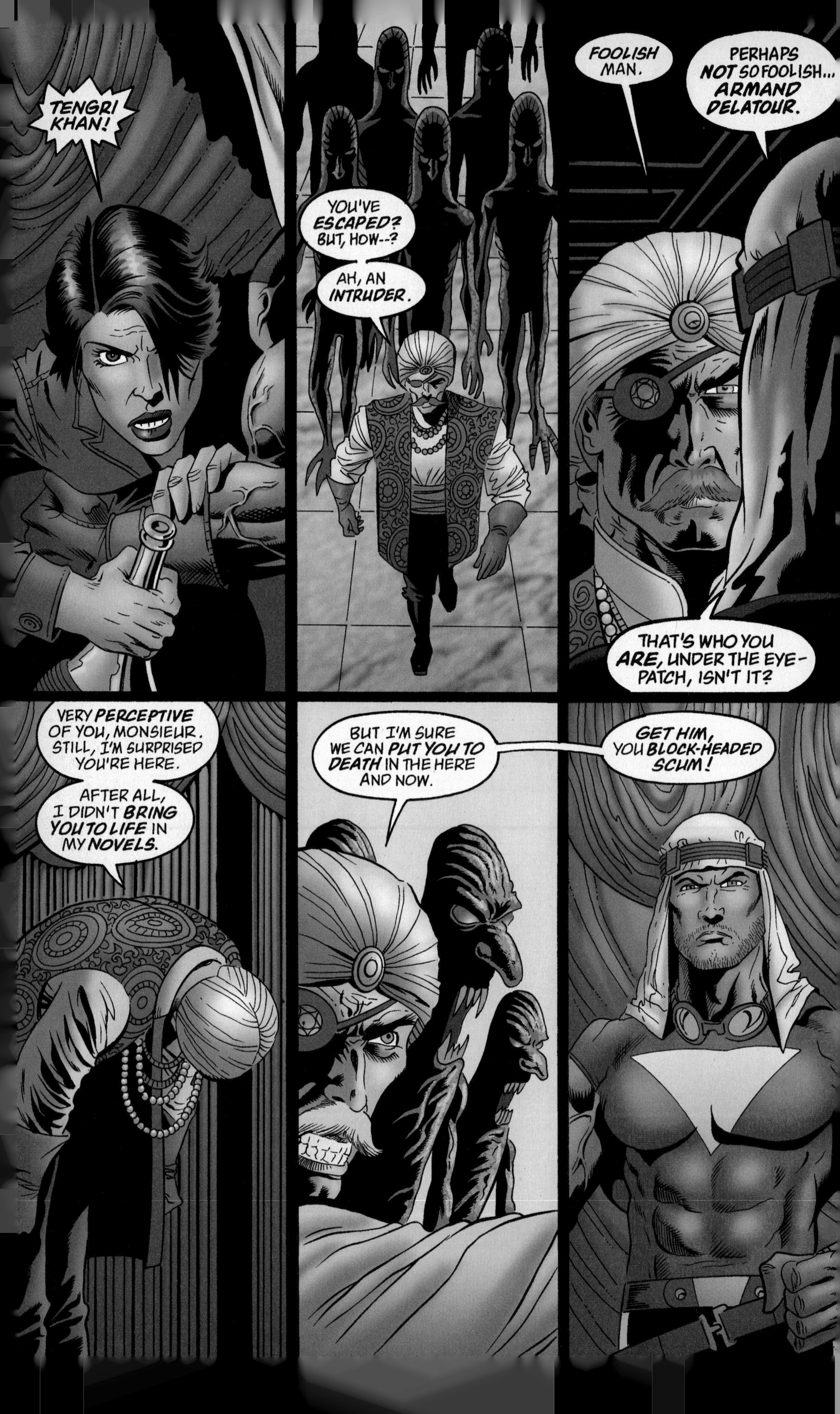
TENGRI KHAN!
YOU'VE ESCAPED? BUT, HOW--?
AH, AN INTRUDER.
FOOLISH MAN.
PERHAPS NOT SO FOOLISH... ARMAND DELATOUR.
THAT'S WHO YOU ARE, UNDER THE EYE-PATCH, ISN'T IT?
VERY PERCEPTIVE OF YOU, MONSIEUR. STILL, I'M SURPRISED YOU'RE HERE.
AFTER ALL, I DIDN'T BRING YOU TO LIFE IN MY NOVELS.
BUT I'M SURE WE CAN PUT YOU TO DEATH IN THE HERE AND NOW.
GET HIM, YOU BLOCK-HEADED SCUM!

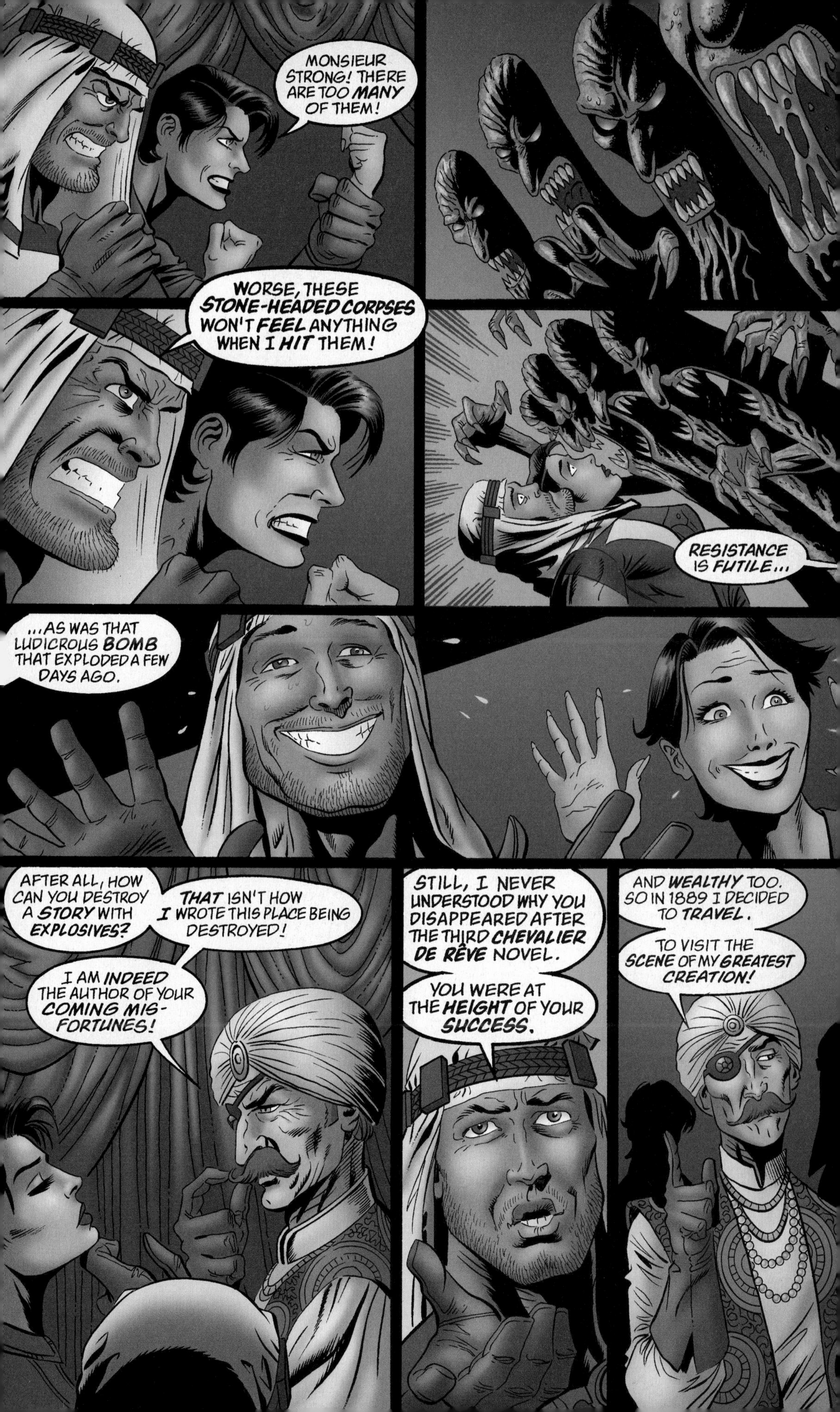
MONSIEUR STRONG! THERE ARE TOO MANY OF THEM!
WORSE, THESE STONE-HEADED CORPSES WON'T FEEL ANYTHING WHEN I HIT THEM!
RESISTANCE IS FUTILE...
...AS WAS THAT LUDICROUS BOMB THAT EXPLODED A FEW DAYS AGO.
AFTER ALL, HOW CAN YOU DESTROY A STORY WITH EXPLOSIVES?
THAT ISN'T HOW I WROTE THIS PLACE BEING DESTROYED!
I AM INDEED THE AUTHOR OF YOUR COMING MIS-FORTUNES!
STILL, I NEVER UNDERSTOOD WHY YOU DISAPPEARED AFTER THE THIRD CHEVALIER DE RÊVE NOVEL.
YOU WERE AT THE HEIGHT OF YOUR SUCCESS.
AND WEALTHY TOO. SO IN 1889 I DECIDED TO TRAVEL.
TO VISIT THE SCENE OF MY GREATEST CREATION!

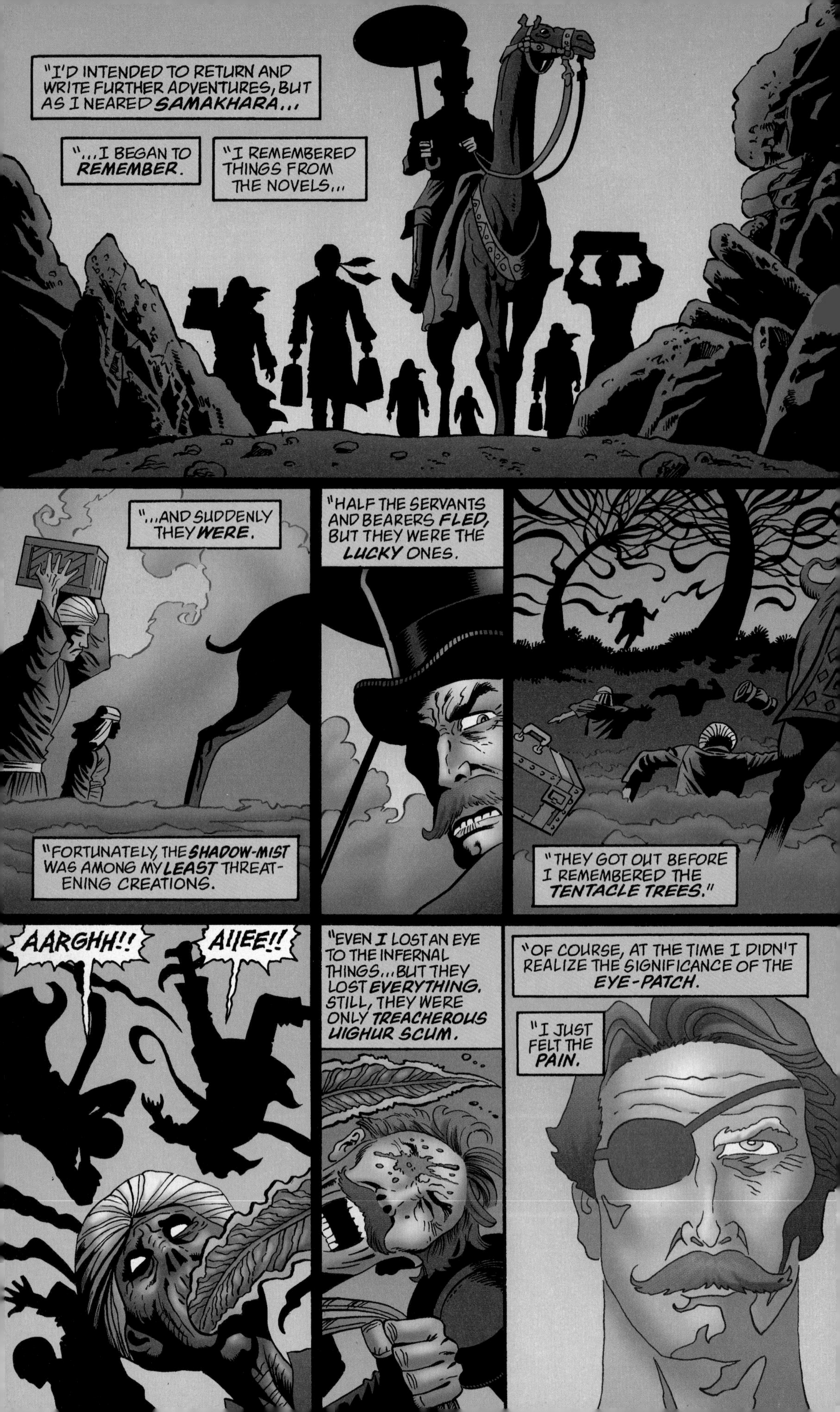

"I'D INTENDED TO RETURN AND WRITE FURTHER ADVENTURES, BUT AS I NEARED SAMAKHARA...
"...I BEGAN TO REMEMBER.
"I REMEMBERED THINGS FROM THE NOVELS...
"...AND SUDDENLY THEY WERE.
"FORTUNATELY, THE SHADOW-MIST WAS AMONG MY LEAST THREAT-ENING CREATIONS.
"HALF THE SERVANTS AND BEARERS FLED, BUT THEY WERE THE LUCKY ONES.
"THEY GOT OUT BEFORE I REMEMBERED THE TENTACLE TREES."
AARGHH!!
AIIEE!!
"EVEN I LOST AN EYE TO THE INFERNAL THINGS... BUT THEY LOST EVERYTHING. STILL, THEY WERE ONLY TREACHEROUS UIGHUR SCUM.
"OF COURSE, AT THE TIME I DIDN'T REALIZE THE SIGNIFICANCE OF THE EYE-PATCH.
"I JUST FELT THE PAIN.

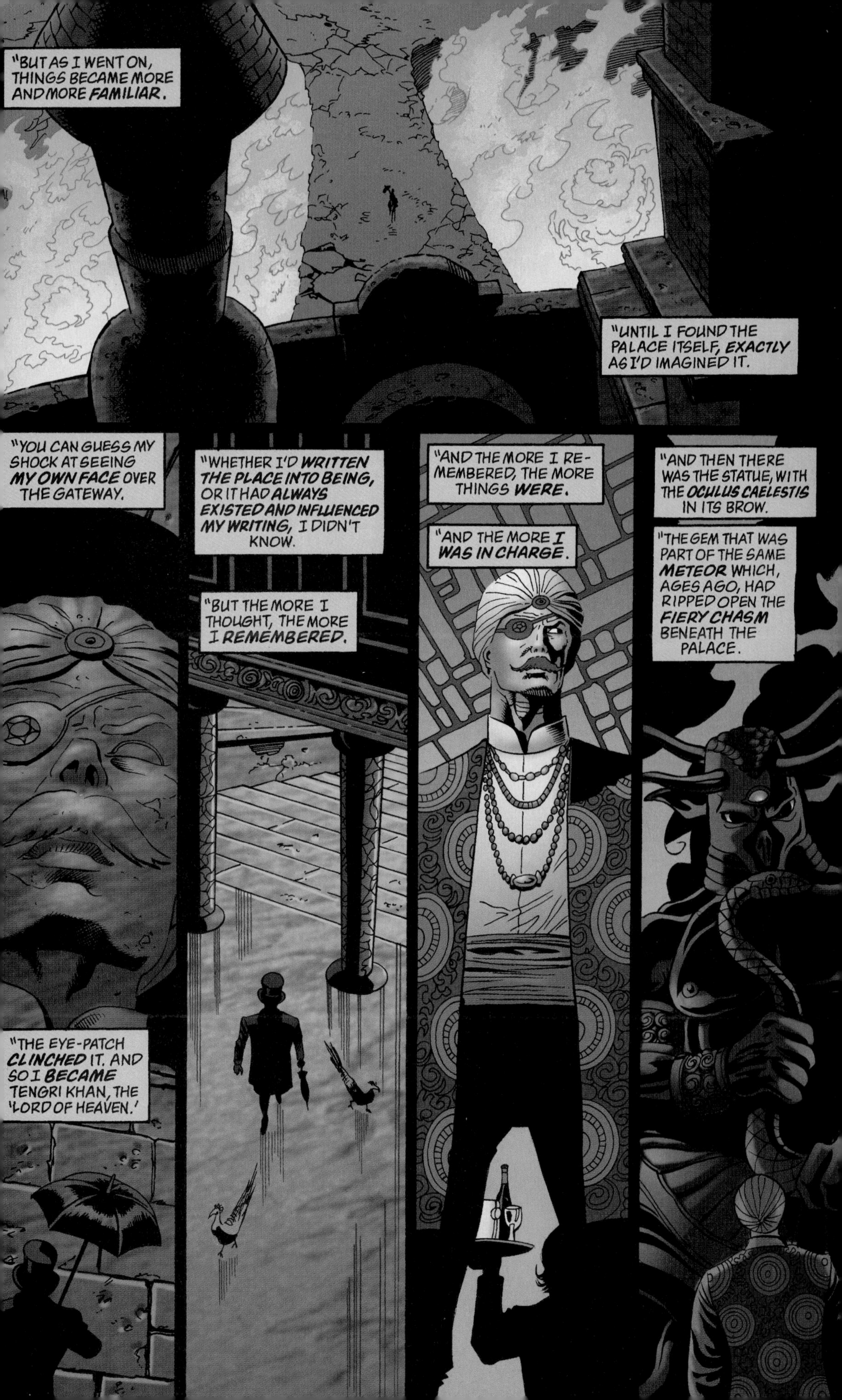
"BUT AS I WENT ON, THINGS BECAME MORE AND MORE FAMILIAR.
"UNTIL I FOUND THE PALACE ITSELF, EXACTLY AS I'D IMAGINED IT.
"YOU CAN GUESS MY SHOCK AT SEEING MY OWN FACE OVER THE GATEWAY.
"THE EYE-PATCH CLINCHED IT. AND SO I BECAME TENGRI KHAN, THE 'LORD OF HEAVEN.'
"WHETHER I'D WRITTEN THE PLACE INTO BEING, OR IT HAD ALWAYS EXISTED AND INFLUENCED MY WRITING, I DIDN'T KNOW.
"BUT THE MORE I THOUGHT, THE MORE I REMEMBERED.
"AND THE MORE I REMEMBERED, THE MORE THINGS WERE.
"AND THE MORE I WAS IN CHARGE.
"AND THEN THERE WAS THE STATUE, WITH THE OCULUS CAELESTIS IN ITS BROW.
"THE GEM THAT WAS PART OF THE SAME METEOR WHICH, AGES AGO, HAD RIPPED OPEN THE FIERY CHASM BENEATH THE PALACE.

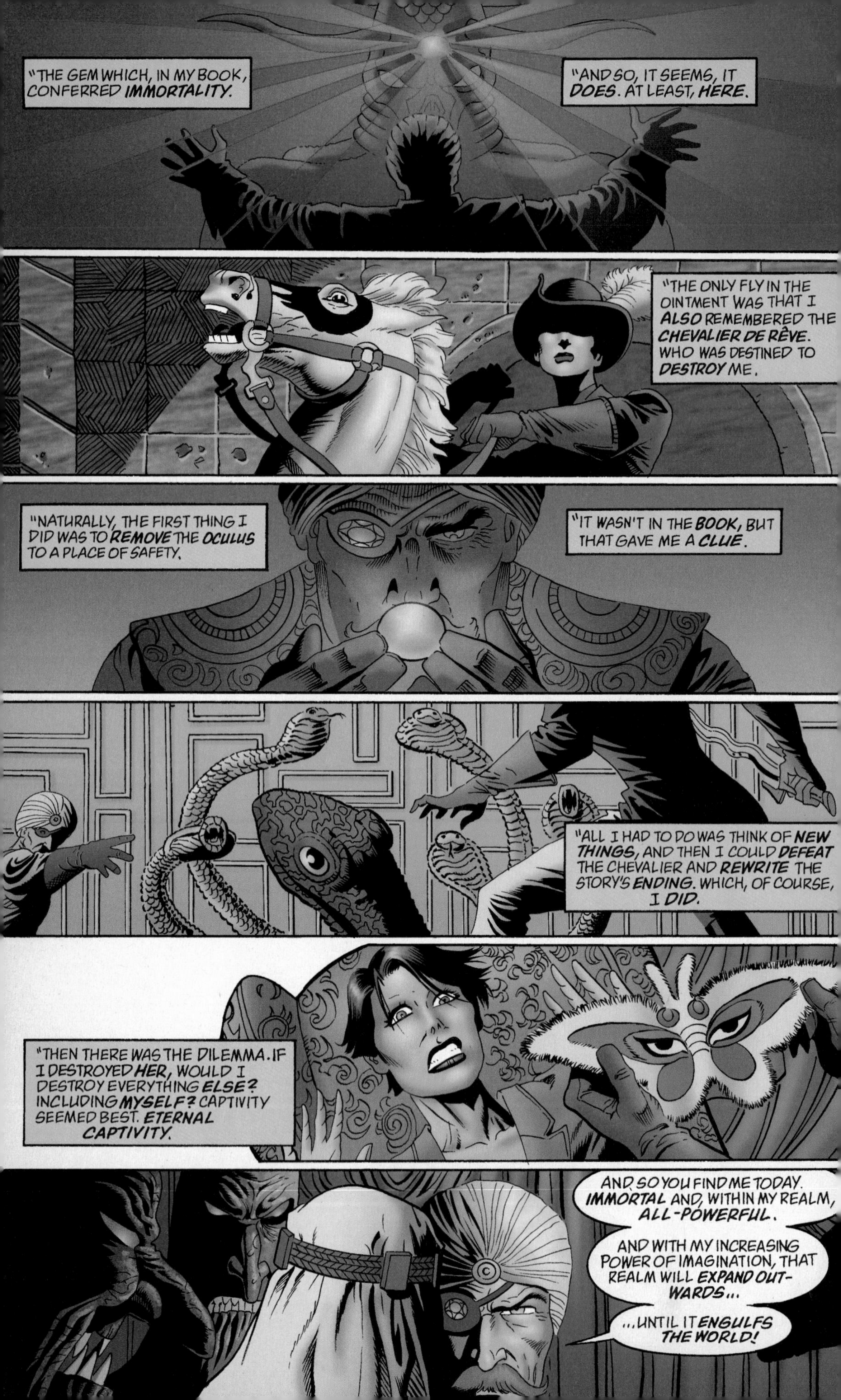
"THE GEM WHICH, IN MY BOOK, CONFERRED IMMORTALITY.
"AND SO, IT SEEMS, IT DOES. AT LEAST, HERE.
"THE ONLY FLY IN THE OINTMENT WAS THAT I ALSO REMEMBERED THE CHEVALIER DE RÊVE. WHO WAS DESTINED TO DESTROY ME.
"NATURALLY, THE FIRST THING I DID WAS TO REMOVE THE OCULUS TO A PLACE OF SAFETY.
"IT WASN'T IN THE BOOK, BUT THAT GAVE ME A CLUE.
"ALL I HAD TO DO WAS THINK OF NEW THINGS, AND THEN I COULD DEFEAT THE CHEVALIER AND REWRITE THE STORY'S ENDING. WHICH, OF COURSE, I DID.
"THEN THERE WAS THE DILEMMA. IF I DESTROYED HER, WOULD I DESTROY EVERYTHING ELSE? INCLUDING MYSELF? CAPTIVITY SEEMED BEST. ETERNAL CAPTIVITY.
AND SO YOU FIND ME TODAY. IMMORTAL AND, WITHIN MY REALM, ALL-POWERFUL.
AND WITH MY INCREASING POWER OF IMAGINATION, THAT REALM WILL EXPAND OUT-WARDS...
...UNTIL IT ENGULFS THE WORLD!

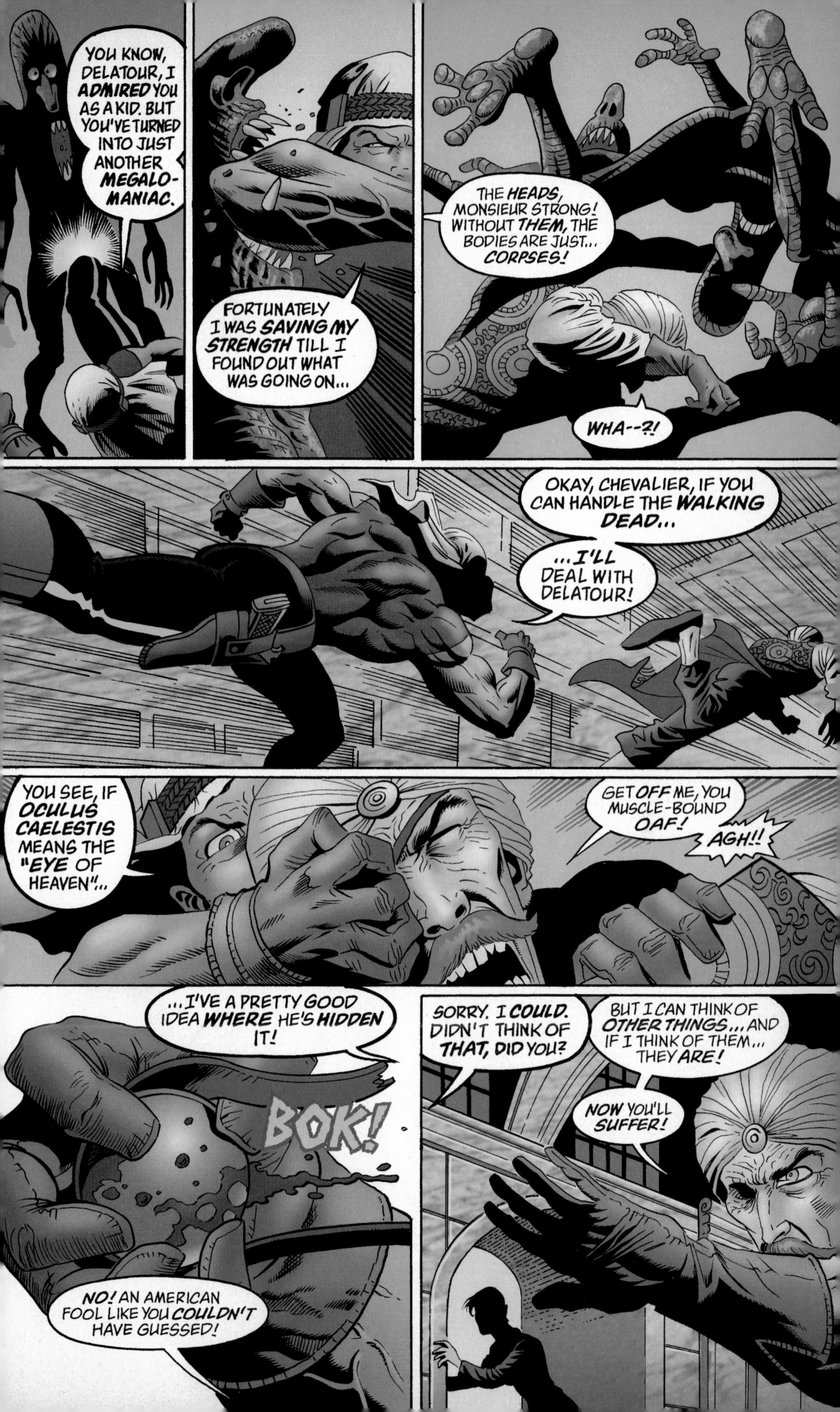

YOU KNOW, DELATOUR, I ADMIRED YOU AS A KID. BUT YOU'VE TURNED INTO JUST ANOTHER MEGALO-MANIAC.
FORTUNATELY I WAS SAVING MY STRENGTH TILL I FOUND OUT WHAT WAS GOING ON...
THE HEADS, MONSIEUR STRONG! WITHOUT THEM, THE BODIES ARE JUST... CORPSES!
WHA--?!
OKAY, CHEVALIER, IF YOU CAN HANDLE THE WALKING DEAD...
...I'LL DEAL WITH DELATOUR!
YOU SEE, IF OCULUS CAELESTIS MEANS THE "EYE OF HEAVEN"...
GET OFF ME, YOU MUSCLE-BOUND OAF!
AGH!!
...I'VE A PRETTY GOOD IDEA WHERE HE'S HIDDEN IT!
BOK!
NO! AN AMERICAN FOOL LIKE YOU COULDN'T HAVE GUESSED!
SORRY. I COULD. DIDN'T THINK OF THAT, DID YOU?
BUT I CAN THINK OF OTHER THINGS... AND IF I THINK OF THEM... THEY ARE!
NOW YOU'LL SUFFER!

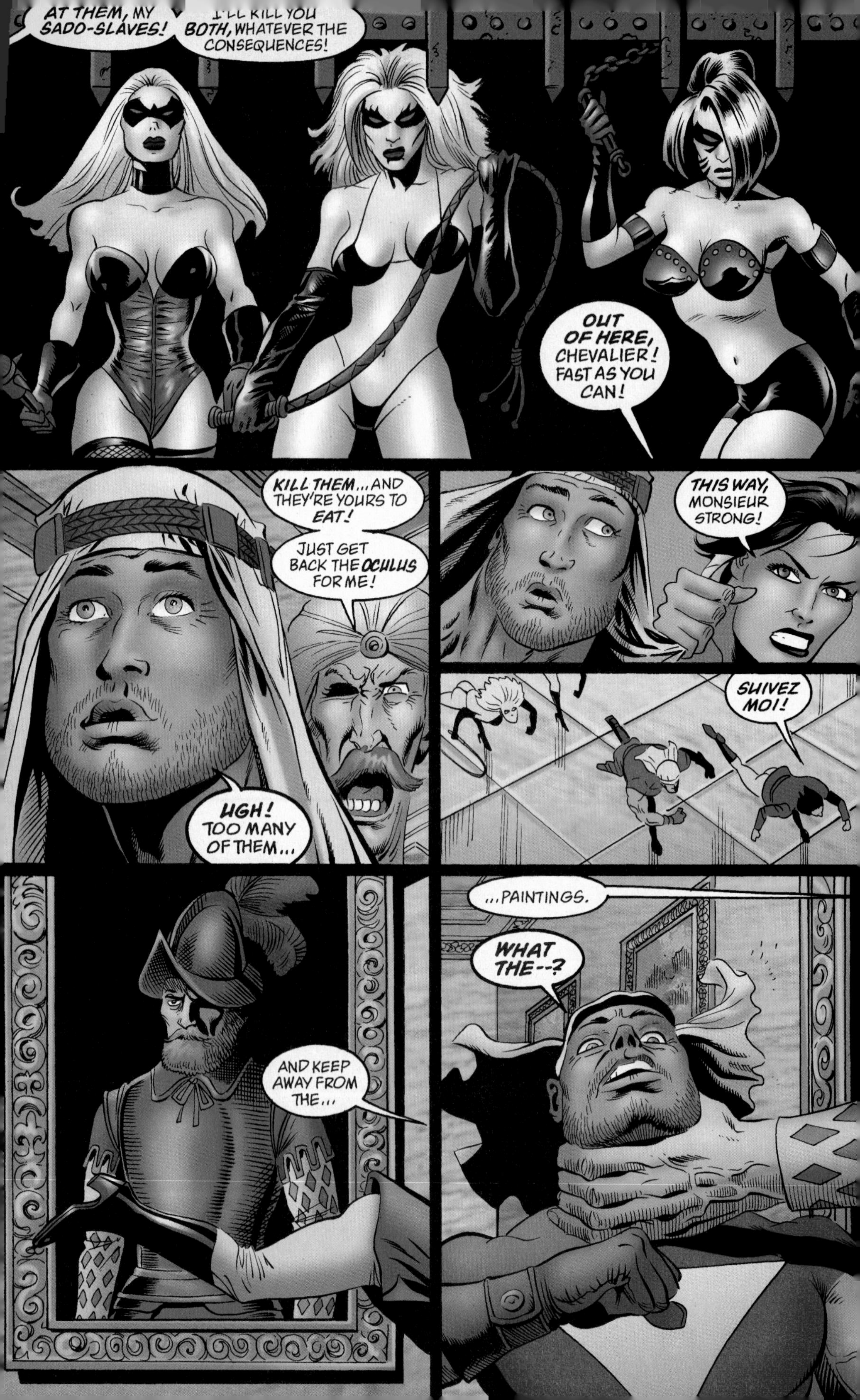
AT THEM, MY SADO-SLAVES!
I'LL KILL YOU BOTH, WHATEVER THE CONSEQUENCES!
OUT OF HERE, CHEVALIER! FAST AS YOU CAN!
KILL THEM... AND THEY'RE YOURS TO EAT!
JUST GET BACK THE OCULUS FOR ME!
UGH! TOO MANY OF THEM...
THIS WAY, MONSIEUR STRONG!
SUIVEZ MOI!
AND KEEP AWAY FROM THE...
...PAINTINGS.
WHAT THE--?

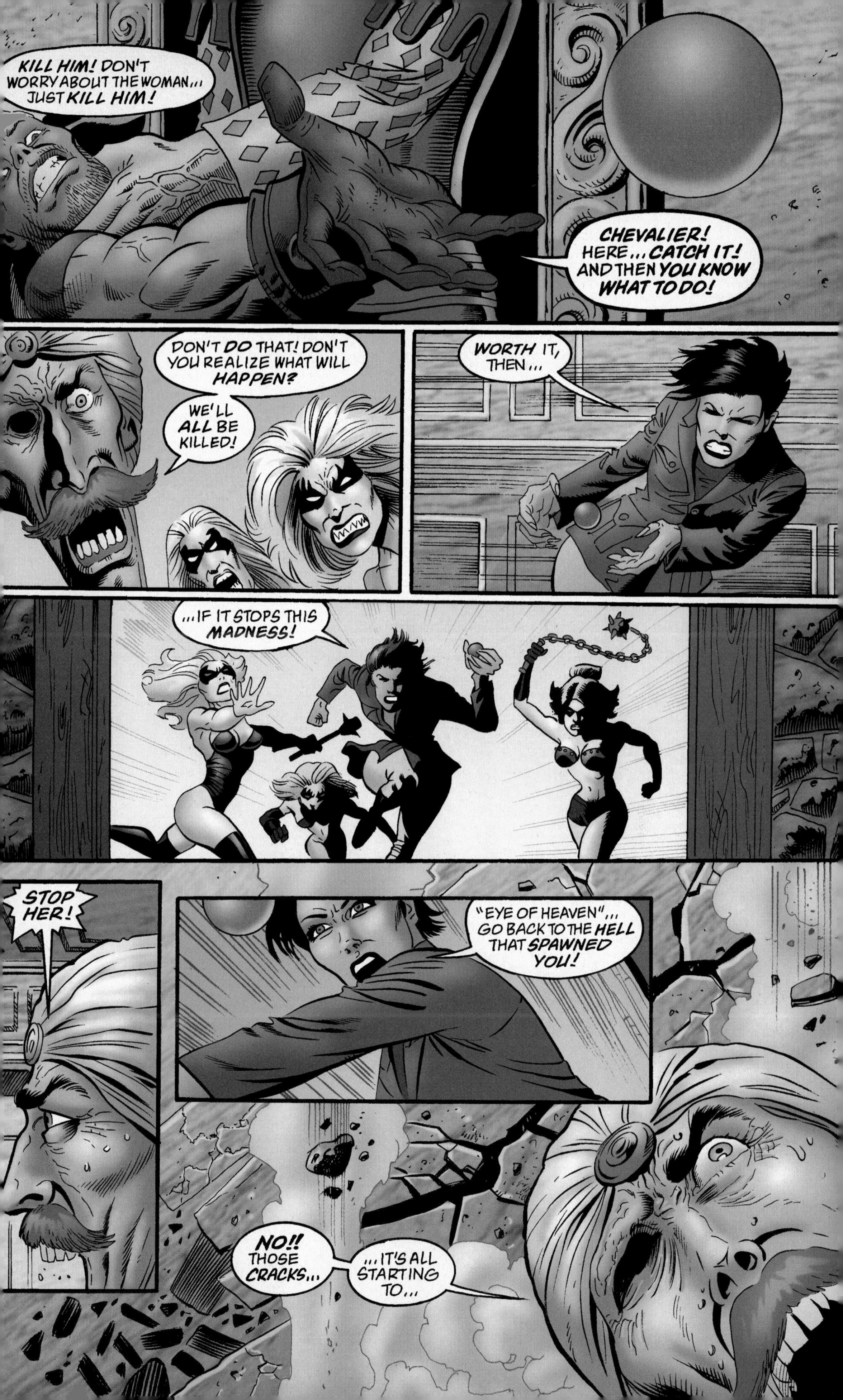
KILL HIM! DON'T WORRY ABOUT THE WOMAN... JUST KILL HIM!
CHEVALIER! HERE... CATCH IT! AND THEN YOU KNOW WHAT TO DO!
DON'T DO THAT! DON'T YOU REALIZE WHAT WILL HAPPEN?
WE'LL ALL BE KILLED!
WORTH IT, THEN...
...IF IT STOPS THIS MADNESS!
STOP HER!
"EYE OF HEAVEN"... GO BACK TO THE HELL THAT SPAWNED YOU!
NO!! THOSE CRACKS...
...IT'S ALL STARTING TO...

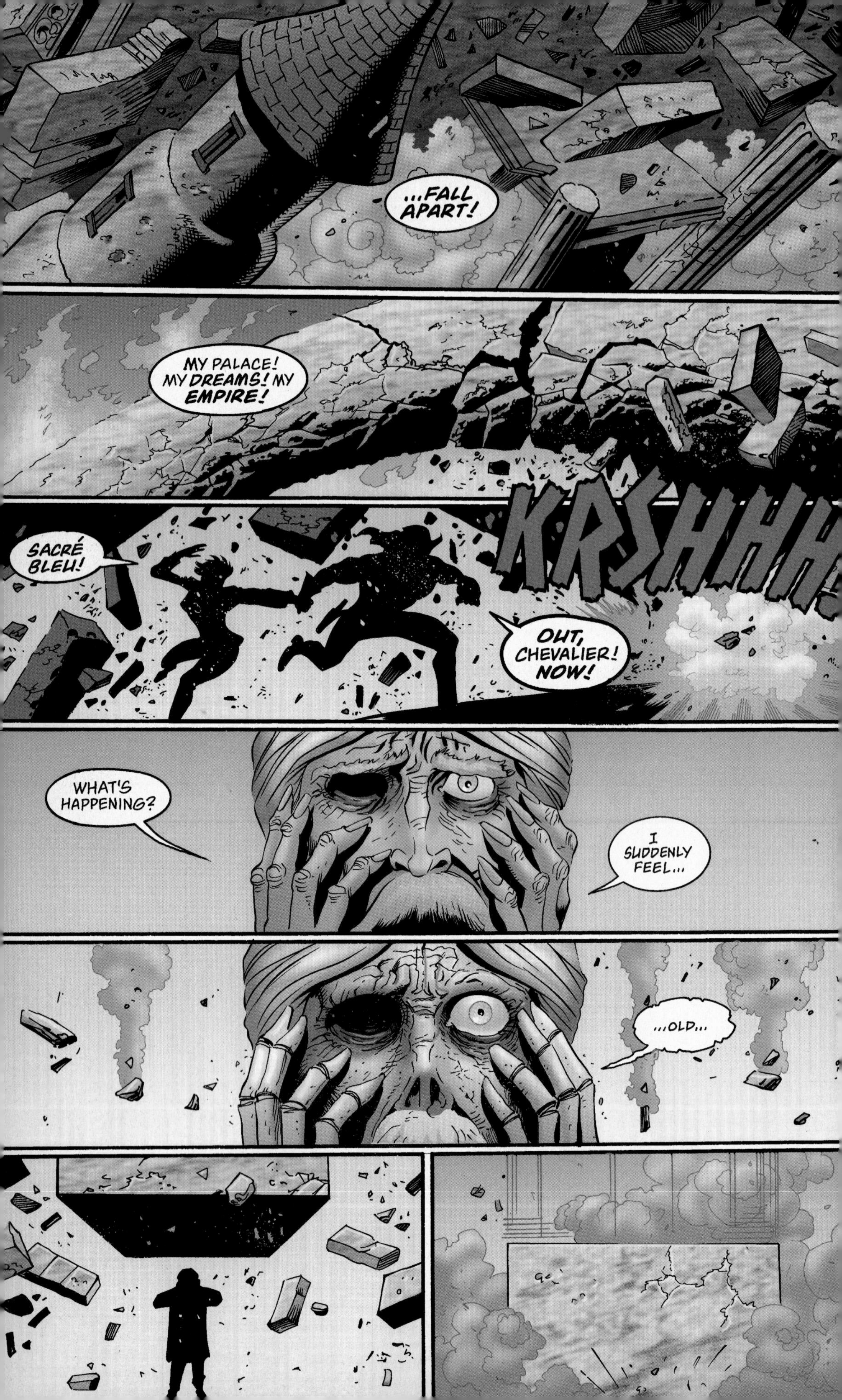
...FALL APART!
MY PALACE! MY DREAMS! MY EMPIRE!
KRSHHH
SACRÉ BLEU!
OUT, CHEVALIER! NOW!
WHAT'S HAPPENING?
I SUDDENLY FEEL...
...OLD...

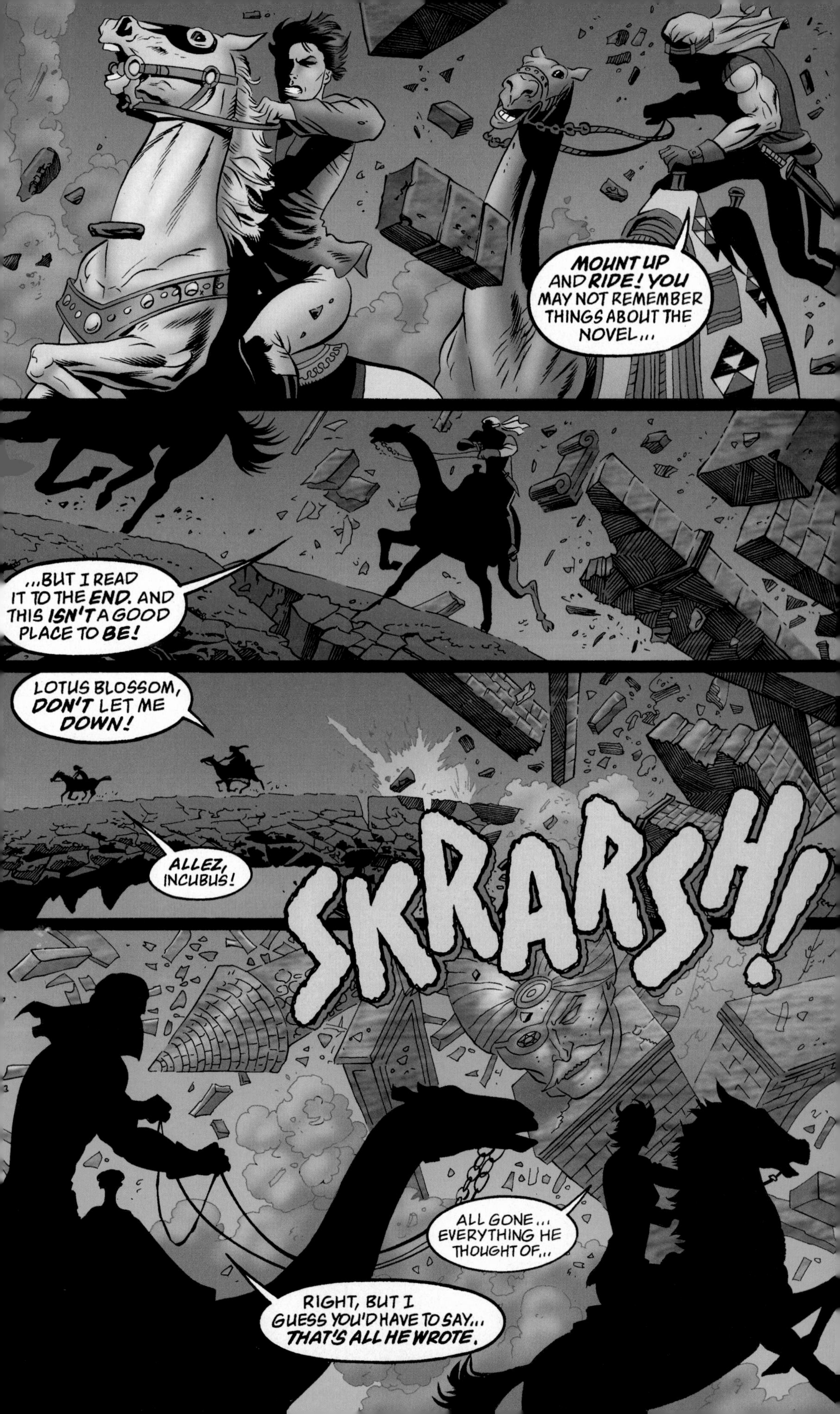
MOUNT UP AND RIDE! YOU MAY NOT REMEMBER THINGS ABOUT THE NOVEL...
...BUT I READ IT TO THE END. AND THIS ISN'T A GOOD PLACE TO BE!
LOTUS BLOSSOM, DON'T LET ME DOWN!
ALLEZ, INCUBUS!
SKRARSH!
ALL GONE... EVERYTHING HE THOUGHT OF...
RIGHT, BUT I GUESS YOU'D HAVE TO SAY... THAT'S ALL HE WROTE.

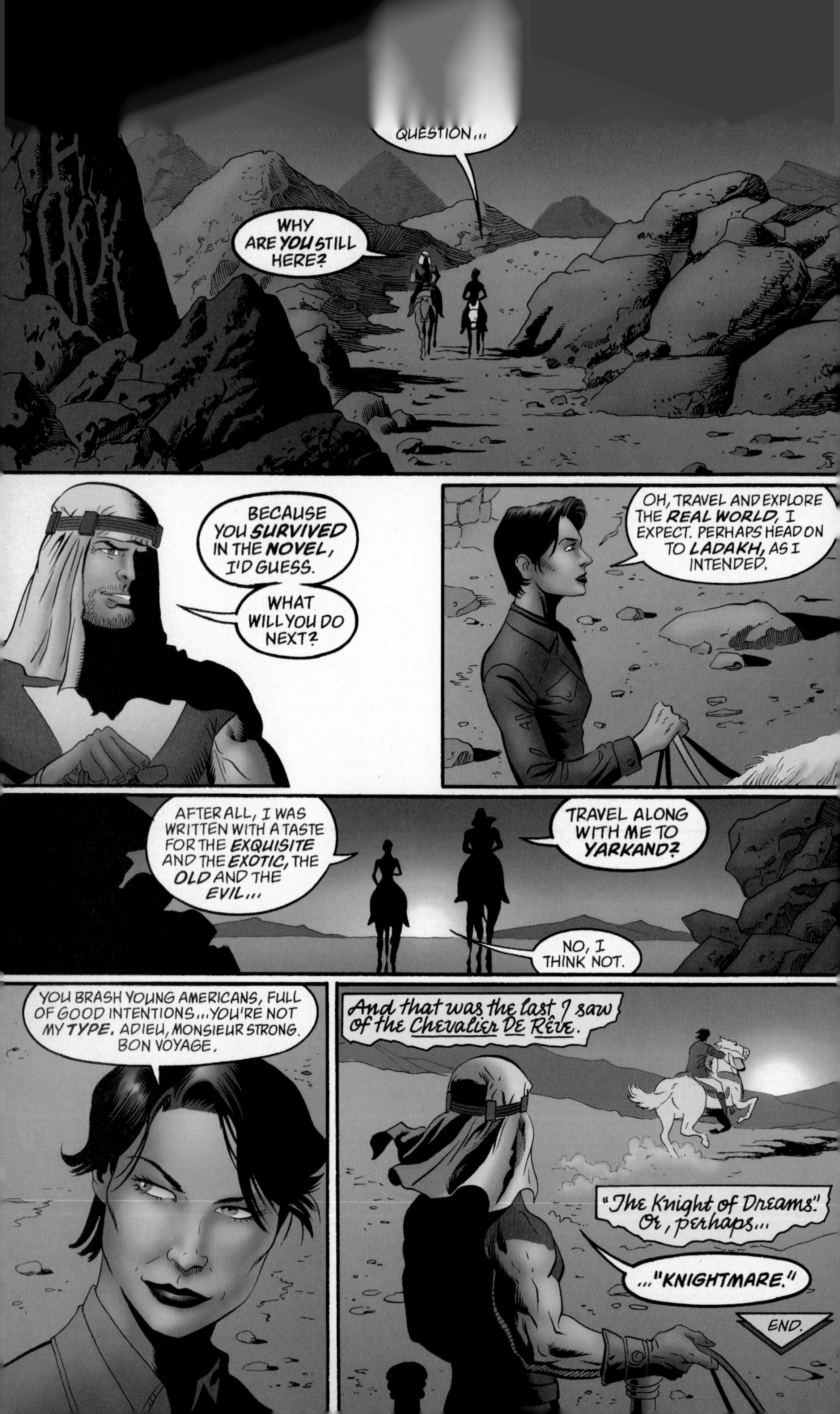
QUESTION...
WHY ARE YOU STILL HERE?
BECAUSE YOU SURVIVED IN THE NOVEL, I'D GUESS.
WHAT WILL YOU DO NEXT?
OH, TRAVEL AND EXPLORE THE REAL WORLD, I EXPECT. PERHAPS HEAD ON TO LADAKH, AS I INTENDED.
AFTER ALL, I WAS WRITTEN WITH A TASTE FOR THE EXQUISITE AND THE EXOTIC, THE OLD AND THE EVIL...
TRAVEL ALONG WITH ME TO YARKAND?
NO, I THINK NOT.
YOU BRASH YOUNG AMERICANS, FULL OF GOOD INTENTIONS...YOU'RE NOT MY TYPE. ADIEU, MONSIEUR STRONG. BON VOYAGE.
And that was the last I saw of the Chevalier De Rêve.
"The Knight of Dreams." Or, perhaps...
..."KNIGHTMARE."
END.

# CHAPTER FIVE

In which a touch of frost returns to Millennium,
forcing Tom and his friends to tackle an icy villain
and bring closure to an old, cold romance.

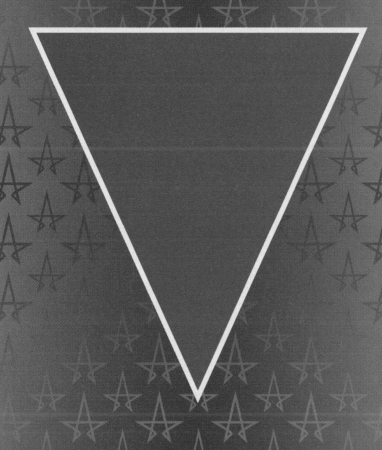

Cover art:
Chris Sprouse & Karl Story
Cover colors:
Randy Mayor

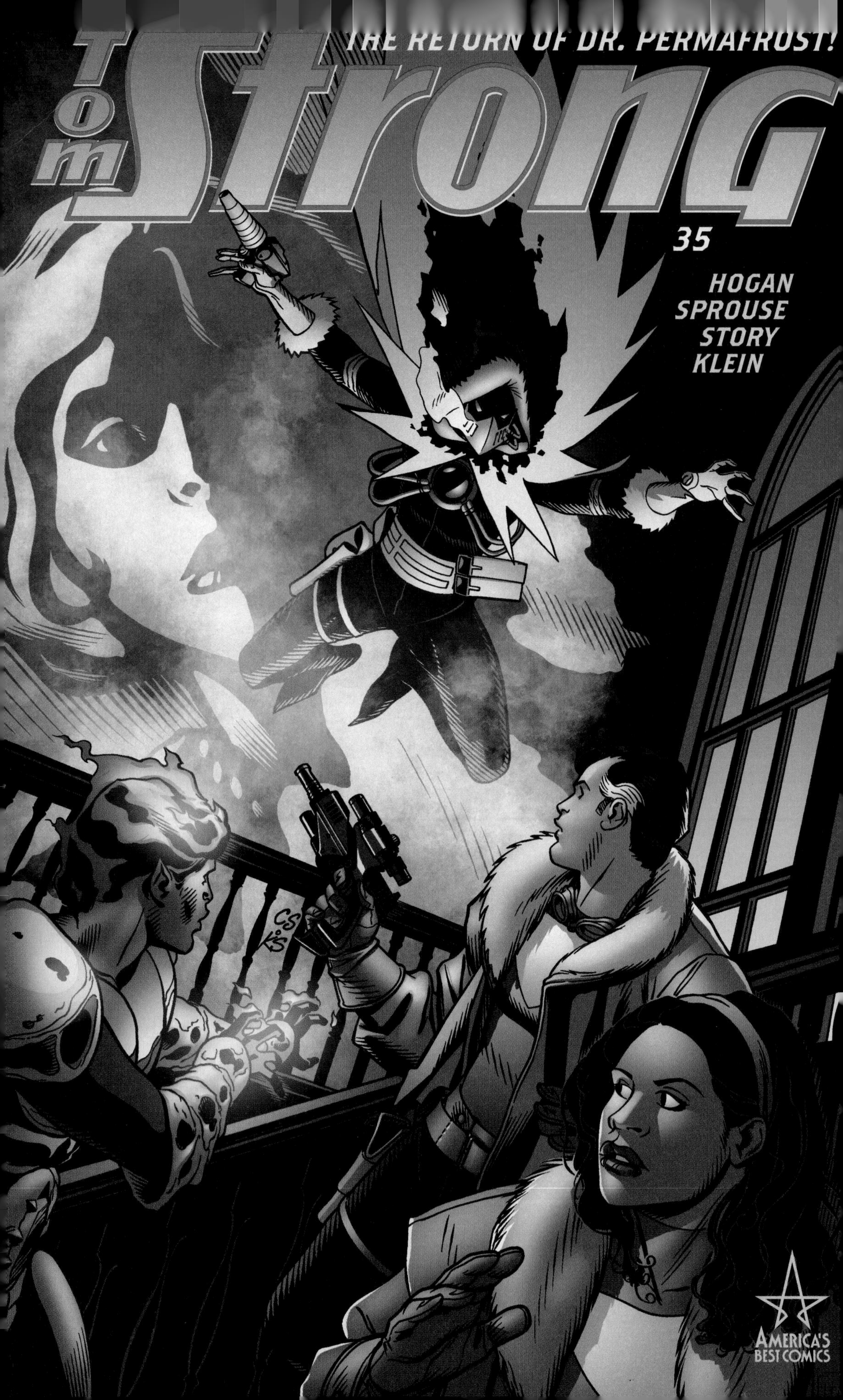
THE RETURN OF DR. PERMAFROST!
Tom Strong
35
HOGAN
SPROUSE
STORY
KLEIN
CS
KS
AMERICA'S BEST COMICS

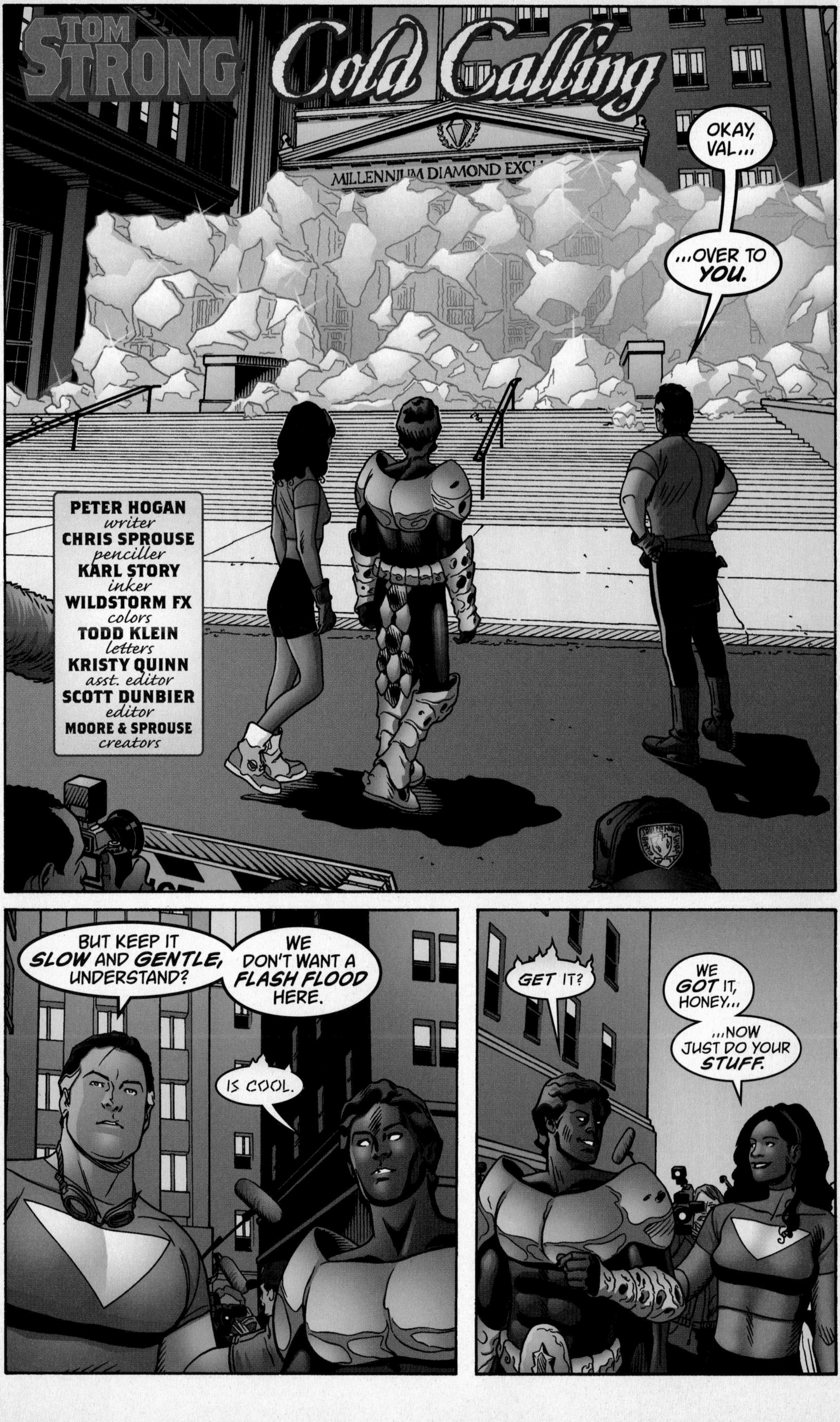
TOM STRONG
Cold Calling
MILLENNIUM DIAMOND EXCH
OKAY, VAL...
...OVER TO YOU.
PETER HOGAN writer
CHRIS SPROUSE penciller
KARL STORY inker
WILDSTORM FX colors
TODD KLEIN letters
KRISTY QUINN asst. editor
SCOTT DUNBIER editor
MOORE & SPROUSE creators
BUT KEEP IT SLOW AND GENTLE, UNDERSTAND?
WE DON'T WANT A FLASH FLOOD HERE.
IS COOL.
GET IT?
WE GOT IT, HONEY...
...NOW JUST DO YOUR STUFF.

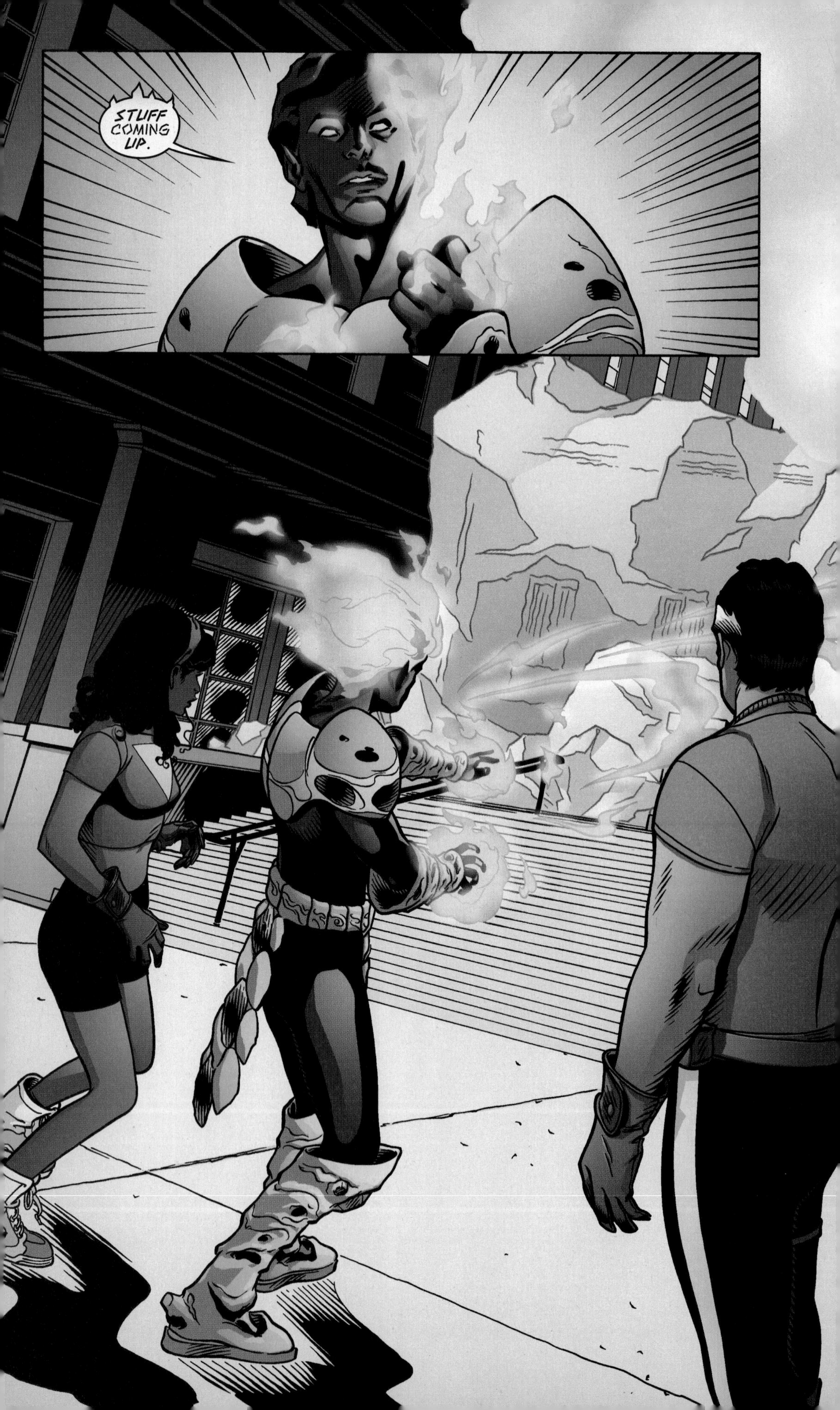
STUFF COMING UP.

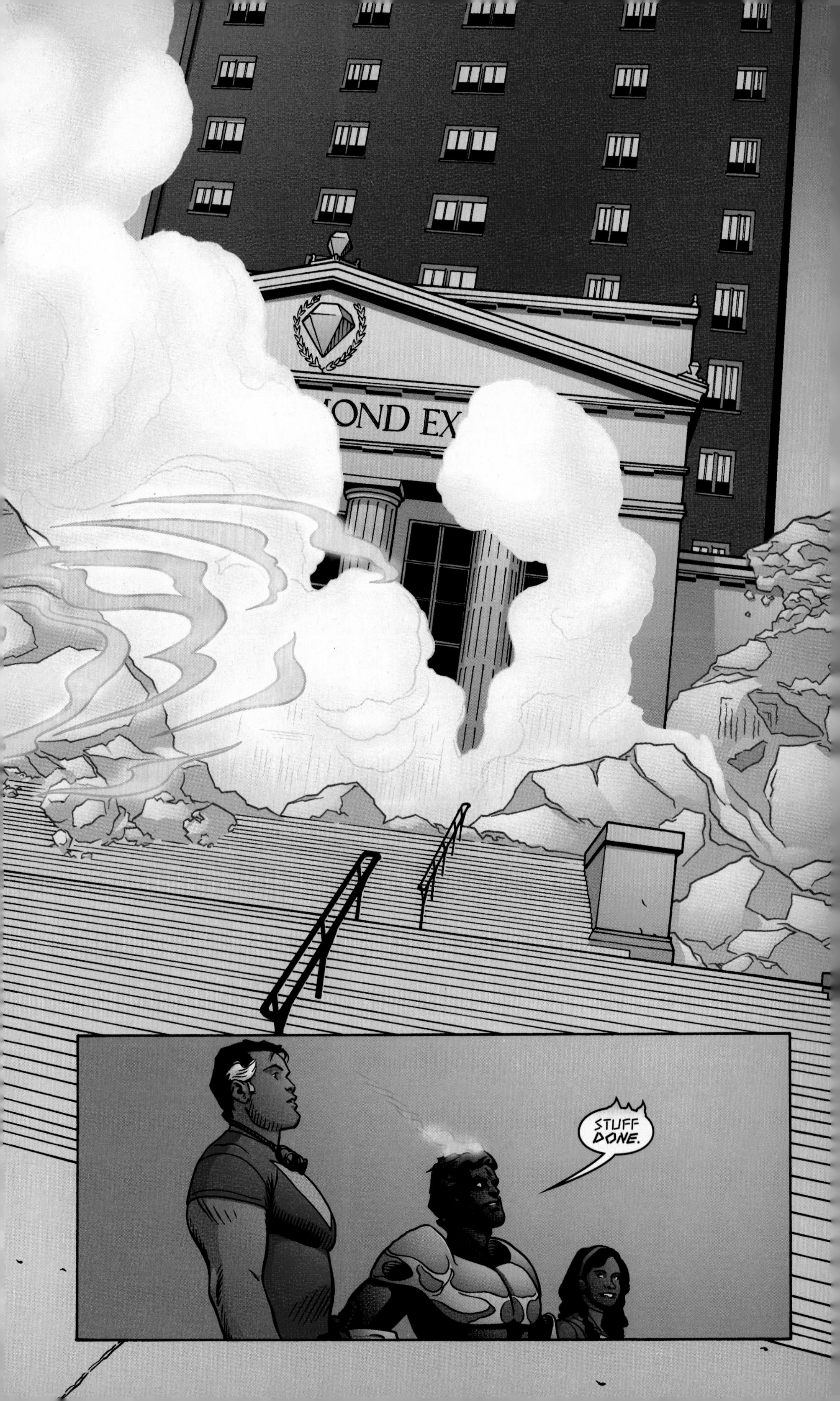
MOND EX
STUFF DONE.

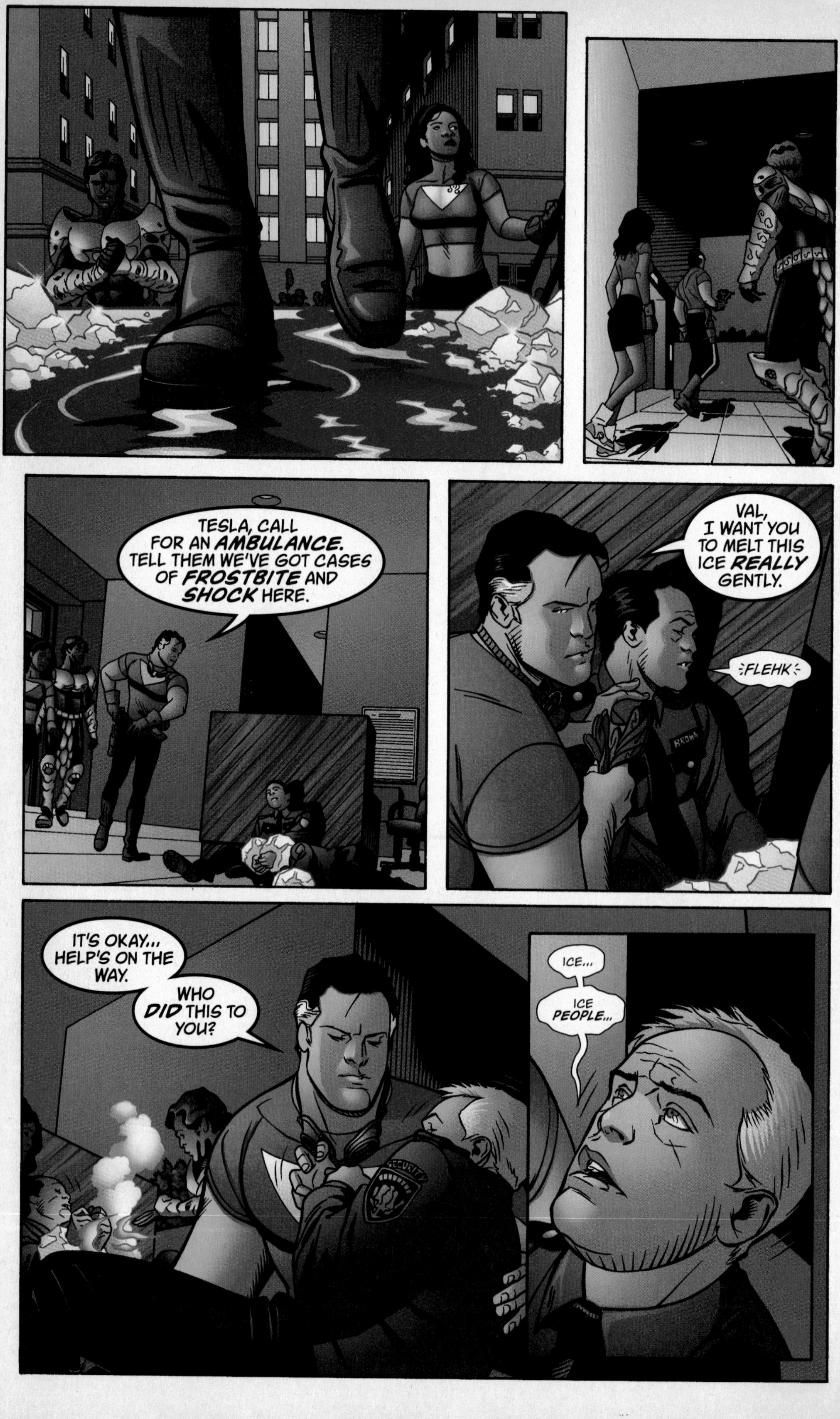
TESLA, CALL FOR AN AMBULANCE. TELL THEM WE'VE GOT CASES OF FROSTBITE AND SHOCK HERE.
VAL, I WANT YOU TO MELT THIS ICE REALLY GENTLY.
FLEHK
IT'S OKAY... HELP'S ON THE WAY.
WHO DID THIS TO YOU?
ICE...
ICE PEOPLE...

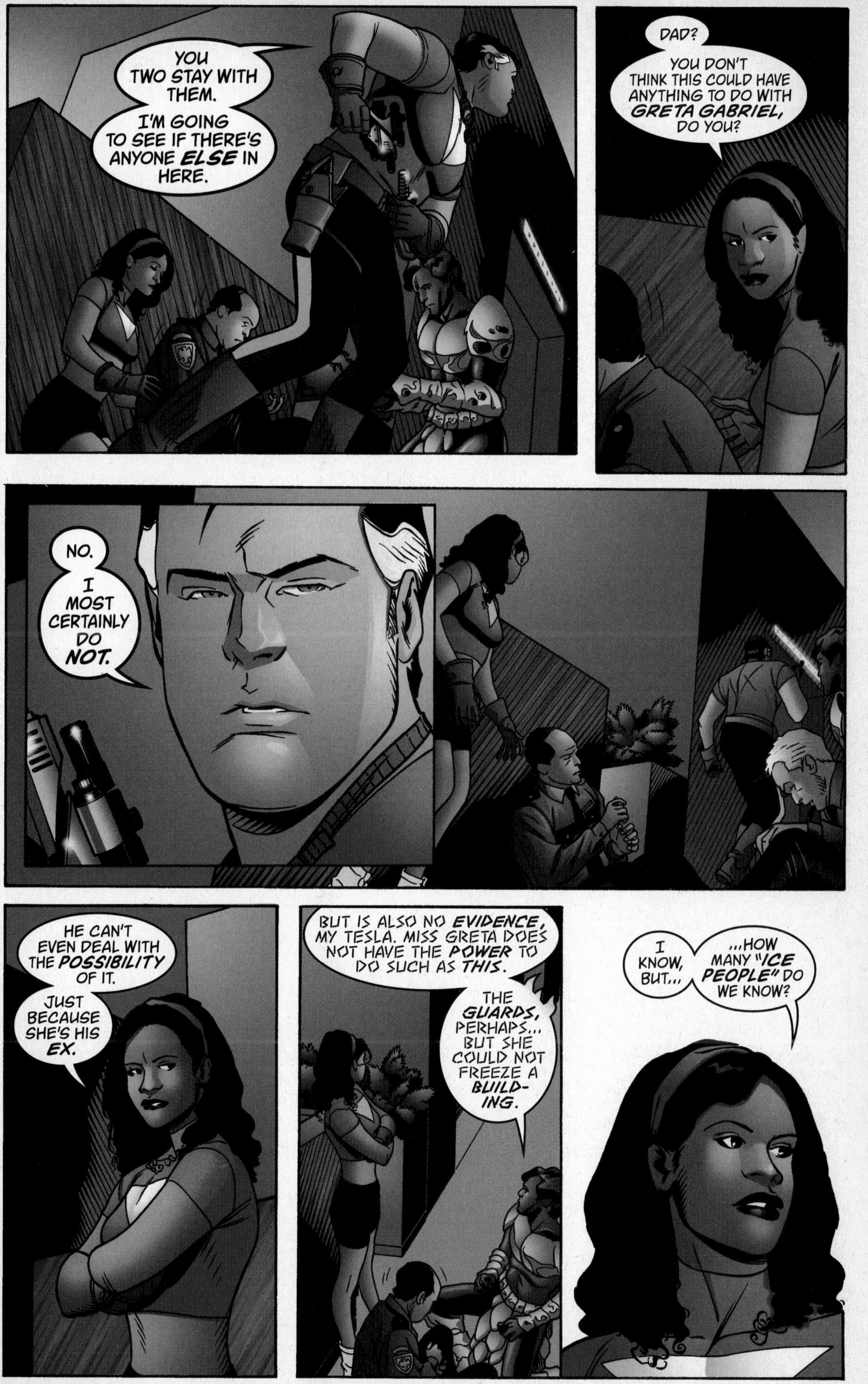
YOU TWO STAY WITH THEM.
I'M GOING TO SEE IF THERE'S ANYONE ELSE IN HERE.
DAD?
YOU DON'T THINK THIS COULD HAVE ANYTHING TO DO WITH GRETA GABRIEL, DO YOU?
NO.
I MOST CERTAINLY DO NOT.
HE CAN'T EVEN DEAL WITH THE POSSIBILITY OF IT.
JUST BECAUSE SHE'S HIS EX.
BUT IS ALSO NO EVIDENCE, MY TESLA. MISS GRETA DOES NOT HAVE THE POWER TO DO SUCH AS THIS.
THE GUARDS, PERHAPS... BUT SHE COULD NOT FREEZE A BUILD-ING.
I KNOW, BUT...
...HOW MANY "ICE PEOPLE" DO WE KNOW?

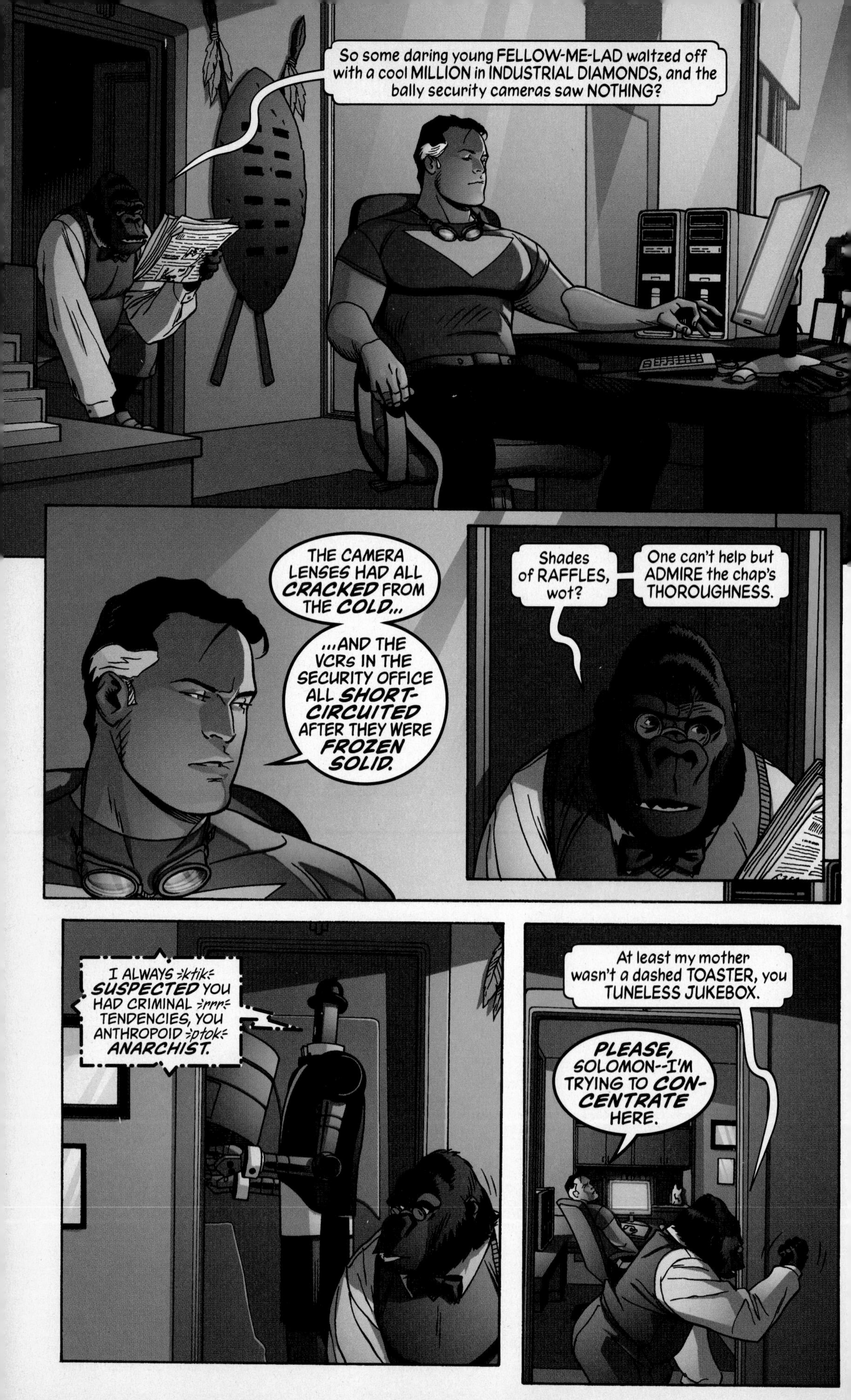

So some daring young FELLOW-ME-LAD waltzed off with a cool MILLION in INDUSTRIAL DIAMONDS, and the bally security cameras saw NOTHING?
THE CAMERA LENSES HAD ALL CRACKED FROM THE COLD...
...AND THE VCRs IN THE SECURITY OFFICE ALL SHORT-CIRCUITED AFTER THEY WERE FROZEN SOLID.
Shades of RAFFLES, wot?
One can't help but ADMIRE the chap's THOROUGHNESS.
I ALWAYS ≥ktik≤ SUSPECTED YOU HAD CRIMINAL ≥rrr≤ TENDENCIES, YOU ANTHROPOID ≥ptok≤ ANARCHIST.
At least my mother wasn't a dashed TOASTER, you TUNELESS JUKEBOX.
PLEASE, SOLOMON--I'M TRYING TO CONCENTRATE HERE.

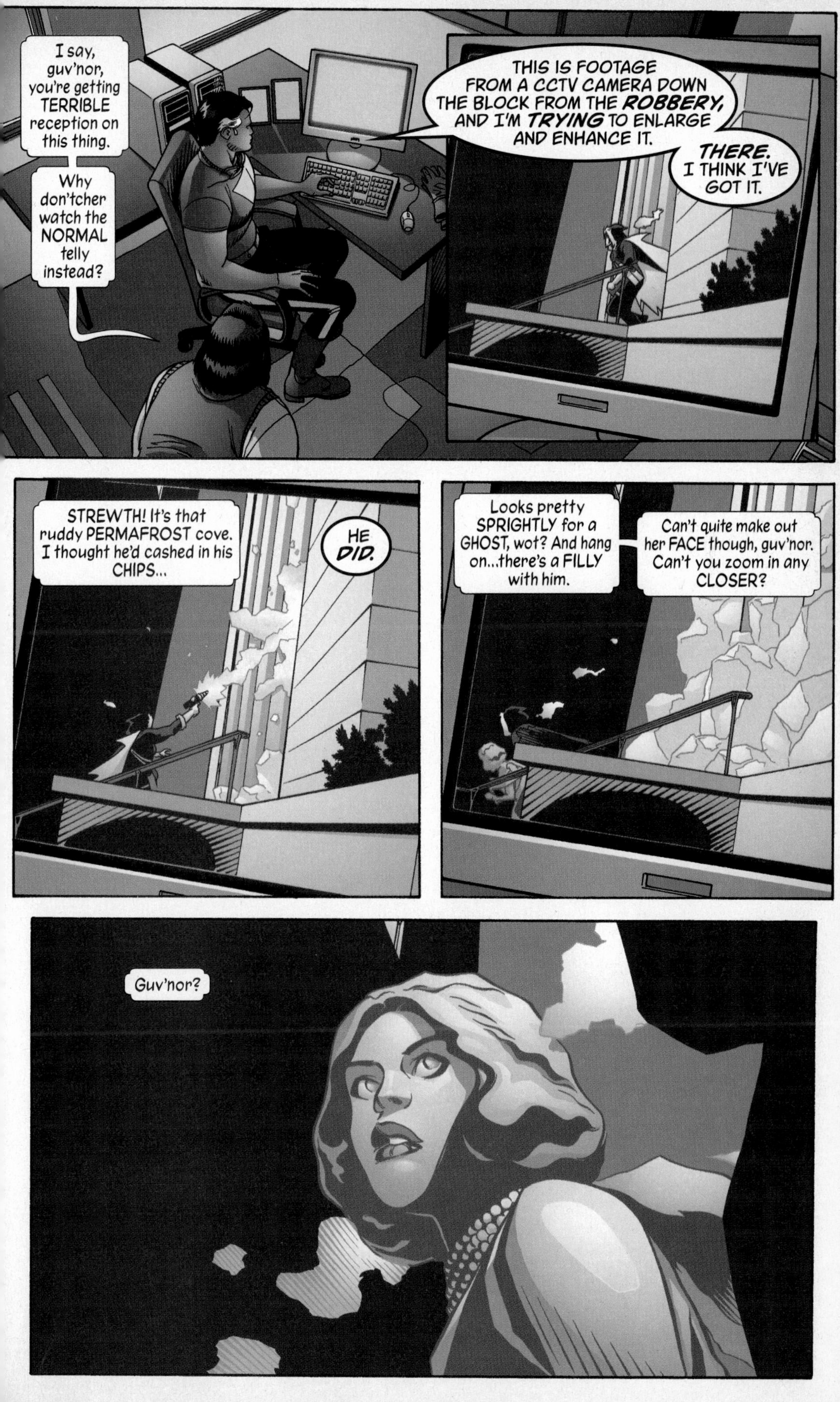
I say, guv'nor, you're getting TERRIBLE reception on this thing.
Why don'tcher watch the NORMAL telly instead?
THIS IS FOOTAGE FROM A CCTV CAMERA DOWN THE BLOCK FROM THE ROBBERY, AND I'M TRYING TO ENLARGE AND ENHANCE IT.
THERE. I THINK I'VE GOT IT.
STREWTH! It's that ruddy PERMAFROST cove. I thought he'd cashed in his CHIPS...
HE DID.
Looks pretty SPRIGHTLY for a GHOST, wot? And hang on...there's a FILLY with him.
Can't quite make out her FACE though, guv'nor. Can't you zoom in any CLOSER?
Guv'nor?

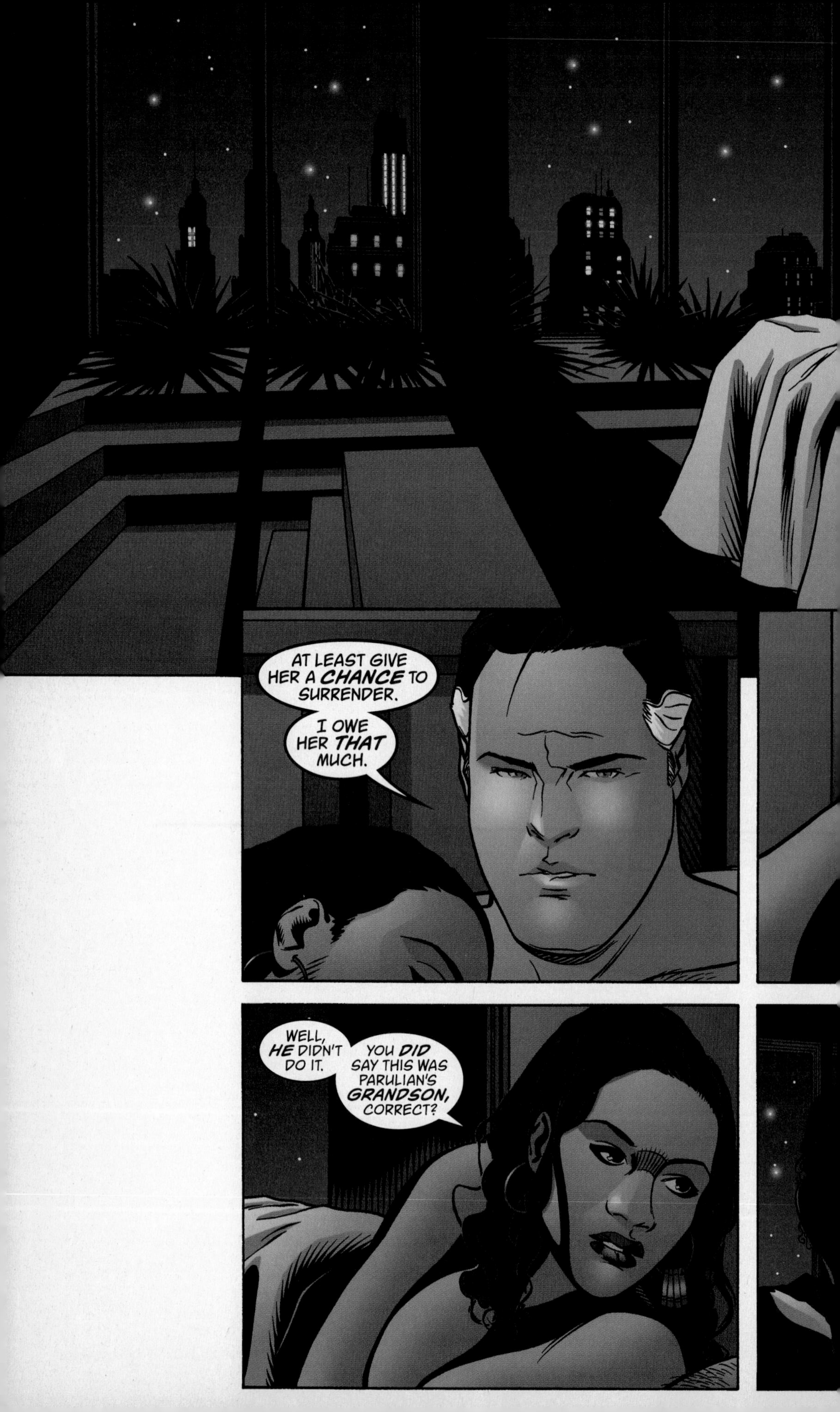
AT LEAST GIVE HER A CHANCE TO SURRENDER.
I OWE HER THAT MUCH.
WELL, HE DIDN'T DO IT.
YOU DID SAY THIS WAS PARULIAN'S GRANDSON, CORRECT?

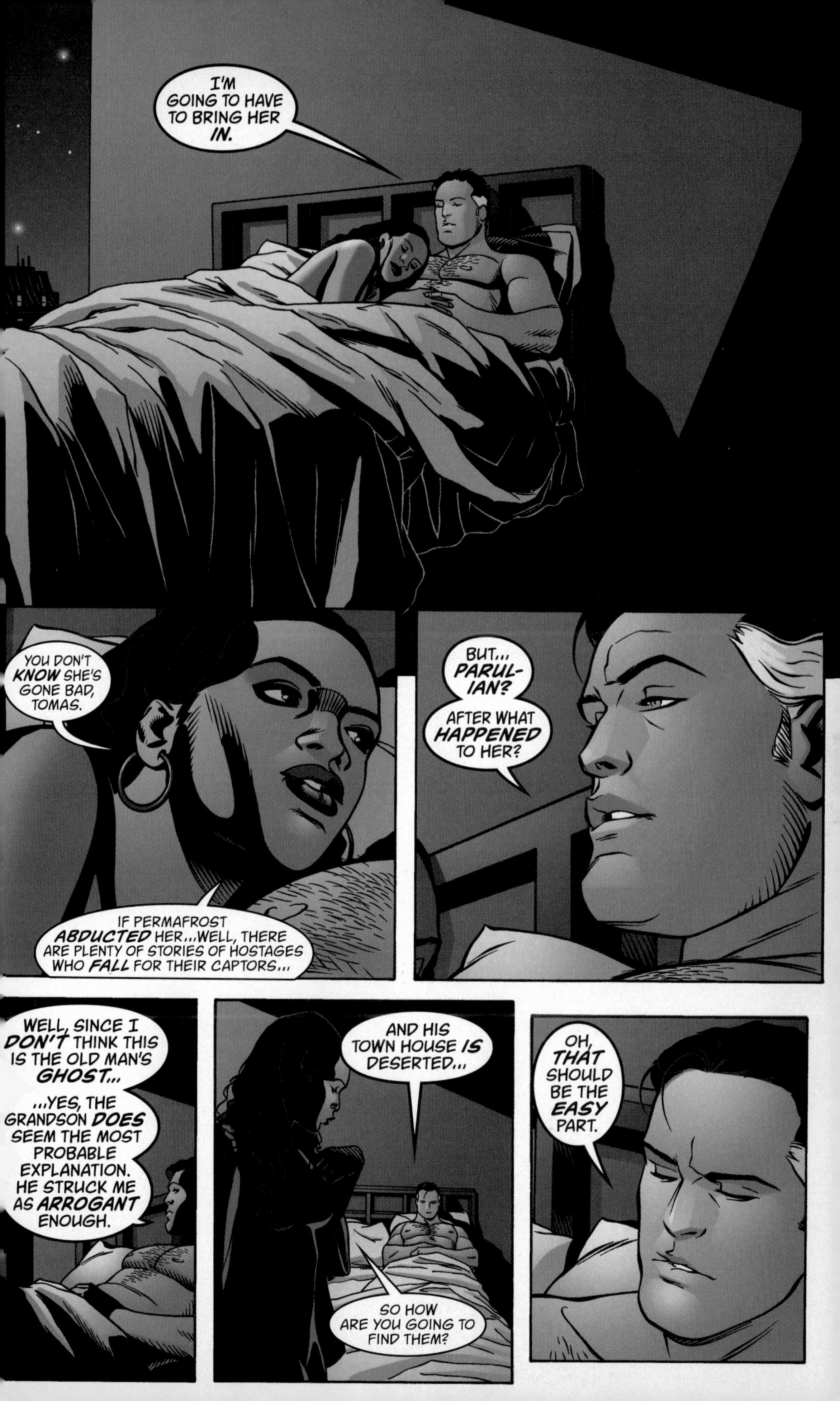
I'M GOING TO HAVE TO BRING HER *IN.*
YOU DON'T *KNOW* SHE'S GONE BAD, TOMAS.
IF PERMAFROST *ABDUCTED* HER...WELL, THERE ARE PLENTY OF STORIES OF HOSTAGES WHO *FALL* FOR THEIR CAPTORS...
BUT... *PARUL-IAN?*
AFTER WHAT *HAPPENED* TO HER?
WELL, SINCE I *DON'T* THINK THIS IS THE OLD MAN'S *GHOST...*
...YES, THE GRANDSON *DOES* SEEM THE MOST PROBABLE EXPLANATION. HE STRUCK ME AS *ARROGANT* ENOUGH.
AND HIS TOWN HOUSE *IS* DESERTED...
SO HOW ARE YOU GOING TO FIND THEM?
OH, *THAT* SHOULD BE THE *EASY* PART.

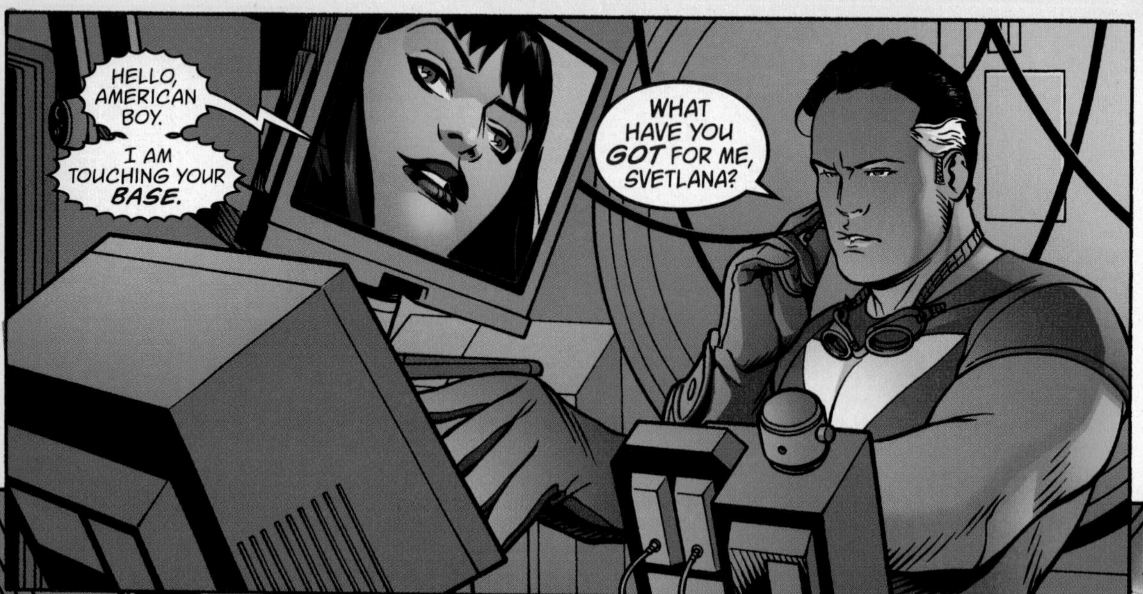
HELLO, AMERICAN BOY.
I AM TOUCHING YOUR BASE.
WHAT HAVE YOU GOT FOR ME, SVETLANA?

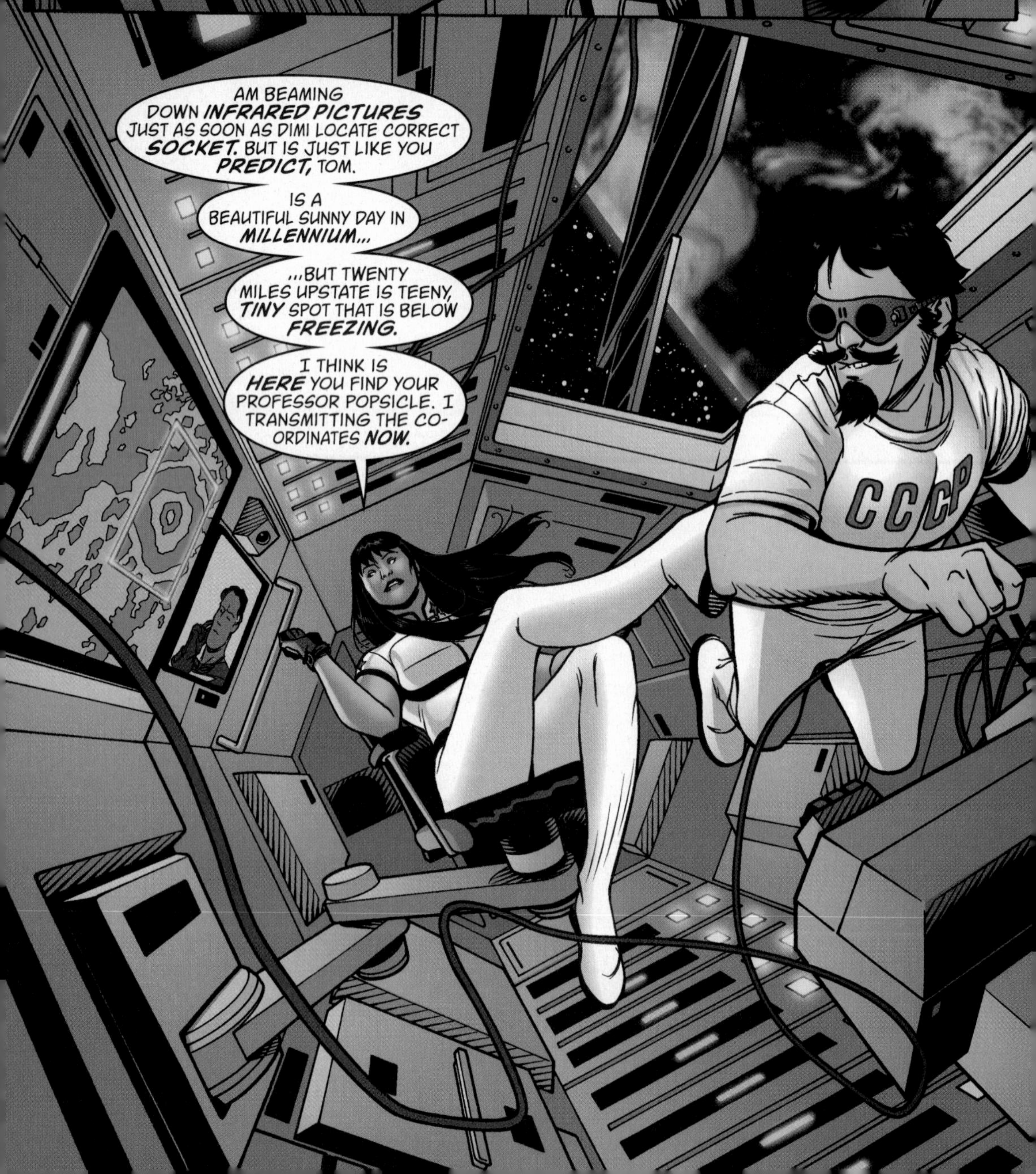
AM BEAMING DOWN INFRARED PICTURES JUST AS SOON AS DIMI LOCATE CORRECT SOCKET. BUT IS JUST LIKE YOU PREDICT, TOM.
IS A BEAUTIFUL SUNNY DAY IN MILLENNIUM...
...BUT TWENTY MILES UPSTATE IS TEENY, TINY SPOT THAT IS BELOW FREEZING.
I THINK IS HERE YOU FIND YOUR PROFESSOR POPSICLE. I TRANSMITTING THE CO-ORDINATES NOW.
CCCP

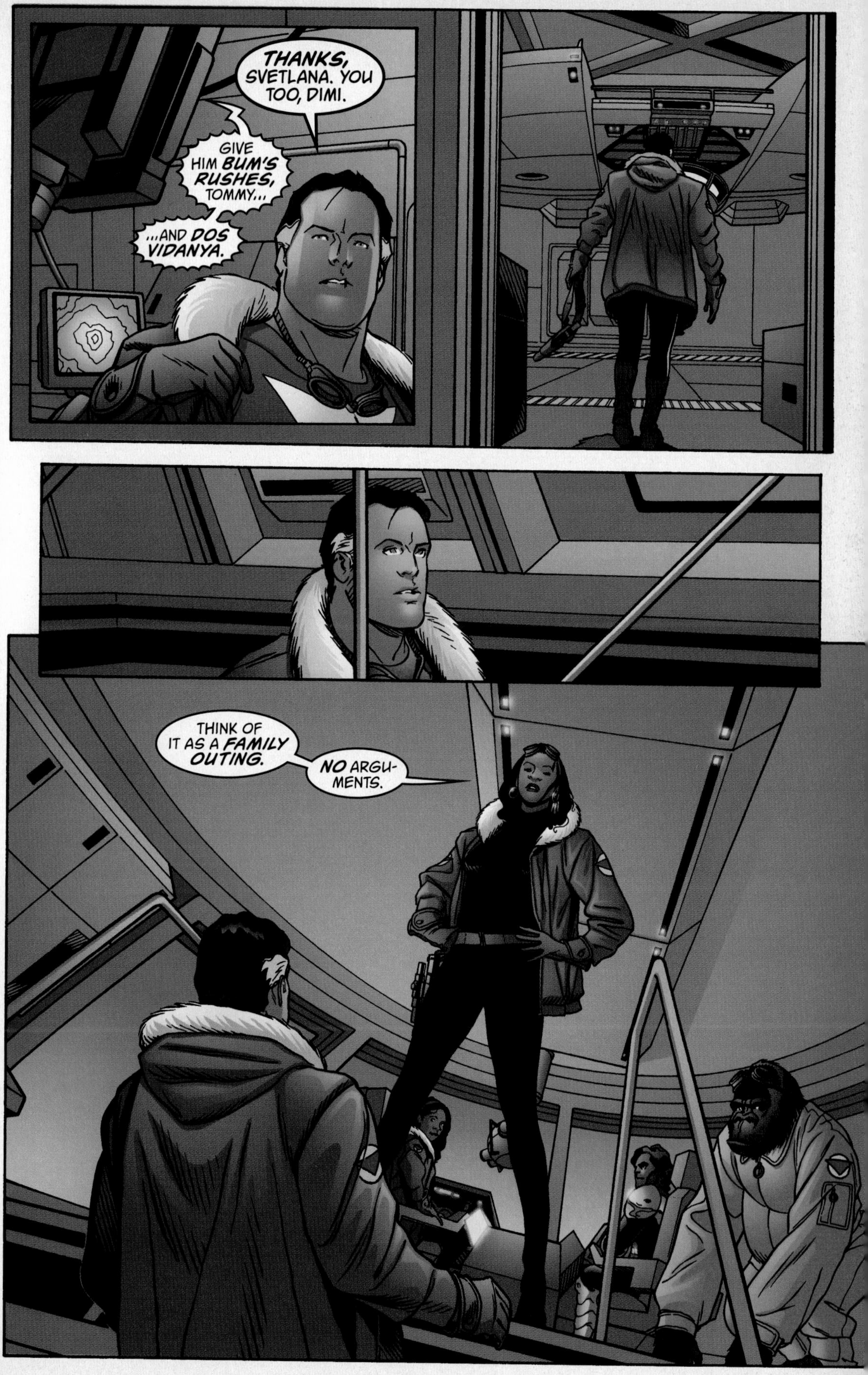
THANKS, SVETLANA. YOU TOO, DIMI.
GIVE HIM BUM'S RUSHES, TOMMY...
...AND DOS VIDANYA.
THINK OF IT AS A FAMILY OUTING.
NO ARGUMENTS.

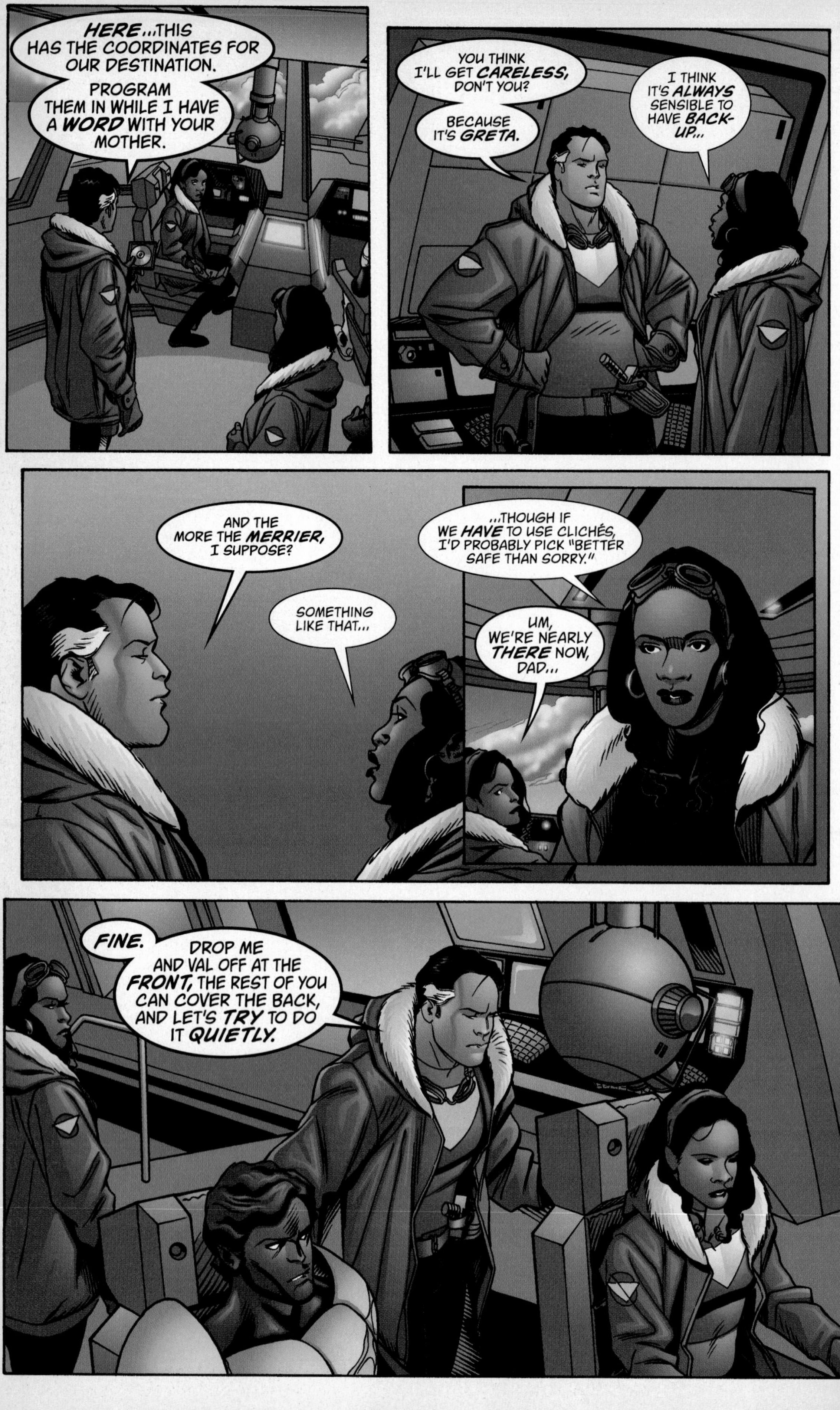
HERE...THIS HAS THE COORDINATES FOR OUR DESTINATION.
PROGRAM THEM IN WHILE I HAVE A WORD WITH YOUR MOTHER.
YOU THINK I'LL GET CARELESS, DON'T YOU?
BECAUSE IT'S GRETA.
I THINK IT'S ALWAYS SENSIBLE TO HAVE BACK-UP...
AND THE MORE THE MERRIER, I SUPPOSE?
SOMETHING LIKE THAT...
...THOUGH IF WE HAVE TO USE CLICHÉS, I'D PROBABLY PICK "BETTER SAFE THAN SORRY."
UM, WE'RE NEARLY THERE NOW, DAD...
FINE.
DROP ME AND VAL OFF AT THE FRONT, THE REST OF YOU CAN COVER THE BACK, AND LET'S TRY TO DO IT QUIETLY.

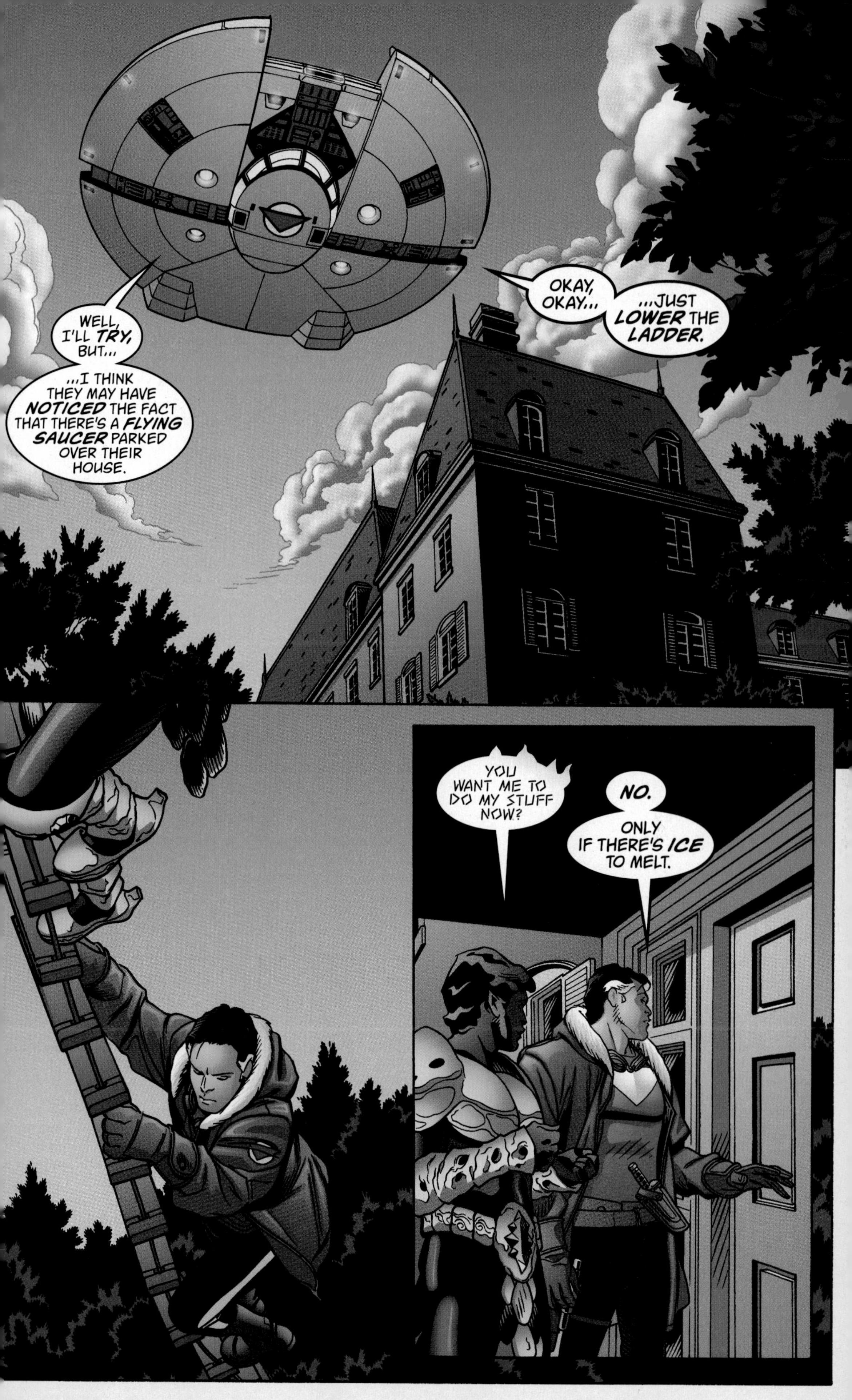
WELL, I'LL TRY, BUT...
...I THINK THEY MAY HAVE NOTICED THE FACT THAT THERE'S A FLYING SAUCER PARKED OVER THEIR HOUSE.
OKAY, OKAY...
...JUST LOWER THE LADDER.
YOU WANT ME TO DO MY STUFF NOW?
NO.
ONLY IF THERE'S ICE TO MELT.

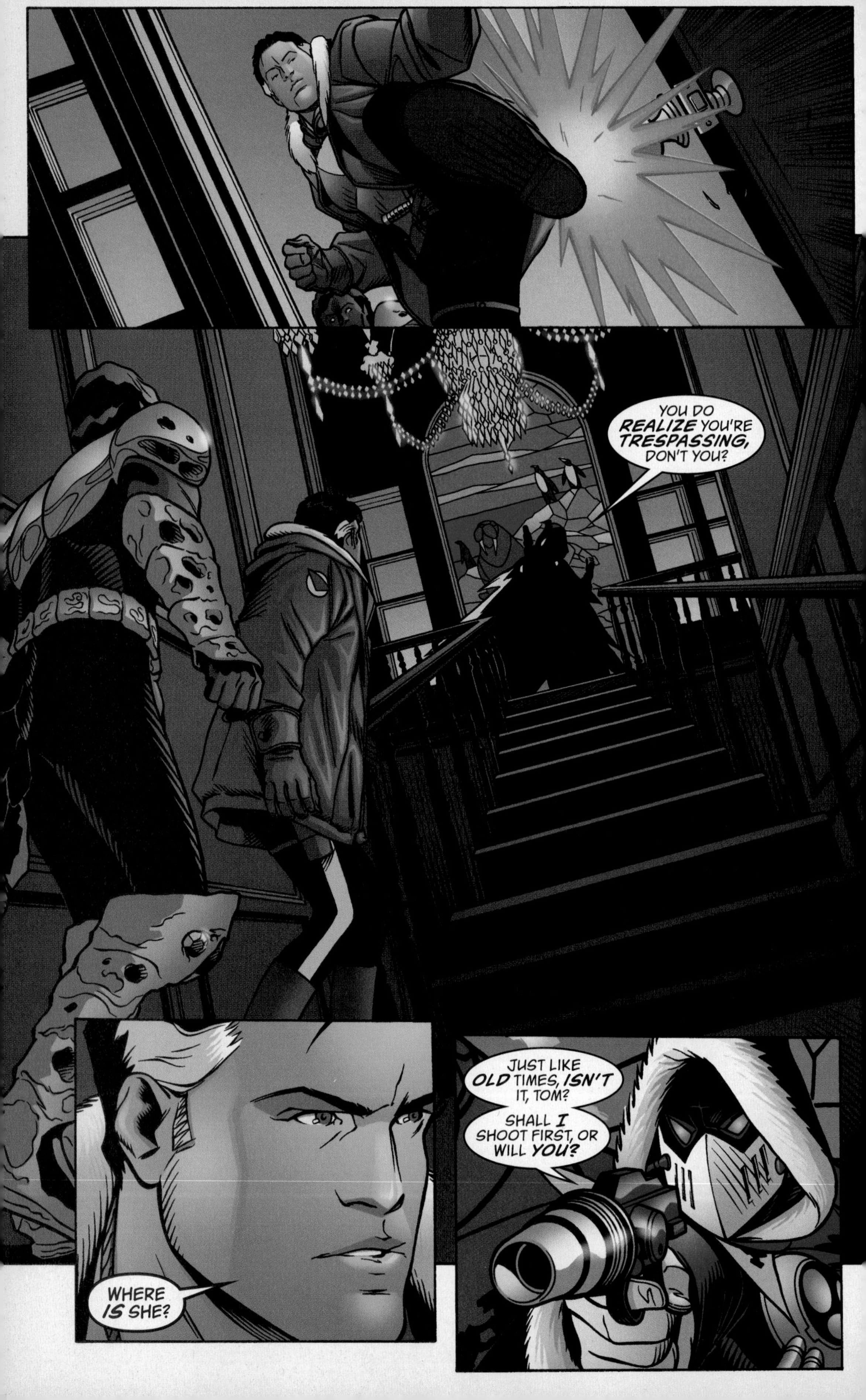
YOU DO REALIZE YOU'RE TRESPASSING, DON'T YOU?
WHERE IS SHE?
JUST LIKE OLD TIMES, ISN'T IT, TOM?
SHALL I SHOOT FIRST, OR WILL YOU?

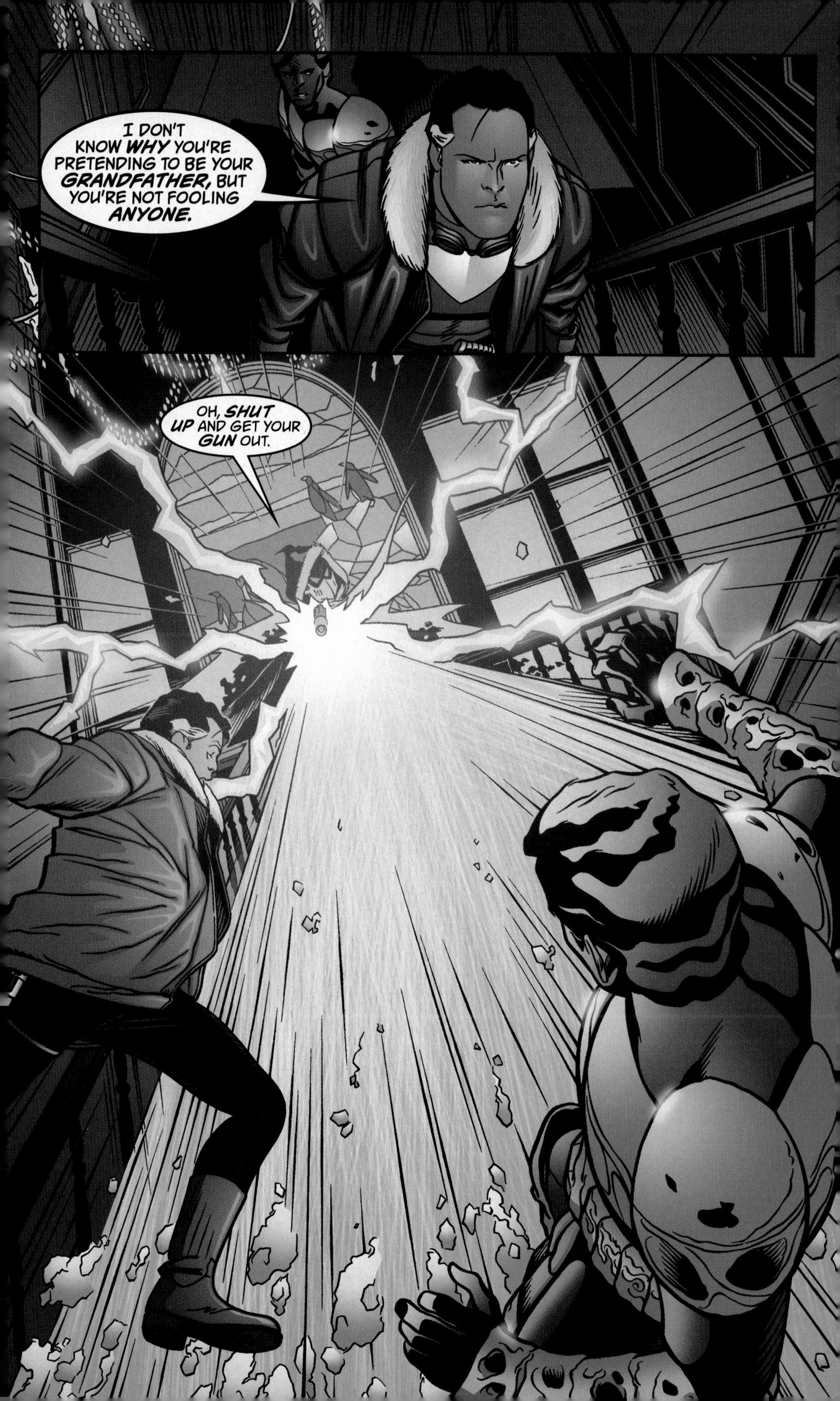
I DON'T KNOW WHY YOU'RE PRETENDING TO BE YOUR GRANDFATHER, BUT YOU'RE NOT FOOLING ANYONE.
OH, SHUT UP AND GET YOUR GUN OUT.

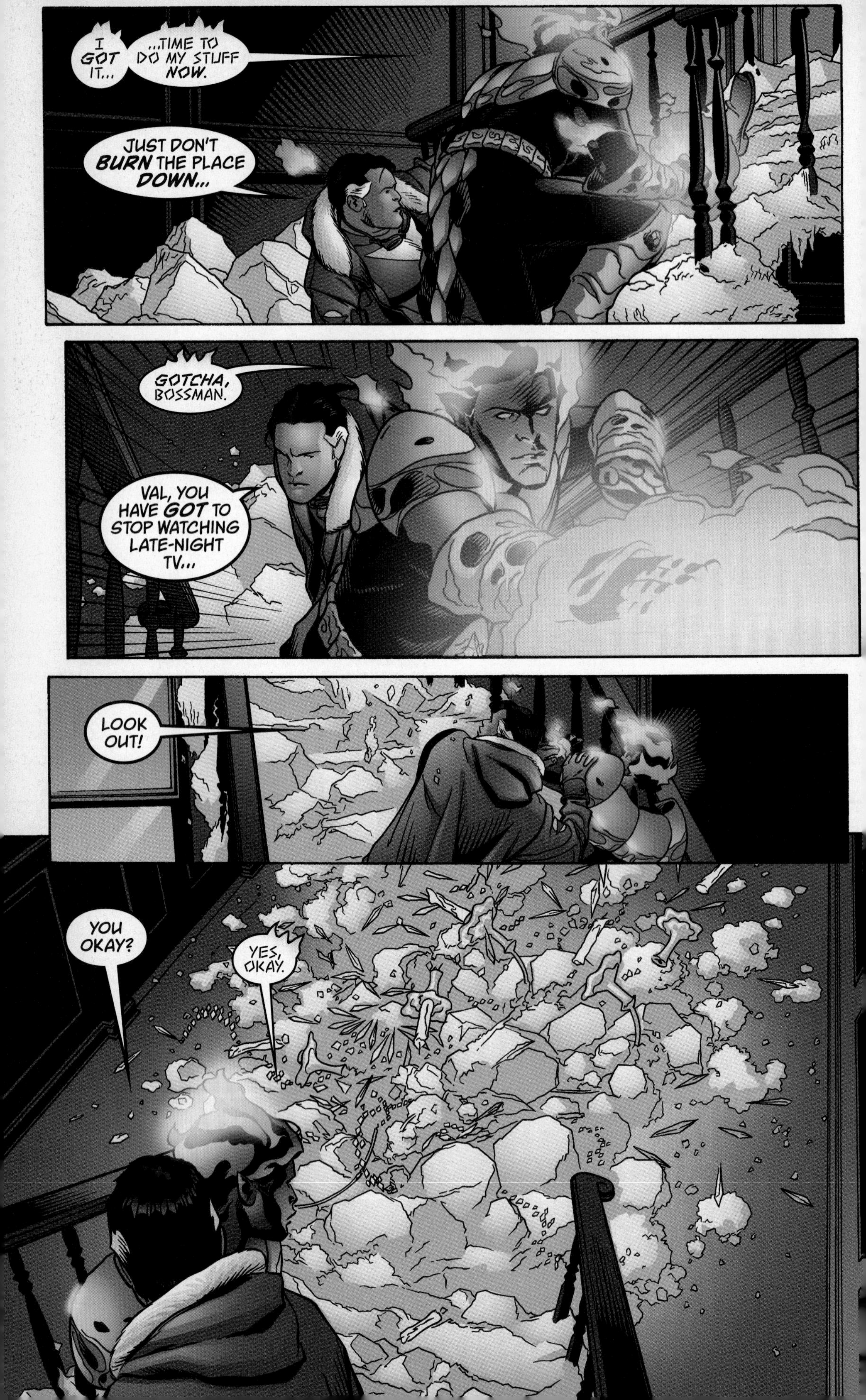

I GOT IT...
...TIME TO DO MY STUFF NOW.
JUST DON'T BURN THE PLACE DOWN...
GOTCHA, BOSSMAN.
VAL, YOU HAVE GOT TO STOP WATCHING LATE-NIGHT TV...
LOOK OUT!
YOU OKAY?
YES, OKAY.

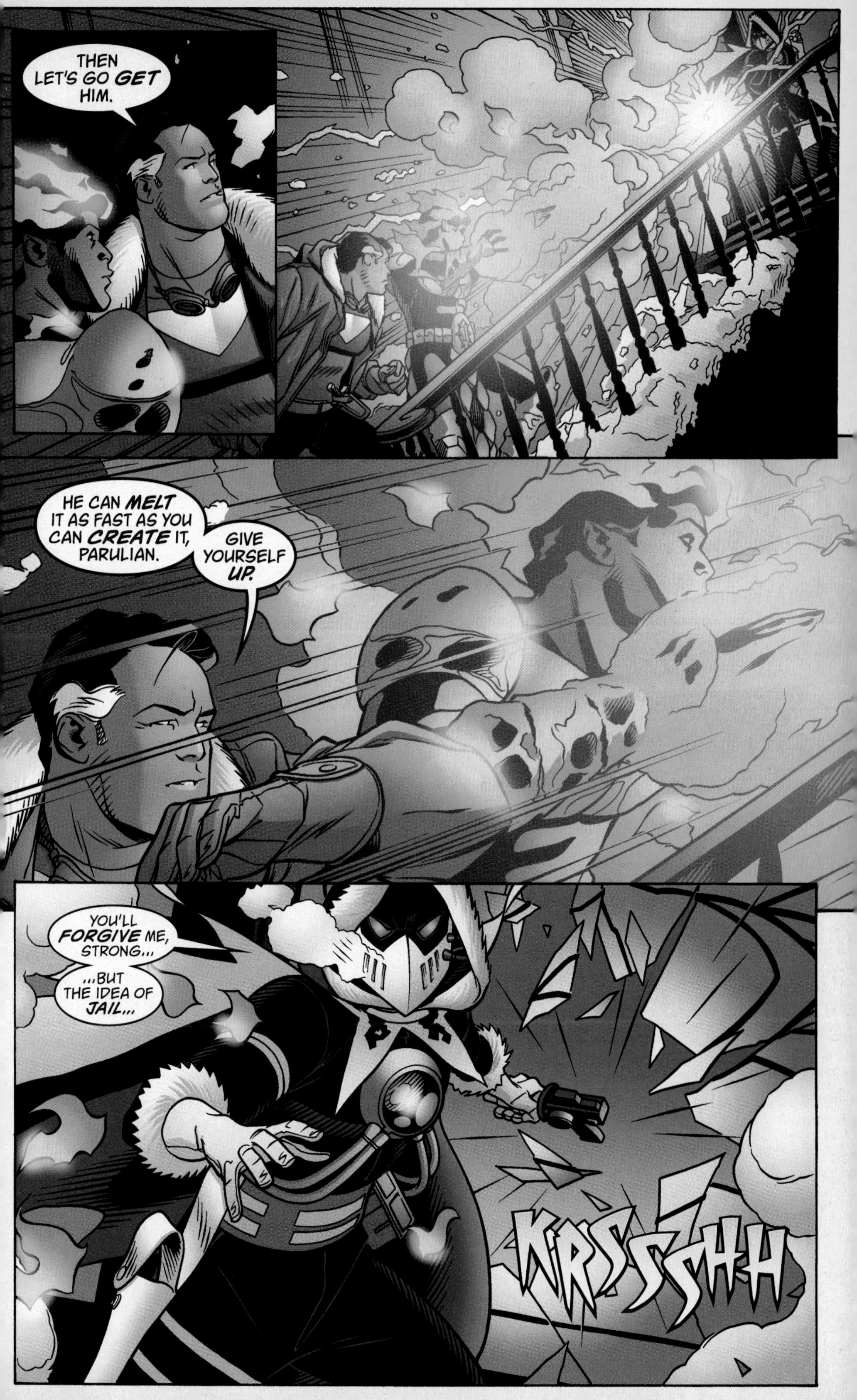
THEN LET'S GO GET HIM.
HE CAN MELT IT AS FAST AS YOU CAN CREATE IT, PARULIAN.
GIVE YOURSELF UP.
YOU'LL FORGIVE ME, STRONG...
...BUT THE IDEA OF JAIL...
KRSSSHH

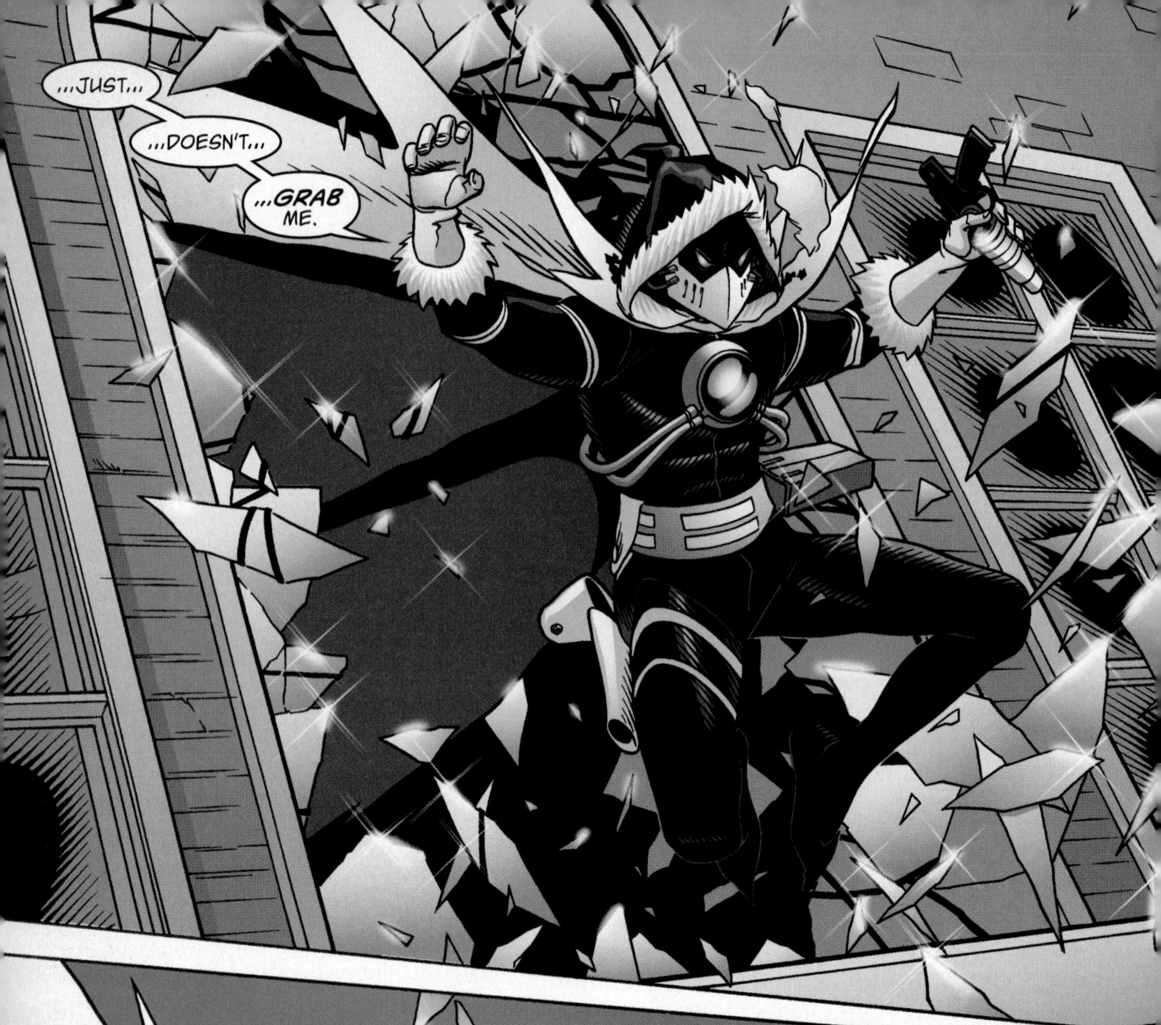
...JUST...
...DOESN'T...
...GRAB ME.

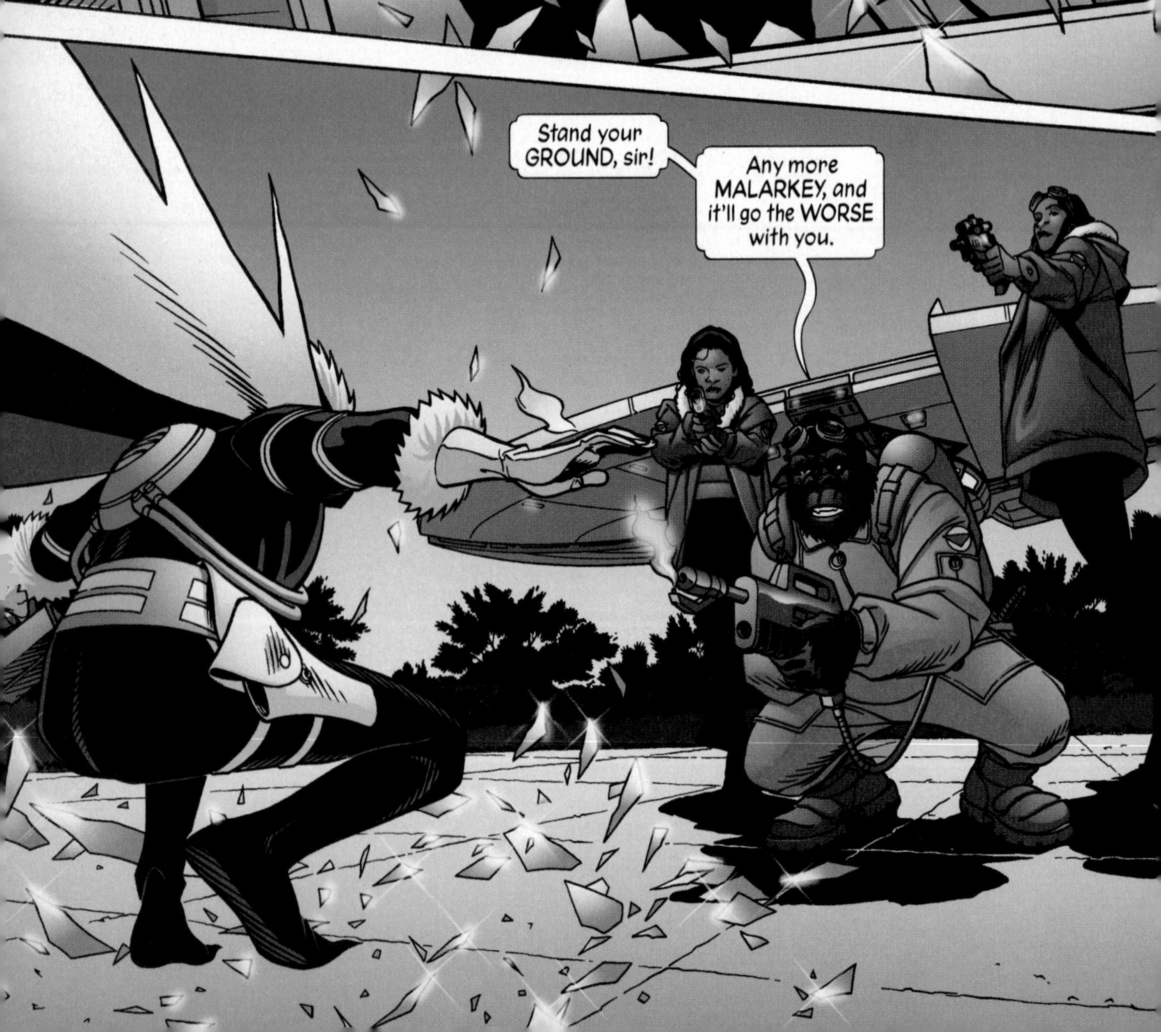
Stand your GROUND, sir!
Any more MALARKEY, and it'll go the WORSE with you.

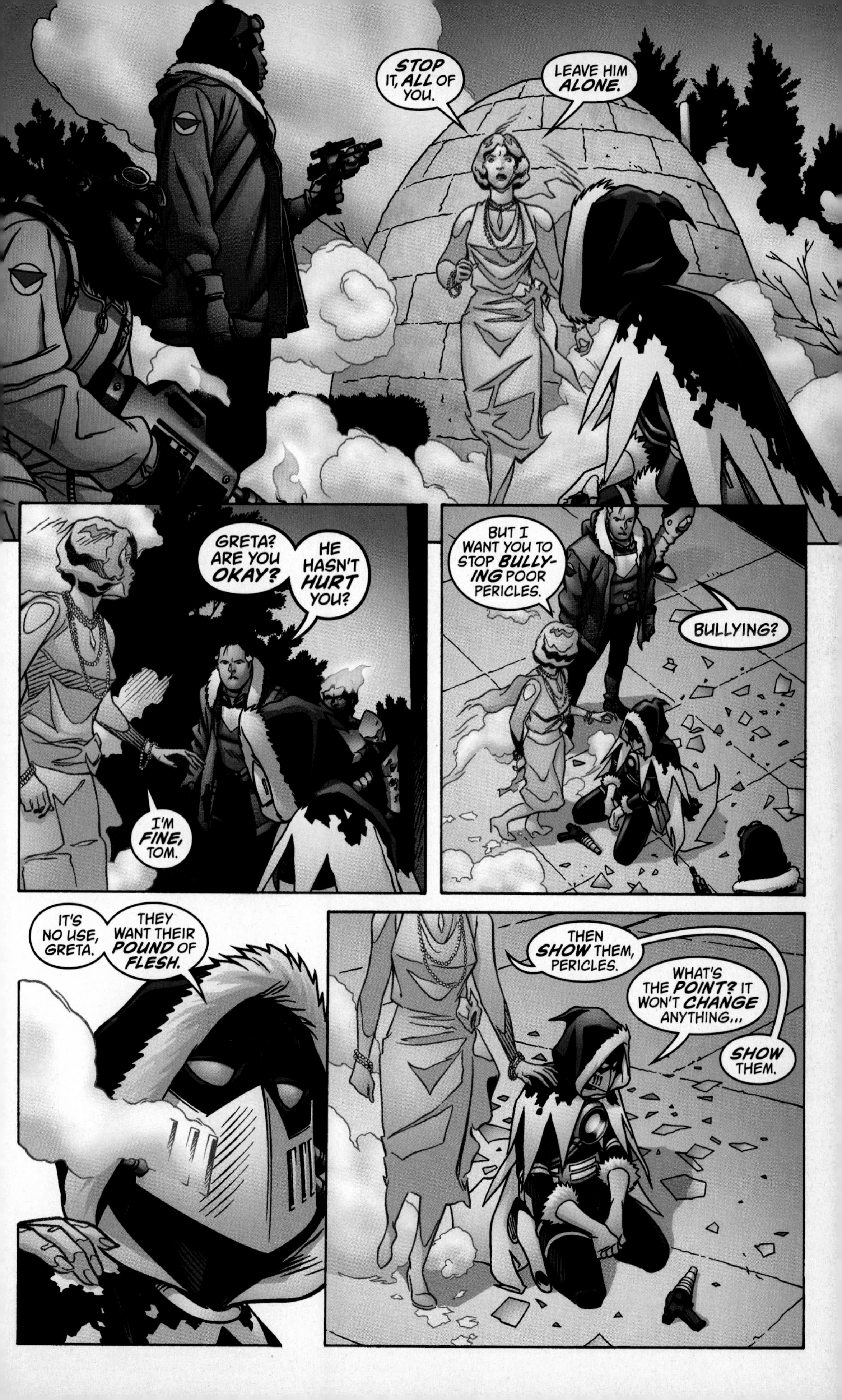
STOP IT, ALL OF YOU.
LEAVE HIM ALONE.
GRETA? ARE YOU OKAY?
HE HASN'T HURT YOU?
I'M FINE, TOM.
BUT I WANT YOU TO STOP BULLYING POOR PERICLES.
BULLYING?
IT'S NO USE, GRETA.
THEY WANT THEIR POUND OF FLESH.
THEN SHOW THEM, PERICLES.
WHAT'S THE POINT? IT WON'T CHANGE ANYTHING...
SHOW THEM.

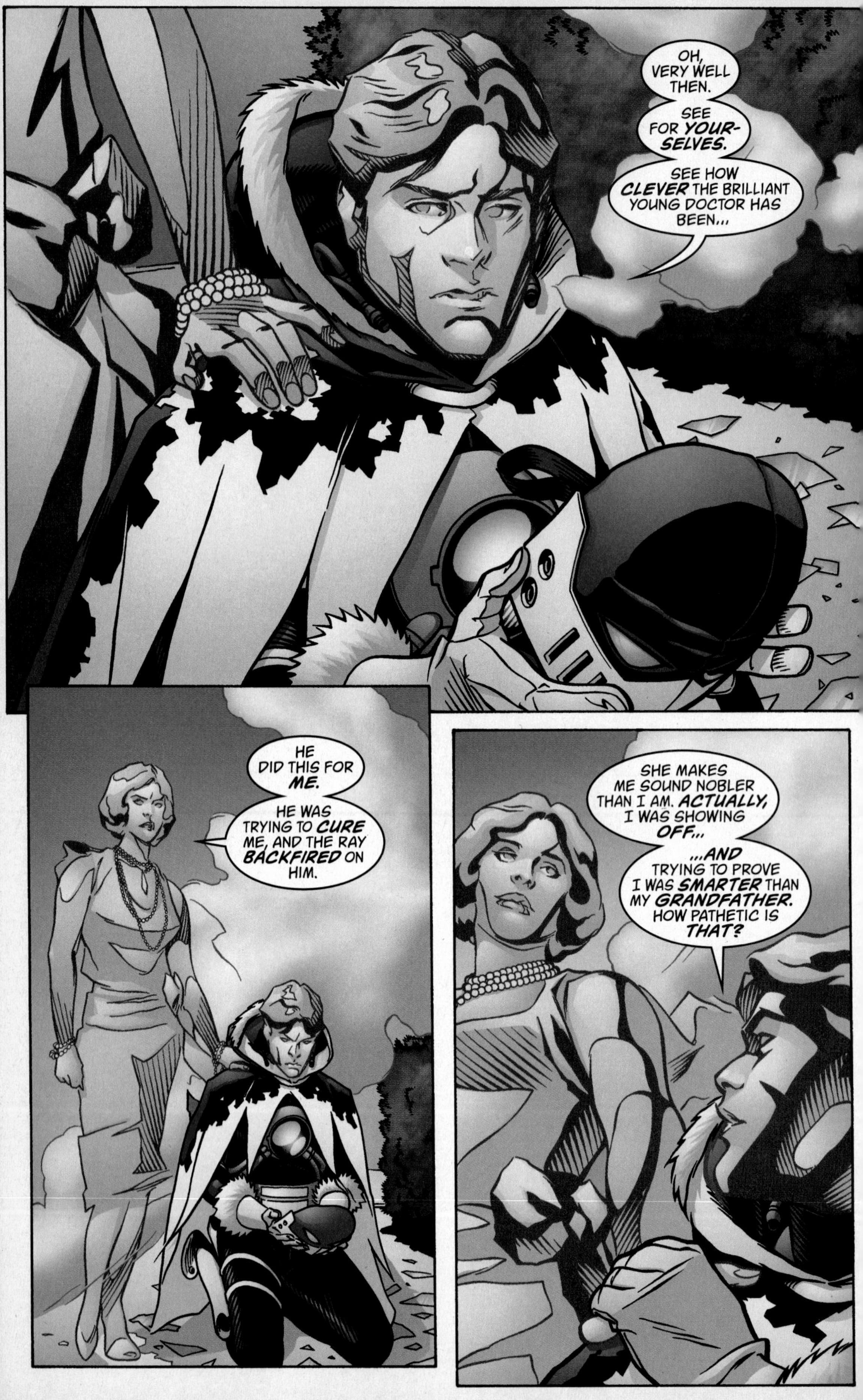
OH, VERY WELL THEN.
SEE FOR YOUR-SELVES.
SEE HOW CLEVER THE BRILLIANT YOUNG DOCTOR HAS BEEN...
HE DID THIS FOR ME.
HE WAS TRYING TO CURE ME, AND THE RAY BACKFIRED ON HIM.
SHE MAKES ME SOUND NOBLER THAN I AM. ACTUALLY, I WAS SHOWING OFF...
...AND TRYING TO PROVE I WAS SMARTER THAN MY GRANDFATHER. HOW PATHETIC IS THAT?

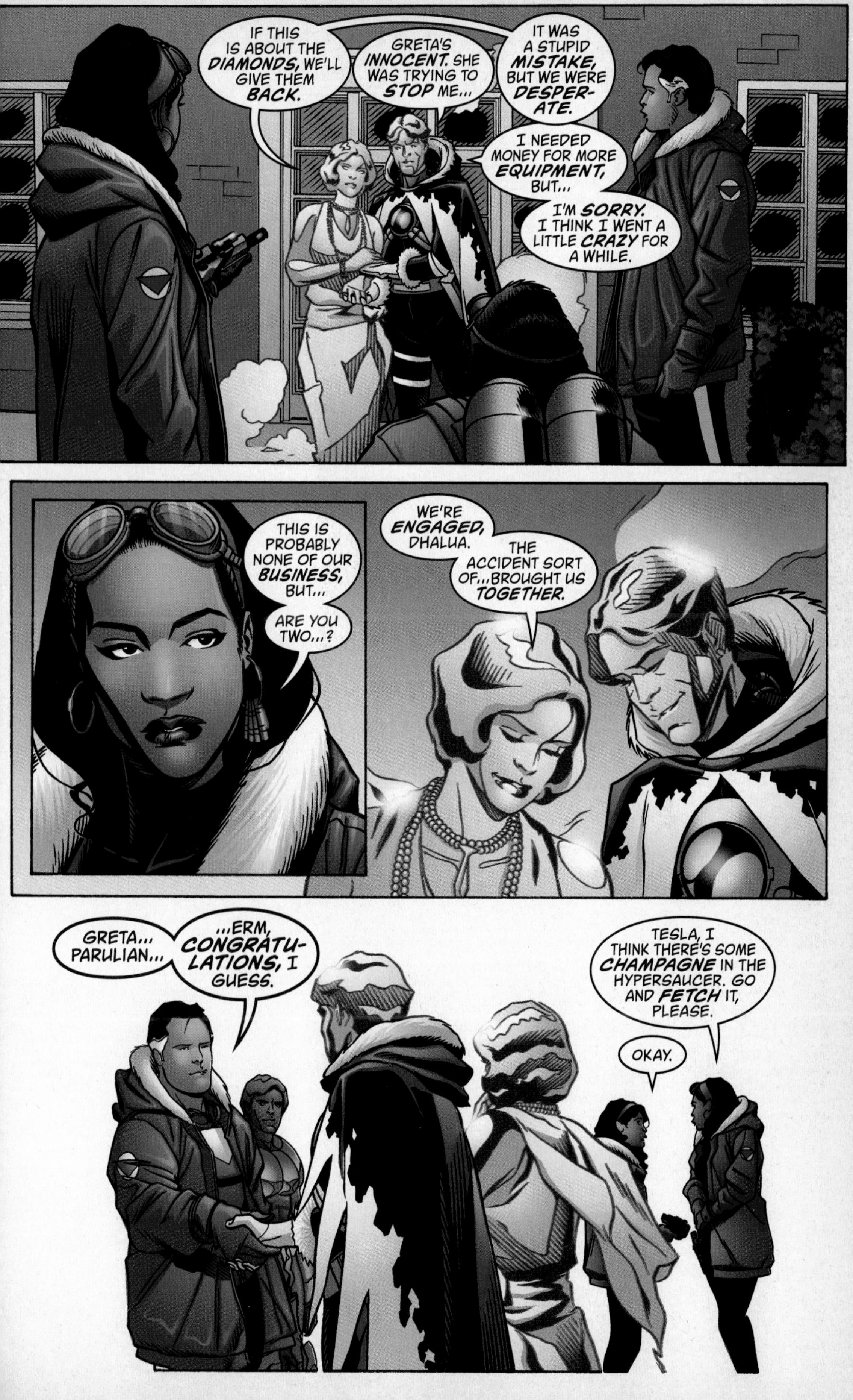
IF THIS IS ABOUT THE DIAMONDS, WE'LL GIVE THEM BACK.
GRETA'S INNOCENT. SHE WAS TRYING TO STOP ME...
IT WAS A STUPID MISTAKE, BUT WE WERE DESPER-ATE.
I NEEDED MONEY FOR MORE EQUIPMENT, BUT...
I'M SORRY. I THINK I WENT A LITTLE CRAZY FOR A WHILE.
THIS IS PROBABLY NONE OF OUR BUSINESS, BUT...
ARE YOU TWO...?
WE'RE ENGAGED, DHALUA.
THE ACCIDENT SORT OF...BROUGHT US TOGETHER.
GRETA... PARULIAN...
...ERM, CONGRATU-LATIONS, I GUESS.
TESLA, I THINK THERE'S SOME CHAMPAGNE IN THE HYPERSAUCER. GO AND FETCH IT, PLEASE.
OKAY.

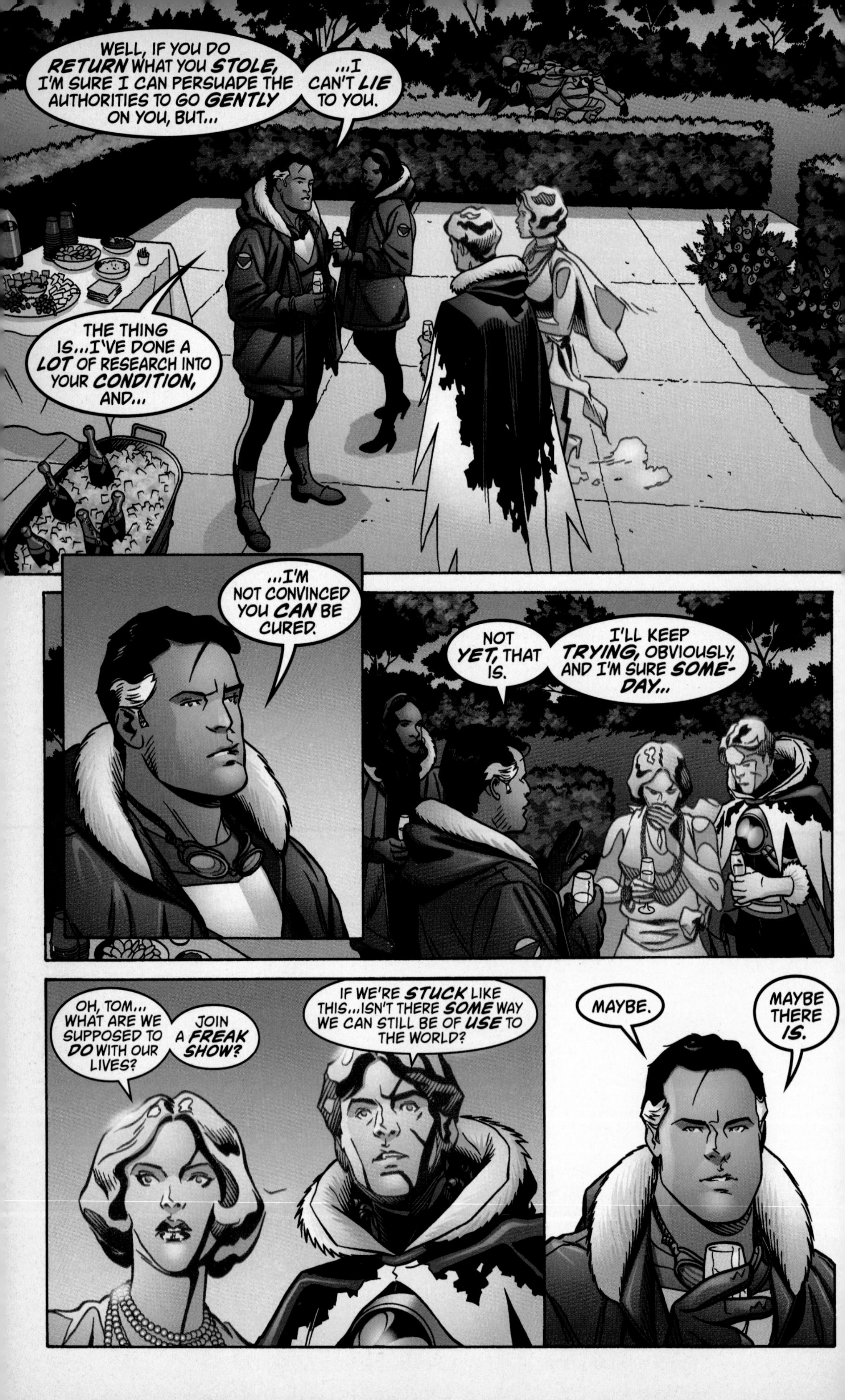

WELL, IF YOU DO RETURN WHAT YOU STOLE, I'M SURE I CAN PERSUADE THE AUTHORITIES TO GO GENTLY ON YOU, BUT...
...I CAN'T LIE TO YOU.
THE THING IS...I'VE DONE A LOT OF RESEARCH INTO YOUR CONDITION, AND...
...I'M NOT CONVINCED YOU CAN BE CURED.
NOT YET, THAT IS.
I'LL KEEP TRYING, OBVIOUSLY, AND I'M SURE SOME-DAY...
OH, TOM... WHAT ARE WE SUPPOSED TO DO WITH OUR LIVES?
JOIN A FREAK SHOW?
IF WE'RE STUCK LIKE THIS...ISN'T THERE SOME WAY WE CAN STILL BE OF USE TO THE WORLD?
MAYBE.
MAYBE THERE IS.

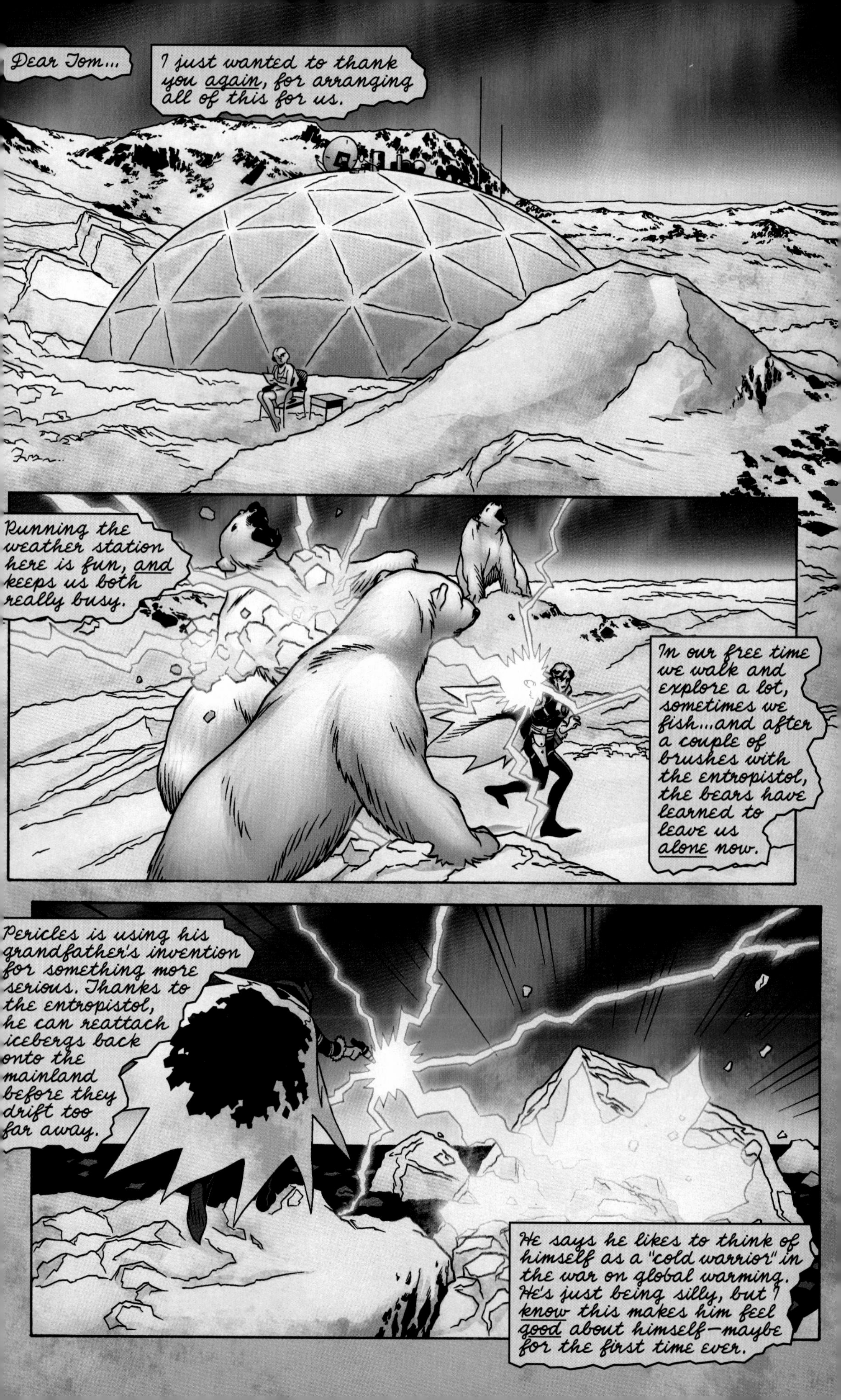
Dear Tom...
I just wanted to thank you again, for arranging all of this for us.
Running the weather station here is fun, and keeps us both really busy.
In our free time we walk and explore a lot, sometimes we fish...and after a couple of brushes with the entropistol, the bears have learned to leave us alone now.
Pericles is using his grandfather's invention for something more serious. Thanks to the entropistol, he can reattach icebergs back onto the mainland before they drift too far away.
He says he likes to think of himself as a "cold warrior" in the war on global warming. He's just being silly, but I know this makes him feel good about himself—maybe for the first time ever.

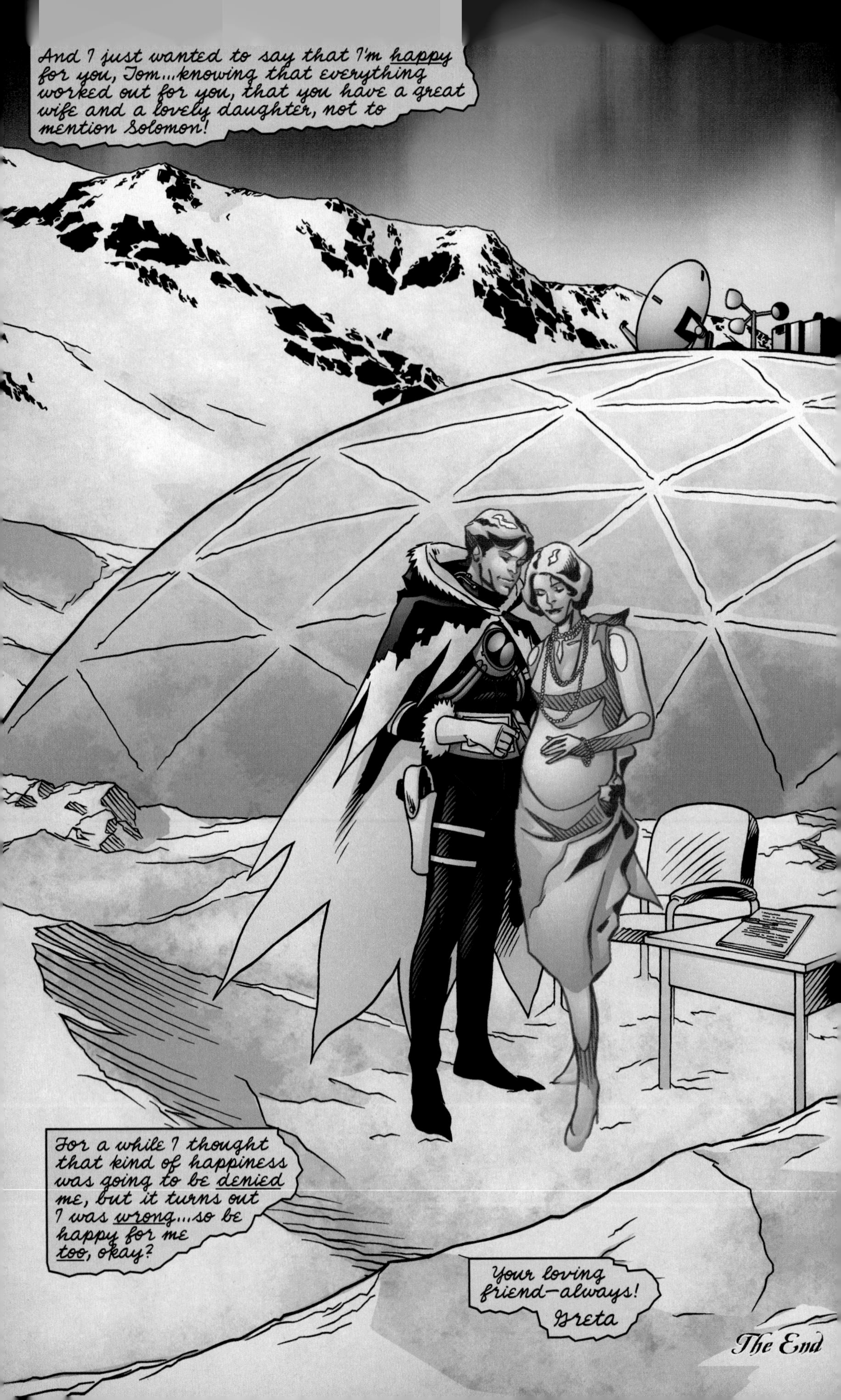
And I just wanted to say that I'm happy for you, Tom...knowing that everything worked out for you, that you have a great wife and a lovely daughter, not to mention Solomon!
For a while I thought that kind of happiness was going to be denied me, but it turns out I was wrong...so be happy for me too, okay?
Your loving friend—always! Greta
The End

# CHAPTER SIX

In which, as must inevitably happen,
all of Tom's stories come to a fitting,
though somewhat unusual conclusion.

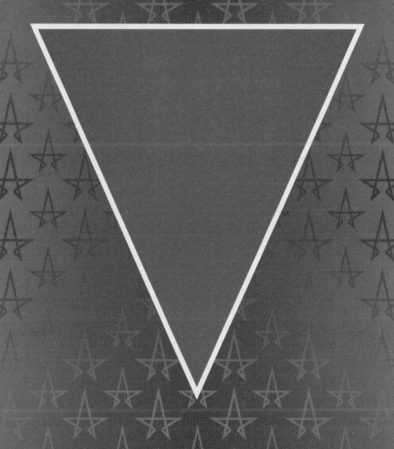

Cover art:
Chris Sprouse & Karl Story
Cover colors:
Jose Villarrubia

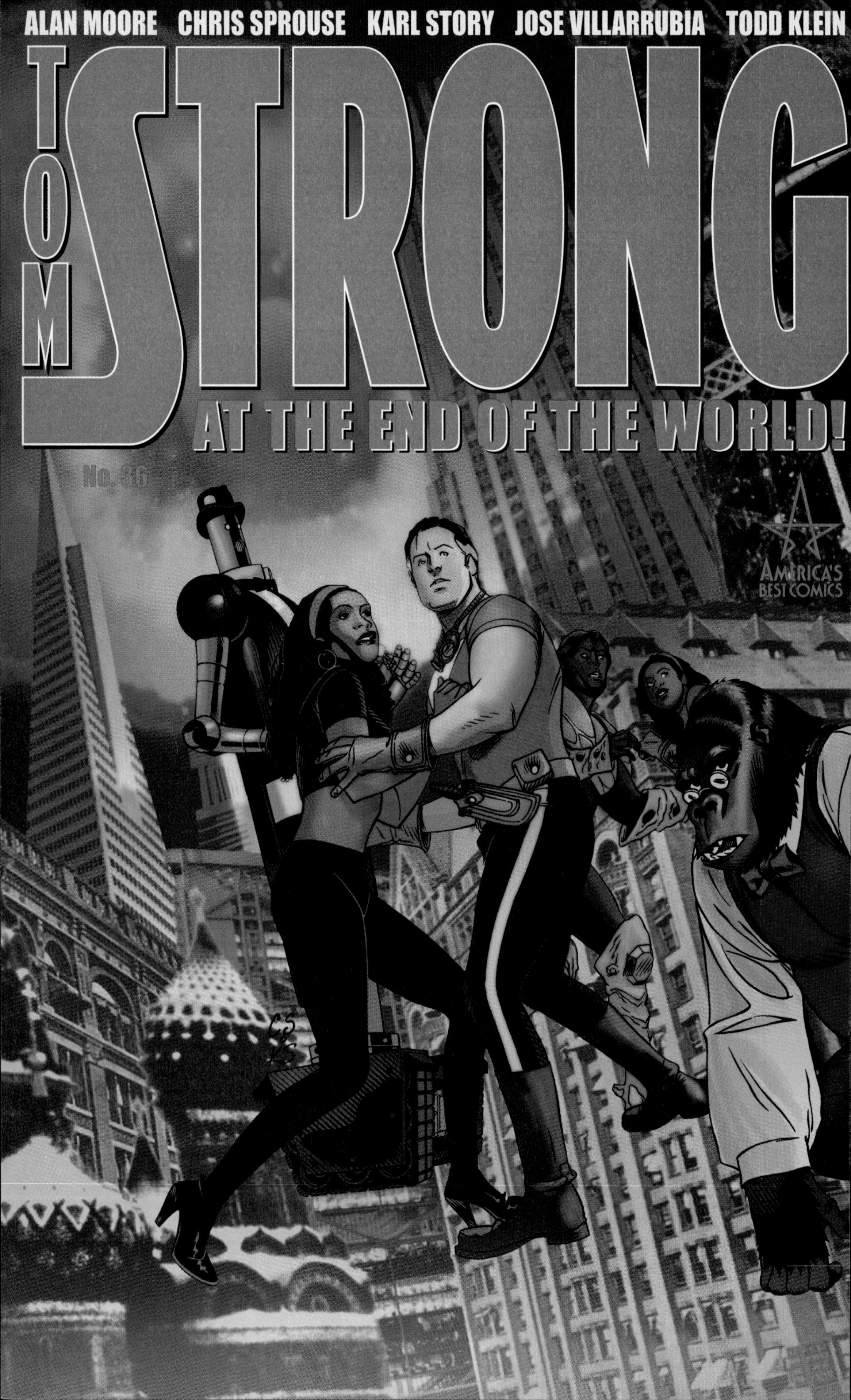
ALAN MOORE CHRIS SPROUSE KARL STORY JOSE VILLARRUBIA TODD KLEIN
TOM STRONG
AT THE END OF THE WORLD!
No. 36
AMERICA'S BEST COMICS

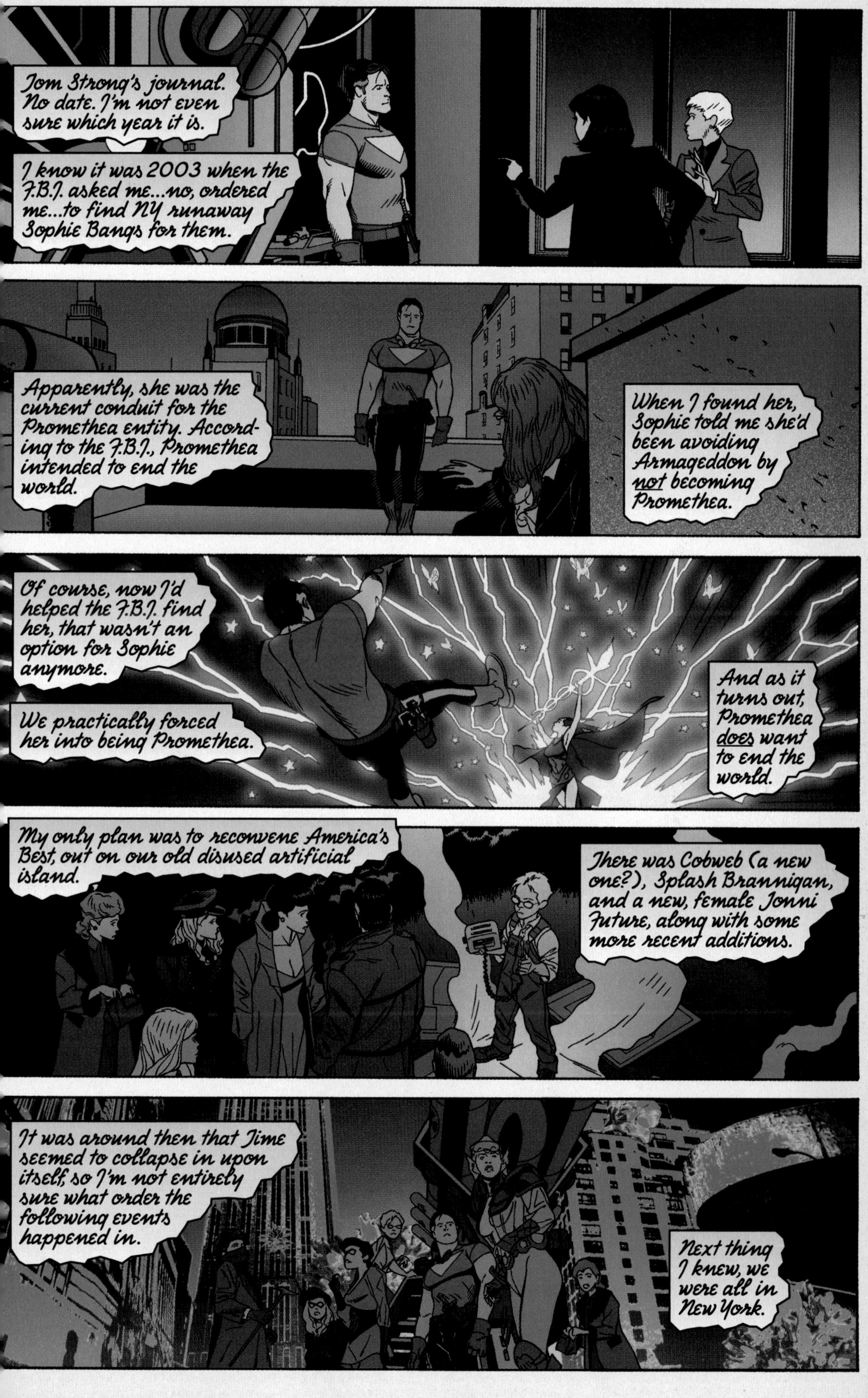
Tom Strong's journal. No date. I'm not even sure which year it is.
I know it was 2003 when the F.B.I. asked me...no, ordered me...to find NY runaway Sophie Bangs for them.
Apparently, she was the current conduit for the Promethea entity. According to the F.B.I., Promethea intended to end the world.
When I found her, Sophie told me she'd been avoiding Armageddon by not becoming Promethea.
Of course, now I'd helped the F.B.I. find her, that wasn't an option for Sophie anymore.
We practically forced her into being Promethea.
And as it turns out, Promethea does want to end the world.
My only plan was to reconvene America's Best, out on our old disused artificial island.
There was Cobweb (a new one?), Splash Brannigan, and a new, female Jonni Future, along with some more recent additions.
It was around then that Time seemed to collapse in upon itself, so I'm not entirely sure what order the following events happened in.
Next thing I knew, we were all in New York.

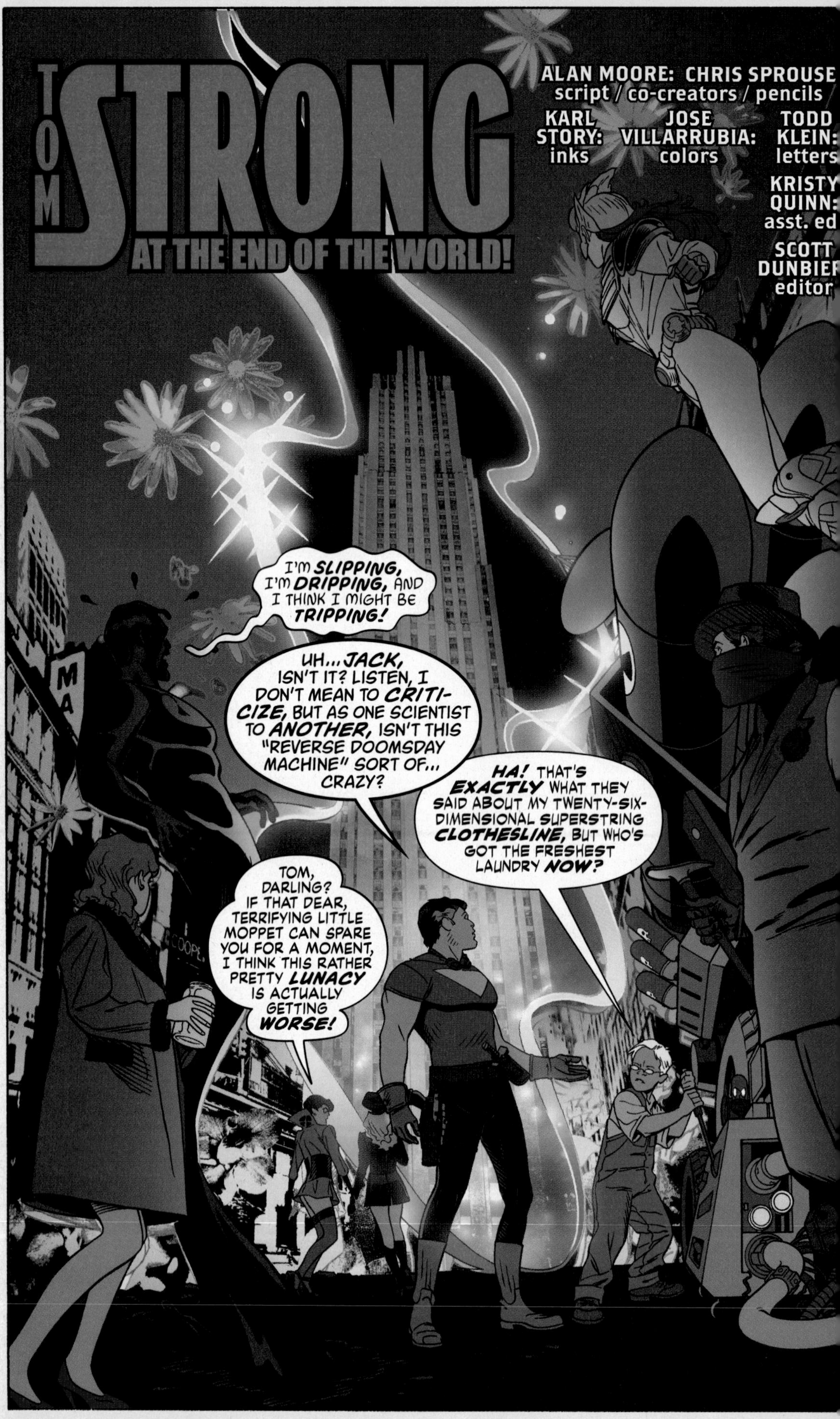
TOM STRONG
AT THE END OF THE WORLD!
ALAN MOORE: CHRIS SPROUSE
script / co-creators / pencils
KARL STORY: inks
JOSE VILLARRUBIA: colors
TODD KLEIN: letters
KRISTY QUINN: asst. ed
SCOTT DUNBIER editor
I'M SLIPPING, I'M DRIPPING, AND I THINK I MIGHT BE TRIPPING!
UH... JACK, ISN'T IT? LISTEN, I DON'T MEAN TO CRITICIZE, BUT AS ONE SCIENTIST TO ANOTHER, ISN'T THIS "REVERSE DOOMSDAY MACHINE" SORT OF... CRAZY?
HA! THAT'S EXACTLY WHAT THEY SAID ABOUT MY TWENTY-SIX-DIMENSIONAL SUPERSTRING CLOTHESLINE, BUT WHO'S GOT THE FRESHEST LAUNDRY NOW?
TOM, DARLING? IF THAT DEAR, TERRIFYING LITTLE MOPPET CAN SPARE YOU FOR A MOMENT, I THINK THIS RATHER PRETTY LUNACY IS ACTUALLY GETTING WORSE!

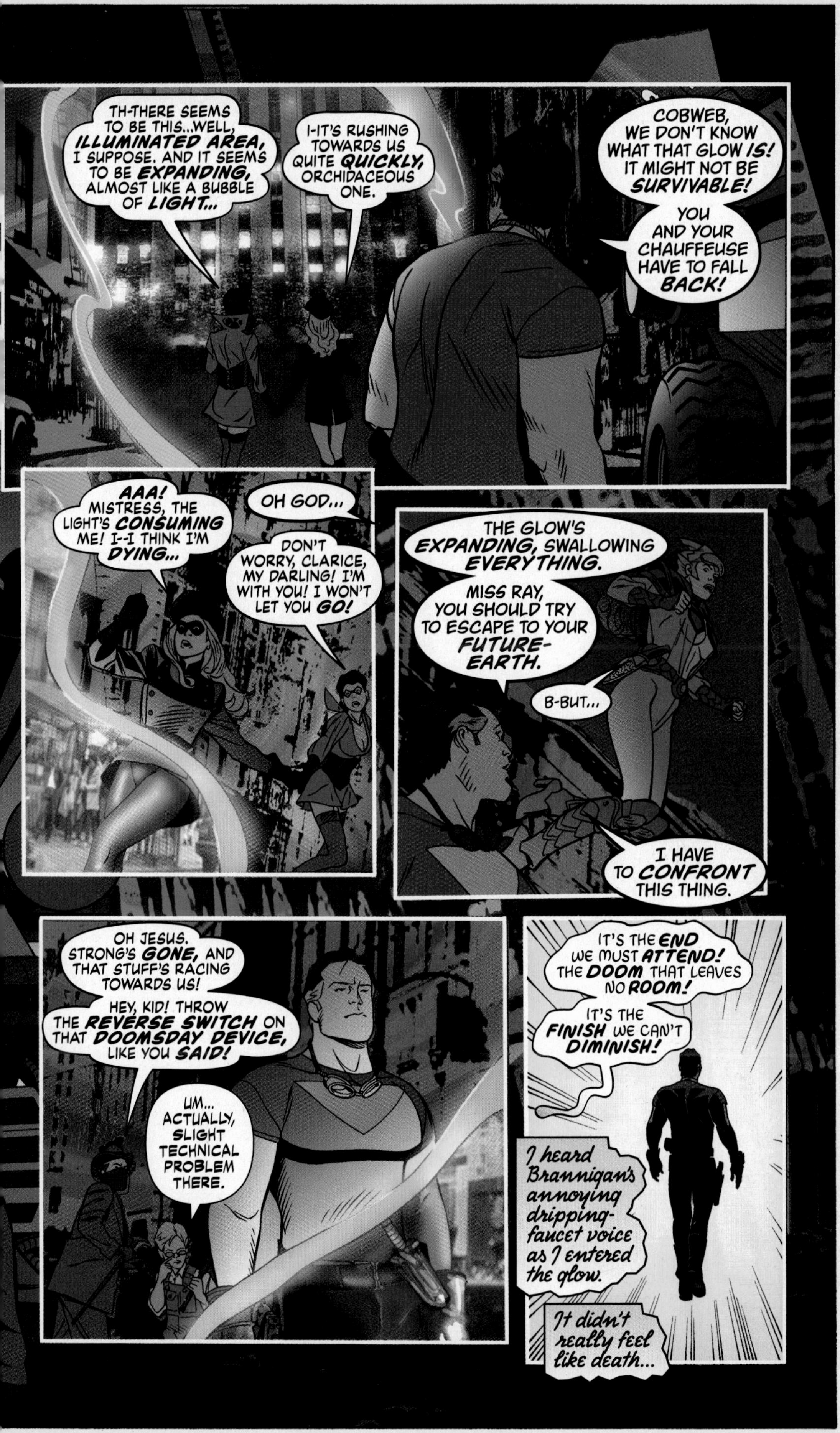
TH-THERE SEEMS TO BE THIS...WELL, ILLUMINATED AREA, I SUPPOSE. AND IT SEEMS TO BE EXPANDING, ALMOST LIKE A BUBBLE OF LIGHT...
I-IT'S RUSHING TOWARDS US QUITE QUICKLY, ORCHIDACEOUS ONE.
COBWEB, WE DON'T KNOW WHAT THAT GLOW IS! IT MIGHT NOT BE SURVIVABLE!
YOU AND YOUR CHAUFFEUSE HAVE TO FALL BACK!
AAA! MISTRESS, THE LIGHT'S CONSUMING ME! I--I THINK I'M DYING...
OH GOD...
DON'T WORRY, CLARICE, MY DARLING! I'M WITH YOU! I WON'T LET YOU GO!
THE GLOW'S EXPANDING, SWALLOWING EVERYTHING.
MISS RAY, YOU SHOULD TRY TO ESCAPE TO YOUR FUTURE-EARTH.
B-BUT...
I HAVE TO CONFRONT THIS THING.
OH JESUS. STRONG'S GONE, AND THAT STUFF'S RACING TOWARDS US!
HEY, KID! THROW THE REVERSE SWITCH ON THAT DOOMSDAY DEVICE, LIKE YOU SAID!
UM... ACTUALLY, SLIGHT TECHNICAL PROBLEM THERE.
IT'S THE END WE MUST ATTEND! THE DOOM THAT LEAVES NO ROOM!
IT'S THE FINISH WE CAN'T DIMINISH!
I heard Brannigan's annoying dripping-faucet voice as I entered the glow.
It didn't really feel like death...

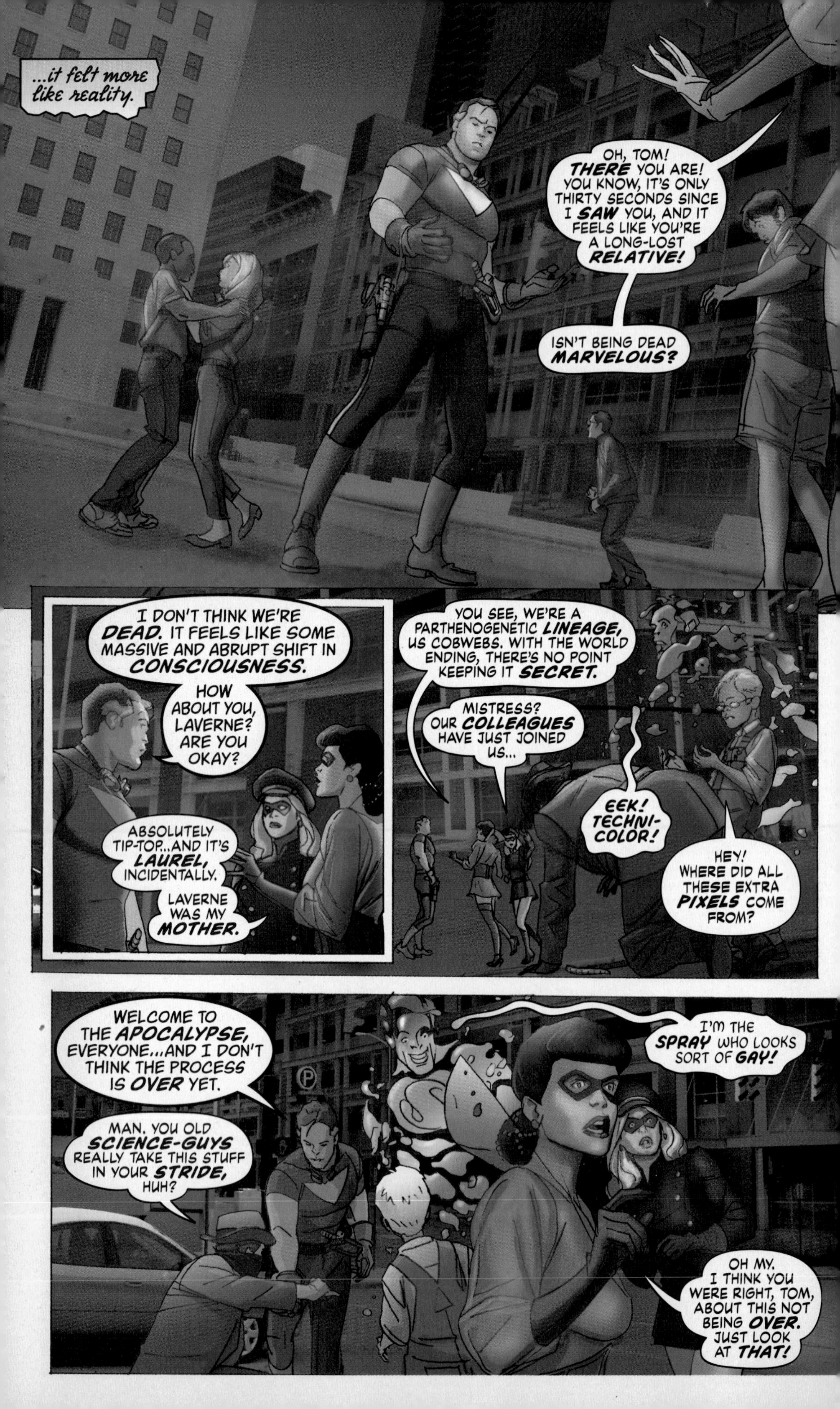
...it felt more like reality.
OH, TOM! THERE YOU ARE! YOU KNOW, IT'S ONLY THIRTY SECONDS SINCE I SAW YOU, AND IT FEELS LIKE YOU'RE A LONG-LOST RELATIVE!
ISN'T BEING DEAD MARVELOUS?
I DON'T THINK WE'RE DEAD. IT FEELS LIKE SOME MASSIVE AND ABRUPT SHIFT IN CONSCIOUSNESS.
HOW ABOUT YOU, LAVERNE? ARE YOU OKAY?
ABSOLUTELY TIP-TOP...AND IT'S LAUREL, INCIDENTALLY.
LAVERNE WAS MY MOTHER.
YOU SEE, WE'RE A PARTHENOGENETIC LINEAGE, US COBWEBS. WITH THE WORLD ENDING, THERE'S NO POINT KEEPING IT SECRET.
MISTRESS? OUR COLLEAGUES HAVE JUST JOINED US...
EEK! TECHNI-COLOR!
HEY! WHERE DID ALL THESE EXTRA PIXELS COME FROM?
WELCOME TO THE APOCALYPSE, EVERYONE...AND I DON'T THINK THE PROCESS IS OVER YET.
MAN. YOU OLD SCIENCE-GUYS REALLY TAKE THIS STUFF IN YOUR STRIDE, HUH?
I'M THE SPRAY WHO LOOKS SORT OF GAY!
OH MY. I THINK YOU WERE RIGHT, TOM, ABOUT THIS NOT BEING OVER. JUST LOOK AT THAT!

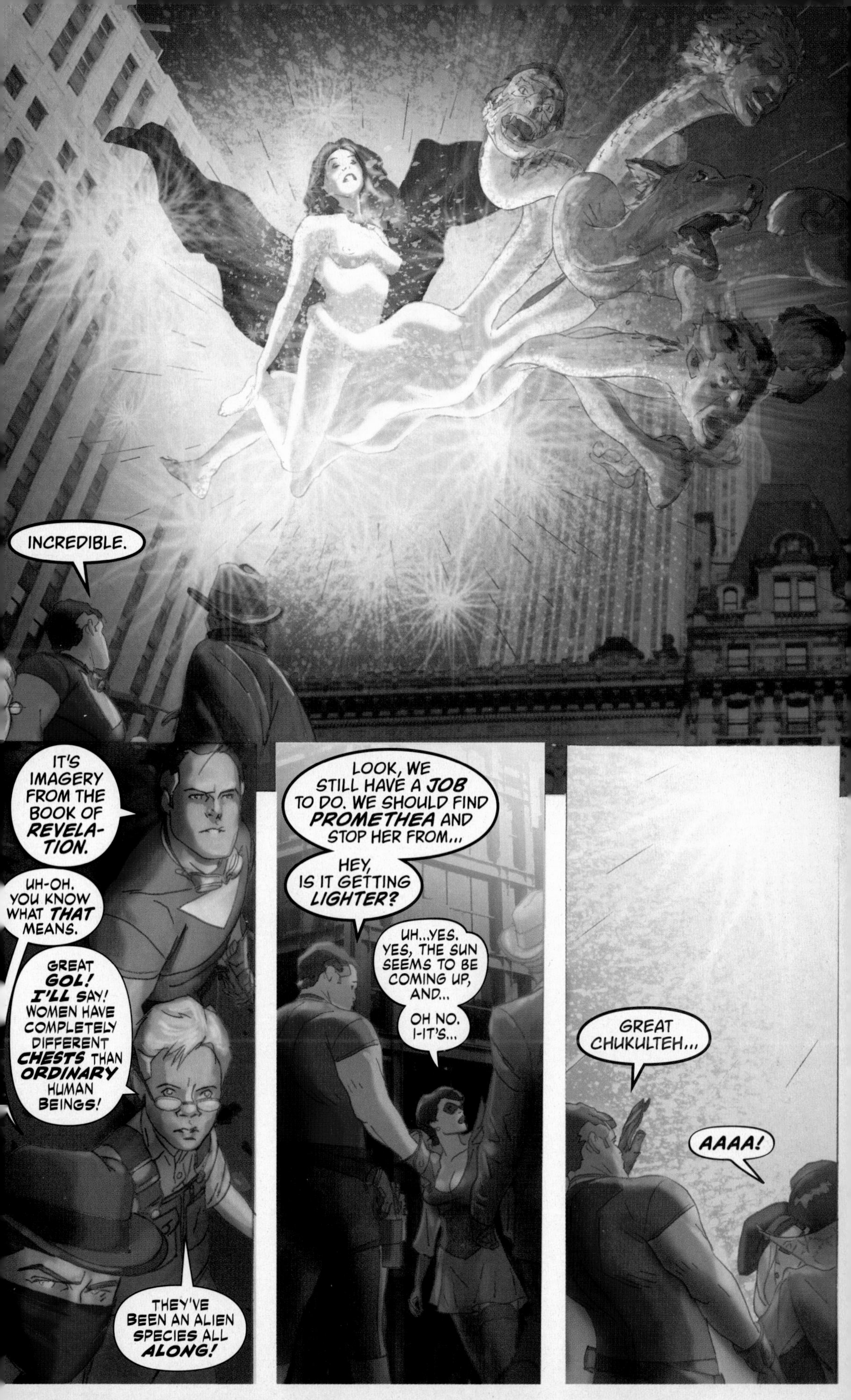
INCREDIBLE.
IT'S IMAGERY FROM THE BOOK OF REVELATION.
UH-OH. YOU KNOW WHAT THAT MEANS.
GREAT GOL! I'LL SAY! WOMEN HAVE COMPLETELY DIFFERENT CHESTS THAN ORDINARY HUMAN BEINGS!
THEY'VE BEEN AN ALIEN SPECIES ALL ALONG!
LOOK, WE STILL HAVE A JOB TO DO. WE SHOULD FIND PROMETHEA AND STOP HER FROM...
HEY, IS IT GETTING LIGHTER?
UH...YES. YES, THE SUN SEEMS TO BE COMING UP, AND...
OH NO. I-IT'S...
GREAT CHUKULTEH...
AAAA!

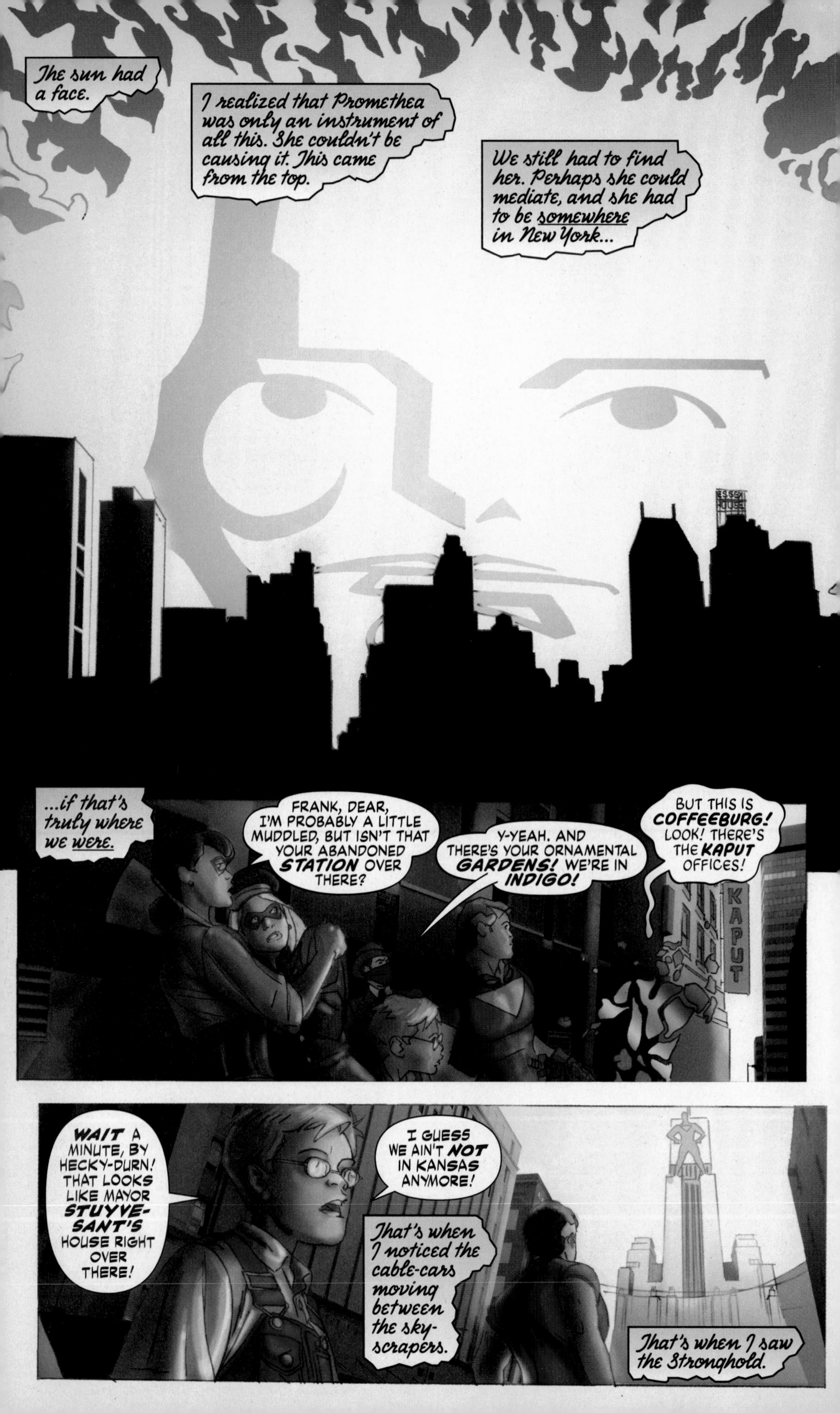
The sun had a face.
I realized that Promethea was only an instrument of all this. She couldn't be causing it. This came from the top.
We still had to find her. Perhaps she could mediate, and she had to be somewhere in New York...
...if that's truly where we were.
FRANK, DEAR, I'M PROBABLY A LITTLE MUDDLED, BUT ISN'T THAT YOUR ABANDONED STATION OVER THERE?
Y-YEAH. AND THERE'S YOUR ORNAMENTAL GARDENS! WE'RE IN INDIGO!
BUT THIS IS COFFEEBURG! LOOK! THERE'S THE KAPUT OFFICES!
KAPUT
WAIT A MINUTE, BY HECKY-DURN! THAT LOOKS LIKE MAYOR STUYVE-SANT'S HOUSE RIGHT OVER THERE!
I GUESS WE AIN'T NOT IN KANSAS ANYMORE!
That's when I noticed the cable-cars moving between the sky-scrapers.
That's when I saw the Stronghold.

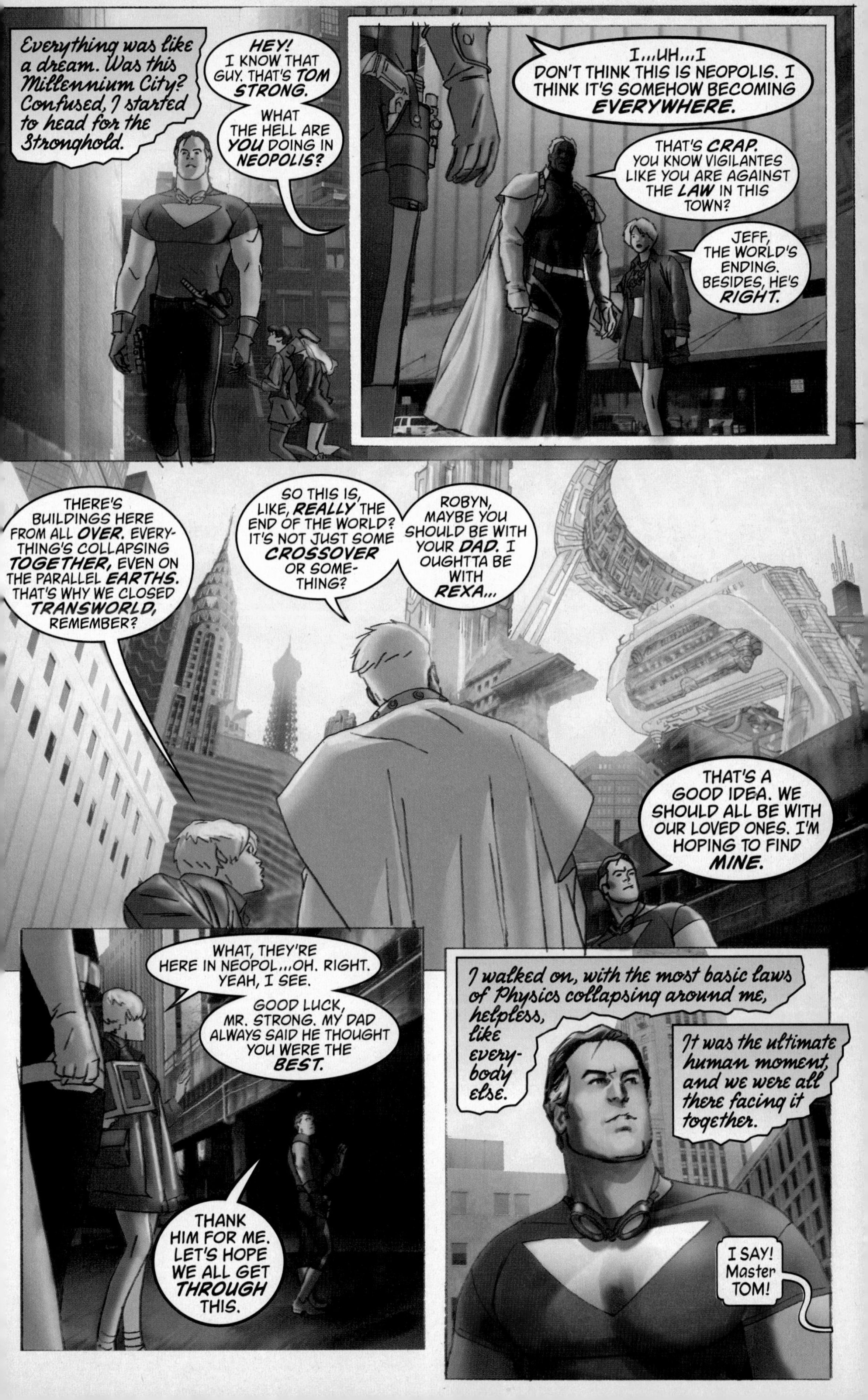
Everything was like a dream. Was this Millennium City? Confused, I started to head for the Stronghold.
HEY! I KNOW THAT GUY. THAT'S TOM STRONG.
WHAT THE HELL ARE YOU DOING IN NEOPOLIS?
I...UH...I DON'T THINK THIS IS NEOPOLIS. I THINK IT'S SOMEHOW BECOMING EVERYWHERE.
THAT'S CRAP. YOU KNOW VIGILANTES LIKE YOU ARE AGAINST THE LAW IN THIS TOWN?
JEFF, THE WORLD'S ENDING. BESIDES, HE'S RIGHT.
THERE'S BUILDINGS HERE FROM ALL OVER. EVERYTHING'S COLLAPSING TOGETHER, EVEN ON THE PARALLEL EARTHS. THAT'S WHY WE CLOSED TRANSWORLD, REMEMBER?
SO THIS IS, LIKE, REALLY THE END OF THE WORLD? IT'S NOT JUST SOME CROSSOVER OR SOMETHING?
ROBYN, MAYBE YOU SHOULD BE WITH YOUR DAD. I OUGHTTA BE WITH REXA...
THAT'S A GOOD IDEA. WE SHOULD ALL BE WITH OUR LOVED ONES. I'M HOPING TO FIND MINE.
WHAT, THEY'RE HERE IN NEOPOL...OH. RIGHT. YEAH, I SEE.
GOOD LUCK, MR. STRONG. MY DAD ALWAYS SAID HE THOUGHT YOU WERE THE BEST.
THANK HIM FOR ME. LET'S HOPE WE ALL GET THROUGH THIS.
I walked on, with the most basic laws of Physics collapsing around me, helpless, like everybody else.
It was the ultimate human moment, and we were all there facing it together.
I SAY! Master TOM!

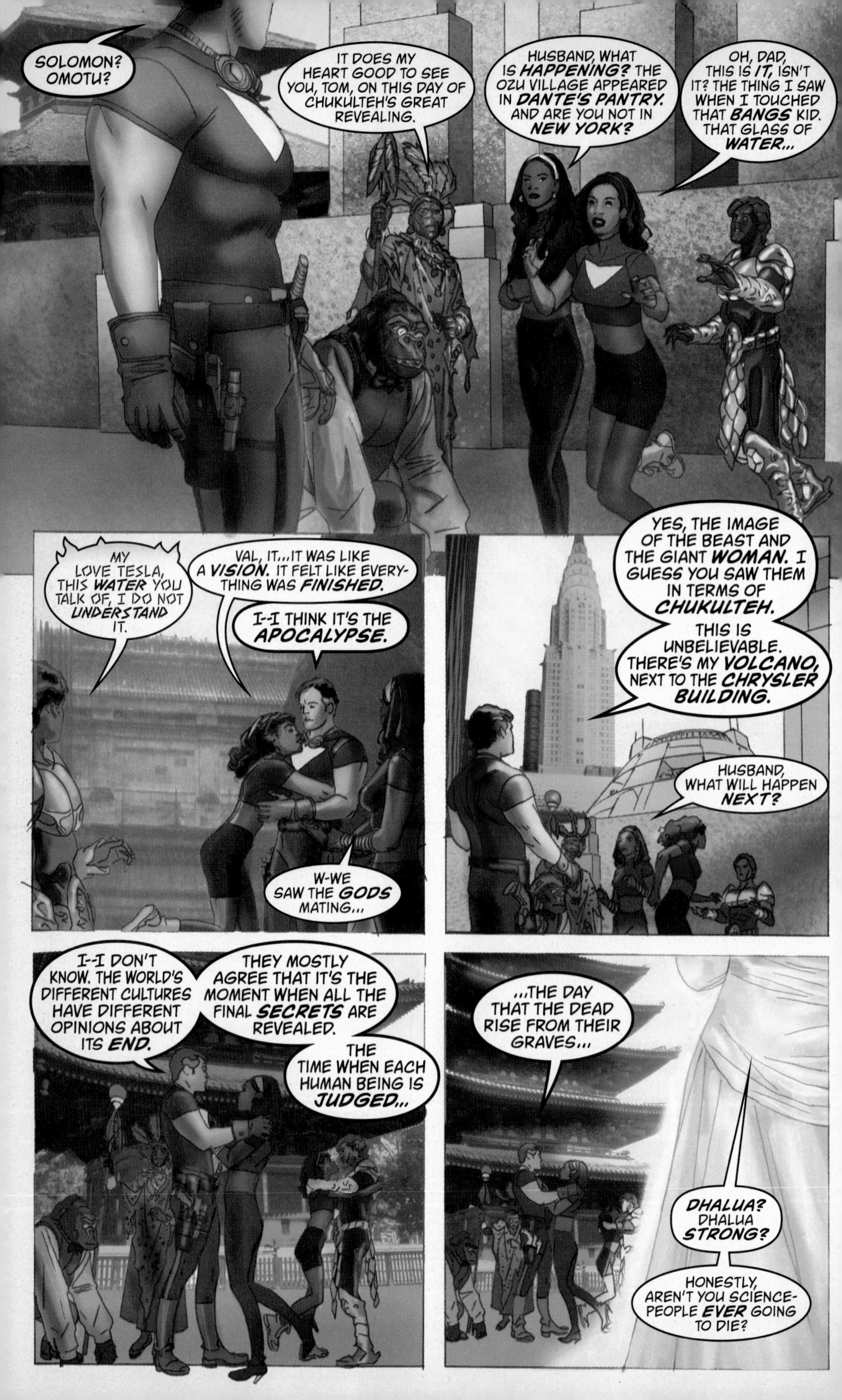
SOLOMON? OMOTU?
IT DOES MY HEART GOOD TO SEE YOU, TOM, ON THIS DAY OF CHUKULTEH'S GREAT REVEALING.
HUSBAND, WHAT IS HAPPENING? THE OZU VILLAGE APPEARED IN DANTE'S PANTRY. AND ARE YOU NOT IN NEW YORK?
OH, DAD, THIS IS IT, ISN'T IT? THE THING I SAW WHEN I TOUCHED THAT BANGS KID. THAT GLASS OF WATER...
MY LOVE TESLA, THIS WATER YOU TALK OF, I DO NOT UNDERSTAND IT.
VAL, IT...IT WAS LIKE A VISION. IT FELT LIKE EVERYTHING WAS FINISHED.
I-I THINK IT'S THE APOCALYPSE.
W-WE SAW THE GODS MATING...
YES, THE IMAGE OF THE BEAST AND THE GIANT WOMAN. I GUESS YOU SAW THEM IN TERMS OF CHUKULTEH.
THIS IS UNBELIEVABLE. THERE'S MY VOLCANO, NEXT TO THE CHRYSLER BUILDING.
HUSBAND, WHAT WILL HAPPEN NEXT?
I-I DON'T KNOW. THE WORLD'S DIFFERENT CULTURES HAVE DIFFERENT OPINIONS ABOUT ITS END.
THEY MOSTLY AGREE THAT IT'S THE MOMENT WHEN ALL THE FINAL SECRETS ARE REVEALED.
THE TIME WHEN EACH HUMAN BEING IS JUDGED...
...THE DAY THAT THE DEAD RISE FROM THEIR GRAVES...
DHALUA? DHALUA STRONG?
HONESTLY, AREN'T YOU SCIENCE-PEOPLE EVER GOING TO DIE?

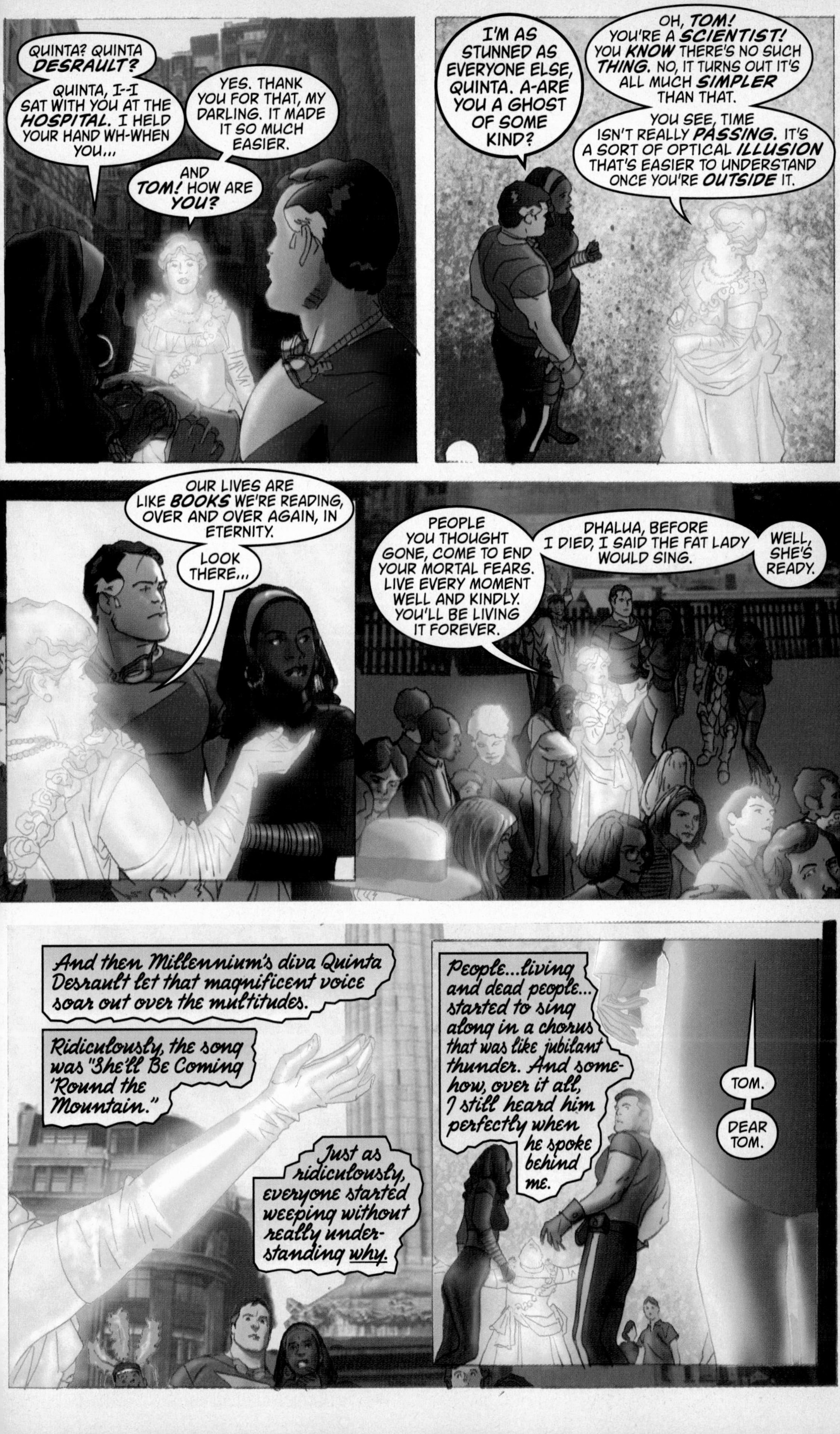

QUINTA? QUINTA DESRAULT?
QUINTA, I-I SAT WITH YOU AT THE HOSPITAL. I HELD YOUR HAND WH-WHEN YOU...
YES. THANK YOU FOR THAT, MY DARLING. IT MADE IT SO MUCH EASIER.
AND TOM! HOW ARE YOU?
I'M AS STUNNED AS EVERYONE ELSE, QUINTA. A-ARE YOU A GHOST OF SOME KIND?
OH, TOM! YOU'RE A SCIENTIST! YOU KNOW THERE'S NO SUCH THING. NO, IT TURNS OUT IT'S ALL MUCH SIMPLER THAN THAT.
YOU SEE, TIME ISN'T REALLY PASSING. IT'S A SORT OF OPTICAL ILLUSION THAT'S EASIER TO UNDERSTAND ONCE YOU'RE OUTSIDE IT.
OUR LIVES ARE LIKE BOOKS WE'RE READING, OVER AND OVER AGAIN, IN ETERNITY.
LOOK THERE...
PEOPLE YOU THOUGHT GONE, COME TO END YOUR MORTAL FEARS. LIVE EVERY MOMENT WELL AND KINDLY. YOU'LL BE LIVING IT FOREVER.
DHALUA, BEFORE I DIED, I SAID THE FAT LADY WOULD SING.
WELL, SHE'S READY.
And then Millennium's diva Quinta Desrault let that magnificent voice soar out over the multitudes.
Ridiculously, the song was "She'll Be Coming 'Round the Mountain."
Just as ridiculously, everyone started weeping without really understanding why.
People...living and dead people... started to sing along in a chorus that was like jubilant thunder. And somehow, over it all, I still heard him perfectly when he spoke behind me.
TOM.
DEAR TOM.

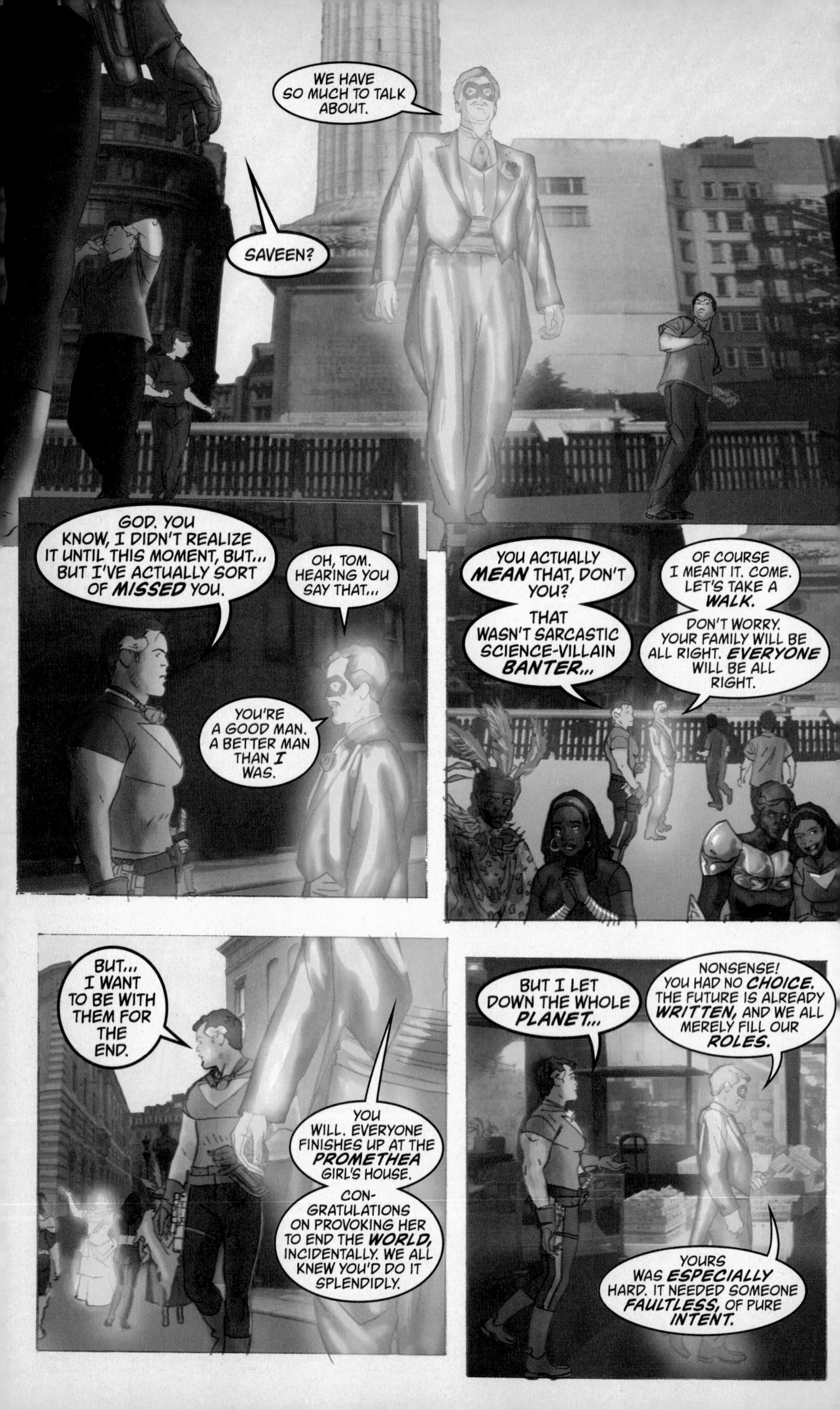

WE HAVE SO MUCH TO TALK ABOUT.
SAVEEN?
GOD. YOU KNOW, I DIDN'T REALIZE IT UNTIL THIS MOMENT, BUT... BUT I'VE ACTUALLY SORT OF MISSED YOU.
OH, TOM. HEARING YOU SAY THAT...
YOU'RE A GOOD MAN. A BETTER MAN THAN I WAS.
YOU ACTUALLY MEAN THAT, DON'T YOU?
THAT WASN'T SARCASTIC SCIENCE-VILLAIN BANTER...
OF COURSE I MEANT IT. COME. LET'S TAKE A WALK.
DON'T WORRY. YOUR FAMILY WILL BE ALL RIGHT. EVERYONE WILL BE ALL RIGHT.
BUT... I WANT TO BE WITH THEM FOR THE END.
YOU WILL. EVERYONE FINISHES UP AT THE PROMETHEA GIRL'S HOUSE.
CON-GRATULATIONS ON PROVOKING HER TO END THE WORLD, INCIDENTALLY. WE ALL KNEW YOU'D DO IT SPLENDIDLY.
BUT I LET DOWN THE WHOLE PLANET...
NONSENSE! YOU HAD NO CHOICE. THE FUTURE IS ALREADY WRITTEN, AND WE ALL MERELY FILL OUR ROLES.
YOURS WAS ESPECIALLY HARD. IT NEEDED SOMEONE FAULTLESS, OF PURE INTENT.

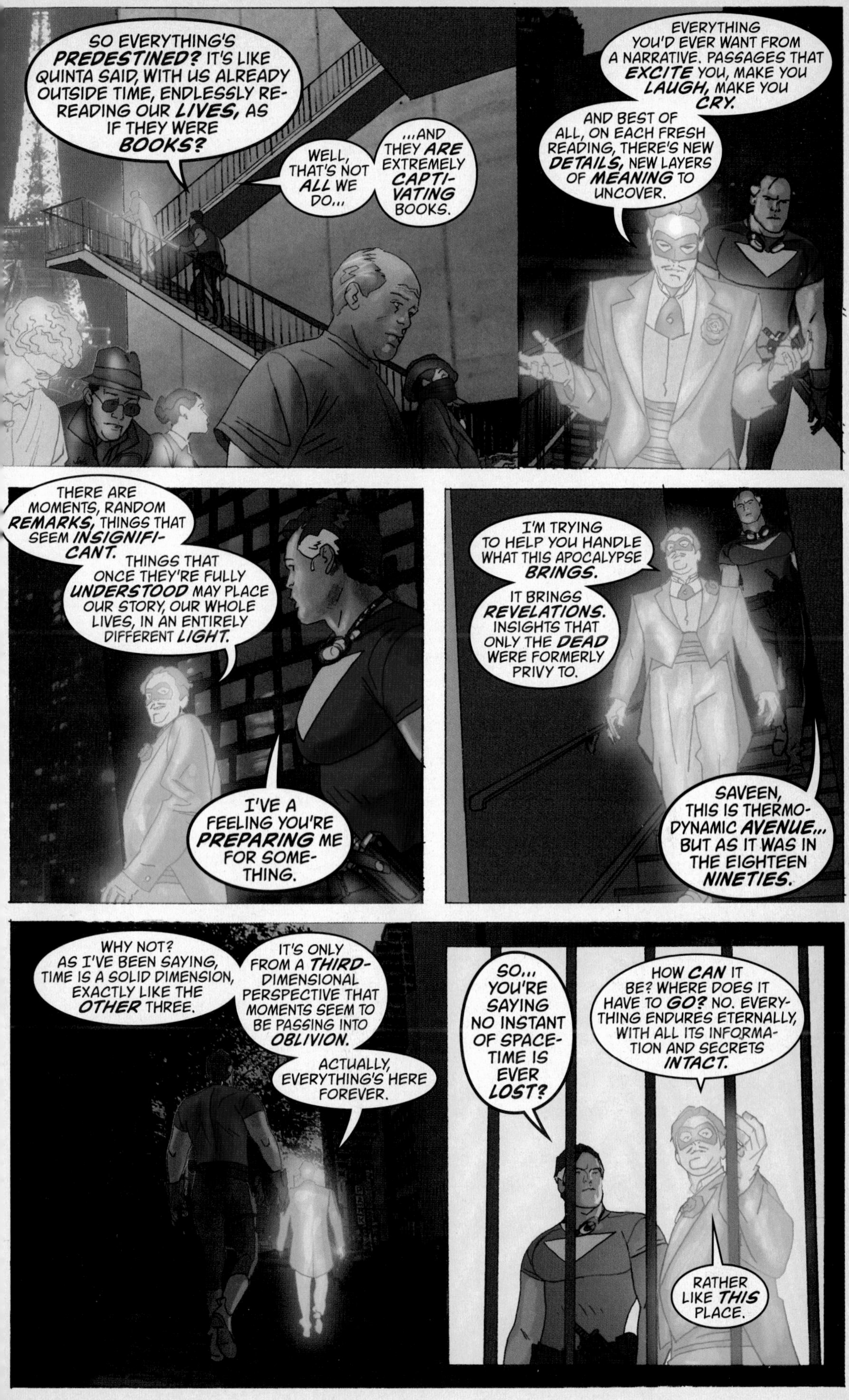

SO EVERYTHING'S PREDESTINED? IT'S LIKE QUINTA SAID, WITH US ALREADY OUTSIDE TIME, ENDLESSLY RE-READING OUR LIVES, AS IF THEY WERE BOOKS?
WELL, THAT'S NOT ALL WE DO...
...AND THEY ARE EXTREMELY CAPTIVATING BOOKS.
EVERYTHING YOU'D EVER WANT FROM A NARRATIVE. PASSAGES THAT EXCITE YOU, MAKE YOU LAUGH, MAKE YOU CRY.
AND BEST OF ALL, ON EACH FRESH READING, THERE'S NEW DETAILS, NEW LAYERS OF MEANING TO UNCOVER.
THERE ARE MOMENTS, RANDOM REMARKS, THINGS THAT SEEM INSIGNIFICANT.
THINGS THAT ONCE THEY'RE FULLY UNDERSTOOD MAY PLACE OUR STORY, OUR WHOLE LIVES, IN AN ENTIRELY DIFFERENT LIGHT.
I'VE A FEELING YOU'RE PREPARING ME FOR SOMETHING.
I'M TRYING TO HELP YOU HANDLE WHAT THIS APOCALYPSE BRINGS.
IT BRINGS REVELATIONS. INSIGHTS THAT ONLY THE DEAD WERE FORMERLY PRIVY TO.
SAVEEN, THIS IS THERMODYNAMIC AVENUE... BUT AS IT WAS IN THE EIGHTEEN NINETIES.
WHY NOT? AS I'VE BEEN SAYING, TIME IS A SOLID DIMENSION, EXACTLY LIKE THE OTHER THREE.
IT'S ONLY FROM A THIRD-DIMENSIONAL PERSPECTIVE THAT MOMENTS SEEM TO BE PASSING INTO OBLIVION.
ACTUALLY, EVERYTHING'S HERE FOREVER.
SO... YOU'RE SAYING NO INSTANT OF SPACE-TIME IS EVER LOST?
HOW CAN IT BE? WHERE DOES IT HAVE TO GO? NO. EVERYTHING ENDURES ETERNALLY, WITH ALL ITS INFORMATION AND SECRETS INTACT.
RATHER LIKE THIS PLACE.

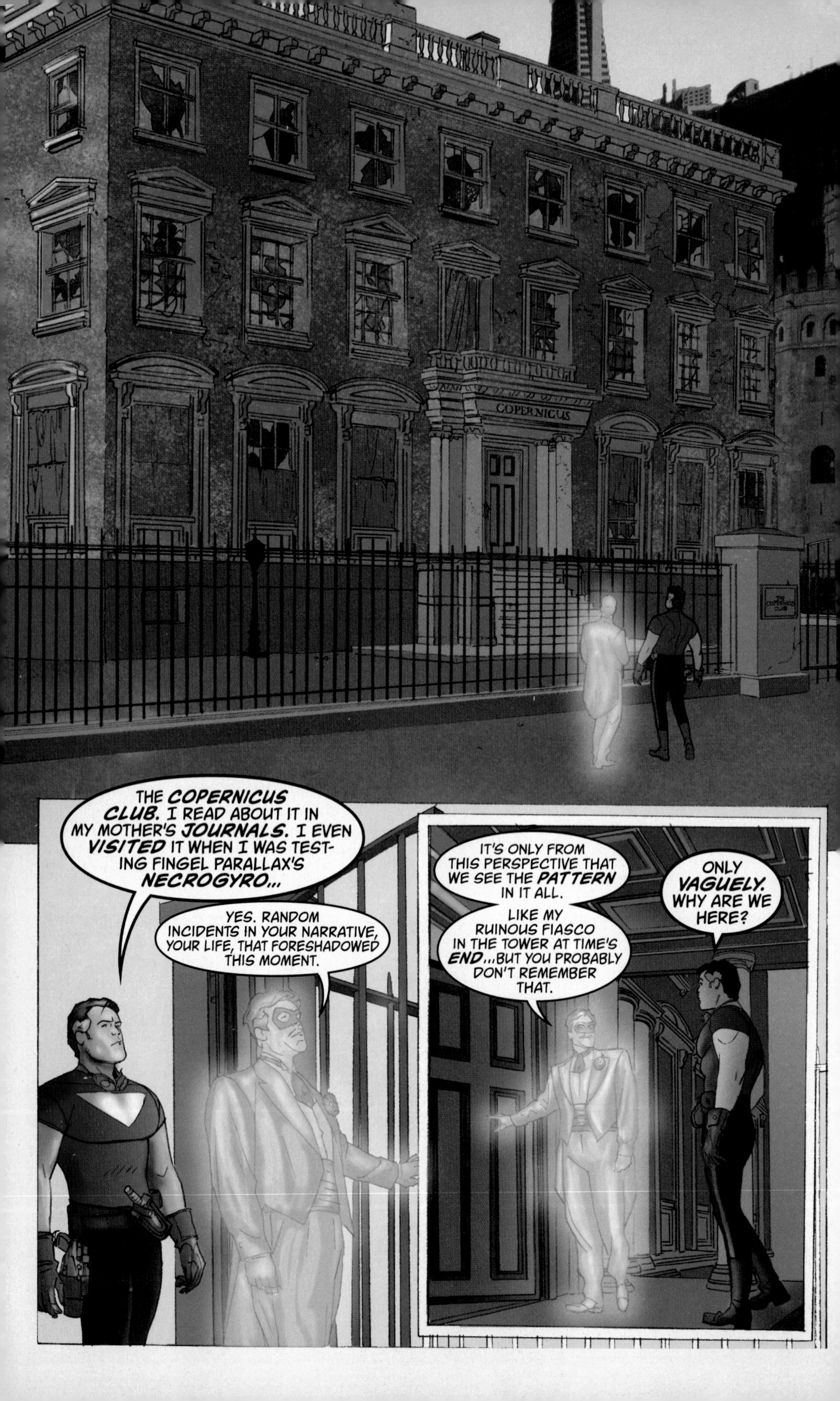
COPERNICUS
THE COPERNICUS CLUB
THE COPERNICUS CLUB. I READ ABOUT IT IN MY MOTHER'S JOURNALS. I EVEN VISITED IT WHEN I WAS TESTING FINGEL PARALLAX'S NECROGYRO...
YES. RANDOM INCIDENTS IN YOUR NARRATIVE, YOUR LIFE, THAT FORESHADOWED THIS MOMENT.
IT'S ONLY FROM THIS PERSPECTIVE THAT WE SEE THE PATTERN IN IT ALL.
LIKE MY RUINOUS FIASCO IN THE TOWER AT TIME'S END...BUT YOU PROBABLY DON'T REMEMBER THAT.
ONLY VAGUELY. WHY ARE WE HERE?

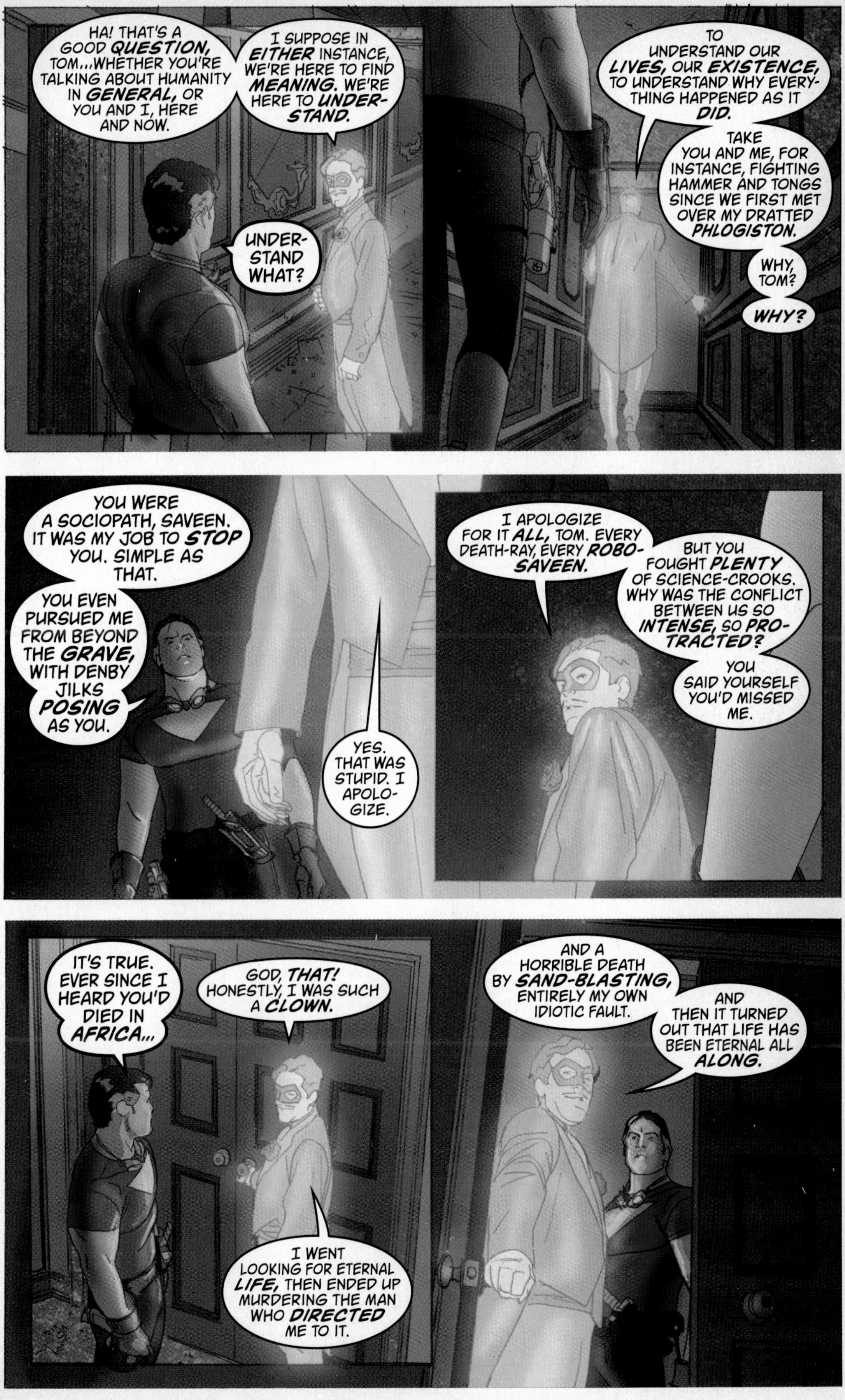
HA! THAT'S A GOOD QUESTION, TOM...WHETHER YOU'RE TALKING ABOUT HUMANITY IN GENERAL, OR YOU AND I, HERE AND NOW.
I SUPPOSE IN EITHER INSTANCE, WE'RE HERE TO FIND MEANING. WE'RE HERE TO UNDERSTAND.
UNDERSTAND WHAT?
TO UNDERSTAND OUR LIVES, OUR EXISTENCE, TO UNDERSTAND WHY EVERYTHING HAPPENED AS IT DID.
TAKE YOU AND ME, FOR INSTANCE, FIGHTING HAMMER AND TONGS SINCE WE FIRST MET OVER MY DRATTED PHLOGISTON.
WHY, TOM?
WHY?
YOU WERE A SOCIOPATH, SAVEEN. IT WAS MY JOB TO STOP YOU. SIMPLE AS THAT.
YOU EVEN PURSUED ME FROM BEYOND THE GRAVE, WITH DENBY JILKS POSING AS YOU.
YES. THAT WAS STUPID. I APOLOGIZE.
I APOLOGIZE FOR IT ALL, TOM. EVERY DEATH-RAY, EVERY ROBO-SAVEEN.
BUT YOU FOUGHT PLENTY OF SCIENCE-CROOKS. WHY WAS THE CONFLICT BETWEEN US SO INTENSE, SO PROTRACTED?
YOU SAID YOURSELF YOU'D MISSED ME.
IT'S TRUE. EVER SINCE I HEARD YOU'D DIED IN AFRICA...
GOD, THAT! HONESTLY, I WAS SUCH A CLOWN.
I WENT LOOKING FOR ETERNAL LIFE, THEN ENDED UP MURDERING THE MAN WHO DIRECTED ME TO IT.
AND A HORRIBLE DEATH BY SAND-BLASTING, ENTIRELY MY OWN IDIOTIC FAULT.
AND THEN IT TURNED OUT THAT LIFE HAS BEEN ETERNAL ALL ALONG.

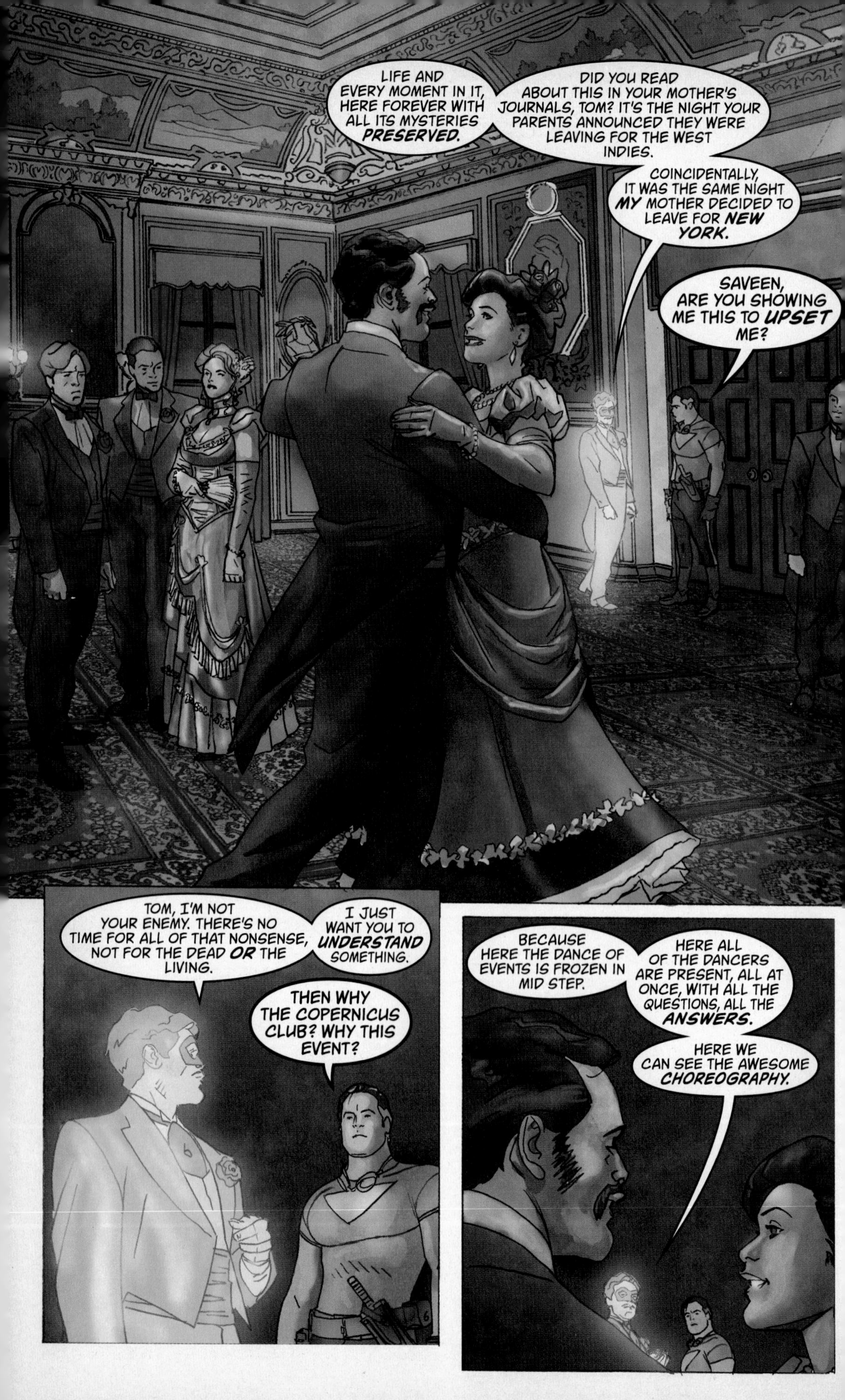

LIFE AND EVERY MOMENT IN IT, HERE FOREVER WITH ALL ITS MYSTERIES PRESERVED.
DID YOU READ ABOUT THIS IN YOUR MOTHER'S JOURNALS, TOM? IT'S THE NIGHT YOUR PARENTS ANNOUNCED THEY WERE LEAVING FOR THE WEST INDIES.
COINCIDENTALLY, IT WAS THE SAME NIGHT MY MOTHER DECIDED TO LEAVE FOR NEW YORK.
SAVEEN, ARE YOU SHOWING ME THIS TO UPSET ME?
TOM, I'M NOT YOUR ENEMY. THERE'S NO TIME FOR ALL OF THAT NONSENSE, NOT FOR THE DEAD OR THE LIVING.
I JUST WANT YOU TO UNDERSTAND SOMETHING.
THEN WHY THE COPERNICUS CLUB? WHY THIS EVENT?
BECAUSE HERE THE DANCE OF EVENTS IS FROZEN IN MID STEP.
HERE ALL OF THE DANCERS ARE PRESENT, ALL AT ONCE, WITH ALL THE QUESTIONS, ALL THE ANSWERS.
HERE WE CAN SEE THE AWESOME CHOREOGRAPHY.

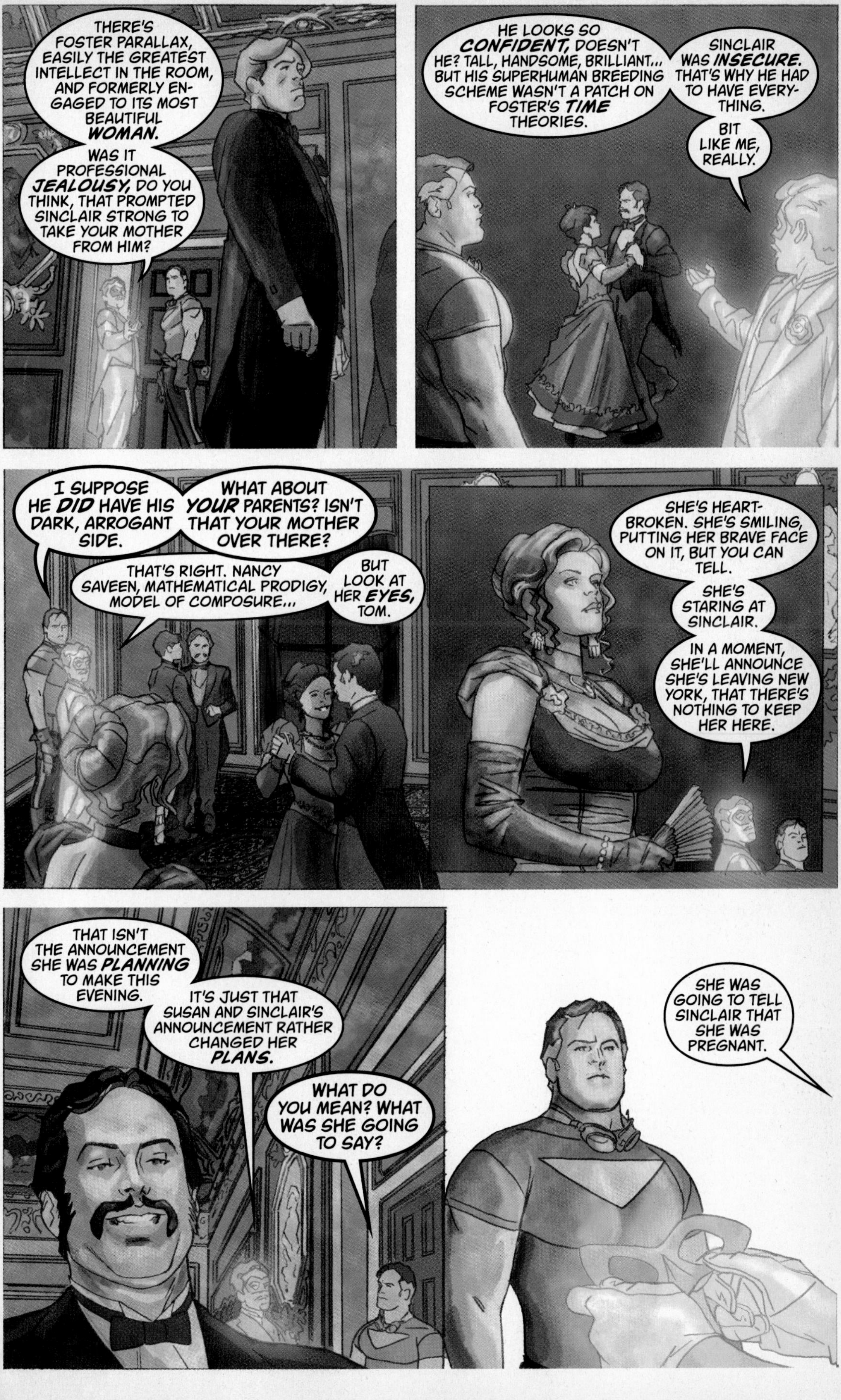
THERE'S FOSTER PARALLAX, EASILY THE GREATEST INTELLECT IN THE ROOM, AND FORMERLY ENGAGED TO ITS MOST BEAUTIFUL WOMAN.
WAS IT PROFESSIONAL JEALOUSY, DO YOU THINK, THAT PROMPTED SINCLAIR STRONG TO TAKE YOUR MOTHER FROM HIM?
HE LOOKS SO CONFIDENT, DOESN'T HE? TALL, HANDSOME, BRILLIANT... BUT HIS SUPERHUMAN BREEDING SCHEME WASN'T A PATCH ON FOSTER'S TIME THEORIES.
SINCLAIR WAS INSECURE. THAT'S WHY HE HAD TO HAVE EVERYTHING.
BIT LIKE ME, REALLY.
I SUPPOSE HE DID HAVE HIS DARK, ARROGANT SIDE.
WHAT ABOUT YOUR PARENTS? ISN'T THAT YOUR MOTHER OVER THERE?
THAT'S RIGHT. NANCY SAVEEN, MATHEMATICAL PRODIGY, MODEL OF COMPOSURE...
BUT LOOK AT HER EYES, TOM.
SHE'S HEARTBROKEN. SHE'S SMILING, PUTTING HER BRAVE FACE ON IT, BUT YOU CAN TELL.
SHE'S STARING AT SINCLAIR.
IN A MOMENT, SHE'LL ANNOUNCE SHE'S LEAVING NEW YORK, THAT THERE'S NOTHING TO KEEP HER HERE.
THAT ISN'T THE ANNOUNCEMENT SHE WAS PLANNING TO MAKE THIS EVENING.
IT'S JUST THAT SUSAN AND SINCLAIR'S ANNOUNCEMENT RATHER CHANGED HER PLANS.
WHAT DO YOU MEAN? WHAT WAS SHE GOING TO SAY?
SHE WAS GOING TO TELL SINCLAIR THAT SHE WAS PREGNANT.

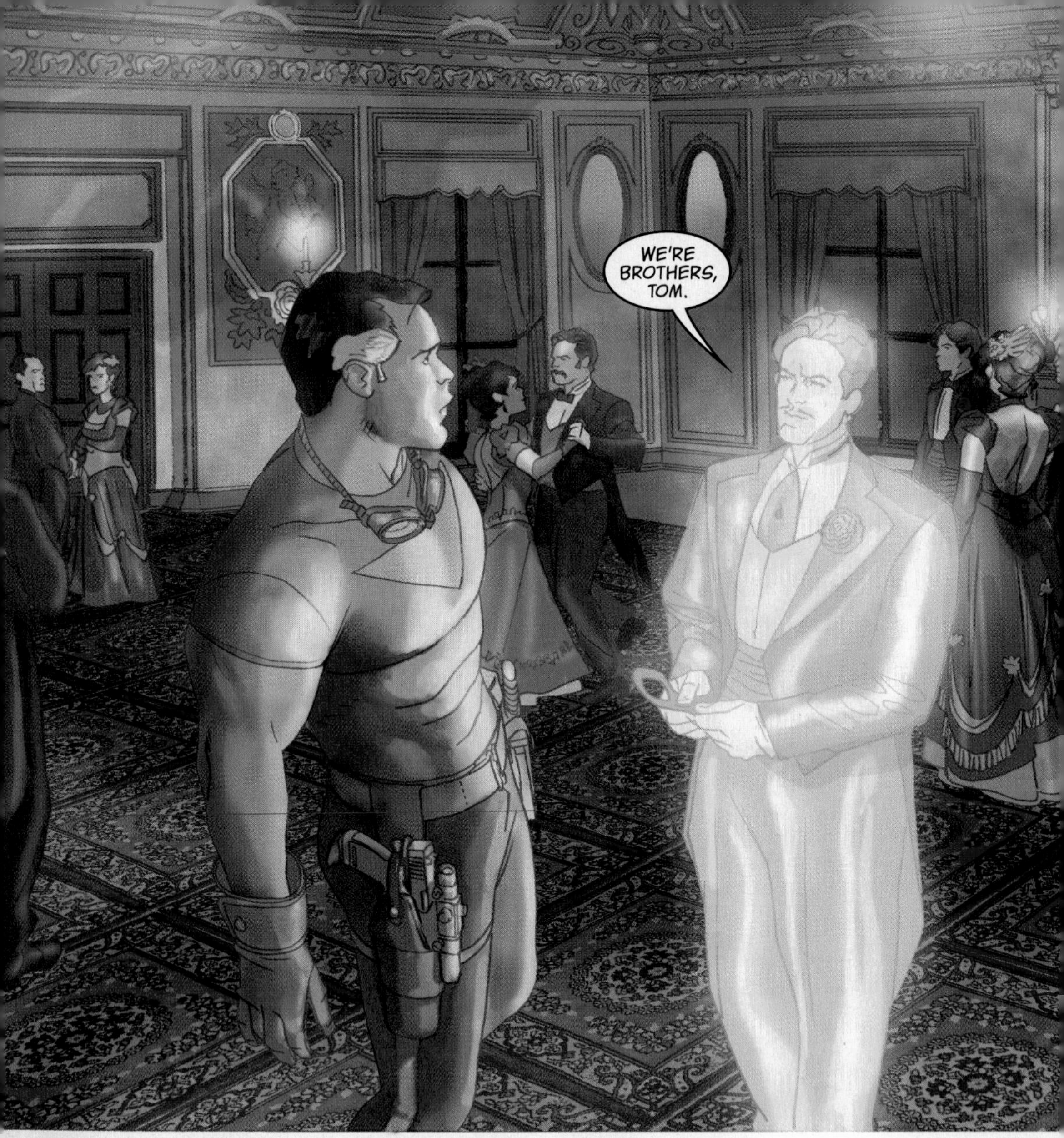
WE'RE BROTHERS, TOM.

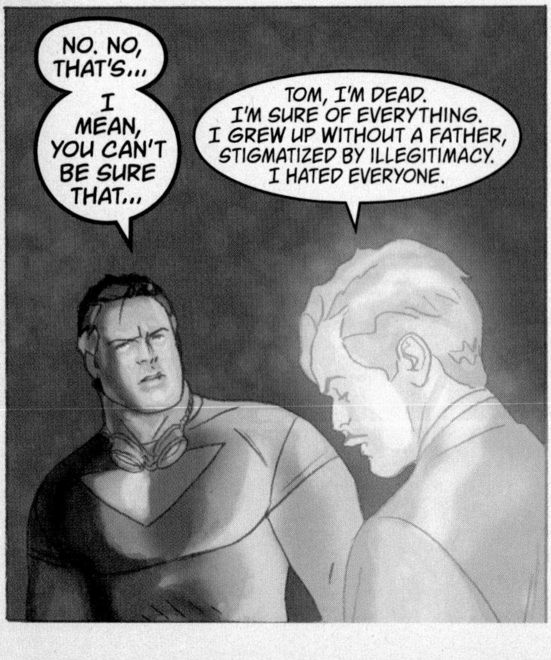
NO. NO, THAT'S...
I MEAN, YOU CAN'T BE SURE THAT...
TOM, I'M DEAD. I'M SURE OF EVERYTHING. I GREW UP WITHOUT A FATHER, STIGMATIZED BY ILLEGITIMACY. I HATED EVERYONE.

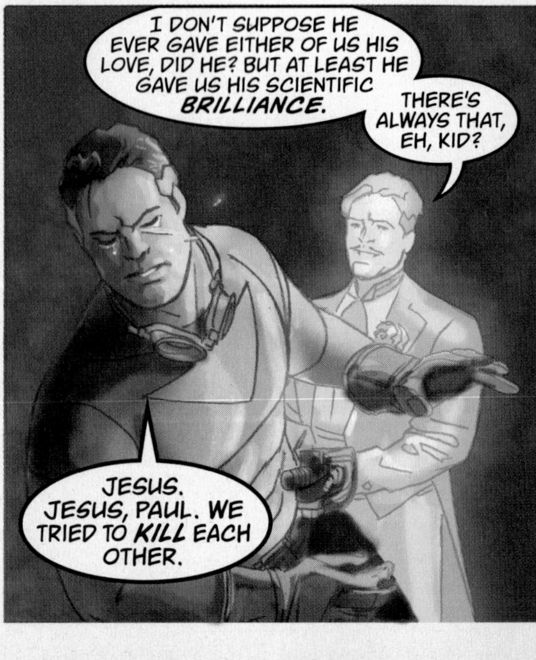
I DON'T SUPPOSE HE EVER GAVE EITHER OF US HIS LOVE, DID HE? BUT AT LEAST HE GAVE US HIS SCIENTIFIC ***BRILLIANCE.***
THERE'S ALWAYS THAT, EH, KID?
JESUS. JESUS, PAUL. WE TRIED TO ***KILL*** EACH OTHER.

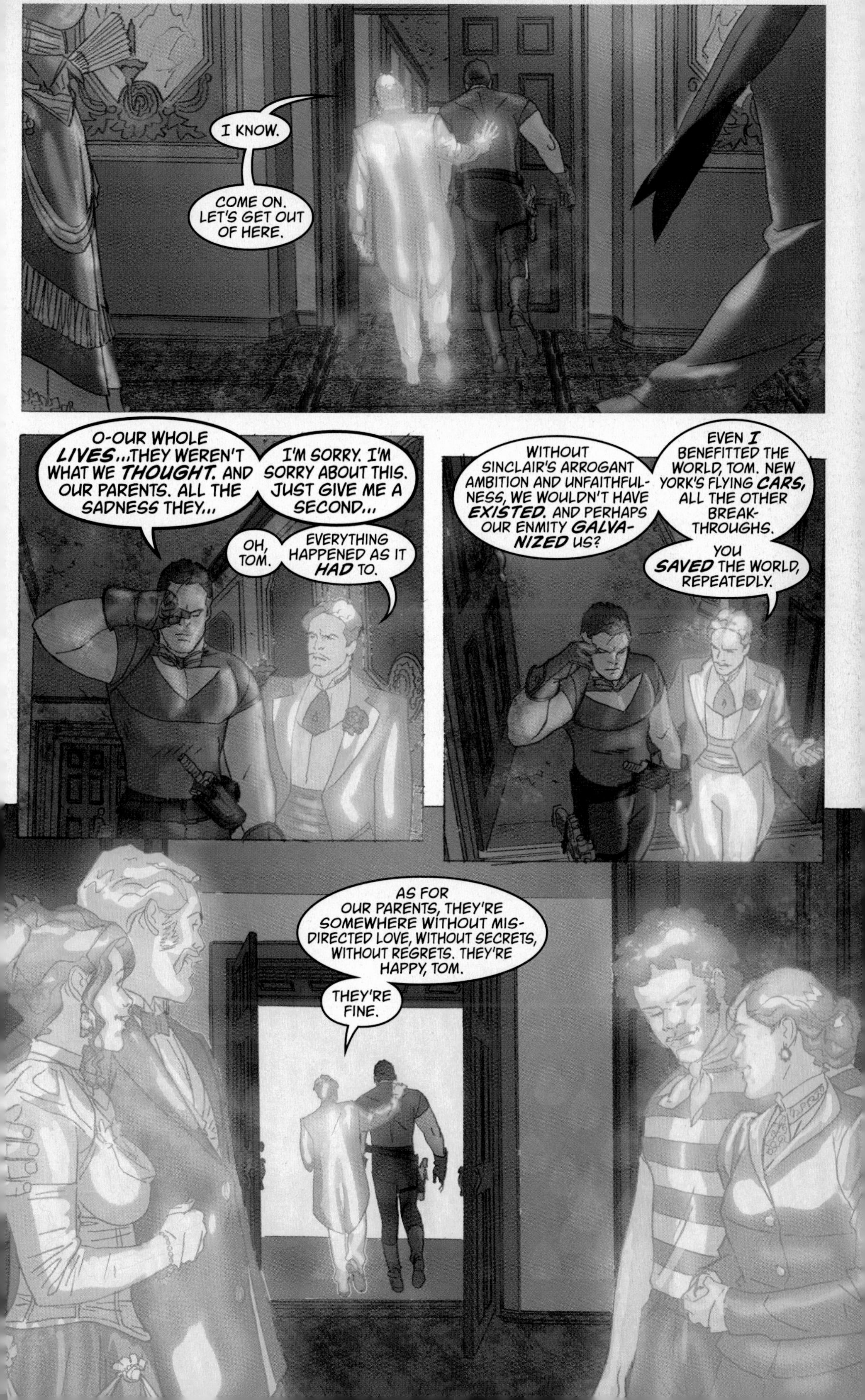

I KNOW.
COME ON. LET'S GET OUT OF HERE.
O-OUR WHOLE LIVES...THEY WEREN'T WHAT WE THOUGHT. AND OUR PARENTS. ALL THE SADNESS THEY...
I'M SORRY. I'M SORRY ABOUT THIS. JUST GIVE ME A SECOND...
OH, TOM.
EVERYTHING HAPPENED AS IT HAD TO.
WITHOUT SINCLAIR'S ARROGANT AMBITION AND UNFAITHFUL-NESS, WE WOULDN'T HAVE EXISTED. AND PERHAPS OUR ENMITY GALVA-NIZED US?
EVEN I BENEFITTED THE WORLD, TOM. NEW YORK'S FLYING CARS, ALL THE OTHER BREAK-THROUGHS.
YOU SAVED THE WORLD, REPEATEDLY.
AS FOR OUR PARENTS, THEY'RE SOMEWHERE WITHOUT MIS-DIRECTED LOVE, WITHOUT SECRETS, WITHOUT REGRETS. THEY'RE HAPPY, TOM.
THEY'RE FINE.

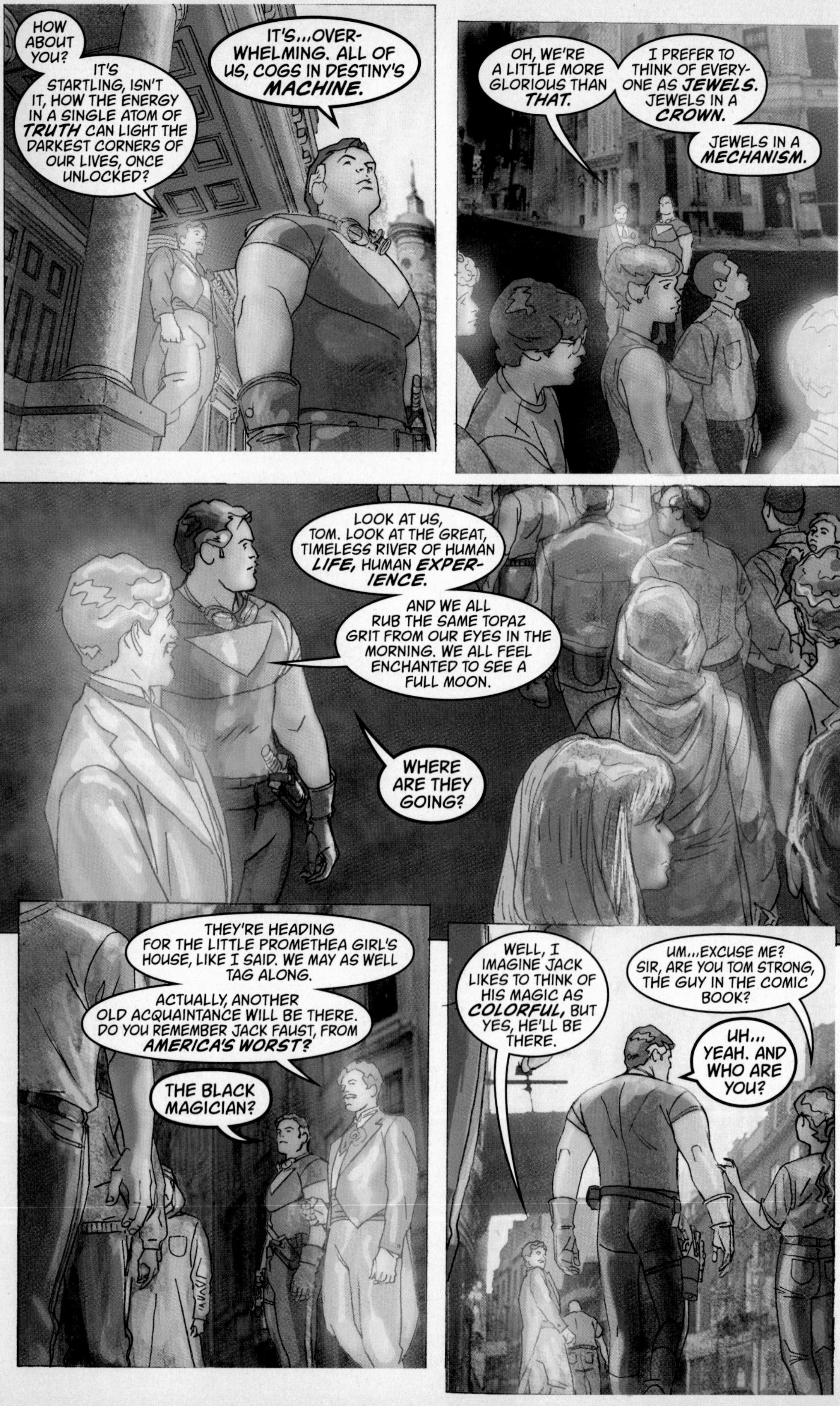
HOW ABOUT YOU?
IT'S STARTLING, ISN'T IT, HOW THE ENERGY IN A SINGLE ATOM OF TRUTH CAN LIGHT THE DARKEST CORNERS OF OUR LIVES, ONCE UNLOCKED?
IT'S...OVER-WHELMING. ALL OF US, COGS IN DESTINY'S MACHINE.
OH, WE'RE A LITTLE MORE GLORIOUS THAN THAT.
I PREFER TO THINK OF EVERY-ONE AS JEWELS. JEWELS IN A CROWN.
JEWELS IN A MECHANISM.
LOOK AT US, TOM. LOOK AT THE GREAT, TIMELESS RIVER OF HUMAN LIFE, HUMAN EXPER-IENCE.
AND WE ALL RUB THE SAME TOPAZ GRIT FROM OUR EYES IN THE MORNING. WE ALL FEEL ENCHANTED TO SEE A FULL MOON.
WHERE ARE THEY GOING?
THEY'RE HEADING FOR THE LITTLE PROMETHEA GIRL'S HOUSE, LIKE I SAID. WE MAY AS WELL TAG ALONG.
ACTUALLY, ANOTHER OLD ACQUAINTANCE WILL BE THERE. DO YOU REMEMBER JACK FAUST, FROM AMERICA'S WORST?
THE BLACK MAGICIAN?
WELL, I IMAGINE JACK LIKES TO THINK OF HIS MAGIC AS COLORFUL, BUT YES, HE'LL BE THERE.
UM...EXCUSE ME? SIR, ARE YOU TOM STRONG, THE GUY IN THE COMIC BOOK?
UH... YEAH. AND WHO ARE YOU?

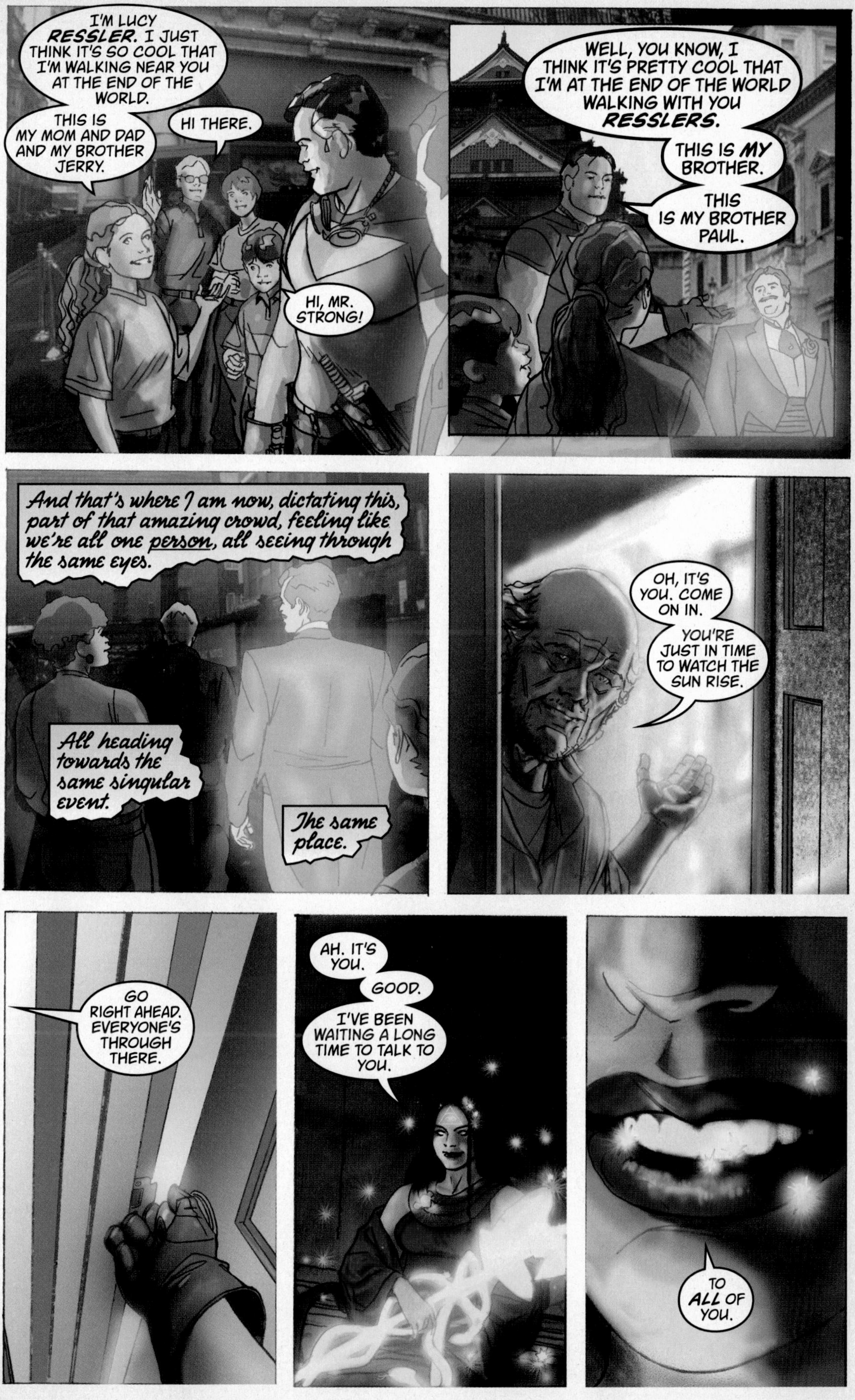
I'M LUCY RESSLER. I JUST THINK IT'S SO COOL THAT I'M WALKING NEAR YOU AT THE END OF THE WORLD.
THIS IS MY MOM AND DAD AND MY BROTHER JERRY.
HI THERE.
HI, MR. STRONG!
WELL, YOU KNOW, I THINK IT'S PRETTY COOL THAT I'M AT THE END OF THE WORLD WALKING WITH YOU RESSLERS.
THIS IS MY BROTHER.
THIS IS MY BROTHER PAUL.
And that's where I am now, dictating this, part of that amazing crowd, feeling like we're all one person, all seeing through the same eyes.
All heading towards the same singular event.
The same place.
OH, IT'S YOU. COME ON IN.
YOU'RE JUST IN TIME TO WATCH THE SUN RISE.
GO RIGHT AHEAD. EVERYONE'S THROUGH THERE.
AH. IT'S YOU.
GOOD.
I'VE BEEN WAITING A LONG TIME TO TALK TO YOU.
TO ALL OF YOU.

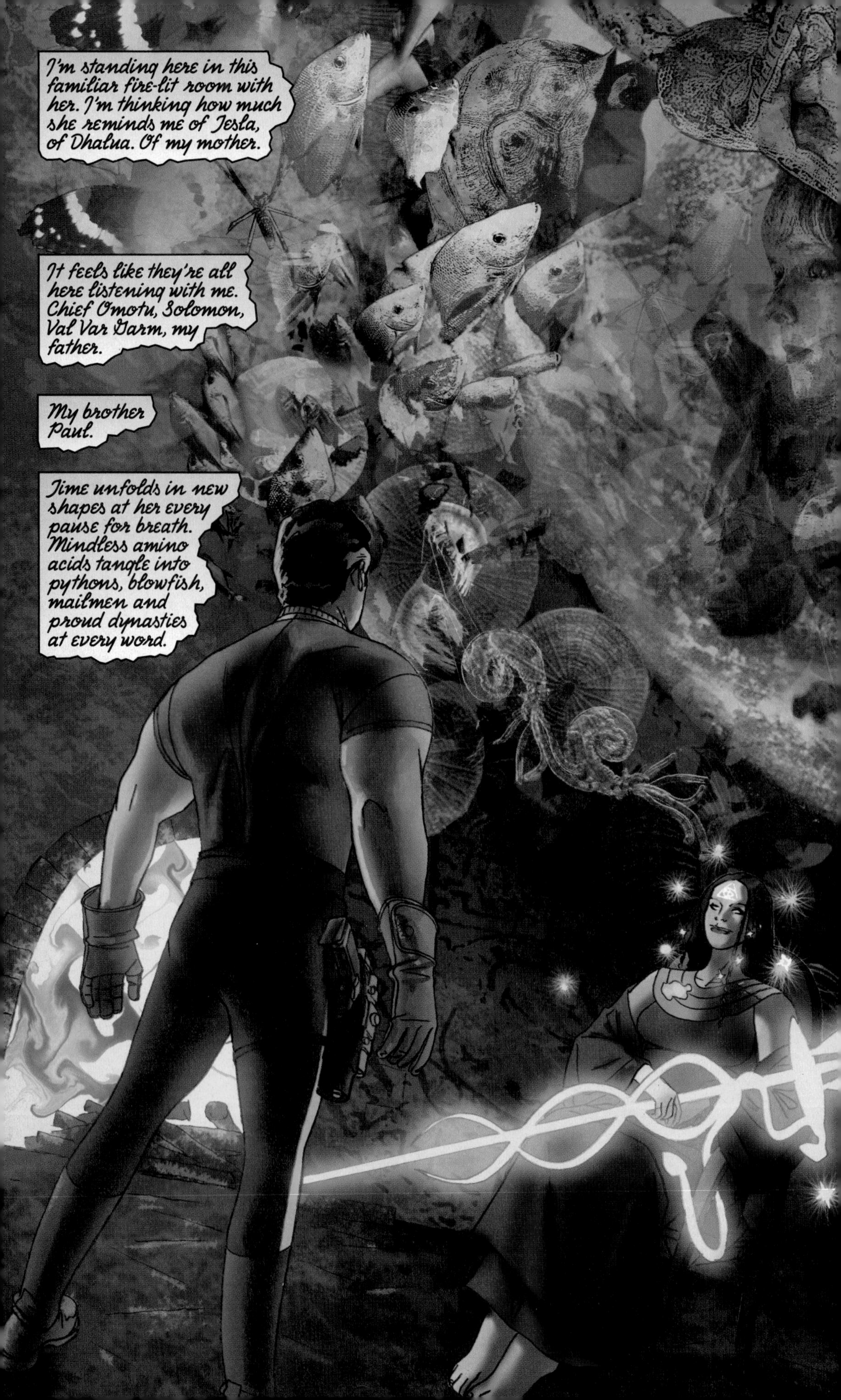
I'm standing here in this familiar fire-lit room with her. I'm thinking how much she reminds me of Jesla, of Dhalua. Of my mother.
It feels like they're all here listening with me. Chief Omotu, Solomon, Val Var Garm, my father.
My brother Paul.
Time unfolds in new shapes at her every pause for breath. Mindless amino acids tangle into pythons, blowfish, mailmen and proud dynasties at every word.

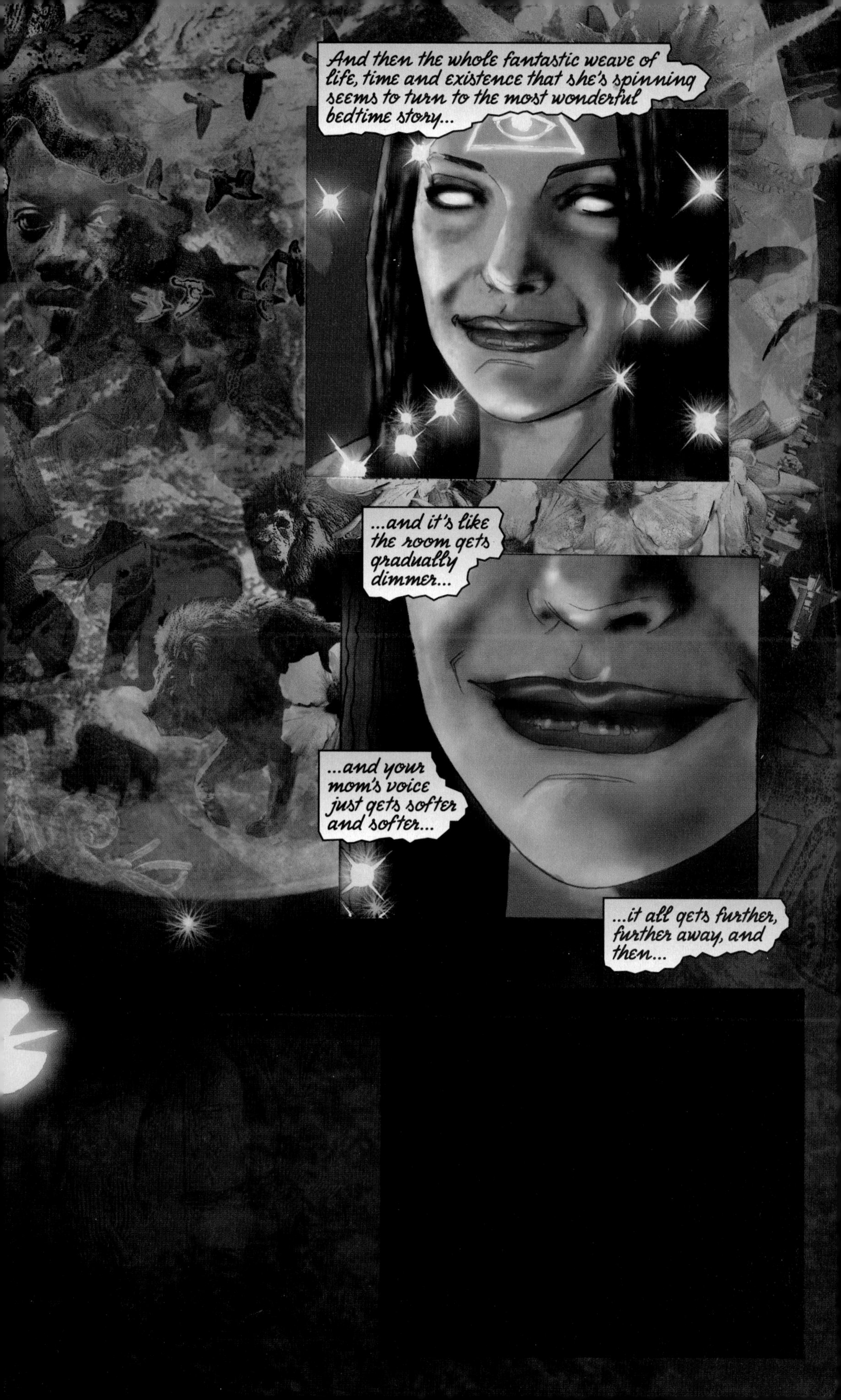
And then the whole fantastic weave of life, time and existence that she's spinning seems to turn to the most wonderful bedtime story...
...and it's like the room gets gradually dimmer...
...and your mom's voice just gets softer and softer...
...it all gets further, further away, and then...

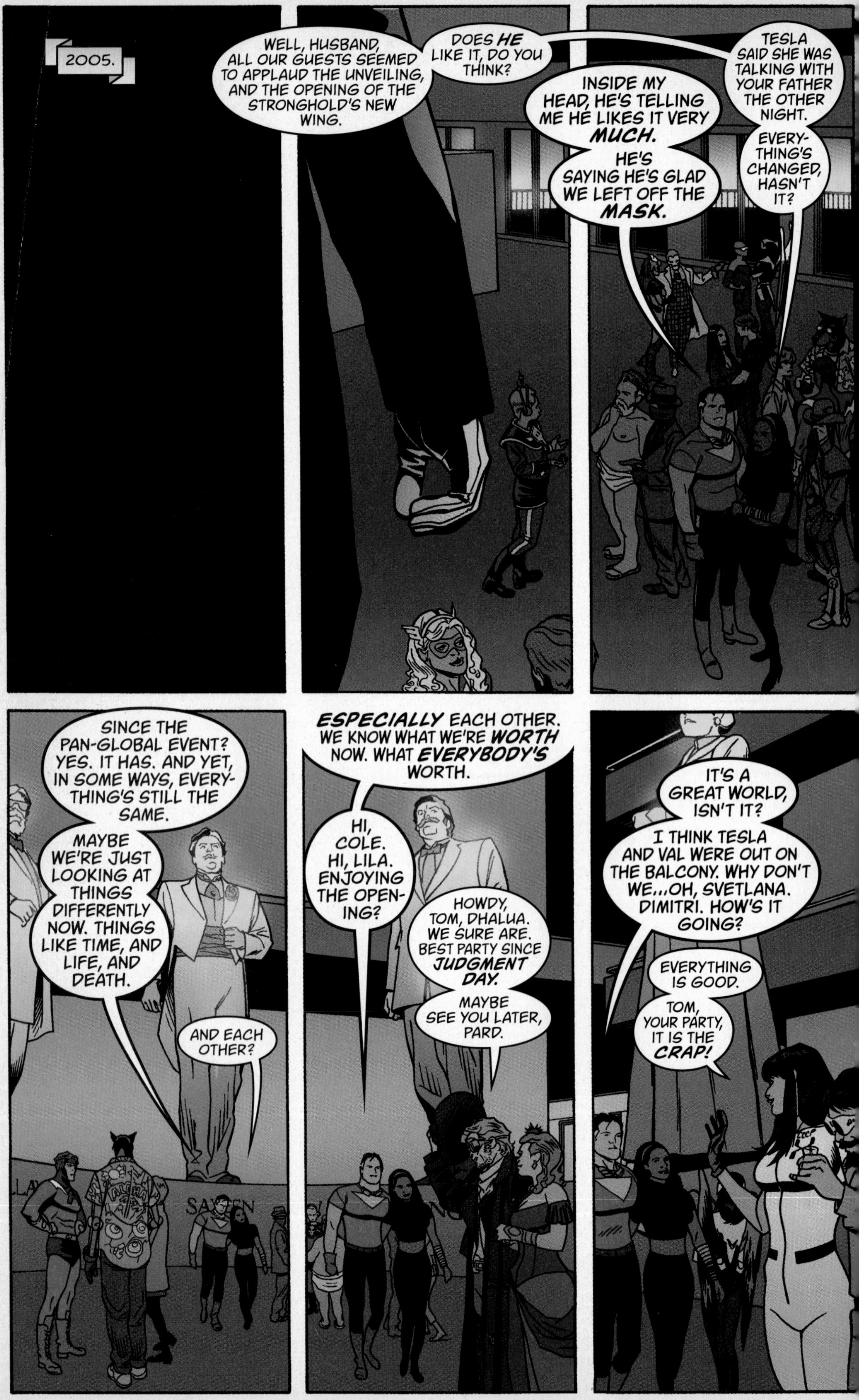
2005.
WELL, HUSBAND, ALL OUR GUESTS SEEMED TO APPLAUD THE UNVEILING, AND THE OPENING OF THE STRONGHOLD'S NEW WING.
DOES HE LIKE IT, DO YOU THINK?
INSIDE MY HEAD, HE'S TELLING ME HE LIKES IT VERY MUCH.
HE'S SAYING HE'S GLAD WE LEFT OFF THE MASK.
TESLA SAID SHE WAS TALKING WITH YOUR FATHER THE OTHER NIGHT.
EVERYTHING'S CHANGED, HASN'T IT?
SINCE THE PAN-GLOBAL EVENT? YES. IT HAS. AND YET, IN SOME WAYS, EVERYTHING'S STILL THE SAME.
MAYBE WE'RE JUST LOOKING AT THINGS DIFFERENTLY NOW. THINGS LIKE TIME, AND LIFE, AND DEATH.
AND EACH OTHER?
ESPECIALLY EACH OTHER. WE KNOW WHAT WE'RE WORTH NOW. WHAT EVERYBODY'S WORTH.
HI, COLE. HI, LILA. ENJOYING THE OPENING?
HOWDY, TOM, DHALUA. WE SURE ARE. BEST PARTY SINCE JUDGMENT DAY.
MAYBE SEE YOU LATER, PARD.
IT'S A GREAT WORLD, ISN'T IT?
I THINK TESLA AND VAL WERE OUT ON THE BALCONY. WHY DON'T WE...OH, SVETLANA. DIMITRI. HOW'S IT GOING?
EVERYTHING IS GOOD.
TOM, YOUR PARTY, IT IS THE CRAP!

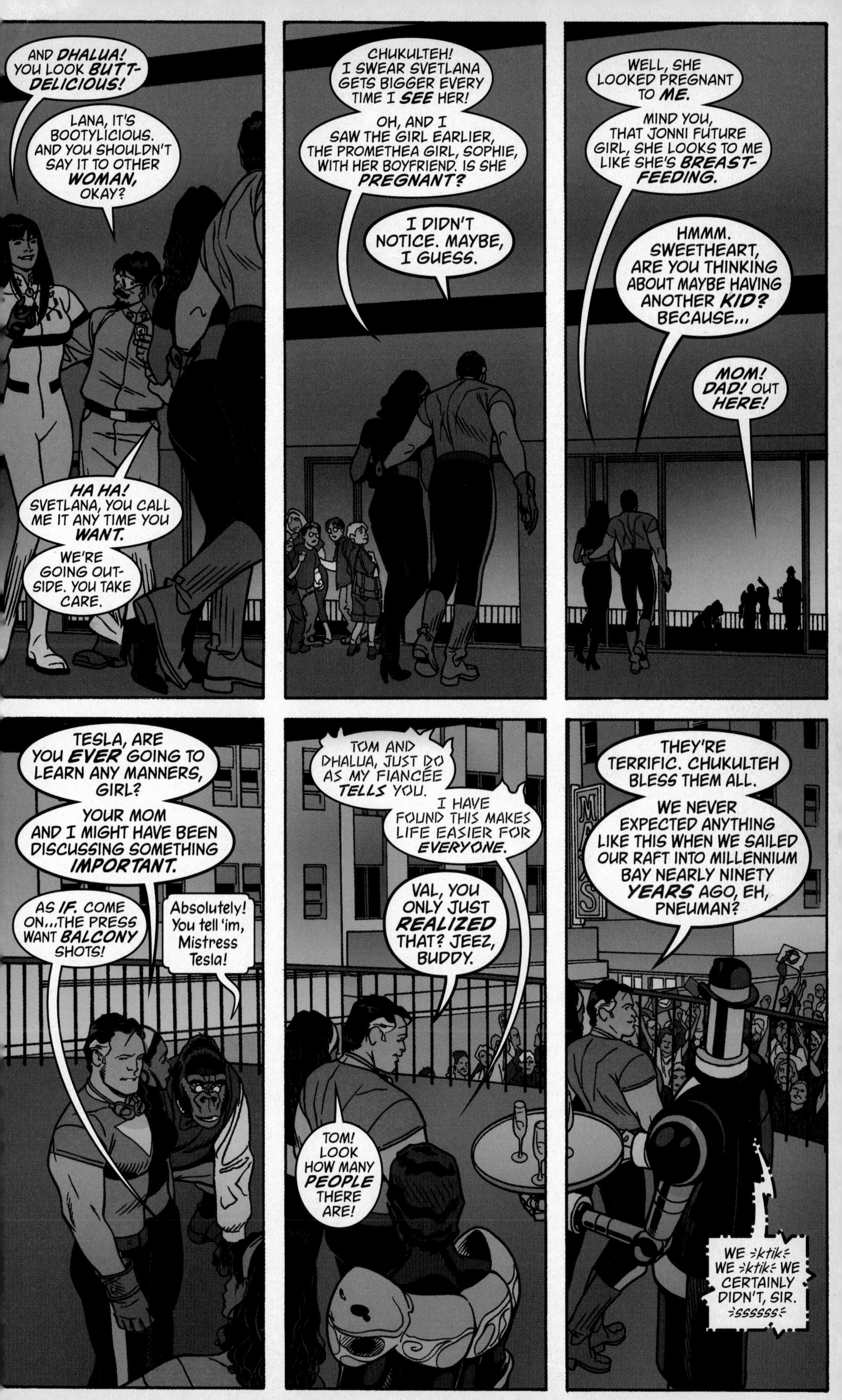

AND DHALUA! YOU LOOK BUTT-DELICIOUS!
LANA, IT'S BOOTYLICIOUS. AND YOU SHOULDN'T SAY IT TO OTHER WOMAN, OKAY?
HA HA! SVETLANA, YOU CALL ME IT ANY TIME YOU WANT.
WE'RE GOING OUT-SIDE. YOU TAKE CARE.
CHUKULTEH! I SWEAR SVETLANA GETS BIGGER EVERY TIME I SEE HER!
OH, AND I SAW THE GIRL EARLIER, THE PROMETHEA GIRL, SOPHIE, WITH HER BOYFRIEND. IS SHE PREGNANT?
I DIDN'T NOTICE. MAYBE, I GUESS.
WELL, SHE LOOKED PREGNANT TO ME.
MIND YOU, THAT JONNI FUTURE GIRL, SHE LOOKS TO ME LIKE SHE'S BREAST-FEEDING.
HMMM. SWEETHEART, ARE YOU THINKING ABOUT MAYBE HAVING ANOTHER KID? BECAUSE...
MOM! DAD! OUT HERE!
TESLA, ARE YOU EVER GOING TO LEARN ANY MANNERS, GIRL?
YOUR MOM AND I MIGHT HAVE BEEN DISCUSSING SOMETHING IMPORTANT.
AS IF. COME ON...THE PRESS WANT BALCONY SHOTS!
Absolutely! You tell 'im, Mistress Tesla!
TOM AND DHALUA, JUST DO AS MY FIANCÉE TELLS YOU.
I HAVE FOUND THIS MAKES LIFE EASIER FOR EVERYONE.
VAL, YOU ONLY JUST REALIZED THAT? JEEZ, BUDDY.
TOM! LOOK HOW MANY PEOPLE THERE ARE!
THEY'RE TERRIFIC. CHUKULTEH BLESS THEM ALL.
WE NEVER EXPECTED ANYTHING LIKE THIS WHEN WE SAILED OUR RAFT INTO MILLENNIUM BAY NEARLY NINETY YEARS AGO, EH, PNEUMAN?
WE =ktik= WE =ktik= WE CERTAINLY DIDN'T, SIR. =ssssss=

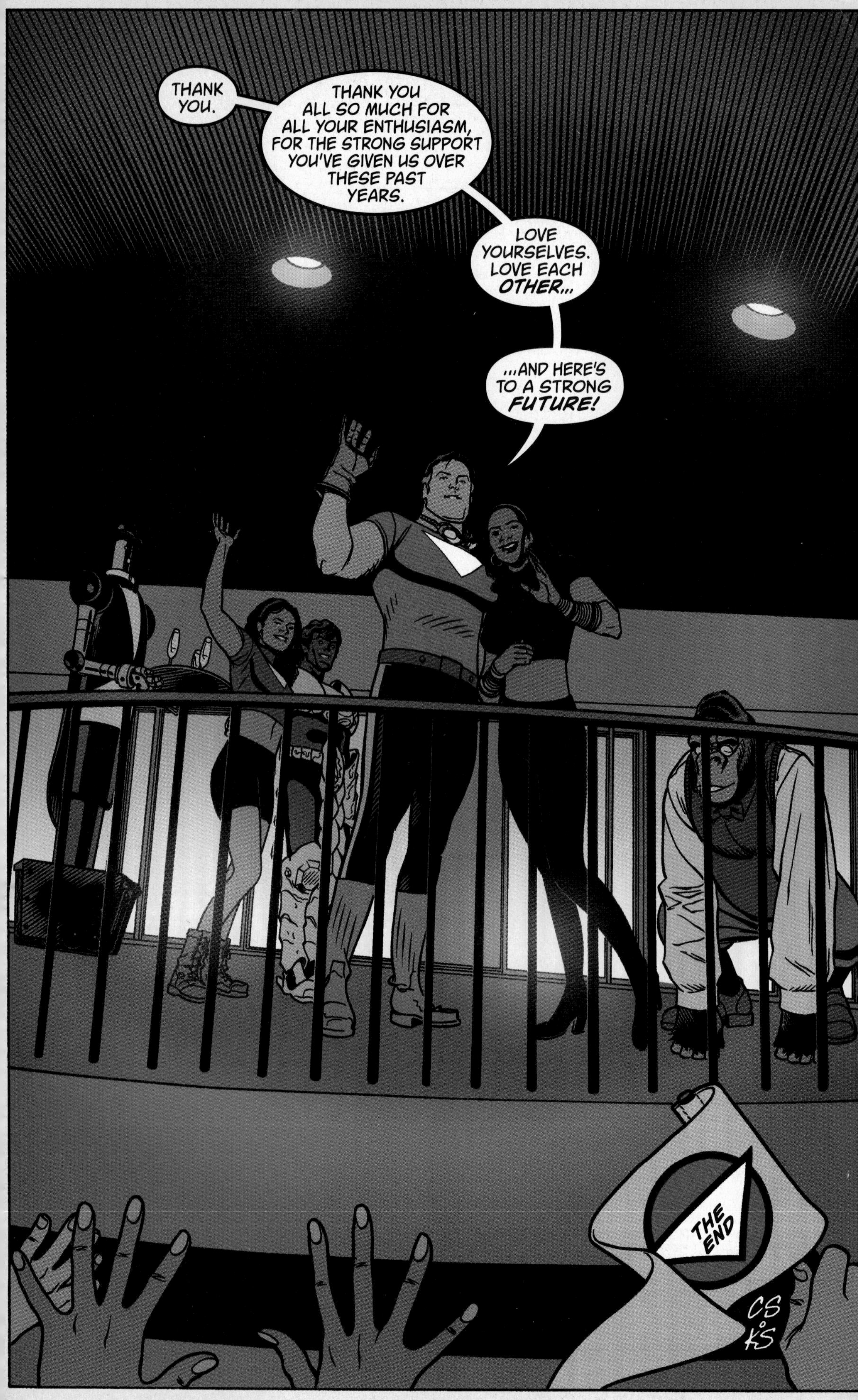
THANK YOU.
THANK YOU ALL SO MUCH FOR ALL YOUR ENTHUSIASM, FOR THE STRONG SUPPORT YOU'VE GIVEN US OVER THESE PAST YEARS.
LOVE YOURSELVES. LOVE EACH *OTHER*...
...AND HERE'S TO A STRONG *FUTURE!*
THE END
CS KS

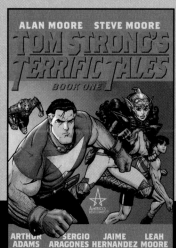
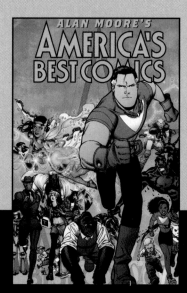

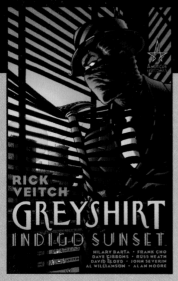

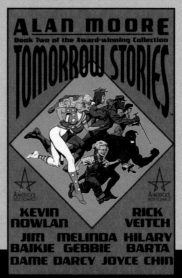
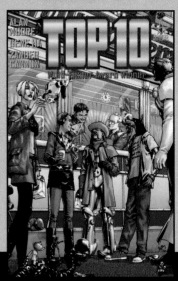